A PSYCHOLOGY SERIES

Edited by

J. MCV. HUNT, PH.D.
UNIVERSITY OF ILLINOIS

MOTIVATION
AND
SOCIAL
INTERACTION

Cognitive Determinants

EDITED BY

O. J. HARVEY
UNIVERSITY OF COLORADO

THE RONALD PRESS COMPANY · NEW YORK

Library of Congress Catalog Card Number: 63-16760

PRINTED IN THE UNITED STATES OF AMERICA

Contributors

Alan R. Anderson, Yale University

William Bevan, Kansas State University

Harold Garfinkel, University of California at Los Angeles

O. J. Harvey, University of Colorado

J. McV. Hunt, University of Illinois

John Lanzetta, University of Delaware

Omar K. Moore, Yale University

Harold M. Schroder, Princeton University

William A. Scott, University of Colorado

Preface

In a large sense the present volume is concerned with some of the motivational and interactional effects of incongruities, both positive and negative, from cognitive baselines. No attempt is made to consider all the problem areas or situations in which such a generic analysis might be appropriate. Nor do we seek detailed agreement on specific theoretical issues. Instead the aim is to present contributions from a group of scholars who, although working on different problems, are pursuing sufficiently similar approaches so that a fairly high degree of theoretical continuity and informational overlap can be provided. This, we feel, has been achieved.

The papers, prepared especially for this symposium, were revised and completed after the conference, enhancing the possibility for each of us to benefit in his own contribution from the discussion of the others.

In addition to the authors, the conference was attended by Luigi Petrullo and Tom Milburne, both of whom contributed materially to the success of the conference. My regret is that their busy schedules did not allow them to prepare formal papers for inclusion in these proceedings.

This symposium was supported financially by the Group Psychology Branch of the Office of Naval Research under Contract Nonr 1147(07) with the University of Colorado. I wish to express my sincere thanks to ONR and to Luigi Petrullo, Head of the Group Psychology Branch, not only for support of this conference but additionally for the support provided me during the past several years for the carrying out of my own research.

O. J. HARVEY

Boulder, Colorado
June, 1963

Contents

MOTIVATION
AND
SOCIAL
INTERACTION

Cognitive Determinants

Chapter 1

Overview

O. J. Harvey

General Orientation

That an individual will come to structure or make sense out of a personally relevant situation is one of psychology's most pervasive tenets. Although perhaps truistic, further implications of this basic assumption are continually being established.

One's concepts or system of meaning serves as a transformer through which impinging events are coded and translated into psychological significance. Without some such internal mediating system, the environing world would remain in a state of irrelevance; or the receiving person would move as a robot impelled solely by the physical attributes of the impingements. But much of the world is relevant and man does not move as a robot, largely because his matrix of definitions filters events through it, stamping personal effects upon it and preventing a 1 : 1 correspondence between input and behavioral outcomes.

Concepts thus render much of the world personally significant, transmute it into meaning and behavioral utility. In so doing they provide a more or less consistent and reliable basis for responding to an otherwise disorganized physical bombardment. Indeed, as we argue later, it is quite probable that without some fairly stable and at least somewhat veridical system of reading and reacting to the situation about him, the individual, both in self structure and biological being, would be doomed to extinction, especially in a capricious and hostile world. To handle the transactions of daily living, at least above the vegetable level, necessitates the ability to detect similarities and differences among impingements, to predict recurrences in them, and to anticipate causal relations among them. Such adaptive requisites tend to be encompassed in one's matrices of concepts or other evaluative schemata.

This is not to say, however, that all definitional frameworks are equally adequate to all environments or task demands. An environment or task characterized by high complexity, change, and variability demands that the system or standards of meaning applied to it must be multidimensional, open to modification from environmental feedback, and even capable of being relinquished in favor of other shadings or qualities of construal. These conditions can be met only by a more differentiated and integrated, a more complex, system. Simpler demands are made by simpler and less variable environments, however, rendering simpler and less flexible conceptual or cognitive makeups fairly adequate to the demands of such a restricted situation.

Veridical or not, however, once a system of ordering has come into being, it becomes the "frame of reference" (Sherif, 1935) in terms of which related events are subsequently gauged, evaluated, and responded to. As Sherif stressed in his early works (1935, 1936), psychological relativity extends to all perceptual and judgmental relationships. Notions of near and far, hot and cold, up and down, of right and wrong, good and bad are comparative effects, anchored to some subjective norm, socially or individually generated, which the perceiver applies to the event. This position can be, indeed has been by many, generalized to say that the effect of any stimulus impingement is determined through its interaction with or dependency on some intraorganismic baseline from which it is perceived and judged. Thus an external treatment might produce one effect on one person and a far different, even opposite, effect on another, depending on the degree of similarity of the subjective norms or filters through which the event was read.

It is within this general S-O-R framework that the papers in this volume should be viewed. All the contributors approach their problem from the common assumption that stimuli do not pass in unaltered form directly from receptors to effectors but instead get converted into psychological dimensions and weight through their relationship to subjective baselines. It is with some of the effects of variations in subjective mediating systems on motivation and social behavior that this volume is mainly concerned.

Maintenance of Internal Standards

Once formed, a concept or evaluative schema displays varying degrees of resistance to change, depending, among other factors, on the magnitude of commitment to it and the nature of the event pressing toward change. Low commitment or minimal involvement toward a particular concept, coupled with a discrepant input from a highly creditable source (in the case of communication effects), would favor conceptual change. With time, any number of circumstances may coalesce to produce marked alteration in our interpretation of an object or occurrence. Stimulus satiation, feedback, and general effects of repetition produce change. Personality differences in conceptual makeup also foster or impede modification. But despite these innumerable factors disposing toward change with time, an individual sampled *at any one narrow cross-section of time* appears to act in ways favorable to keeping his current system of ordering as maximally intact as the situation will permit.

Caught in the situation of conflict between two or more evaluative predilections or choices, the dissonance or asynchrony seems to be resolved in ways that favor the concepts or definitional possibilities of greater personal relevance and centrality. Distortions, dissociation, discrediting, redefinition, and enhancement of the commitment to the target concept are only some of the psychological gerrymanderings that may be employed as a buffer against too much strain and stress on one's ways of ordering. Motivationally colored responses are not restricted to highly central concepts, however. Distortions and redefinitions, along with other "defensive" responses have been found to occur in less striking form in relation to psychophysically derived concepts about weights and distance (Harvey and Caldwell, 1959).

One might think, for example, that adult human beings would be little involved in the definitions and rules of such informal games as ticktacktoe, especially under conditions of minimal threat or reward. That this is not the case, however, is shown clearly in several lifelike experiments by Garfinkel (Chapter 7). Responses of doubt, dismay, hostility, and attribution of malevolence were some of the consequences that resulted from plays that, technically, were legitimate but which deviated from the customary and commonly assumed ways of playing.

Negative reactions to the different and the unexpected, moreover, seem not to be restricted to human beings. Hebb (1955) has reported that young chimpanzees reacted with strong fear and disturbance at the sight of their familiar keeper in unfamiliar dress, when seeing a model of a human head, or when seeing the anesthetized body of a fellow chimp. Others have reported parallel observations.

Possible Bases for Negative Reactions to Incongruity

Why do most of us seemingly react so negatively to events and situations that run counter to our more or less habitual modes of construal and response, particularly when these relate to cherished values and definitions? This question, as are all "why's," doubtlessly is open to as many equally plausible explanations as there are levels and vantage points from which it might be approached. Thus while today many psychologists are discussing the tendency for the organism to maintain the world as he has come to define it and react to it, this is being done in different languages and from rather historically disparate bases.

The more widespread answer to this question today probably would be in terms of some kind of general system theory, although not necessarily to the extent suggested by such authors as Bertalanffy (1950) and Miller (1955). Many of the prevalent notions represent a kind of adventitious wedding of cybernetics, information theory, field theory, and thermodynamics. It is probably from the latter two areas that more psychologists have borrowed more directly and have attempted to apply more widely.

Field Theory and Thermodynamics. Field theory and thermodynamics, being of historically common parents, have given rise to certain parallel assumptions. The one most relevant to our question is that all systems are endowed with inherent organizational tendencies which flow toward the establishment of stabilized relations of parts and toward maintenance of the equilibrium or state of synchrony between them. Incursion from external sources or malfunctioning of some internal part upsets the balanced relationships and by so doing generates states of increased tension and energy. This results in activity aimed at restoration of equilibrium, a state of harmony and balance that might or might not be identical to the relationships and tension level existing prior to the disruptive displacement from the steady state.

The notions of organization and equilibrium implied that once it has come into being a system is endowed with the tendency toward self-preservation, or "dynamic self-regulation" as Katz (1950) termed it. This assumption was basic to three lines of thought that are particularly important for the present question: the theory of psychodynamics advanced by Freud; the field theory of Gestalt psychology, especially as this was elaborated and popularized by Lewin; and the "wisdom of the body" or homeostasis hypothesis developed by physiology but borrowed by psychology.

Freud, with his subsystems of id, ego, and superego, was mainly concerned with ways in which the various defense mechanisms operate through unconscious means to protect the ego system from the forces disposing toward the tension state of anxiety. Lewin, on the other hand, more experimentally inclined and influenced by the avowed goals of operationalism, concentrated on the effects of disequilibrium and psychic tensions produced through such situational manipulations as interruptions of tasks, blocking of goals, and failure in attainment of levels of aspiration (Lewin, 1935). Both Freud and Lewin, as well as their theoretical cousins in physiology, assumed that the tension generated by threat and displacement from the steady state was resolved in ways most compatible with the welfare or functioning of the total system. Under some conditions this might lead to considerable change in the relationship between some of the weaker and less potent parts. Miller (1955), in his discussion of the applications of general systems theory, expressed a derivation of this notion this way: "Systems which survive employ the least expensive defenses against stress first and increasingly more expensive ones later" (p. 528).

The impact of field theory and Lewin's thinking is very evident today in such works as Festinger's (1957) treatment of cognitive dissonance, in Heider's (1946, 1958) treatment of balance, in Newcomb's (1953, 1961) treatment of symmetry, in Osgood and Tannenbaum's (1955) treatment of congruity, as well as in numerous other related articles and books. Freud's thinking thus far has been applied very little to the experimental investigation of conceptual refutation or other baseline-event incongruities. Yet it is quite probable, as Hunt argues in Chapter 3, that many of the reactions obtained from the refutation of highly central concepts would qualify as "defense mechanisms," should one choose to use that label. For example, it has been found, in ways doubtlessly less striking than Freudians might postulate, that when having their self derogated by another person subjects may distort both their perception and recall of the negative information, discredit its source, resort to denial and excuses, become less favorable in their opinions toward both themselves and the source (Harvey, Kelley, and Shapiro, 1957; Harvey, 1962), or even more positive toward the person doing the derogating (Wright, 1958).

Homeostasis and Wisdom of the Body. The idea that a system mobilizes its defenses to ward off or in other ways cope with disruptive forces portending threat and too much tension, expressed commonly but in different languages by Freud and Lewin, was also central in the homeostatic doctrine of the physiologists. Upset of the equilibrium of the internal system was assumed to bring into action the necessary forces for restoration of balance. Cannon quotes Claude Bernard, whom he credits as being first to suggest that the internal environment operates in terms of equilibration, as saying: "'It is the fixity of the *milieu interieur* which is the condition of the free and independent life . . . and all the vital mechanisms, however varied they may be, have only one object, that of preserving constant the conditions of life in the internal environment'" (Cannon, 1932, p. 38).

The work of Cannon, such as that reported in *Wisdom of the Body* (1932), contributed heavily to documentation and popularization of the theory of homeostasis as a principle of system adaptation and survival.

Organisms were shown to engage involuntarily and automatically in a wide range of adjustive activities in response to an upset of such internal constancies as those surrounding temperature, blood sugar, acidity, water content of the blood and lymph, oxygen, blood sodium, blood calcium, protein, and other dietary elements. As P. T. Young summarizes this work:

> The internal conditions, as Cannon said, are not rigidly fixed, but they vary within limits according to the demands of the external environment. Thus if the existence of the total organism is threatened with an encounter with an enemy, there are prompt alterations within the internal fluid matrix that tend to assist the organism in a struggle for existence. For example, if a cat is threatened by a barking dog, there is a rise in the level of blood sugar, thus providing a source for increased energy during vigorous muscular exertion; the circulation of blood in muscles and brain is speeded up; the processes of digestion are temporarily checked; adrenin is poured into the blood stream by the adrenal glands thus stimulating the heart and producing other adaptive changes; oxygenation is accelerated through action of the spleen, etc. All such changes prepare the cat for a life-and-death struggle in the face of a crisis. Thus internal changes meet the demands of external conditions [Young, 1961, p. 112].

Richter extended the principle of homeostasis to show how overt behavior facilitates the maintenance of physiochemical steady states. Homeostatic imbalance leads to behavior which compensates for the disturbance and tends to restore the steady state. Richter sought to illustrate this principle through the effects of removal of several of the ductless glands in rats. Removal of the pituitary gland, which renders the body incapable of producing adequate heat, resulted in the operated animals compensating by building larger and warmer nests (Richter, 1942). Adrenalectomized rats, which would normally die through loss of sodium chloride through the urine, compensated for this loss and maintained seemingly good health by marked increases in salt intake when given free access to a 3 per cent sodium chloride solution (Richter, 1936). Similarly, animals which had had their parathyroid glands removed were able to maintain a fairly normal life, instead of the usual weight loss, tetany, and death, by taking in increased calcium when it was made freely available to them (Richter and Eckert, 1939). From these and theoretically parallel results, such as the apparent tendency to avoid poisons and select proper diets in cafeteria type feedings, Richter concluded that ". . . in human beings and animals the effort to maintain a constant internal environment or homeostasis constitutes one of the most universal and powerful of all behavior urges or drives" (Richter, as quoted by Young, 1961, p. 113).

Until the recent upswing in the frequency of balance, consonance, and congruity "models," the concept of homeostasis was applied to a wide variety of psychological problems. Thus Freeman (1948) broadened it to include most of the traditional problems surrounding motivation or "energetics," as he preferred to call it. It was his thesis "that objective descriptions of total neuromuscular homeostasis (in terms of the interaction of isolable overt and covert part-reaction systems) offer independent and direct measures of dynamic behavior wholes which in themselves will ultimately "outfield" the field theories of the Gestaltist, psychoanalyst, and other exponents of psychic energetics and phenomenological description" (Freeman, 1948, p. 506). Perhaps even more expansive was the attempt made by Stagner (1951) and Stagner and Karwaski (1952) to interpret the typical issues encountered in the introductory psychology course within the framework of homeostatic doctrine.

Cortical Stimulation. If the question of why do man and animals react negatively to events that deviate too far from the habitual and typical were put to a neurophysiological psychologist or a Neo-behaviorist, his answer, if he deemed the question a meaningful one in the first place, would probably involve some notion of arousal or activation level. Since Hebb's *Organization of Behavior* (1949), it has become increasingly more prevalent to view organisms as disposed toward maintenance of some more or less standardized and optimal level of cortical activity (see Fiske and Maddi, 1961). This optimal, as Berlyne conceives it and others concur, "will normally be some distance from both the upper and the lower extreme" (1960, p. 194). Marked deviation from the optimal level of stimulation in either direction, toward either increased or decreased arousal, is assumed to result in negative reaction to the input. Stimuli are generally assumed to be maximally positive in their effects when they are slightly but not too discrepant from the baseline, in line with the affective arousal hypothesis offered by McClelland *et al.* (1953). Repeated stimulation at or near the adaptation level (the term used by McClelland *et al.*) results in stimulus satiation and a less than optimal level-input disparity. Too low a level of arousal is assumed to lead to boredom, even to hallucinations in the case of extreme sensory deprivation, and to activity directed toward bringing in more stimulation. Hence the person or animal under stimulus satiation or less than optimal arousal would experience as positive slightly discrepant events, expressed in curiosity and a tendency toward exploring his environment in search of complexity and novelty in order to increase his level of activation (Hebb, 1955; Glanzer, 1958; Berlyne, 1960). The "exploratory-curiosity-manipulatory drive," avers Hebb (1955, p. 247), "essentially comes down to a tendency to seek varied stimulation." "The significance of this relation," he continues, "is a phenomenon of the greatest importance for understanding motivation in higher animals. This is the *positive attraction of risk taking,* or mild fear, *and of problem solving, or mild frustration . . ."* (1955, p. 250). Too varied a pattern of stimulation, too much complexity, too high a level of arousal, on the other hand, leads to efforts at reducing the stimulation by withdrawing from the different and more complex toward the simpler and the familiar, even in freezing and other strongly avoidant responses.

Most of the arousal level hypotheses, including those relating to curiosity and exploration, remain essentially ideas on drive reduction (Hebb, 1955; Berlyne, 1960), although many of the writers in the area, including Hebb in his earlier work, assumed they were not. Instead of restoration of tissue depletions driving behavior, as Hull and his followers conceived it (1943), the need to maintain optimal levels of stimulation and arousal has been posited. Deviation from the optimal is still assumed to create tension and discomfort which motivates the organism toward its removal; but not to complete zero, as early Hullian theory implied. The idea that an organism is curious, seeks novelty, and explores just because of factors "intrinsic" in its makeup is being more and more rapidly replaced, it would seem, by the as yet unarticulated assumption that such behavior after all is instrumental to the maintenance of levels of optimal excitation, tension, and arousal.

Arousal level theories, in addition to being aberrant drive reductions hypotheses, also imply a kind of homeostatic or equilibrium principle. But, in these more neurophysiologically tinged notions, that which is being maintained has shifted from field tensions and blood chemistry balance to the optimal level of excitation in the "conceptual nervous system" (Hebb, 1955). The determinants of this assumed optimal, however, have yet to be worked out, even at the theoretical level. Presumably the assumption is that the volume of past stimulation determines the base line of the optimal. Seemingly untreated are the effects of motivational selectivity and idiosyncratic makeups that may render highly relevant some relatively infrequent impingement out of the total volume and give it disproportionate weight in the ultimate level or base line. According to Glanzer (1958, p. 312), "The increase or decrease with respect to parts of the environment is a function of the difference between the average amount of information the individual is accustomed to and the current rate of flow of information from the environment."

The Need for Meaning and Self Structure. Negative reactions to events that depart radically from the customary conception of them might be explained in terms of yet another, a fourth, theoretical alternative. Without too much absurdity from a functionalistic point of view, a biogenic need for structure or meaning could be postulated and hostility to alien events be accounted for in terms of threat to the structure or meaning attached to the situation. It is not necessary to posit the tendency to structure as a biological imperative, because, native or not, the making of some kind of sense out of a situation appears invariable and unquestionably essential to the prediction of recurrences and differences in the surrounding world. To cope adequately with the environment, even to survive in it, seems to necessitate the ability to read it or define it in some degree of veridicality at least. To satisfy even the simpler motives requires that the organism be able to see relevant means-ends relationships, that is, be able to "know" what objects or stimuli are motive relevant and to be capable of delineating and engaging appropriate courses of action for their attainment. One's conceptual system goes a long way toward embodying these essentials. Curiosity, searching, and going beyond the customary are ways in which these construal networks can be further differentiated, refined, and organized into both more sensitive and more general metering systems. Development toward greater differentiation and integration, toward greater cognitive complexity or abstractness, renders the individual less dependent on the physical attributes of the stimulus world, more capable of transcending these both in space and time. It allows the perception of more varied goals and more means to their attainment. It provides a more adequate means of fate control, greater independence from the pressures of the physical world, a greater mastery over what otherwise would be an omnipotent environment. It is quite probable that man especially seeks control over his fate, the keys to satisfaction of his motives and the development of his self.

Elsewhere (Harvey, Hunt, and Schroder, 1961), we have made the self synonymous with one's totality of concepts. To the extent this is correct, threat to definitions of a situation would be equivalent to threat to the self, would portend negation of the perceived means-ends relationships, and would, if severe enough, render inoperative the means of fate control and adaptation. The importance of conceptual systems for mooring oneself in space and time, for meaningful existence, seems to be indicated by brainwashing, marginality, sensory deprivation, or overly homogeneous environments. Without heterogeneity of some degree, no information is yielded of the world. Without some kind of stimulus variation, growth and self development appear retarded. And with systematic severance of the usual ways of reading the world and anchoring oneself, the dramatic effects of brainwashing and sensory deprivation occur.

Such effects as those produced by sensory deprivation would be explained very differently by a self-oriented psychologist and one operating from an optimal stimulation hypothesis. This is clearly apparent from two studies carried out from these different orientations.

Under the assumption that the self is comprised of one's network of meaning in relation to differentiated aspects of his environment, Sherif and Harvey (1952) studied the effects of sensory deprivation, or "the elimination of stable anchorages," as they called it, on self disorganization. Subjects were placed in a large and totally darkened auditorium where, through mazelike paths, they sought their way to points in the environment from which they made judgments of autokinetic movement. Disorganization was reflected in heightened judgmental variability as well as in verbal reports the subjects made voluntarily and in interview. Representative of the subjects' comments were such expressions as:

"'Very unsure and a little afraid, not of anything in particular, just of a strange and totally unexplained situation.'"

"'Felt helpless and ill at ease—was very puzzled'" (Sherif and Harvey, 1952, p. 300).

The cortical stimulation hypothesis was tested in the well-known sensory deprivation study of Bexton, Heron, and Scott (1954). Here, numerous expressions of confusion and discomfort were made by the subjects, some of whom displayed varied patterns of hallucination after extended deprivation.

While these two studies point to effects of different theoretical orientations on what was hypothesized and observed, they may at the same time suggest something quite different: that equally valid measures could be taken simultaneously from different levels. Instead of the social psychologist or the physiologist assuming his was *the* valid observation, perhaps it would make more sense to say that to any situation the individual responds in a myriad of ways that are open to measurement at numerous levels and from divergent theoretical stances. If indeed the organism does react negatively to events that deviate too far from whatever baseline he gauges the situation by, the effects of this should be accessible from both the more molar and molecular levels, from physiological indexes to indications of self functioning. If measures that were simultaneously obtained from different levels, different instruments, and different assumptions were considered together, a more complete and accurate picture of behavior surely should be provided.

How Evaluative Schemata Affect Motivation

In one language or another, this is the issue with which this volume is mainly concerned. Hence only a few general comments will be made here.

McDougall (1908) defined an instinct as an innate predisposition to perceive an object or class of objects in a particular way, to experience certain affect, positive or negative, in the presence of the object, and to engage appropriate goal behavior in relation to it. If "innate" were deleted from the preceding, this characterization would be applicable to all motives, both biogenic and sociogenic, its being generally agreed that motives in some way initiate, select, and direct behavior.

Internalized social norms, adaptation level, cognitive structures, conceptual and self systems satisfy these criteria. They render the individual selective in what *kinds* of stimuli are relevant and hence which stimulus class will effect certain perceptual, affective, and behavioral outcomes. Their activation not only affects the kind of stimulus events that are relevant to the system, and hence the ones that are actively warded off or permitted entrance, they also sensitize the individual toward intensity, resulting in either lowered or raised thresholds for certain kinds of inputs. The differential lowering and raising of threshold toward certain stimuli is, of course, the same old question as perceptual defense and offense. It has come to be a general hypothesis that portending negation or threat to the evaluative system disposes toward heightened threshold and perceptual defense. It is apparent that this is not necessarily compatible with coping adequately with threat. Closing one's eyes to adversity and danger, displaying the ostrich effect, might in certain environments work at complete cross-purposes with problem solution, and even survival. This does not mean, however, that organisms always pursue the best of all possible courses toward solution of a problem and grappling with threat and difficulty. It is but to suggest that most of the perceptual defense hypotheses arc too simple; that in some cases a person might be disposed toward lowered thresholds in the face of potentially refuting or threatening information or happenings. The solution of this question ultimately will probably be synonymous with effects of confirmation and refutation of conceptual systems and schemata.

It might be offered as a general hypothesis that all motivational arousal is the consequence of disrupting certain relationships between the outside world and the metering system encompassed in the intraorganismic norms. While this should hold at the genotypic level for both biogenic and sociogenic motives, there are important differences between these cores of motivation at the more phenotypic level. Sociogenic motives, such as attitudes, values, and other concepts, tend to be more enduring and stable across time than do the biogenic motives. Hence the former are more likely to be triggered off by discrepancies that result from alteration in the *external environment*. Biogenic motives, on the other hand, are more likely to become active and influence behavior due to physiochemical changes in the *internal environment*. In both cases optimal discrepancies between the internal-external environments are surpassed, but by different mechanisms. The behavior directed toward satisfaction of these different motives may also reflect these differences in the activating mechanisms. In the case of sociogenic motives the individual may be more disposed toward transforming the outside world to make it conform to the conceptual moulds of the inside, whereas in the case of biogenic motives the aim is more likely to be to change the inside. Whether the inside is changed or the outside is transformed, either technique may serve to re-establish the pre-existing relationship between the intraorganismic baseline and the environment and in so doing reduce the motivational arousal.

What form do evaluative schemata and conceptual matrices take when discrepant events are not present to produce arousal and consequent behavior? We could say that one's concepts, his values, prejudices, and the like, lie dormant and inert until certain relevant events call them into play. While this probably would not be entirely incorrect, it probably would be far from the whole story because, if one's ways of ordering were completely inactive, it would be as if they did not exist and their selective and directing influences would be nullified. Hence it is probably more correct to assume that once concepts come into being they vary on the dimension of passivity-activity, from low activity in consonant environments to high activity in discrepant and deviant environments. Presumably at low levels of activity, which may or may not coincide with Hebb's (1949) notions of cortical activity, it would take a more intense or discrepant stimulus input to produce the effect that could be obtained by a less intense treatment at higher levels of activity. Further, the more central the concepts, the greater the likelihood that they shall be more active and hence the lower the threshold toward certain kinds of stimuli or the lower the stimulus intensity necessary to effect certain outcomes.

It is a typical practice among many psychologists to make sharp distinctions between cognition and affect, the implication being that the two are independent. Such practice is not in line with the wealth of experimental evidence accrued during the past three decades showing that such cognitive activities as perception, judgment, and learning are greatly colored and affected by needs, attitudes, and emotions. It is our assumption that conceptual functioning is highly affective, both being influenced by existing affective states and in turn influencing affective states. As McClelland et al. (1953) have stressed, affective arousal and emotion in general become more meaningful when viewed in terms of relationships between impinging events and internal baselines or adaptation levels of the recipient. Feelings of success, failure, pleasure, and pain have been found to be a function of the aspiration level or height of the subject's goal and not of objective accomplishment or stimulus intensity alone. The vast amount of work in social psychology on reference group theory, the heart of which is the assumption of stimulus relativity, has made it quite clear that so many of our social motives, the end points we strive for, are markedly influenced by the reference group norms which we take as standards of comparison. James (1890), in one of his many acute observations, noted that self-esteem = success/pretensions, or accomplishments in relation to some ideal standard. The parallel of this has been expressed repeatedly in level of aspiration research as well as in certain notions of personality. It has become a basic tenet of Roger's (1959) philosophy that one's feeling of self-adequacy and worth is a function of the discrepancy between the ideal and perceived self.

Hence the individual doesn't strive for the attainment of universal levels. Most persons direct their efforts toward ensuring accomplishments consonant with personal standards which have been derived from the social dicta of reference groups or from more direct individual experience with the object class to which the baseline relates. Despite the diversity of their etiological determinants, whether they be taken from ready prescribed social dicta or obtained through direct experience, the conceptual standards affect heavily, in some cases are the sole determinants of, what the target level is. This seems to hold for all perceptual and judgmental phenomena, whether in relation to heaviness, distance, right and wrong, good and bad, evil or pure. Reality is construed in terms of such standards. And individuals move toward behaving compatibly with their own subjective worlds. Compatible events are permitted into the system, produce positive affect, generate approach tendencies, and foster reinforcement. Events that are too deviant refute the conceptual standards and dispose toward negative affect and avoidance which may take the form of attack and attempted destruction or some form of modification of the different to make it fit the bounds of the imposed conceptual standards. The activity of zealots, who feign to save the world from the forces of the evil or misguided, illustrates dramatically the attempts to make the world fit their standards of rightness. Unable to alter their concepts to fit the world, such persons must transform the world to fit their definitions of what it should be.

The Chapters

No attempt has been made to employ identical languages and points of view. There is, however, a broad common point of view that prevails throughout this volume. This has already been noted. The value of stimuli is viewed as not being absolute in their effects but dependent upon the base line or internal standards to which the receiving subject compares them in the process of evaluating them and responding to them. Different ones of us treat such base lines differently, both in terms of what they are conceived to be and the effects of events deviating from them.

In Chapter 2 Bevan concerns himself mainly with the dependence of a treatment's reinforcement value upon its relationship to the subject's adaptation level. The need for modifying reinforcement theory away from strict stimulus determinants in the direction of organismic states and norms is made clear.

In Chapter 3 Hunt deals with the broad problem of motivation inherent in information processing. In so doing, he provides a review and an analysis of most of the prevailing notions in motivation, including homeostasis, balance, tension reduction, and optimal levels of arousal. These, as well as recent findings and developments in the study of brain arousal and motivational systems, are integrated into a coherent and theoretically consistent treatment of motivation and behavior.

In Chapter 4 Harvey and Schroder concentrate on the effects of structural variations in conceptual and self systems upon cognitive and motivational outcomes. The self is depicted as a kind of evaluative filtering system, differing in such structural attributes as concreteness-abstractness, that determines what aspects of the world are of relevance and whether or not they shall be of positive or negative motivational consequence. Brief application of these assumptions are made to such areas as interpersonal relations, reinforcement, creativity, and exploratory behavior.

In Chapter 5 Schroder and Harvey attempt to draw certain parallels between group structure and conceptual structure. The possibility that groups as well as individuals may be viewed as operating at more concrete or more abstract levels is examined and some of the consequences of such possibilities for groups and international relations are suggested. Some of the environmental and training conditions that seemingly affect the level of individual and group abstractness are also described.

In Chapter 6 Moore and Anderson are also concerned with structural aspects of personality. Instead of reasoning from structure to behavior, as is typical, they reverse the direction. They note such behavior as relates to solutions of puzzles, games of chance, games of strategy, and creation of various art forms. They then reason backward to what personality attributes would be requisite to the evolvement of such games and activities, or "folk models" of behavior. As other contributors to this volume believe, these authors also feel that traditional drive reduction and instrumental theories of motivation need to be drastically revamped or replaced to be compatible with the evolvement of activities that apparently are pursued in all cultures for seemingly intrinsic reasons.

In Chapter 7 Garfinkel shows the psychological consequence of refuting implicit but not necessarily articulated aspects of social norms. This is done by observing reactions to violation of "commonsense culture," those unformalized rules and regulations which members of a group or society tend to follow and which are assumed to be followed by other members. The importance of negating the "commonsensically ordered and ordering routines of every day actions" to anomie, alienation, and deviance is also discussed.

In Chapter 8 Lanzetta treats problem solving as a situation in which the individual is faced with the different and the unexpected. Both situational and individualistic determinants of search behavior, risk taking, and general approach to problem solution are treated. Reactions to such discrepant situations are considered within the general paradigm of dissonance theory.

In Chapter 9 Scott continues the focus on cognitive or conceptual structure, with the emphasis on problems surrounding definition and measurement of relevant cognitive dimensions and attributes. As his chapter makes clear, many of us use the same terms for different behavioral or phenomenal constructs while others of us commit the reverse practice. Some methodological approaches to clearing up both linguistic and constructual confusion and ambiguity are described. Moreover, the point is made clear that while certain meaningful inferences may be made about the theoretical construct under test by samples of behavior at removed levels it is advantageous, both theoretically and methodologically, to measure the construct as directly as possible, a practice that is fairly rarely followed in work with cognitive and conceptual structure.

In Chapter 10 Harvey comments briefly on issues of some degree of theoretical accord and then describes what appear to him to be some of the more important unsolved questions relating to effects of incongruous inputs.

Chapter 2

The Pooling Mechanism and the
Phenomena of Reinforcement

WILLIAM BEVAN

The historian of the psychology of learning some day may very well characterize the present period as the reinforcement era. For several decades—but particularly during the past one or two—this concept has held the attention of an impressive array of extremely able minds (e.g., Thorndike, Hull, Tolman, Muenzinger, Spence, Skinner, and Estes). Thus, it is surely presumptuous for a perceptionist with only the most superficial knowledge of learning to address himself to the question of how reinforcing agents achieve their effects upon performance. Without admitting any responsibility for elaborating or reviewing extant reinforcement theories, I should like to begin with the assumption that these conceptual treatments are generally ineffective in accommodating certain rather important reinforcement phenomena. These latter relate to the way in which performance efficiency varies as a function of complex patterns of reinforcement stimulation: its association with intensive changes in the reinforcing agent, the relative frequency with which the agent is applied, the temporal characteristics of the reinforcement program, its randomness or non-randomness, etc. There are empirical data which bear on these matters and certain facets of the question of schedules have been systematically dealt with by Skinner and his followers (cf., e.g., Skinner and Ferster, 1957). Meanwhile, the problem of the relationship between performance efficiency and the intensive aspects of reinforcement has received relatively little systematic attention until the decade of the 1950's and attempts to fit it to existing learning theories have not been altogether impressive.

The purpose of this paper is to explore the possible fruitfulness of adapting a conceptual formulation from the realm of psychophysics—the pooling model of adaptation-level theory—to the explanation of these reinforcement phenomena. Beyond this brief introduction, it will consist of a description of the important properties of reinforcement and of the pooling model, and, finally, a review of certain of the evidence available to substantiate this position.

The Properties of Reinforcement

The reinforcement system is an intervening mechanism that has as its major property the capacity of either enhancing or hampering performance efficiency for those aspects of the response complex to which it relates.[1] Under optimum conditions it increases the likelihood that certain reactions will occur, while it decreases the likelihood that other responses will be evoked. Under other conditions it may not only fail to facilitate improved performance but actually contribute to its deterioration. Thus, when motivation in a task reaches emotion-provoking proportions, the addition of either reward or punishment may lead to a breakdown of behavior. Reinforcement is difficult to classify as a variable. While it has been common to think of it in the context of energetics—i.e., drives, needs, urges, etc.—on the one hand and in terms of affectivity—i.e., as somehow related to the pleasant or unpleasant consequences of an act—on the other, it also appears to be related to cognitive functions: for example, to the variable, knowledge of results.[2] As an intraorganismic process or set of processes, it is influenced not only by the motivational status of the organism, but also by its past experience with reinforcers. Perhaps most important of all, it has integrity over time in the same sense that memory processes, for example, have integrity over time. As a determinant of behavior, its most characteristic property is intensity. While particular reinforcing agents may be qualitatively different, their influence upon performance must be described as either great or small. A particular reward and a particular punishment may be opposites as affective consequents of an act; at the same time, they may be equivalents as reinforcing agents. Finally, it appears most parsimonious to identify reinforcement with performance rather than with learning. In specific instances, of course, this is easier said

[1] The present writer recognizes that performance efficiency is a looser concept than is immediately apparent. What it implies varies with the situations to which it refers; in general, it connotes what is commonly meant by good and bad performance. When the acquisition of responses is a prominent feature of the behavior under consideration, performance efficiency is indicated by time and/or error scores; when operant behaviors are involved, rate or speed defines efficiency; when the behavior is a motor skill, precision is the index.

[2] Woodworth some years ago (1947) postulated a will to perceive and theorized that the achievement of an organized perception constitutes reinforcement in the service of this need. More recently Hebb (1955), from a consideration of the McGill studies on sensory isolation (e.g., Bexton, Heron, and Scott, 1954) as well as Harlow's work on manipulation (e.g., 1953) and Berlyne's on curiosity (e.g., 1950), has concluded that the immediate drive value of cognitive experience is established.

than done, for in most observable behaviors learning and performance variables are confounded to greater or less degree.

Much of what has just been stated is not readily discernible in the prevalent current views regarding reinforcement. For example, it has been common practice to equate reinforcement with the reinforcer. Thus, Kimble (1956) in his introductory text uses the terms reward and reinforcement interchangeably. It is, therefore, also not surprising that in experiments dealing with the relationship between performance and reinforcement magnitude the most widely used design has involved independent groups receiving different but fixed magnitudes of reinforcer. Indeed, with certain exceptions, experimenters on reinforcement have tended to beg the problem of reinforcement magnitude and have concerned themselves more often with the variable of reinforcer frequency. This is epitomized by a great interest in schedules of reinforcement and the performance phenomena associated with these. Finally, implicit in most views appears to be the assumption that reinforcement is discontinuous and temporally confined to the periods when reinforcing agents are applied. To paraphrase Thorndike (1949), rewards stamp in responses; to paraphrase Muenzinger (1946), punishment alerts the subject to the critical cues at the choice-point. This assumption means that reinforcement, in its effect at any specific moment, is virtually independent of the organism's past history of reinforcement. It implies what Hobhouse (1901) long ago recognized as the retroaction paradox.

Adaptation-Level and the Principle of Pooling

Helson (1959), in his chapter in Koch's recent first volume, has formally enumerated ten postulates upon which his theory of adaptation level is based. A brief summary of certain of these provides a readily grasped description of what is meant by the principle of pooling: First of all, it is assumed that every instance of behavior is defined with reference to some appropriate adaptation level or internal norm. This intraorganismic reference level is derived from an interaction of all relevant present stimuli (simultaneous pooling) as well as from a combination of present and past inputs (successive pooling). The existence of the adaptation level furthermore implies a bipolarity within response systems. Stimuli above it evoke one kind of response, those below it, the opposite reaction. Finally, because patterns of input typically are variable, the adaptation level is a changing value. This, in turn, means that the effect of any particular stimulus upon this organism will be variable, for its properties depend upon its scalar relationship to the prevailing norm.

Adaptation level is formally defined by the expression

$$AL = S^p B^q R^r$$

where S represents the magnitude of present stimulation, B, the relevant scalar values of the background, and R, the contribution of unassessed variables including such inputs as motivation and past experience. The exponents, p, q, and r, are weighting coefficients which indicate the contribution of each class of variable to the norm. The precise mathematical statement of these relationships, of course, will differ with the stimulus and response dimensions under consideration and other factors. The scalar value of particular responses may, meanwhile, be identified by the expression

$$R = K(S - AL)$$

where R indicates the scalar value of the response, K is a psychophysical constant, S is the scalar value of present stimulation, and AL, that of the appropriate internal standard.

Helson was led to his formulation of the adaptation-level principle by his observations of color constancy and contrast (Helson, 1938). He discovered that he could specify successfully the hue, brightness, and chroma of achromatic patches in colored light in terms of the dominant wavelength of the ambient illumination, the lightness of the background, and the reflectance of the patch itself. He later (Helson, 1947) found that the indifference point (adaptation level) for other psychophysical dimensions could be predicted accurately in this same fashion. Thus, for example, if you present a series of weights, regularly spaced between 200 and 400 grams, for single-stimulus judgment, each weight appearing equally often in the order of presentation, you may expect the indifference point (IP—the stimulus magnitude judged neither heavy nor light, but medium or neutral) to be about 250 grams and predictable by the expression, $\log (AL - .75d) = \log \Sigma Xi/N$. If a weight weighing 90 grams is next added to the order of presentation as a standard, the IP will be seen to drop to about 190 grams. Conversely, if the additional weight is 900 grams, the IP will be a higher 340 grams. The apparent loudness of a tone, the brightness of a light, the heaviness of a weight, etc., is thus not simply a function of its physical magnitude but depends also on the nature of the background, the properties of the stimulus series, and other conditions.

The essential nature of pooling may be further illustrated by the application which Darby and I (Bevan and Darby, 1955) have made of adaptation-level theory to the problem of stimulus equivalence in the psychophysical setting. This involved fixing the left side of Helson's equation at an arbitrarily selected value. Also held constant were the relative frequency of presentation and the physical magnitude of all but one stimulus represented on the right side of the equation. Then, by successively changing the relative frequency of presentation for this item over a wide range and by solving for its corresponding magnitude, values were obtained from which to construct a curve of equivalent inputs. The several points on this curve specified the relative frequency with which a stimulus of some particular magnitude must be presented without causing a shift in adaptation level. An empirical test of the limits of the curve revealed it to hold over an unexpectedly wide range. For every twelve trials of a series of four weights, it was found possible to add to the order a fifth weight, varying in heaviness over a range of 1000 grams and in frequency of presentation between once and 100 times, without producing a difference between predicted and obtained AL's of more than 1 or 2 per cent. These data are of interest because they represent not only the successful prediction of a set of equivalence relationships but also a new type of "constancy" that holds in the face of changing patterns of stimulation.

Performance Efficiency and Level of Arousal

Another relationship warrants comment before exposition of the present position is possible. This concerns level of directed arousal and performance efficiency. A great variety of experiments involving such variables as magnitude of incentive, task difficulty, drive level, and degree of vigilance all point to its being curvilinear in nature. It is seen, for example, in the data that led to the formulation of the Yerkes-Dodson principle in the early 1900's (Yerkes and Dodson, 1908). It may be inferred from Pavlov's identification of excitable, central, and inhibitable types of dogs (Pavlov, 1928). It has been made explicit by Hebb (1955) in his discussion of the relation between effectiveness of cue function and level of arousal. This relationship between tension level and performance involves both the somatic and the vegetative processes. Thus, while Courts (1939) some years ago reported that the recall of nonsense syllables was first enhanced and later fell below control level as the subject increased the force with which he squeezed a hand dynamometer during the course of learning, Meyer and Noble (1958) more recently have found that dynamometer tension facilitates the learning of a verbal maze by subjects with low scores on the Taylor Manifest-Anxiety Scale while it causes the performance of high-anxiety subjects to deteriorate.

The Relation of Reinforcement to Performance

The following interpretation of the relation of reinforcement to performance was first presented by Adamson and myself several years ago (Bevan and Adamson, 1958). Since that time we have had further opportunity to collect supporting evidence from studies carried out in our own and other laboratories. A revised statement has appeared as a chapter in Volume II of *Decisions, Values, and Groups* (Bevan and Adamson, 1961). Our point of view is best presented as a set of eight statements, some assumptive and some axiomatic:

1. Reinforcing agents are stimuli (S) which vary, as do other stimuli, in frequency of occurrence, have temporal duration, and differ in intensity. Whether or not a stimulus acts as a reinforcer depends upon a number of considerations that need not be made explicit in this presentation. For persons like the present writer, prone to think in cognitive terms, one important factor concerns the subject's identifying the stimulation in one way or another as associated with the task at hand.

2. Upon application, S gives rise to stimulation processes (s) within the organism, these processes having the property of intensity.

3. The organism is selective, differentiating stimulation (s) into two classes: primary stimulation (s_p) and background stimulation (s_b). These processes are inferred stimulus variables roughly corresponding to the Gestalt dichotomy of figures and ground or Helson's categories of focal and contextual stimuli.

4. The organism is a norm-creating system, averaging stimulation over time to produce an internal standard or referent ($\bar{s}$), defined by the expression

$$\bar{s} = \left[\frac{(s_{b_1} s_{b_2} \ldots s_{b_n})^x}{N_b} \quad \frac{(s_{p_1} s_{p_2} \ldots s_{p_n})^y}{N_p} \right]$$

where the first term on the right side represents the average magnitude of the background processes over a series of inputs, the second stands for the average intensity of primary stimulation of the reinforcement sequence, and the exponents indicate the relative contributions of s_b and s_p to the norm.

5. The magnitude differential between s_p and $\bar{s}$ at the time (t) that S is applied relates directly to the judged magnitude of S, expressed as (R_{j_t}). This differential is identified as Δ_s. It is reinforcement magnitude as distinct from the magnitude of the reinforcing agent (S). The expression, $\Delta_s = s_p - \bar{s}$, may be positive, negative, or zero. Accordingly, R_{j_t} is strong, weak, or medium (neutral).

6. The occurrence of behavior presupposes an organism which is aroused or under tension. Like $\bar{s}$, tension level ($\bar{t}$) is regarded as having temporal continuity. It is an average which, at any given moment, presumably represents the actions of a multiplicity of variables, only one of which (Δ_s) is considered in the present formulation. Factors such as deprivation and physiological status contribute heavily to $\bar{t}$, but the present concern is limited to the specific effects of the reinforcement process upon it.

7. The relationship between tension level and a generic class of indices labeled response-efficiency is held to be curvilinear, poorer performance being associated with both high and low values of $\bar{t}$ about an intermediate optimal level.

8. The effectiveness of a reinforcer in altering performance is held to be a function of the concurrent magnitudes of Δ_s and residual $\bar{t}$.

There are then three major assumptions that define our point of view: (a) The organism averages stimulation, including that associated with reinforcing agents; (b) it reacts with reference to an internal norm based on this average; and (c) response efficiency is a curvilinear reflection of tension level. Furthermore, certain considerations must be kept in mind as implications of this formulation are reviewed. First, concern is with the relationship between performance and reinforcement magnitude over trials. Secondly, since the present formulation is not, in itself, a theory of learning, certain issues of significance to learning theory are of little concern to this discussion. Thus the question of latent learning presents no problem, for, since the occurrence of reinforcement has not been identified as a sole, necessary, or even sufficient condition of learning, learning may or may not occur in the absence of discrete reinforcing agents. Similarly, no distinction is drawn between primary and secondary reinforcement. Since reinforcement is identified as an intervening system capable of influencing performance through shifts it induces in tension level, the terms "primary" and "secondary" are regarded as labels which identify reinforcing agents in terms of their etiology. The functional distinction between "positive" and "negative" reinforcement also disappears with a recognition of the empirical problem of ordering a repertoire of reinforcing agents in terms of their relative effectiveness. Finally, the present approach circumvents the controversy concerning whether reinforcement is related to drive induction or drive reduction, because it maintains that any series of events that induces a change in tension level will be effective in changing performance. By the same token, it accommodates data (e.g., those of Zimbardo and Miller (1958)) to the effect that hungry rats run faster than sated animals even when food and water are absent in the goal box and there is no evidence of acquired fear that indicate that "irrelevant" drives facilitate performance.

Some Implications of the Present Point of View

This final section discusses particular reinforcement phenomena within the context of the formulation just outlined. Appropriate references to the empirical literature will be included, although no attempt has been made to be encyclopedic in coverage.

Reinforcing Agents as Psychophysical Stimuli. Before exploring the applicability of the adaptation-level model to the phenomena of reinforcement, it seemed wise to examine the proposition that reinforcing agents possess certain properties that characterize the stimuli of psychophysical experiments: particularly, the capability of being ordered along a dimension or judged intensity for which a neutral point may be derived, and sensitivity to anchor or series effects. Adamson and I (1960) made such an examination of electric shock, a commonly used reinforcer. Subjects were asked to make rating-scale judgments of five physical intensities of shock under three different conditions. In one, each intensity was presented the same number of times; in another, the frequency distribution was skewed so that the weaker intensities were presented more often than the strong; in the third, the frequency distribution was subjected to more severe positive skewing. The specific expectation of the experimenters was that if electric shock behaved like more conventional psychophysical stimuli in the adaptation-level experiment, the stimulus value corresponding to a judgment of medium would decrease as the degree of positive skewness increased. The data confirmed this expectation.

Effective Intensity of Reinforcement and Performance Efficiency. An obvious inference from the present position is that the effectiveness of a particular reinforcing agent is not a fixed value, since the differential between the magnitude of the stimulation process associated with it and the reinforcement AL will change as a result of prior pooling. This inference will evidence itself in a variety of ways in the following paragraphs. Meanwhile, since it is assumed that there is a direct relationship between this differential and the judged magnitude of the reinforcing agent, a simple way of describing the relationship is to state that performance efficiency relates directly to the judged, in contrast to the physical, magnitude of the reinforcing agent. Physical magnitude has its influence upon performance as it reflects itself through apparent magnitude.

Several experiments carried out in our laboratory provide empirical support for this interpretation (Bevan and Adamson, 1960; Black, Adamson, and Bevan, 1961). In these, the research strategy was to demonstrate that the effect upon performance of some particular intensity of reinforcer differed as a function of the intensity of pretest stimulation to which the subject was exposed. One experiment involved human maze learning, the other white rats in a straight-away. In the former, three groups of subjects, prior to performing the maze task, were required to judge the intensities of 30 presentations of a brief shock. For one the shock was physically weak, for another it was of medium strength, and for the third, it was physically strong. Next, all groups made a fixed number of trials in a two-choice bolt head maze problem and received the medium shock as punishment for each erroneous choice. Performance curves constructed from the data of the three groups revealed the influence of the pretest treatment. On the early trials all groups performed at chance level, but with further trials the curves diverged revealing different rates of progress. The best performance was obtained from the group adapted to the weak pretest shock. Performance was poorest in the group that received the strong pretest shock. The performance of the group both adapted to and tested with medium shock plotted between these two extremes. Statistical tests indicated the poor performance group to be significantly poorer than the other two, although the superiority of the best over the intermediate failed demonstration at conventionally accepted confidence levels. These results indicate, in line with expectation, that the effectiveness of a reinforcing agent is not a simple matter of its physical intensity but depends upon the background of reinforcement upon which it occurs.

Meanwhile, recognizing that maze performance is a complex product of both learning and motivation, we decided to reproduce the paradigm of the maze experiment with a simple task. In order to check the generality of the maze results, it was decided to use other than human subjects. Accordingly, the situation selected was the white rat in the straight-away. Four groups of animals were involved. Three received ten trials a day in a shuttle box, one group with weak, one with medium, and one with strong shock. Immediately after its shuttle box trials, each animal received ten trials in the straight-away with the medium intensity of shock. The fourth group was tested in the straight-away alone to provide information on habituation to shock. The performance curves of the three groups receiving pretest shock corroborate the results of the maze study. The best performance (fastest running) occurred in the group adapted to the weak pretest shock. Again, the performance of the group receiving medium intensity shock in both the shuttle box and the straight-away was of intermediate efficiency. Here also, the difference between the superior and the intermediate group was suggestive but not statistically demonstrated. Over-all, however, it would appear that speed of running, like maze performance, varies with the apparent, in contrast to the physical, strength of the reinforcing agent.

An earlier study of Lawson (1957) suggests support for this conclusion with positive reinforcers. Rats were required to perform concurrently for food in two brightness discrimination problems. Some subjects received a relatively large amount of food for each correct response on each problem; others received a small amount for both problems; still others received a large amount on one problem and a small amount on the other. There were no significant differences among the scores for the groups receiving the same magnitude of reinforcer on both problems. Meanwhile, as we would have predicted, the animals receiving the large amount on one problem and the small amount on the other made reliably fewer errors on the large-reward than on the small-reward task.

In the studies just described, the reinforcement context arises from the serial patterning of reinforcing inputs. Another interesting facet concerns the intensitive structure of the stimulus complex within which the reinforcing agent appears. If the intensive level of the reinforcing agent is sufficiently above the level of its background, it will appear as an intense stimulus; if it is below, it will be judged weak; and if the physical intensities of the agent and its background are about the same, the reinforcer will be medium or neutral in quality. The fact that light onset may be used as a reinforcer for the operant bar-pressing response provides a convenient device for exploring this figure-ground relationship. Some particular intensity of s_p should be more effective when it is greater than s_b than when it is less intense than s_b. An experiment of Hurwitz (1960) has some bearing on this point. Two groups of rats were subjected to a series of daily periods in Skinner boxes with the bar available. For one group the boxes were illuminated, for the other kept dark. Then both groups were tested in dark boxes, with bar pressing resulting in light onset. Reasoning from the present point of view that exposure to illumination during the operant sessions would produce an internal standard that would reduce the effectiveness of the light-onset reinforcer, Hurwitz expected greater bar-pressing activity during tests from the animals adapted in dark boxes. This is exactly what he found. A more elaborate examination of these context relationships would involve using different levels of ambient illumination in the box, both before and during tests, and allowing the reinforcer intensity to vary to different extents both above and below these ambient levels.

Effectiveness of Reinforcement and the Distinctiveness of the Reinforcing Agent. Following from the above discussion of context is the proposition that the more readily the reinforcer may be distinguished from its context, that is, the greater the intensitive difference between s_p and s_b, the greater its effectiveness as a reinforcer will be. A psychophysical analogue is found in the AL studies of color constancy and contrast: The more removed the stimulus is from the neutral point, the more saturated it appears. Support for this prediction is found in a conditioning study of Kessen (1953). Working with an avoidance response, he held the US constant and varied the magnitude of the CS and reported both latency and the number of CR's evoked to be a positive function of the CS intensity. If we may assume that the CS appeared within an essentially constant context, then the magnitude of the corresponding stimulation process may be described as a differential between s_p and s_b.

Adaptation to Repeated Reinforcement. It is a commonly observed fact that with repeated application a reinforcer of fixed magnitude loses its effectiveness. This may be accounted for as follows: Since s_p is not only differentiated from $\bar{s}$ at moment t, the time of application, but also has been assimilated into $\bar{s}$ at $t+1$, the differential between s_p and $\bar{s}$ is gradually reduced. Thus the reinforcer gradually takes on neutral quality. Since each subsequent presentation of s_p adds a small increment to $\bar{s}$, the loss in effectiveness may be expected to be a negatively accelerated function of the number of presentations. This means that in order to maintain the effectiveness of a reinforcer, it is necessary to change its intensity at the same rate that it is neutralized through pooling. A special case in point would appear to be the loss of the orienting reflex, first noted by Pavlov and more recently the subject of intensive study by Russian investigators of conditioning, with repeated presentations of the unconditioned stimulus that originally aroused it (Razran, 1961).

Patterns of Intermittent Reinforcement and Performance Efficiency. The present explanatory scheme predicts that certain patterns of intermittent reinforcement have a greater effect upon performance than continuous application of the reinforcing agent. If a non-reinforced trial is viewed as a trial on which the organism receives reinforcement of zero intensity, then such trials should have the effect of reducing $\bar{s}$ and thus of enhancing the magnitude of Δ_s. Depending upon the length of the reinforcement series at the moment the agent is applied, a single non-reinforcer may have a great or small effect upon the magnitude of the reinforcement. Generally, it may be expected to have a relatively small effect. Since the apparent magnitude of the agent on the trial following zero reinforcement should be enhanced (i.e., the $s_p - \bar{s}$ differential should be greater), performance, under optimum conditions, with an intermittent schedule should be superior to that for a continuous schedule. Meanwhile, if we recognize the curvilinear relationship between average tension level and performance efficiency, then the best performance may be expected from subjects on some schedule of intermediate intermittency, with poorer performance associated with continuous reinforcement, on the one hand, and with infrequent reinforcement, on the other. This is what Grant and Schipper (1952) found in a study of partial reinforcement in eye-blink conditioning. The largest number of CR's *per reinforcement* were associated with the 50 and 75 per cent schedules, poorer performance with the 25 and 100 per cent schedules.

A special aspect of the problem of intermittent reinforcement is the use of non-random programs of partial reinforcement. For example, Bloom and Capaldi (1961) have recently studied the relative effectiveness of the single and double alternation of reinforced and non-reinforced trials. The adaptation-level interpretation of reinforcement, extending the reasoning of the above paragraph, would anticipate superior performance under the double-alternation program. Bloom and Capaldi report faster running in rats on both reinforced and non-reinforced trials of the double-alternation schedule than on the non-reinforced trials of the single-alternation schedule. In the early stages of testing, performance on the reinforced trials of the single-alternation schedule were inferior to that on double alternation, but after about eight days of testing, these became practically identical with the double-alternation speeds.

Related to the question of intermittent schedules is that of performance changes during extinction, for, in terms of the experimental operations used, the acquisition and extinction phases of testing may be described as a block of reinforced trials followed by a block of non-reinforced trials. Considering them in this light, we would expect that the most abrupt shift in performance would occur with a continuous schedule followed by extinction trials, since the differential between the reinforcement norm and the extinction condition (zero reinforcement) would be maximal. Less marked changes should be observed with partial schedules. An experiment by Bowers (1960) supports this prediction. Using escape from a charged runway as reinforcement, he found a marked and abrupt reduction in running speed in animals which had received 100 per cent reinforcement, when the goal box was charged during extinction trials, while rats on a 50 per cent schedule showed very little difference in running speed between the final stages of acquisition and the extinction phase.

The Temporal Spacing of Reinforced Trials. Since this view of reinforcement contends that each application of a reinforcer of fixed magnitude brings its effective value some increment closer to an indifference point, it follows that rapid repetition of the agent should be accompanied by relatively rapid neutralization with an attendant decrement in performance efficiency. Meanwhile, the curvilinear function describing the tension level-performance relationship prompts the expectation that too wide spacing of reinforcements also will be identified with poorer performance, for regardless of how intense reinforcement is on a single trial, extended periods of zero reinforcement cannot be supportive of tension at an effective level for good performance. The loss of effectiveness just predicted is frequently seen in conditioning (Deese, 1953). It was identified some twenty-five years ago by Hovland (1936) as inhibition of reinforcement. Some recent data of Cotton and Lewis (1957) on runway behavior are in line with expectation, although they lack statistical verification. Animals were run to food at intervals of either one-fourth, two, eight, or sixteen minutes. The fastest runners were the two-minute animals, and the next were the one-fourth-minute animals, with the eight- and sixteen-minute animals making still poorer scores.

An interesting facet of the problem of spacing involves the variable of delay of reinforcement and the consideration that the subject may treat this as he does the substantive dimensions of the reinforcer, integrating delays and deriving expectancy norms just as he derives magnitude norms. An experiment is currently planned for our laboratory program and data on this point should be available shortly.

Performance with Shifts in Reinforcement Magnitude. An interest in the effects of changing reinforcement magnitude during training first led Adamson and me to consider the possible fruitfulness of conceptualizing reinforcement in adaptation-level terms, for the analogy between this operation and the use of an anchor is readily apparent. It is to be expected that subjects exposed to such shifts downward or upward will drop below or rise above the performance of controls on a comparable but single magnitude of reinforcer. This is, of course, the contrast effect reported by Crespi (1942) and described in many papers since that time. An interesting example of contrast in differential conditioning has been reported by Bower (1961). Rats were trained concurrently in two runways. In one they were reinforced with eight pellets per trial and in the other with one pellet per trial. Control groups received either one or eight pellets in both alleys. The animals receiving differential reinforcement did reliably poorer than the one-pellet animals on the one-pellet alley. Performance in the eight-pellet alley, meanwhile, was slightly but not significantly less than that of the eight-pellet group, suggesting but not confirming a kind of regression toward the reinforcement mean in the differentially reinforced subjects.

An experiment from the series carried out by Adamson and me (1960) demonstrates very nicely that subjects integrate reinforcement magnitudes over trials. Four groups of subjects were tested on a bolt head maze task. Five intensities of shock were used in varying combinations as reinforcing stimuli. Group A received a positively skewed, randomly sequenced distribution, with the average intensity below the midpoint of the series. Group B was given a negatively skewed distribution with the average above the series midpoint. Group C received a symmetrical distribution with the average intensity at the midpoint. And Group D was a control group receiving the midpoint intensity on all trials. All reinforcements were for errors, the subject shocking himself automatically each time he made an incorrect choice. The poorest performance was obtained from Group A, the group receiving the lowest mean intensity of shock, the next poorest from Group B, the subjects given the highest average intensity of shock. The best performance was given by Groups C and D, which did not differ reliably from each other. Not only did the three different average levels of shock yield different average performances, they also displayed reliably different rates of learning, a fact that tends to refute Hull's early contention that amount of reinforcement affects the final asymptote of performance, but not the rate of approach to this value (Hull, 1943). The fact that curves for Groups C and D are almost superimposed, one upon the other, is especially convincing evidence for pooling. Ancillary to the main purpose of this experiment, these data also provide support for earlier statements about the relationship between tension level and performance, for, if average performance is plotted against average intensity, the curve will be bowed upward with the best performance coinciding with moderate shock levels.

Performance with Combinations of Different Types of Reinforcement. The point of view outlined in the present paper makes no functional distinction between different classes of reinforcer. All are characterized in terms of their effective magnitude and have their effect through their influence on the level of arousal. But it does recognize that different classes may interact and these interactions may be expected to reveal themselves in changes in effective magnitude. For example, rewards and punishments are both reinforcing. Both may be defined in terms of their facilitative influence upon performance, and both may be scaled in terms of their effectiveness in this regard. And, while their respective ranges of influence may not coincide, they at least overlap to a marked degree. The present position implies that it is each's intensity relative to the reinforcement norm—not its beneceptive or nociceptive quality—which determines its effectiveness in altering performance. Meanwhile, rewards and punishments lie on opposite sides of the neutral point of a psychophysical dimension of affectivity, and this fact may produce contrast effects when they are used in combination. Thus, the effective intensity of some specific physical intensity of punishment may be enhanced if it has been preceded by a sequence of rewards. Conversely, some particular reward may be more effective as a reinforcer if it has been preceded by punishment.

An experiment in our laboratory, involving the learning of nonsense syllables, is being carried out to explore these possibilities.

Performance with Reinforcement for Errors Versus Reinforcement of Correct Responses. The above section has stressed the intensive level in contrast to the quality of reinforcement. If affectivity associated with reinforcers relates to performance efficiency, it is because of its general arousal value—i.e., because it is capable of causing a shift in tension level. Thus, it follows that a consideration of which should be reinforced—correct responses or errors—is of little theoretical consequence. Any difference in effect may be presumed to be due to a difference in the temporal point in training at which each predominates, or in some other empirical consideration. Muenzinger's studies of T-maze performance (1946) would appear to provide evidence for this conclusion, although the situation perhaps is complicated by the fact that the correction method was used. When rats were run in a brightness discrimination problem with the correct goal box baited with food, it required, on the average, 114 trials to reach criterion. When shock was added for errors, performance efficiency was enhanced, criterion being reached in 39 trials. Meanwhile, when shock was presented on the correct turn, performance to criterion occurred in 49 trials and, when given for both correct and incorrect responses, criterion performance averaged 40 trials. Performance under each of three shock conditions was reliably better than under the control (food alone) condition. However, there were no significant differences among the three shock groups.

Resistance to Extinction and Reinforced Performance Following Extinction. In the discussion of the intermittent application of reinforcers and its relation to performance, reference was made to the place of extinction within this conceptual framework. If the period of extinction is considered as a sequence of zero or some minimum reinforcement trials, then tension may be expected to return toward its initial level, with a consequent reduction in performance efficiency. At the same time, the usual period of deprivation that is interposed between extinction sessions may be expected to enhance tension level and thus make possible spontaneous recovery as well as the disinhibitory effect of "irrelevant" stimuli.

It has been observed (e.g., Perin, 1942) that extinction occurs more readily following a short sequence of reinforced trials than after a long sequence. This fact is consistent with expectation. In the case of the short series, as contrasted to the long, the reinforcement norm lies closer to the pretest level and each extinction trial has proportionately greater weight and thus tends to more quickly return the norm to this level. Meanwhile, resistance to contrast-induced shifts in performance may be expected to be greater for smaller than for larger changes in level of reinforcement. The change from low level reinforcement to extinction trials is perhaps a special case of this relationship. When small magnitudes are used, the maximal value at which the reinforcement norm may stabilize following a course of reinforcements is necessarily closer to the pretest level than if an intense stimulus is used. Thus Δ_s associated with the extinction trials is less intense and therefore less effective. Put in phenomenological language, the shift from low level of zero reinforcement is marked by low-level contrast. The same reasoning may be applied to the problem of extinction following continuous and partial reinforcement. Since the reinforcement norm for an aperiodic schedule after some arbitrary number of trials must lie closer to zero than that for continuous reinforcement, the Δ_s associated with extinction must be weaker and, therefore, resistance to extinction greater. Lawson (1960) suggests that the first prediction may have empirical support while the greater resistance to extinction associated with partial reinforcement is well known (cf., e.g., Jenkins, McFann, and Clayton, 1950).

Finally, the larger the number of extinction trials employed, the greater the $s_p - \bar{s}$ differential must be when reinforcement is again instituted. This suggests that enhancement effects of the contrast variety also should follow periods of extinction. Adamson, Maier, and I (1961) investigated this possibility with the bar-pressing response. While our data are not in every way definitive, they indicate that the inflection of the performance curve for a post-extinction period of reinforcement occurred sooner than that in the pre-extinction curve and at a higher level. The higher rate of responding persisted through the second reinforcement period. Finally, the initial drop in response rate in a second extinction period was clearly greater than its counterpart in the first.

Conclusion

Any theory of reinforcement, to be of ultimate value, must explicate the role of reinforcing stimuli in the great variety of complex situations that characterize human behavior. Before this is possible, a great deal of information must be acquired. The significant properties that identify a great diversity of stimuli as reinforcers must be identified and scaled. Indeed, stimuli used as reinforcers must be placed on common dimensions. How they behave as they share different degrees of contingency with responses, how they relate to each other when they occur in combination, how their strength varies as a function of their immediacy—these are things which must be better known. Eventually, it should be possible to state precisely, given a typical subject, how performance will fare under the great range of reinforcement conditions met by human beings outside the laboratory. Meanwhile, we are confident that the analogy of perceptual contrast and the principle of pooling are worthy of exploration by students of reinforcement.

Chapter 3

Motivation Inherent in Information Processing and Action

J. McV. Hunt [1]

The questions about the springs of human action that motivational theory attempts to answer are at least as old as the generalized thinking of such Greeks as Plato (see his *Philebus*), but the term *motive*, according to the *Oxford Universal Dictionary*, came with the Renaissance. It derives from the medieval Latin word *"movere,"* meaning "to move," and it is defined as "that which tends to move a person to a course of action." The conception had its beginnings in Descartes' (1649) attempt to explain the behavior of animals on mechanistic principles, but this derives in turn from ancient Greek notions that material (the bodies of animals and men) and motion (behavior) are separate orders of existence and that material moves only when motion is imparted to it by force. This conception put the springs of organismic action outside organisms, made them extrinsic. In spite of Claude Bernard's (1859) discovery of, and emphasis on, the internal milieu as one source of these springs of action, they have continued, largely, to be conceived of as extrinsic, at least to cognitive process and to action per se. The purpose of this paper is to review a variety of lines of evidence implying intrinsic motivation, i.e., springs of action that inhere in cognition (information processing) and action.

The questions that motivation theory has attempted to answer have never been fully agreed upon, but the various theories have typically attempted to answer some portion of eight major questions. The first question concerns why organisms are active at all. What instigates their activities, and what stops them? This may be termed the *instigation* question. The second concerns what factors control the vigor of activity. This may be termed the energization question. The third concerns what

[1] This paper is part of a project supported by a grant from the Carnegie Corporation of New York. I acknowledge this support with gratitude.

controls the direction of behavior, whether an organism will approach
or avoid a given situation, and what will be the hedonic value of the
situation. This may be termed the *direction-hedonic* question. The
fourth concerns what factors determine whether organisms become attached to certain objects, places, and persons, and come to seek them
rather than others. This is the *cathexis* question. The fifth concerns
the choice of response, and the sixth concerns the choice of goals. These
may be termed the *choice* questions. The seventh concerns the factors
underlying behavioral and conceptual change, and it may be termed the
learning question. The eighth concerns why organisms persist in utilizing responses that fail to achieve their goals and why they persist in
seeking goals they do not achieve. This may be termed the *persistence*
question.

The Traditionally Dominant Conceptual Scheme

Although debate has never been wanting concerning motivation, a
pattern of beliefs that answer these questions has been growing and
developing dominance from shortly after the turn of the twentieth
century up through the sixth decade. First, according to this dominant
conceptual scheme, organisms are instigated to act by strong and painful
external stimuli, by such homeostatic needs as hunger and thirst, by sex,
or by innocuous stimuli which have been associated with (conditioned
to emotional responses evoked by) the strong painful stimuli or the
homeostatic needs and sex. Behavior is instigated by some combination
of these conditions that are presumed to produce a generalized inner
state of excitement which, since Woodworth (1918) first introduced the
term in America, has been called *drive*. The drive impels action. When
these conditions cease to operate, the drive ceases, and the behavior
stops.[2]

[2] Space prohibits full documentation of the statements in this synopsis of the traditionally dominant theory. It should be noted, nevertheless, that this answer to the
instigation question has both historical and empirical roots in the classic work of
Claude Bernard (1859), the investigations and theorizing of Walter B. Cannon
(1915), and the investigations of Curt Richter (1922, 1927). One can say that this
answer to the instigation question and those indicated below have been dominant
by virtue of the wide variety of theorists who have shared them. This answer to
the instigation question, for instance, has been shared essentially not only by the
originators but also by Carr (1925), Dashiell (1925, 1928), Dollard and Miller
(1950), Freeman (1934, 1948), Freud (1900, 1915), Guthrie (1938), Holt (1931),
Hull (1943), Melton (1941), Miller and Dollard (1941), Moss (1924), Mowrer
(1950), Thorndike (1913), Warden (1931), and Wood (1908). The notion of acquired or conditioned drive appears almost full-blown in Freud's (1915) *Instincts
and their Vicissitudes* and is shared in varying degrees of explicitness by Dashiell
(1928), Freeman (1934), Holt (1931), Tolman (1925), even though its explicit
formulations come from the Yale group of the fourth and fifth decades (see: Hull,
1943; Miller, 1948, 1951; Miller and Dollard, 1941; Mowrer, 1939).

Second, this traditionally dominant conception has found the determinants of the vigor of activity in the intensity of painful stimulation, or in the degree of homeostatic need, or in the intensity of the emotional responses that were originally part of the total response to such stimulation but which have come via conditioning to be evoked by originally innocuous stimuli. The gist of this statement concerning the primary painful stimuli and homeostatic needs has been widely accepted in varying degrees. In many cases, acceptance came before relevant empirical data were available to corroborate the belief, but supportive empirical evidence has been found (see Brown, 1961; Spence, 1956; Young, 1936, 1961). The relationship is far from perfect, however, and this fact induced Hull (1943) to consider the vigor, the likelihood, and the persistence of response to be a multiplicative function of the strengths of drive and of habit.[3]

Third, the answer to the direction-hedonic question has come in terms of drive reduction. Organisms are presumed to seek and to approach situations which will reduce the level of drive, and to withdraw from and to avoid situations which will increase the level of drive. Approach responses are presumed to be associated with positive hedonic

[3] Beyond the gist of this statement for the so-called primary drives, disagreement abounds. Whether homeostatic needs produce painful stimuli which not only instigate activities but energize them as well (Dollard and Miller, 1950; Freud, 1915; Hull, 1943; Miller and Dollard, 1941) or instigate the activation of "central motive states" which prime the organism for the exciting incentive value of receptor inputs that lead toward consummatory acts (see Beach, 1942; Lashley, 1938; Morgan, 1943, 1959; Spence, 1956; Stellar, 1954; Tolman, 1925) is still a matter of debate and investigation. The recognition of the relation of conditioned emotional excitement to its role in energization has been slower in coming. Although it was crudely recognized by Freud (1915) and by Dashiell (1928), and although Duffy (1934, 1941) had forcefully argued the role of emotion in the energization of behavior as late as the mid-1940's, Young and Leeper had a controversy over whether "emotion is acute disturbance or upset" (Young, 1943, p. 51) or "emotional processes . . . arouse, sustain, and direct activity" (Leeper, 1948, p. 17). More recently the role of emotion in the energization has been clearly formulated (Duffy, 1951, 1957; Lindsley, 1951, 1957; Miller, 1951; Mowrer, 1947, 1960; Solomon and Brush, 1956; Spence, 1956). Experimental investigations have demonstrated clearly that emotional arousal composing part of the total response to noxious stimulation can serve to motivate new acts (Gibson, 1952; Miller, 1948, 1951; Solomon and Brush, 1956). Probably Spence (1956, p. 180) has given the most explicit formulation of a quantitative relationship between the intensity of emotional arousal from painful stimuli and the vigor of conditioned responses, and McDonald (1946) has shown that at least in the case of the eye-blink to a puff of air and the finger withdrawal from electric shock, the vigor of the conditioned response is indeed a function of the intensity of the emotional excitement at the time of conditioning. This is to say that the vigor of the conditioned responses was weaker among subjects for whom conditioning took place after the GSR to repeated stimulation with air puffs to the eye or electric shocks to the finger had shown adaptive reduction than in subjects for whom no such opportunity for such adaptation had been allowed. For all the debate, clearly this traditionally dominant answer to the energization has a basis in experimental fact.

value, and withdrawal and avoidance with negative hedonic value. From the standpoint of this dominant conception, all motivation is aversive in character.[4]

Fourth, the answer to the cathexis question has come in these same terms of drive reduction. An organism is presumed to develop emotional attachments for those objects, places, and persons that are associated with drive reduction or lead to the anticipation of drive reduction. Thus, the human infant is presumed to become attached to the mother who serves to reduce the anxieties aroused by its hunger and other discomforts (Freud, 1926).[5]

Fifth, the choice of response has been conceived to be a function of the drive operative and the past experience of the organism with this drive. Each drive-stimulus presumably has an hierarchy of responses innately associated with it, and the one that is manifested is the one that has served effectively to reduce the drive in such situations in the past (Hull, 1943; Miller and Dollard, 1941).

Sixth, from the generic standpoint, the goal, or what Freud (1905, 1915) termed the "aim," of behavior is drive reduction. In the short-run sense, the goal-choice question becomes equivalent to the direction question already answered, but in the long-run sense, it concerns those relatively distant objectives distinctive of human action. Since a major share of the empirical information upon which the dominant conceptual scheme is based has come from either the observation of human beings in psychotherapy or experiments with such laboratory animals as rats, the answers to the long-run goal-choice question have been either indirect or extrapolative. The extrapolative answers have come largely in terms of the notion of acquired drives (see, e.g., Dollard and Miller, 1950; Miller and Dollard, 1941), but the extrapolations of acquired drives pose quandries, as Brown (1953) has pointed out.[6]

[4] Those believing in exciting and pleasurable incentives have not been wanting (see Bühler, 1918, 1928; Crespi, 1942; McDougall, 1923; McClelland et al., 1953; Spence, 1956; Thorndike, 1913; Tolman, 1925; and Young, 1936, 1961), but the dominant position has made pleasure a matter of drive-reduction (see Hull, 1943; Dollard and Miller, 1950; Miller, 1951; Miller and Dollard, 1941), or of the anticipation of drive-reduction (Mowrer, 1960). Although Freud (1905) wrote of pleasures deriving from the stimulation of the erogenous zones in his *Three Contributions*, Freud (1915), the more formal theorist, explicitly made pleasure a matter of reducing excitation. Moreover, at one place, Mowrer (1952, p. 423) has written, "At the level of ego-psychology, there may be said to be only one master motive: anxiety."

[5] For the most part, experimental psychologists have not been concerned with the cathexis question, but inadvertently they have produced evidence consonant with this dominant answer in the work on "secondary reinforcements" (see, e.g., Hilgard, 1956; Hull, p. 95; Hunt, 1945; and Mowrer, 1960).

[6] Nevertheless, the beginnings of empirically tested information about the bases for goal choices have been coming in the form of experiential developmental determinants of such motivational traits as aggression (Bandura and Walters, 1959); Levin and Sears, 1956; Sears, Whiting, *et al.*, 1953), dependency (Sears, Whiting, *et al.*,

Seventh, the basis for behavioral change or learning in the dominant conceptual scheme has been frustration. When any given mode of response ceases to reduce the drive, that mode is presumed to be weakened relative to the other responses in the ready-made hierarchy, and these are tried out in turn until one serves to reduce the drive (Hull, 1943; Melton, 1941; Miller and Dollard, 1941).[7]

Eighth, the answer to the persistence question has been seen as the number of times that a course of action has met with success in reducing the drive (Hull, 1943, pp. 102, 112). However, the fact that the habits of laboratory animals which have met with such success only part of the time regularly persist longer than habits which have regularly met with success belies this beautifully succinct answer (see Humphreys, 1939, and review by Jenkins and Stanley, 1950). Moreover, pathological persistence in the form of the "repetition compulsion" suggested to Freud (1920) a basis for motivation "beyond the pleasure principle" and led him to posit his concept of the "death instinct."

Implications of Activity Without Primary or Acquired Drive

This traditionally dominant theory is a conceptual edifice of ample dimensions and intricate detail. The succinctness of its answers to the motivation questions give it a considerable degree of elegance. A substantial body of experimental work appears to give most of these answers a bulwark of empirical support. In what follows, there is no intent to deny these facts. Painful stimulation is undoubtedly prepotent over homeostatic needs, and the latter are prepotent over the kinds of motivation to be discussed. It must be noted, however, that, according to this dominant conceptual scheme, all behavior is motivated by forces extrinsic to that behavior. Moreover, without these extrinsic forces of painful stimuli and homeostatic needs, organisms will presumably become quiescent. Even though it is difficult to rule out the possibility of the operation of acquired drives, a substantial body of evidence indi-

---

1953; Sears, Maccoby, and Levin, 1957), the need for achievement (Winterbottom, 1958), and others (see Becker, 1962). But the answer to the question of what controls the choice of long-term goals from the dominant conceptual scheme has not been succinct, or clear, or empirically well founded.

[7] As Amsel (see 1958), Brown and Farber (1951), and Young (1943) have noted, such frustration is fraught with emotional disturbance. As Young (1943) has noted, this emotional disturbance is associated with disruption of the habitual pattern of action, and Hebb (1949) has contended that emotional disturbance is the disruption of the central processes which mediate habitual patterns of action. But, as Leeper (1948) has noted, this emotional drive shapes the new structure of habitual response, and, as Bindra (1955, 1959) has contended, whether emotion is seen as a disruption or a shaper of response is a matter of when in the course of a series one looks at an organism's encounters with a given situation.

cates that organisms do not become quiescent in the absence of these extrinsic forces. This evidence does not deny the validity of all the answers from the dominant conceptual scheme, but it denies their claim to completeness, and it is likely that the motivation inherent in information processing and action is more important for the psychological development and the education of young human beings than are the extrinsic factors which have been utilized to motivate the learning of animals in the laboratory.

Evidence of Activity in the Absence of Drive or Need. Various observers have long pointed to the delight which children take in their new accomplishments and have seen it as motivationally significant even when play was conceived in terms of the recapitulation theory (Appleton, 1910; Gross, 1896). Also, Bühler (1928) long ago urged the concept of "function pleasure" precisely because play with new accomplishments appears to occur in the absence of either homeostatic need or painful stimulation, but a major share of the evidence implying intrinsic motivation has appeared since World War II. In 1945, Beach surveyed the observations of play in animals to show that animals are most likely to exhibit playful activities in the absence of homeostatic need, of painful stimulation, and of the innocuous stimuli which might presumably have been associated with these. Harlow, Harlow, and Meyer (1950) found that "monkeys would learn to un-assemble a three-device puzzle with no other 'drive' and no other 'reward' than the privilege of un-assembling it." In another study, Harlow (1950) found that two well-fed and well-watered monkeys worked repeatedly at un-assembling a six-device puzzle for ten continuous hours even though they were quite free of painful stimulation and quite well fed and well watered. Moreover, at the tenth hour of testing, according to Harlow, they were still "showing enthusiasm for their work." In an extended series of studies beginning in 1950, Berlyne (see 1960) found that well-fed and well-watered rats will explore areas new to them if only given an opportunity and that the more varied the objects in the region to be explored, the more persistent the rats' exploration. Berlyne has also found that variations in innocuous receptor-inputs will instigate and sustain looking or listening and that novelty, incongruity, and complexity will reinforce behavior in human beings. In another extended series of experiments, Montgomery (1952) has shown that the spontaneous tendency for rats to go alternately to the opposite sides of a T- or Y-maze is not a matter of fatigue of a given response as Hull (1943) contended, but rather one of avoiding the place that the animals have most recently experienced, that the choice of place goes to the one less familiar (Montgomery, 1953a), and that rats will learn in order to get an opportunity to explore (Montgomery, 1955; Montgomery and Segall, 1955). In this same vein, Butler (1953) has shown that monkeys will learn discriminations in order only to obtain the privilege of peeking through a window in the opaque walls of their cages or (Butler, 1958) of listening to sounds from a tape recorder.

All of these various activities occur in the absence of strong or painful stimulation and homeostatic need, and presumably in the absence of stimuli which have been associated with such primary drive conditions. Moreover, Montgomery (1953b) has obtained evidence indicating that the effect of hunger or thirst may be that of decreasing rather than that of increasing exploratory behavior. Furthermore, since it is the unfamiliar stimuli which are most effective in eliciting exploratory behavior, it is hardly likely that such stimuli could have become conditioned to the consummatory activities that may be the source of arousal when an organism is hungry or thirsty. Similarly, Montgomery and Monkman (1955) and others have found that stimuli that have been associated with painful stimulation tend to inhibit rather than to increase exploratory behavior.

Limitations of space notwithstanding, the evidence of the famous McGill studies of stimulus deprivation should be noted (see Bexton, Heron and Scott, 1954; Heron, Doane, and Scott, 1956). Even though McGill students were well fed, free of pain and strong stimulation of any sort, and without the usual allusions to sex, and even though these students were paid $20 a day, they would not remain quiescent in a room where stimulus variation was minimized. These various kinds of evidence appear to demand that theoretical recognition be given to some new kind of motivation.

Modes of Theoretical Recognition. Several modes of theoretical recognition have been given to these observations. One is "drive naming." Beach (1945) wrote of an instinct (equivalent, in this instance, to drive) of play, but later (1955) he disavowed instincts as a useful explanatory principle. Various others have named drives in terms descriptive of the activities which these drives are presumed to motivate. Thus, Nissen (1930), Mote, and Finger (1942), Montgomery (1954), and others have written of an *exploratory drive*. Harlow et al. (1950), Harlow and McClearn (1954), and others have written of a *manipulative drive*. Butler (1953) has noted a "drive for visual exploration." Berlyne (1950, 1960), like Dashiell (1925), Romanes, and Thorndike long before him (see Dennis, 1955), has emphasized a "curiosity drive" and used it to explain both exploratory and manipulative behavior. Moreover, Erikson (1950), the child psychoanalyst, has postulated an "urge for contact" and an "urge for locomotion." Finally, Nissen (1930, 1954) and Glanzer (1953) have mentioned a "need for stimulation." In fact, Nissen (1954) has asserted that just as the stomach needs food, the brain needs stimulation. Such drive naming may be useful as a way to indicate topical areas, but it is a theoretical blind alley. The drive naming of today appears to be revisiting the instinct naming of McDougall (1908). Just as McDougall's instinct naming went down under the criticism of such psychologists as Knight Dunlap (1919), Watson (1924), and Woodworth (1928), and such sociologists as Bernard (1924), drive naming should probably go down for the same reasons. Insofar as the drives named are accepted as explanations of the activities they name, they are logical shuttles that may delay the thought and investigation that should ultimately lead to genuine explanation and understanding. Actually, of course, not all of those who have named drives have been satisfied with pure drive naming. Beach (1955), Berlyne (1960), and Montgomery, for instance, have all been much concerned with the nature of the underlying mechanisms of these activities. Moreover, Harlow (1950) is among the first to use the term "intrinsic motivation" for the notion that a basis for motivation inheres within activity itself.

A second mode of theoretical acknowledgment of the evidence of activities in the absence of painful stimulation and homeostatic need consists of naming their *telic significance.* Thus, Ives Hendrik (1943) has conceived the delight which children take with their new-found accomplishments to be the basis for an "urge to mastery," and White (1959), in his excellent review of the evidence under discussion, has called the springs of these activities "competence motivation." Terms of telic significance may even be helpful as classification and mnemonic devices, but they provide no means of developing hypotheses about antecedent-consequence relationships, and, if accepted as explanations, they too may delay fruitful thought and investigation.

A third mode of theoretical recognition has consisted in the postulation of *spontaneous activity.* It has become almost fashionable during the last several years to say that "to be alive is to be active." Hebb (1949) pointed out that inasmuch as the electroencephalogram appeared to indicate that brain cells are always active, the instigation required no answer. Later, however, he appears to have seen a gap between the intrinsic activity in aggregates of his own (Hebb, 1955). Others like Hunt (1960), Miller, Galanter, and Pribram (1960), and Taylor (1960) have also recently accepted this notion of spontaneous activity in their published papers. However, as L. I. O'Kelly has pointed out in a personal communication, the notion of *spontaneous activity* may be just as malevolent as the notions of instinct and drive, and for precisely the same reason. Moreover, the notion that brain cells are continually acting without external stimulation may be wrong. The work of Burns (1958) appears to indicate that aggregates of brain cells may not indefinitely sustain their activity, as indicated by the electroencephalogram, without inputs of stimulation. The fact that Burns's recording electrodes were placed on the surface of the brain may have made them too insensitive to catch all signs of intrinsic firing. Even so, a single shock applied directly to the disengaged aggregate of cortical cells (with blood supply intact) yielded evidences of reverberative activity that endured for seconds, and a dozen stimulations separated by a second would reverberate for perhaps half an hour. Thus, apparently the brains of mammals are kept active by inputs from peripheral receptors which are so constructed that they send impulses even in the absence of the sort of stimulation to which they are conceived to be reacting. For instance, Granit (see 1955) has noted that retinal cells of a certain variety fire in the dark and that they increase their rate of firing with time of exposure to complete darkness. For a long time, such firing was attributed to stray light, but Granit (1955) has lately conceived of these cells having the function of keeping the level of arousal within the brainstem reticular formation above that minimal level required to keep the organism responsive to inputs from the distance receptors.

It follows that if organisms do not become inactive in the absence of painful stimulation and homeostatic need, or in the absence of innocuous stimuli which have been associated with these, and if brain cells must be sustained in their activity by inputs from peripheral receptors, one must assume the existence of some mechanism of *intrinsic motivation*. To put it another way, one must assume that there must be some mechanism for motivation that is inherent within the organism's perceptual inter-action with the environment. It is in this context that the terms "intrinsic motivation" and "motivation inherent in information processing and ac-ion" are proposed.[8]

Bases for "Motivation Inherent in Information Processing." I like the notion of "intrinsic motivation" and the too long, uneuphonious term, "motiva-tion inherent in information processing and action," for three reasons. First, it provides a direct contradiction to the dogma that all behavior is extrinsically motivated by strong or painful stimulation and homeostatic need, or by innocuous stimuli which have been associated with these. Second, it recognizes the origins of this motivation in the basic changes which have been going on since World War II in our conception of how the central nervous system works. Third, it provides a rubric for a basic

[8] These terms are not original with me. Harlow (1950), as already noted, has used the term "intrinsic motivation," and Taylor (1960) has come very close to "motivation inherent in information processing" with his "information processing theory of motivation." Neither of the users of the terms, however, has described the mechanism of motivation to be discussed. But even this mechanism is not original; it derives from a synthesis of investigative fact and theoretical concept scattered in the literature.

mechanism of motivation and for the evidence for this mechanism.

The conception proposed under these terms has much in common with past cognitive theories of motivation. Unlike these, however, it can contribute at least something toward answers to most of the major motivational questions. Moreover, it provides an hypothesis concerning mechanism that helps to integrate several lines of investigation and that suggests still other lines of empirical research that may prove to be considerably more important for child-rearing and education than are the traditionally dominant motivational mechanisms based on painful stimulation and homeostatic needs (including sex).

In what follows, the discourse will indicate the hypothetical nature of the mechanism and the way in which it participates in answers to the various questions asked of motivational theory.

Intrinsic Motivation and the Instigation Question

The basis for an answer to the instigation question, a question which has always been troublesome for cognitive theories, derives in large part from two major categories of change in conceptions of the functioning of the central nervous system. One of these concerns the concept of the functional unit. Here, the change is from the reflex arc to the feedback loop. The second is a concept of over-all brain functioning in the mediation of behavior. Here, the change is from the notion of the brain as a static switchboard to the notion of the brain as an anatomical setting for active information processes. With these changes comes the notion of *incongruity* as an instigator of behavior and the notion of *congruity* as the stopper of behavior.

From Reflex Arcs to Feedback Loops. Historically, the notion of the reflex arc has conceptual roots in Descartes's (1649) conviction that the bodies of animals are machines energized by forces of the external world, and in Thomas Willis' (1672) conception of involuntary movements. The notion has anatomical foundations in Bell's (1811) discovery of the separate ventral and dorsal roots of spinal nerves, and in Magendie's (1822) discovery that the dorsal roots have sensory functions while the ventral roots have motor functions. After Marshall Hall (1843) formulated the principle of the reflex and identified it with the anatomical conception of the reflex arc, Sechenov (1863) extrapolated the notion to brain function and laid the foundation for Pavlov's (see 1928) conditioned reflex. The extension of reflexive connections of sensory inputs with motor outputs through the brain received strong empirical support when Fritsch and Hitzig (1870) discovered that the application of galvanic currents to the cortex in the region of the gyrus anterior to the central sulcus elicited movements of muscles of the opposite side of the body. It was presumed that this region of the cortex was wholly motor in function, the large cells therein giving rise to the long fibers of the direct pyramidal tracts. When Caton (1875) and Beck (1890) found electrical potentials in the primary sensory areas of the cerebral cortex evoked by sensory stimulation, the empirical foundations for transcortical, reflex-analogous connections between sensory input and motor output were apparently established. In fact, even though Caton and Beck both discovered also the intrinsic electrical activity of the brain, this was temporarily lost because the conceptual equipment to appreciate it was lacking. Only much later, when Berger (1929) rediscovered these intrinsic rhythms, did electroencephalography come into being. Even so, it was largely the work of Sherrington, beginning in 1893 and culminating in 1906 with his *Integrative Action of the Nervous System,* that established the concept of the reflex. Sherrington established it so well, in spite of Dewey's (1896) trenchant criticism, that it is generally forgotten that Sherrington worked only with spinal preparations in which the brain did not participate and that, even so, he clearly recognized the reflex as only an abstraction.

One trenchant defect in the capacity of the concept of reflexive action to answer the instigation question has been its inability to handle the matter of set or attention. In his discussion of attention, William James (1890) called notice to the fact that the relatively loud clicking of a grandfather clock would produce neither a response nor an awareness until it stopped. Conversely, a faint sound of a child's distant cry can bring a mother up short in the face of louder noises, so long as that cry is not completely masked. Such facts have implied that the instigation of activities cannot be completely a matter of the onset of drives or acquired drives. Moreover, neurophysiologists have recently demonstrated that efferent impulses from the brain feed back through motor fibers in nerve tracts previously thought to be completely sensory in function, and they serve to regulate the level of discharge in these sensory nerves at a point close to the peripheral receptors. Excellent reviews of this evidence of central regulation of afferent inputs have been done by Granit (1955) and by Lindsley (1956).

Perhaps the instigative import of such central influence on afferent input is best dramatized in a study of hearing in cats. Hernandez-Peon, Scherrer, and Jouvet (1956) have found that the neural activity recorded with electrodes at the cochlear nucleus in unanaesthetized cats evoked by exposure to tones of moderate intensity is markedly reduced whenever the cats are exposed to the sight of mice in a bell-jar or to the odor of fish. Such neurophysiological evidence clearly implies that there must be a direct feedback loop through which central processes can regulate receptor inputs. Bruner (1957a) makes much of such central regulation of receptor inputs for perceptual organization, and the implications are just as great for the instigation question in motivation.

There is also evidence that the anatomical equipment for feedback loops exists. It appears that the Bell-Magendie Law, defined as *sensory nerves* in terms of *afferent* fibers in the dorsal-spinal roots and *motor nerves* in terms of *efferent* fibers in the ventral-spinal roots, was much overgeneralized (see Pribram, 1958b). Moreover, the sensory projection areas, which have been presumed to receive only incoming fibers from the thalamus, also contain cells giving rise to motor fibers. In the case of vision, Walker and Weaver (1940) have found that eye movements can be elicited by stimulating any portion of the visual receptive center in the occipital lobe of monkeys. Moreover, these eye movements can be elicited by electrical stimulation of the olfactory receptive area (Kaada, Pribram, and Epstein, 1949; Pribram and Kruger, 1954). Correspondingly, fibers of the thalamus connecting with other fibers originating in the receptors of muscle and skin come to the motor cortex of the precentral gyrus (Pribram, 1958b). It is thus that the stretch receptors in the muscles have a direct connection with which to influence the firing from these motor areas over the pyramidal tracts. With such evidence from both neurophysiology and neuroanatomy for direct feedback control of both input and output from the brain, the reflexive notion of brain function (where input is presumed to go to a given region, to travel across the association areas of the cortex, to be associated with other incoming inputs, thence to go to the motor areas whence it is relayed back to the muscles and glands) is no longer consonant with the known facts.

The TOTE Unit and Incongruity Instigation. With the feedback loop replacing the reflex arc as the concept of the functional unit of the nervous system, *incongruity* provides a basis for instigating actions and *congruity* provides a basis for stopping these actions. It has been the merit of Miller, Galanter, and Pribram (1960) to suggest what they term the "Test-Operate-Test-Exit (TOTE) unit" as the successor to the concept of the reflex arc (see Fig. 3–1). Perhaps the most familiar feedback mechanism, or servomechanism, is the home thermostat. In this device, the *test*, or sensing mechanism, is a thermometer. When the temperature of the room falls below the standard for which the thermostat is set, the electrical circuit that operates the furnace is closed. The furnace continues to *operate* until the temperature rises to the standard; then the mechanism breaks the circuit, and this constitutes the *exit*. In the TOTE sequence, the testing device starts the operation when there is an *incongruity* between conditions (temperature in this illustration) and some standard (the temperature at which the thermostat is set, here), and the operation continues until, as so tested, *congruity* ensues between conditions and standard. It is as thus conceived that incongruity becomes the basis for starting the organism on some given operation and that the return to congruity becomes the basis for stopping the organism's operation. In this fashion, the existence of the concept of the feedback loop provides an answer to the instigation question.

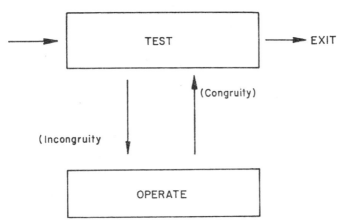

Fig. 3–1. Diagram of the TOTE unit (after Miller, Galanter, and Pribram, 1960, p. 26).

This principle of incongruity and congruity can be broadly generalized. Elaborating the operational possibilities of their TOTE unit, Miller, Galanter, and Pribram (1960) made the arrows in Fig. 3–1 represent three levels of abstraction, namely, energy, information, and control. At the first level, the arrows represent neural impulses. At the second, they represent information flowing from one place to another. At the third level, they represent control in such terms as a list of instructions that comprise the program for an electronic computer. In the case of a simple reflex, these arrows represent all three levels of abstraction simultaneously. Incongruity, also, can be conceived in terms of these three levels. In the case of defensive reactions, the sensing mechanism may be conceived to be the receptors, and the standard may be conceived to be relatively fixed as the threshold of discomfort or pain. In the case of such homeostatic needs as hunger and thirst, the sensing mechanisms appear to consist of the specialized receptors localized along the walls of the third ventricle in the hypothalamus that respond to chemical changes within the blood stream and the cerebral-spinal fluid. For hunger (see

Stellar, 1954), for instance, incongruity probably consists of a blood-sugar level below that for which the sensing mechanisms are probably innately set within quite narrow limits, and the operation probably consists of a kind of scanning mechanism in which the organism becomes "set" for receptor inputs which have been sequentially organized with (conditioned to) the consummatory act of eating. For hunger, moreover, there appears to be another sensing mechanism which serves to stop the consummatory activity. For the activities leading to eating, and even for this consummatory act itself, a stimulus control is required, and presumably this control consists of a hierarchy of operations based on other sorts of incongruities.

In the control of complex activities, Miller, Galanter, and Pribram (1960) have conceptualized the brain mechanisms of control in terms of a hierarchical organization of TOTE units. They illustrate the principle with one of Woodworth's (1958, p. 37) two-phase motor units: the banal process of hammering (see Fig. 3–2). Hammering consists of lifting and striking. The incongruity which starts hammering is seeing that the head of the nail sticks up. The congruity which stops hammering is seeing that the head is flush with the surface. They depict the sequence as follows:

Test nail. (Head sticks up.) Test hammer. (Hammer is down.) Lift hammer. Test hammer. (Hammer is up.) Strike nail. Test hammer. (Hammer is down.) Test nail. (Head sticks up.) Test hammer. . . . And so on until the test-of-the-nail reveals that its head is flush with the surface of the work, at which point control can be transferred elsewhere. Thus, while the compound TOTE unit unravels itself simply enough into a coordinated sequence of tests of actions, the underlying structure that organizes and coordinates the behavior is itself hierarchical, and not sequential [1960, p. 34].

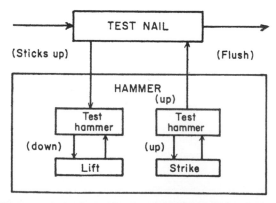

Fig. 3–2. Diagram of the hierarchical arrangement of the TOTE units in a plan for hammering nails. The operational plan consists of two hypothetical TOTE units, lifting and striking (after Miller, Galanter, and Pribram, 1960).

It should be noted that this principle of hierarchical organization of TOTE units is nicely consonant with the manner in which computers are programmed to solve problems (Newell, Shaw, and Simon, 1958), with Ashby's (1952) design for a mechanical brain, with Piaget's (1936) observations of the hierarchical development of intellectual functions in children, and with observations on the learning of conceptual skills in the work of Gagné and Paradise (1961).

From Static Switchboard to Active Information Processing. The principle of hierarchical organization shows up best in complex functioning. Moreover, the meaning of incongruity for the instigation of complex functioning takes on special properties.

Historically, when C. Lloyd Morgan (1894) was calling into question the faculties with which Romanes (1893) had been explaining the evolution of intelligence in animals, and when Thorndike (1898) was trying to explain the problem solving of animals without recourse to faculties, they had at hand the concept of the reflex and that dramatic new invention, the telephone. The telephone switchboard provided a mechanical model for changes in connections between stimulus and response. The switchboard notion provided not only a conception of how various stimulus inputs could be connected with given responses but also a conception of how chaining one reflex to the next might account for complex activities. The model was teachable, and it served as a kind of explanation which persisted in spite of the fact that Lashley (1917) early pointed out that, given the speed of the nervous impulse, it would be impossible for the movement of a pianist's finger to be the stimulus for the motion of the next finger in the execution of a rapid cadenza. Nevertheless, in 1943, even Hull considered it self-evident that the brain "acts as a kind of automatic switchboard" (p. 18, p. 384). In view of the professions of objectivity and rigor of the early behaviorists, it is ironic that in a logical sense this automatic switchboard had essentially the same properties as Romanes's mental faculties. The fact that it is only with the advent of the electronic computer, the dramatic mechanical model of the mid-twentieth century, that the notion of the switchboard is being displaced by the notion of active information processes nicely illustrates Conant's (1947) principle of progress in science that "a theory is only overthrown by a better theory, never merely by contradictory facts" (p. 48). The same point is relevant for the engineers' invention of the servomechanism as a replacement for the simple switching mechanism in the case of the concept of the reflex. At any rate, no sooner had electronic computers been developed than Wiener (1948) and others were struck by the analogy between computer processes and thought. Moreover, the programing of electronic computers to solve problems has led to a generalized consideration of what kinds of processes must go on in the brain to permit animals and human beings to do what they are observed to do. They solve problems. When computers solve problems, they are said to process information. It is this fact that has suggested to me the too long and uneuphonious term, "motivation inherent in information processing."

It is useful to consider directly some of these conceptions suggested by the programing of computers to solve logical problems. Newell, Shaw, and Simon (1958) have identified the following components:

1. A control system consisting of a number of memories, which contain symbolized information and are interconnected by various ordering relations . . .
2. A number of primitive information processes, which operate on the information in the memories. Each primitive process is a perfectly definite operation for which no physical mechanisms exist . . .
3. A perfectly definite set of these processes [organized] into whole *programs* of processing. From a program it is possible to deduce unequivocally what externally observed behaviors will be generated.

After programing their "logic theorist" to solve relatively simple identities in symbolic logic, Newell, Shaw, and Simon (1958) put down what they saw as the implications of their programing for the functioning of the central nervous system. They wrote as follows:

The picture of the central nervous system to which our theory leads is a picture of a more complex and active system than that contemplated by most associationists. The notions of "trace," "fixation," "excitation," and "inhibition" suggests a relatively passive electro-chemical system (or, alternatively, a passive "switchboard") acted upon by stimuli, or altered by that action, and subsequently behaving in a modified manner when later stimuli impinge upon it. In contrast, we postulate an information-processing system with large storage capacity that holds, among other things, complex strategies (programs) that may be evoked by stimuli. The stimulus determines what strategy will be evoked; the content of these strategies is already largely determined by the previous experience of the system. The ability of this system to respond in complex and highly selective ways to selective stimuli is a consequence of this storage of programs and this "active" response to stimuli.

Such suggestions have prompted certain neurophysiologists and neuro-psychologists to look for counterparts to these computer components within mammalian brains.

Pribram (1958b, 1960) suggests that the loci of the analogs of the computer control-system components may be the intrinsic systems of the cerebrum. The term *intrinsic systems* derives from Rose and Woolsey (1949), who coined it in their attempt to classify thalamocortical relationships. It was noting that the dorsal nuclei of the thalamus received no inputs from outside the telencephalon that suggested the term *intrinsic*. In their gross functional significance, these intrinsic regions show considerable correspondence with the association areas, and one might translate Hebb's conception of the A/S ratio into an intrinsic/extrinsic or I/E ratio, where the extrinsic systems are comprised of the direct sensory projection systems through the ventral and geniculate nuclei of the thalamus to the various sensory receptive centers on the cortex and of the traditional motor areas of the precentral gyrus giving rise to the direct pyramidal tracts (see Fig. 3–3). It is such evidence combined with that for feedback loops which led Pribram to argue (1960) that "the cerebral mechanism does not work by way of some simple trans-

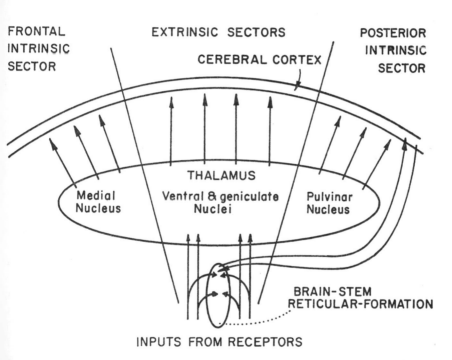

Fig. 3–3. Schematic diagram to illustrate the division of the cerebrum into intrinsic and extrinsic sectors on the basis of their afferent connections. The ventral and geniculate nuclei of the thalamus receive the major direct afferents from the receptor systems outside the cerebrum, and they project to the various extrinsic sectors of the cortex for visual, auditory, somaesthetic, etc., systems. The medial and pulvinar nuclei have no such afferents, and they project, respectively, to the frontal and posterior intrinsic sectors of the cortex. Included also are the interacting connections between the posterior intrinsic sector of the cortex with the brainstem reticular formation (after Pribram, 1958, with modifications).

cortical reflex that transfers input from sensory centers to output via motor areas after integration has taken place in the association areas" (pp. 15 ff.). Rather, it appears to work via systems of connections between the central core and the cortex of the brain. This conclusion is based also upon the finding that the cross-hatching of sensory and motor areas of the cortex produces relatively little change in behavior, whereas disrupting the input and output fibers by undercutting the so-called association areas produces profound disturbances in both skilled action and in recognitive functions. The intrinsic systems are composed, thus, of the cortex and of tracts leading from the cells in the cortex to the thalamus and other central structures, and back. It is in these intrinsic sectors that Pribram (1960) finds the likely counterparts of the computer control system comprised of its memories, its operations for processing information, and its hierarchically arranged sets of these operations analogous to the programs for information processing inferred by Newel, Shaw, and Simon (1958).

The intrinsic systems are two: one frontal, one posterior. The basis for this division is both anatomical and functional. Anatomically, the frontal system contains the dorso-medial nucleus of the thalamus, the frontal association areas of the cerebral cortex, the limbic system with its various connections to the centers of homeostatic need around the internal core of the brain, and the hypothalamus. In this frontal intrinsic sector, Pribram localized hierarchical arrangements of TOTE mechanisms that mediate executive functions. These comprise the "intentions" or "plans" and the mechanisms for ordering the utilizing information that resides in test sensitivities to incongruities between past and present perturbations of the dispositional states within the organism. The behavioral evidence for the notion that the frontal sector mediates intentions and plans comes from the fact that lesions in this sector tend to produce confusions of executive functions. One example is the disorganization of delayed reaction and double alternation found to result from frontal lesions in primates by Jacobsen et al. (1935) and in a human patient by Nichols and Hunt (1940). Another kind of example is the inability of patients with lesions of the medial structures of the temporal lobe to carry out a sequence of actions. Although their memory for events prior to surgery may be normal and these patients may have immediate recall for a series of digits or of instructions, they are unable to continue and may be unable to remember, following a distraction in the course of a task, that there was any task at all (Milner, 1958). Such lesions presumably interrupt the connections between subsystems of TOTE units in the limbic formations of the telencephalon which, in turn, are interconnected with what Pribram calls the "biased homeostats of the brain-stem core" (1960, pp. 12, 22). The hypothetical hierarchical arrangement of these subsystems would permit trial-and-error changes to occur in them whenever the error signal should be such that corrective change is no longer uniquely specified. As conditions change, and not too rapidly, the mechanism would permit the organism to search for additional instructions. So long as the search went on, the organism might be said to be frustrated. It would be gratified only when further change in the representations came to be precluded by unique specification from the error signal, i.e., "only when [the organism] can do things pretty much as [it] intends to do them" (Pribram, 1960, p. 21).

The posterior intrinsic sector consists anatomically of the pulvinar nucleus of the thalamus and the association areas of the cerebral cortex posterior to the central sulcus. It includes the parietal, temporal, and occipital lobes minus those specific reception centers for the various modalities. This posterior section is also connected with the brainstem reticular formation (see Lindsley, 1957). Whereas lesions in the anterior intrinsic sector disrupt executive functions, lesions in the posterior intrinsic sector interfere with the recognitive intelligibility of receptor inputs. While injury to the various regions of the posterior intrinsic system close to the various receptive centers shows behavioral effects that are related to one or another of the receptor modalities (Pribram, 1958b), these behavioral effects are quite different from those of lesions in the projection systems or receptive centers themselves. For instance, as Klüver (1941) has demonstrated, lesions in the visual projection system or reception center result in inability to make discriminations based on such properties as contour and brightness. Monkeys with such lesions can discriminate only total light intensity. On the other hand, Chow (1952) and Mishkin (1954) have shown that monkeys with lesions in the posterior intrinsic sector can make such discriminations, but they cannot identify objects or make alternative responses to variations in contour or pattern or luminance. For instance, a monkey with a lesion in the posterior intrinsic sector can catch a gnat in mid-air, evidence of his capacity to discriminate contour and brightness, but loses discrimination habits based on the identification of objects.

One can conceive of this posterior intrinsic system containing a hierarchically arranged store of coded representations of the various invariant properties of receptor stimulation from objects and situations and persons viewed from all their various angles. This, which corresponds to Hebb's (1949) cell assemblies that derive from "primary learning," will be referred to as "the storage."

The mechanism of storage is unknown, but Hyden (1959, 1960) has suggested that information might be stored in central neurons through excitation-induced specificity of ribonucleic acid molecules. In a series of hypothetical steps, these molecules might control the release of transmitter substances that would, in turn, excite the postsynaptic membrane and thereby restrict the activity of the neuron to appropriately coded inputs. The search for the "engram" so assiduously pursued by Lashley (see 1952) must, however, continue. As Pribram (1960) points out, the coded representations of the constancies of reception must be established according to the rules derived from the structure of the nervous system and from experience, which constrain the otherwise random properties of the neural network. These representations, and perhaps, also, the rules, must be gradually modifiable by changes in situational variables.

In the information processing of this posterior intrinsic system, incongruity must have special properties. The test component of the TOTE unit must be sensitive to incongruities between present receptor inputs and the residues of past receptor inputs in the storage. This means that the standard of the sensing mechanism is itself a function of past experience and could well have the properties of what Helson (1959) has termed the adaptation level (AL). If an investigator knew or could control an organism's commerce with a given category of objects, it should be possible to specify such incongruities in terms of the difference between those with which the organism has become familiar and those of his present encounter. It should become possible to quantify such incongruities in the terms of information theory (see Attneave, 1954), but this may be considerably complicated by the category-construction process that Bruner (1957a) has shown to exist in connection with perceptual readiness.

Such incongruity between present inputs and past constancies in receptor stimulation could be expected to start operations of search for additional information. Such search may be illustrated by the adjustment of the receptors made, as Woodworth (1947) has pointed out, to achieve clear vision. It may also be illustrated by the continued scrutiny of novel objects to which Berlyne (1960) has applied the term curiosity. This search, that is, the operational phase of the TOTE unit, can be said to exit when some representation becomes available in the storage which is consonant with the inputs of the moment, that is, when the object is recognized and identified. To quote Pribram (1960, p. 22), "the organism is satisfied when it is fully informed." At any rate, again one can see how incongruity can instigate the search within the storage for something to match the input, or the search of circumstances to lead to full information. Again, one can also see how congruity can stop this process. This is at least a provisional answer to the instigation question.

Incongruity and Energization

This answer to the instigation question based on incongruity or congruity of centrally based information and inputs can probably be classed as a cognitive theory of instigation. Cognitive theories of the control of behavior have been notoriously "cold." Although the computer-based conceptions of information processing suggest that the brain houses a variety of active processes rather than a set of static processes in an automatic switchboard, those who have thus far attempted to explain behavior in terms of information processing have presented a "cold" picture of living and behaving. Although Miller, Galanter, and Pribram (1960) have provided a clear, if provisional, answer to the instigation question, they too have said little about the vigor of activities and little about emotion. On the vigor of activity, the note that "what we call an 'effort of will' seems to be in large measure a kind of emphatic inner speech" (p. 71). On emotion, they have remarked that "in any situation where a successful plan suddenly becomes useless, the reluctant desertion of the plan is accompanied by strong emotions" (p. 98). Also they have noted that "the more or less sudden realization that an enduring plan must be changed at a strategic level is accompanied by a great deal of emotion and excitation. When this excitation can find no focus in either the Image or in action, the person experiences 'anxiety.' The patient may then develop plans to cope with the anxiety (defense mechanisms) instead of developing new Plans to cope with reality" (p. 116). In other words, they acknowledge the existence of emotions but supply only these hints of principles to answer the energization question. In what follows, evidence from various sources is marshaled to show that an important basis for energization and emotion appears to be inherent in information processing and action.

A Taxonomy of Incongruities for Action and Informal Processing. Pribram's (1958b, 1960) discovery of two separate intrinsic systems—one anterior where executive plans and functions predominate, and one posterior where recognitive functions and intelligibility predominate—suggests a taxonomy of incongruities of relevance to the energetic and emotional aspects of information processing. In the case of the frontal intrinsic system, energization and emotion appear to derive from the frustration of, and conflict among, plans where the incongruity resides between input and the expectations integral to the plan. In the case of the posterior intrinsic, energy mobilization and emotions appear to derive from incongruity between the information coded in the inputs of the moment and the expectations based upon information coded in the residues of past inputs in the storage, or from dissonance among such information systems as beliefs and attitudes.

Energization Inherent in Frustration and Conflict. Commonsense observation, clinical observation, and experimentation all indicate that frustration of plans or conflict among plans constitutes a source of emotional disturbance, energization, and arousal.

Frustration occurs when an obstacle of some sort interferes with achieving the goal of a plan (Dollard, Doob, et al., 1939; Rosenzweig, 1944). One has only to recall the last time one went to one's favorite restaurant for a favorite repast only to find it absent from the menu, or the last time one stepped into one's automobile to go somewhere only to discover that it would not start, to get evidence that such frustration is emotionally disturbing. Furthermore, clinical observation is replete with instances in which unfulfilled desires appear to be the source of emotional disturbance. In fact, Freud's (1917, p. 335) early theory of anxiety as a "souring" of unsatisfied libido is a frustrative conception of this form of emotional disturbance. Even earlier, Dewey (1894) formulated a frustrative theory of emotional disturbance.

Experimental evidence of frustration being an antecedent of energization comes from the work of Amsel (1958) and his collaborator, who have developed the conception that the absence of an anticipated goal object ("frustrative non-reward") produces an emotional drive state like that postulated by Brown and Farber (1951) which increases the vigor of that behavior that immediately follows the frustrating events. In the original experiment of this series, Amsel and Roussel (1952) arranged two mazes in tandem. Hungry rats were trained to run down one straight alley-maze into a first goal box for food, then to leave this goal box and run down a second alley into a second goal box which was distinctively different from the first. The time required to run between goal box I and goal box II was measured. After this measure had achieved an asymptotic stable minimum, the animals in the experimental group were frustrated by the omission of food in goal box I on intermittent trials. The animals thus frustrated ran considerably faster through maze II on those trials when food was omitted from goal box I than they did on trials when food was present there. Moreover, they ran faster on the average than did controls on the same numbered trials. Such phenomena have been reproduced repeatedly and Amsel (1958) has summarized the results of the series of studies.

The importance of the relation of arousal to frustration calls for some theoretical interpretation. For more than twenty-five years, Duffy (1934, 1941, 1951, 1957) has been arguing and assembling the evidence to show that the so-called "expressive indicators" of emotion constitute the core of energy mobilization within the organism. Lindsley (1951, 1957) has accepted much of this argument in what he has termed "an activation theory of emotion," and he has marshaled the evidence, much of it from his own laboratory, to show that the electroencephalogram (EEG) in both momentary emotion and chronic states of anxiety manifests "an activation pattern" consisting of abolition of the synchronized (alpha) rhythms and the induction of high-frequency waves of low magnitude. Similarly, direct stimulation of the brainstem reticular formation evokes an EEG pattern of activation (Moruzzi and Magoun, 1949), as do also administrations of adrenalin and noradrenalin, which are the hormones conceived to be most directly associated with fear and anger (Dell, 1956). Furthermore, Lindsley (1951, 1957) has also marshaled the evidence to show that in deep sleep or coma the EEG pattern is one of slow waves of large magnitude, that this pattern is approached whenever soporific drugs are administered (Lindsley, 1944), and that it results also from destruction of the basal diencephalon. This is the rostral end of the brainstem reticular formation which appears to be the cerebral center for a continuum of activation or arousal that extends from deep sleep, at the low end, to anxious panic, at the high end. Other investigators like Schlosberg (1954), Hebb (1955), and Malmo (1958) have accepted this conception of a continuum of arousal as both a central aspect of emotion and the central factor underlying energy mobilization. This may also be identified with the generalized drive that Hull (1943) and others [9] have conceived to combine in multiplicative fashion with habit strength to determine the vigor of performance. Whereas most of Lindsley's work has been based on the EEG, all of the customary "expressive indicators"—including palmar conductance (or the PGR), pulse rate, blood pressure, volume of peripheral blood vessels as measured by the plethysmograph, and tension in skeletal muscles as measured by the electromyograph (ENG)—provide indications of arousal which, however, are far from perfectly intercorrelated (Wenger, 1948; Lacey, 1959). In various combinations, these are the indicators used by the Russian investigators of the attention giving which they term the "orienting reflex" to be discussed further below (see Berlyne, 1960; Razran, 1961).

Studies employing these physiological or "expressive" indicators of emotional arousal in subjects submitted to frustration are few, but two Japanese investigators (Yoshii and Tsukiyama, 1952) have reported that omitting food from the goal box of a maze of rats that have come to expect food results in an increase in frequency and a decrease in amplitude of EEG waves. This is precisely the kind of change that goes with increasing arousal, so this finding lends support to the findings of Amsel.

More studies of this kind are needed, but those that exist tend clearly to confirm the commonsense and clinical observations that frustration

[9] See, e.g., Brown and Farber (1951), Brown (1953), Farber (1954), Spence (1956).

brings emotional arousal. On the other hand, it is not clear that this emotional arousal comes, as claimed by Miller, Galanter, and Pribram (1960), from a mere interference with a plan per se. If one takes the position of the drive reductionist, the activity being interfered with is presumably reducing some primary or acquired drive. If this be true, interfering with the progress of the activity would be conceived merely to reinstate the original drive. Moreover, such an interpretation is quite tenable for these experiments reported because each one is dependent upon homeostatic need as the source of motivation in the animal subjects concerned.

Conflict occurs as interference between or among plans. Or, in the language of behavior theory, conflict occurs as interference among responses. In the sense that one of these plans serves to frustrate the other, conflict may be seen to involve frustration (Rosenzweig, 1944). Again, commonsense observation, clinical observation, and experimentation are all sources of evidence appearing to indicate that conflict may be a source of emotional arousal and energization. One need only recall the last time one experienced a troublesome decision between two alternative courses of action to get evidence from commonsense observation that conflict can be a source of emotional arousal. Moreover, on the basis of their clinical observations, both Janet (1925, Vol. I, p. 450) and Freud (1917, p. 302), as well as many others, have thought they saw conflict as one of the crucial factors in the functional disorders of personality where emotional disturbance is one of the outstanding symptoms.

Although the classic experimentation on conflict is the work of Miller (1944), he explicitly left open the issue concerning whether conflict might be a source of drive. It must be remembered, however, that the first experimentally induced neurotic disturbances appeared to result from conflict. The first of these appeared when one of Pavlov's dogs was attempting to discriminate between a luminous circle which was repeatedly accompanied by feedings and an ellipse which was not accompanied by feedings. He wrote:

> When, in the course of this training, the ratio of the semiaxes of the ellipse had been reduced, from what was originally 2/1 to 9/8, the behavior of the animal underwent an abrupt change that indicated emotional disturbance. The hitherto quiet dog began to squeal on the stand, kept wriggling about, tore off with its teeth the apparatus for the mechanical stimulation of the skin, and bit through the tubes connecting the animal's room with the observer [1927, p. 290].

For most observers, such behavior would clearly imply disturbing emotional arousal.

In a much more recent study, Fonberg (1956) has obtained evidence indicating that the state produced in a dog by such conflict is functionally equivalent to that induced by painful stimulation. What Fonberg did first was to train her dogs to perform distinctive defensive responses to terminate such aversive stimuli as electric shocks. Next, she presented these dogs in another situation with the problem of discriminating between tones. One of these tones was regularly followed by food powder, and the other was not. Whenever, in the course of this training, the negative tone was made more like the positive, the dogs would manifest the distinctive defensive reactions that they had learned to terminate the noxious shock. Thus, from the point of view of these dogs, the inner state produced by the conflict of "plans" appears to have been functionally equivalent to that produced by the pain of electric shock.

Studies recording directly the "expressive" physiological indexes of arousal in subjects submitted to conflict have been few, but in the study by Yoshii and Tsukiyama (1952), the choice point in the maze, where presumably the rat would be subject to a conflict in "plans," was a source of change in the EEG record consisting of an increase in fast waves and a decrease in their amplitude: the indicators of emotional arousal. Moreover, in dogs trained to raise a paw at the sound of a metronome to avoid electric shock, Poleshayev (1958) reports that the appearance of a piece of meat while the metronome was sounding evoked quicker and deeper breathing along with an increase of fast waves and a decrease in the magnitude of EEG waves. If one assumes that the appearance of meat evoked a food-getting plan which conflicted with the defensive plan being trained, one can see these dogs as having been put in conflict, a conflict which appeared to increase arousal.

A study by Lanier (1941) appears to indicate that "affective conflict" may be a source of arousal. What Lanier did was to have his subjects individually classify words into the categories "pleasant," "unpleasant," "indifferent," and "mixed." When they were presented with the words from their own individual classifications, it was the "mixed" words that evoked the largest GSR's.

Again, even though there be evidence of emotional arousal in these experimentally induced conflicts, it is always possible for the drive reductionist to say that the arousal derives from the unrequited drive evoking and energizing the conflicting responses ("plans"). In the case of conflict, moreover, where interference frustrates both plans, one might expect the summation of the emotional arousal involved in their instigation and energization.[10]

[10] In this discussion of arousal in frustration and conflict and in that below concerning arousal in incongruity and dissonance, I am very much indebted to the excellent survey of the evidence made by Berlyne (1960). Even though my theoretical synthesis differs substantially from his, his fine book has been an excellent source of both references and ideas.

Arousal from Incongruity and Dissonance. Evidence of emotional arousal from incongruity and dissonance derives from a variety of sources. Moreover, the nature of this evidence makes it clear that the arousal is indeed *inherent* in the information processing.

The terms *incongruity* and *dissonance* are generic. They refer to a variety of organism-environment interactions which have been seen by others in various related ways. As will be reported below, Hebb (1946) has found that chimpanzees will withdraw in fear from familiar objects which have never been associated with either painful stimulation or homeostatic need but which appear in an unfamiliar guise. The familiarity derives from the *primary* learning that established the "cell assemblies" and "phase sequences" which, from the standpoint of the conception of the TOTE unit, constitute the standard against which new inputs are matched for recognition. When familiar objects are seen in an unfamiliar guise, the discrepancy between the familiar standard and the unfamiliar guise constitutes the incongruity. The organism-environment relationships have also been subsumed under what Berlyne (1960, p. 44) called "collative variables" because their evaluation requires a comparison between stimuli which have already been experienced and the stimuli being experienced. Such commonsense terms as surprise, novelty, uncertainty, and complexity have their basis in such comparisons. Finally, most of these organism-environment relationships have also been subsumed under what Festinger (1957) has called "cognitive dissonance." Festinger has defined *dissonance* and *consonance* as relationships which exist between pairs of elements, or, as the relationships that exist between the bits of information that are attitudes, opinions, and beliefs, and the communications received (see 1957, p. 9). Two elements of information are said to be dissonant "if, considering these two alone, the obverse of one element would follow from the other" (1957, p. 13). Festinger's formulation, however, makes *dissonance* include relations not only between informational inputs and stored inputs but also between organizations of information already stored in the form of attitudes, beliefs, and opinions. Here the terms *incongruity* and *dissonance* include this whole gamut of organism-environment relationships.

SHORT-TERM AND LONG-TERM INCONGRUITIES. Human ingenuity can probably develop any number of systems for classifying incongruities. Investigation may ultimately require a complex taxonomy (see, e.g., Smock and Holt, 1962, for variations in reactions to various kinds of novelty), but even immediately it will be useful to distinguish short-term incongruities from long-term incongruities.

Short-term incongruities occur with sudden changes in the nature of receptor inputs or when the inputs of the moment lead to expectations which fail to match those which come. Here the standard of the TOTE unit is determined by the on-going state of affairs, and the change constitutes the incongruity which, as will be seen, starts the arousal function and apparently shifts attention. Long-term incongruities differ only in degree from the short-term variety. They occur when the expectations derived from the previous past experience with objects, situations, persons, and sequentially organized events fail to match the inputs that come. Here the information in the storage, based upon past inputs for the given context, supplies the standard of the TOTE unit, and the failure of match from the new input constitutes the incongruity. Hebb's anesthetized infant chimpanzee is an example; in the past experience of adult chimpanzees with infants, the form is accompanied by characteristic postures and motions that evoke fear which are absent in the anesthetized infant.

AROUSAL WITH SHORT-TERM INCONGRUITY. The evidence for intrinsic emotion arousal from short-term incongruity is abundant. Ever since the galvanometer was first utilized to measure the conductivity of the skin (see Landis, 1932), it has been evident that sudden changes in a wide variety of stimulus inputs would serve to lower the resistance of the skin, i.e., increase the conductance of the skin as a consequence of sweating. Moreover, when other "expressive indicators" of emotional arousal were employed, it became clear that all of them would show evidences of emotion in connection with sudden changes of stimulus input. Pavlov early noted these reactions to what he called "indifferent stimuli" and subsumed them under what he called the "orienting" or "what-is-it?" reflex (see Razran, 1961). In recent years, a group of Russian investigators have studied this orienting reflex (OR) extensively. In these studies, they have radically altered the traditional design of conditioning experiments. In the place of studying the pairing of a single innocuous stimulus (CS) with another stimulus which is immediately effective in evoking some response (US), to study the OR they have employed a wide variety of response indicators to repeated exposure to some given stimulus. Thus, on the side of overt response, the OR may consist operationally of such changes in sense organs as the dilation of the pupil, photochemical changes in the retina, of such changes in skeletal muscles as those directing the sense organs, the arrest of on-going actions, an increase in muscle tonus (indexed myographically— ENG), and of the various "expressive indicators" of emotion already described.

From these Russian investigations, it appears that the OR is the mammalian organism's first reaction to any change in the stimulation impinging at any given moment. The bigger the change, i.e., the greater the degree of incongruity, the greater is the degree of emotional arousal. Also, the quicker the change, the greater is the degree of emotional arousal as indicated by the complex of reactions described. It would appear that the function of the OR in information processing is one of shifting attention from the old and on-going to new stimulation. This complex of reactions appears to comprise what Piaget (1936) has termed the "looking schema" and the "listening schema," both reflex-like schemata that are present in newborn human infants. Similar observations have been made by Bühler, Hetzer, and Mable (1928). Thus, the OR appears to be both an arousing and directing mechanism which prepares the organism to receive stimulation that is new in the situation and that may be of a significance in adaptation.

It is the fact that this OR tends to decrease and even to disappear with repetition of the same stimulation that permits a clear demonstration that emotional arousal is inherent in such information processing. The reviews by Berlyne (1960) and Razran (1961) are replete with experimental demonstrations of this adaptive diminution of arousal which comes with repetitive stimulation and of the fact that change in the adapted stimulation brings a return of arousal. In a sense, these demonstrations are a confirmation of the commonsense observation that one does not hear the clock tick until its stops. Consider two of the more dramatic experimental demonstrations.

First, one by Sharpless and Jasper (1956). With needle electrodes implanted in the brainstem reticular formation, Sharpless and Jasper presented their cat-subjects repeatedly with loud sounds which lasted for about three seconds. At first, each presentation evoked a burst of irregular, high-frequency EEG waves of low magnitude like those commonly associated with anxiety or with great effort. With each succeeding presentation, the EEG arousal reaction became shorter, and changes in frequency and in magnitude became less in degree. By the end of thirty trials, this arousal reaction had essentially disappeared. It was, so to speak, extinguished. When this experiment was repeated on the same cats day after day, the arousal reaction tended to recover spontaneously on each successive day, but the adaptation to it became more and more rapid. Following adaptation, however, a change in any characteristic of the stimulus brought back the fast EEG waves of low magnitude. A reduction in loudness was as effective in restoring the arousal reaction as an increase in loudness. Moreover, changes in pitch were as effective as changes in loudness. Such findings are clearly dissonant with the traditional theoretical expectation that arousal must come from strong or painful stimulation, homeostatic need, or from innocuous stimuli which have previously been associated with such primary drive stimuli. It is in this sense that one can say that the case for emotional arousal intrinsic in short-term incongruity is much stronger than that for intrinsic arousal in either frustration or conflict.

Second, one by Vinogradova (1958), known only from the secondary accounts of Berlyne (1960) and Razran (1961), which is even more spectacular in its theoretical import. Vinogradova is reported to have presented repeatedly to her human subjects a tone, paired in sequence with an electric shock, until the vascular component of the OR, assessed with a plethysmograph, had been extinguished. Then, with omission of the shock, which by traditional theoretical expectations would certainly be considered the noxious and painful portion of the stimulus complex, the presentation of the sound alone brought a return of the vascular component of the OR. From such an experimental finding, it is exceedingly difficult to see how the vascular indication of arousal could be anything other than inherent in the short-term incongruity of information processing. It is, indeed, the omission of the noxious electric shock that brings about the return of the emotional arousal. In the conceptual scheme employed here, the test or sensing-mechanism of the TOTE unit has been set by the repeated presentation of the tone-shock sequence to have shock follow tone, and the absence of the traditionally conceived drive stimulus from this sequence serves to instigate the operation that manifests itself as emotional arousal indexed by the plethysmograph. This operation is no plan of action. It seems to consist in an alerting of the organism for information intake.

AROUSAL IN LONG-TERM INCONGRUITY. Following this demonstration of emotional arousal inherent in short-term incongruity, the evidences from commonsense observation, clinical observation, and experimentation of emotional arousal inherent in long-term incongruities become more plausible.

Commonsense observation would appear to indicate that the subjective state associated with long-term incongruity in the sense of information which fails to correspond with existing beliefs and attitudes is one that has been called by a number of names that include "bewilderment," "confusion," "perplexity," and "puzzlement." In the terms of the Young (1943, 1948b)-Leeper (1948) controversy, these terms may represent the emotional-intellectual condition associated with reorganization of the information in the storage. Typically, perplexity gives way to a new view of the matters concerned as, presumably, the information in the storage gets reorganized. The emotional quality of such intellectual operations as coming through bewilderment to a new conception is evidence of motivation inherent in the long-term incongruity of information processing. In fact, it may well be that this emotional arousal is the subjective side of the energization required for reorganization of information in the storage.[11]

Clinical observations are also a source of plausible evidence. In fact, the theories of anxiety put forth by Kelly (1955) and Rogers (1951) are at least highly consonant with this notion of emotional arousal inherent in long-term incongruity. In Kelly's (1955) formulation, the arrangement of information in the storage consists of "personal constructs." These represent active efforts on the part of an individual to make sense out of his observations, and they derive both directly from idiosyncratic personal experience with reality and from what the individual is taught in the course of his communications with others. Thus, an individual may be led by information coming through communications so to construe the world that the information coming via his idiosyncratic perception is incongruous with this construing. The consequence of this incongruity is seen by Kelly to be emotional distress, or anxiety.

In the formulation of Rogers (1951), the source of anxiety, which he terms psychological tension or maladjustment, arises out of an inconsistency between the self concept and various concrete perceptions. According to Rogers, this self concept, which corresponds to what is here called again the arrangement of information in the storage, has two experiential origins. It derives, first, from direct, idiosyncratic perceptual interaction with the environment and with people, and, secondly, from evaluations (information) which are "taken over from others, but perceived in distorted fashion as if they had been experienced directly" (1951, p. 498). Rogers writes further, "as experiences occur in the life of the individual, they are either (a) symbolized, perceived, and organized into some relationship to the self, (b) ignored because there is no perceived relationship to the self-structure, (c) denied symbolization and given a distorted symbolization because the experience is inconsistent with the structure of the self" (1951, p. 503). Whenever the individual attempts to satisfy needs which are not admitted to the self concept and whenever he attempts to react to experiences which are denied by his self concept, there is a basic or potential psychological tension, and the individual feels anxious. He feels that he is not united or integrated and that he is unsure of his direction. Contrariwise, Rogers writes, "psychological adjustment exists when the concept of self is such that all the sensory and visceral experiences of the organism are, or may be assimilated on a symbolic level into a consistent relationship with the concept of self" (1951, p. 513). Roger's term *inconsistency* is synonymous with incongruity and especially with long-term incongruity. Inasmuch as these two conceptions of the basis for anxiety have derived from

[11] This formulation is highly similar to Hebb's (1949) disruption hypothesis, but it has the advantage of incongruity being potentially measurable.

observing neurotic patients undergoing psychotherapy, they are distillations of evidence from clinical observation of emotional arousal inherent in the long-term incongruity of information processing.

In connection with these conceptions of anxiety proposed by Kelly and Rogers, it is interesting to recall Freud's (1926) expressions of dissatisfaction with both his earlier and his later formulations of the basis for anxiety. Freud apparently developed the first of his theories in his observations of the anxiety neuroses (1894) and elaborated it as he developed his libido theory (1898) in which he construed anxiety as a transformation of libido blocked by repression. In his *Introductory Lectures*, Freud referred to this anxiety as a "souring" of the frustrated libido (1917, p. 335). Freud's later theory of anxiety appears to have had its beginnings in his observations concerning the origins of guilt. He attributed guilt to conflict between the ego and the super-ego, and the origins of this conflict were conceived to arise from the child's experience of castration threats for masturbation and his fantasies of paternal competition in connection with his Oedipal wishes (Freud, 1923). Still later, Freud (1926) wrote that "instinctual demands often become an (internal) danger only because . . . their gratification would bring about an external [danger]" and still later, in the *New Introductory Lectures*, Freud (1932) became quite explicit about the source of anxiety residing in such past punishments as castration threats and experiences of losing parental love. Moreover, these painful experiences presumably came in connection with impulses toward drive satisfaction. Thus, these impulses became the conceptual equivalents of conditional stimuli for the anxiety response; the anxiety response was seen to inhibit the impulses, and repression was thereby accounted for in terms of anxiety (see 1932, p. 118). Freud's (1926) dissatisfaction with both of these formulations came in connection with his observations of emotional distress in children as fear of being alone, fear of the dark, fear of strangers. These observations failed to fit his conceptual models, and he considered the possibility that they might represent a racial heritage of innate preparation against real danger. It is precisely such fears that appear to be independent of homeostatic need and painful stimulation; they appear to inhere in information processing as incongruity deriving from the absence of accustomed and expected receptor input.

The experimental work of Hebb on the origins of fear in chimpanzees lends, perhaps, the strongest empirical support for this proposition. The experiments of Hebb and Riesen (1943) and of Hebb (1946) were prompted by the Watson-Rayner (1920) conception of emotional disturbance as conditional responses. According to this notion, which is a forerunner of the notion of acquired drives, such an emotion as fear is a native response to such stimuli as loud sounds and pain, and these native responses can be conditioned to a variety of originally neutral receptor inputs. Although this notion is apparently close to "common-sense," in proposing it Watson and Rayner were apparently utilizing conceptions derived from Watson's (1916) extensive familiarity with the pioneering work of Pavlov. This traditional conception of fear met with sharply dissonant evidence when Hebb and Riesen (1943) observed that the infant chimpanzee's fear of strangers does not appear in chimpanzee infants reared in the nursery of the Yerkes Primate Laboratory, where their histories were known, until these infants approached about four months of age. Later, Hebb (1946) found that even intense panic reactions could be induced in laboratory-reared chimpanzees by showing them the sculptured head of a chimp, where the expected remainder of the body was absent, or by showing them an anaesthetized infant chimpanzee, where the customary postures and motions were absent. Near panic could be induced in young chimpanzees by having the familiar experimenter appear in a Halloween mask or even in the coat of the familiar "keeper" or, vice versa, by having the "keeper" appear in the coat of the experimenter. Such observations have been interpreted to mean that emotional reactions arise in a predetermined fashion directly out of organismic maturation (Jones and Jones, 1928; Jersild and Holmes, 1935). When these observations are coupled with the observation that Riesen's (1947) chimpanzees reared in darkness show no fear of strange people or of objects at ages much greater than the "normal" four months, however, this maturation interpretation breaks down. It was probably Hebb (1946) who first formulated the idea, if not the language, that incongruity could be the basis for fear. One can describe the chief characteristic of all of these fear-evoking situations in Hebb's (1946) experiment as "the familiar in an unfamiliar guise." As Hebb (1946, 1949) has pointed out, the role of experience (i.e., the primary learning) is to establish the familiarity (i.e., the "cell assemblies" and "phase sequences") that constitutes the standard of the TOTE unit against which the incongruity of "unfamiliar guise" is detected.[12]

Emotional disturbances in children and pets which have puzzled many people appear understandable in these terms. The fears of the dark and of solitude in the human child that puzzled Freud and in the chimpanzee that puzzled Köhler (1925, p. 251) can be seen as the incongruity

---

[12] Hebb (1949) conceived the emotional disturbance to be disruption of the reverberative circuits comprising the "cell assemblies" and "phase sequences" by the unfamiliar inputs. This identification of emotional disturbance with disruption of cerebral firing had the merit of providing an explanation of emotional disturbance in diseases in which the disruption of timing may have a biochemical basis. On the other hand, inasmuch as Hebb also recognized that lesser degrees of unfamiliarity could be attractive, this formulation failed to provide conceptual leads for the quantifying of incongruity necessary for investigation. I shall return to this issue in discussing incongruity and the direction-hedonic question.

which results from the absence of accustomed receptor inputs within any context. Other examples are the child who becomes disturbed when a familiar nursery rhyme is altered in the reading, the pet dog that barks excitedly and whines when his young master walks on his hands, the cat that loves to be petted by his child-mistress and by a familiar neighbor in whose house he was raised but runs frantically to hide at the sight of the neighbor carrying the child on his shoulders. Without being especially concerned about the point, moreover, Piaget (1936) notes that his children showed emotional distress in seeing radically altered versions of things that they had come to recognize.

Experimental investigations of opinion and attitude change have produced a body of evidence indicating that the incongruity between attitudes and beliefs held and information received through communication is "a motivating factor in its own right" (Festinger, 1957). Incongruity in this sense is what Festinger calls "cognitive dissonance." Festinger's basic hypothesis states that "the existence of dissonance, being psychologically uncomfortable, will motivate a person to reduce the dissonance and achieve consonance . . . [and] when dissonance is present, in addition to trying to reduce it, the person will actively avoid situations and information which would be likely to increase the dissonance" (1957, p. 3). A person may reduce dissonance by changing his beliefs, and this is the common effect, but when beliefs are especially strong, dissonance may lead to changes in behavior that will change circumstances and thereby make them more nearly consonant with belief. It is thus that "a person who is habitually very hostile toward people [and who believes that people are universally hostile] may surround himself with persons who provoke hostility" (1957, p. 20). It is also thus that a person who believes his own behavior is poor cannot accept a compliment without looking behind it for some ulterior motive in the individual from whom it comes.

Although Festinger (1957) reviews a number of investigations that illustrate the various aspects of his theory, his focus on opinion and attitude change has led him to no direct evidence of emotional arousal in connection with cognitive dissonance. The clinical observations of Kelly (1955) and Rogers (1951) and the experiments of Hebb (1946) with chimpanzees, however, indicate that recording the "expressive indicators" of emotional arousal in studies of attitude change would probably yield evidence confirming the deduction that receiving information incongruous with opinions held will evoke arousal. In fact, Haywood (1962) has already found that a confusing message will increase palmar sweating as indicated by the colorometric method of Kuno (1956).

It is highly likely that both the degree of incongruity and the abruptness or rate at which incoming information appears to demand reorganization of information in the storage will be factors determining the degree of emotional arousal. A study of Ewing (1942) is highly suggestive and illustrative in this connection. It indicates that the information with which a message opens can be highly important in determining the impact of that message, apparently because the nature of the opening phrases determines both the degree and the rate of accommodation that the listener anticipates. Ewing presented his random groupings of Duke students with a message much more unfavorable to Henry Ford than were the beliefs held by most of these students. One group was led to expect information dissonant with their opinions, i.e., information unfavorable to Ford, by the following opening: "Numerous people have pointed out that Ford represents big business at its best. However, some of the following facts hardly justify this view" (1942, p. 80). The other group was led to expect information consonant with their already established beliefs, i.e., a message favorable to Ford, by the following opening: "Numerous people have pointed out that Ford represents big business at its worst. However, some of the following facts hardly justify this view" (1942, p. 80). Now, with the remainder of the messages going to the two groups exactly alike, the immediate change in opinion, based upon a measure of attitude taken before and after presentation of the message, was considerably less than half as great under the first or dissonant opening than under the second or consonant opening. Moreover, when the opinion of the students was measured again a week later, those who had been led by the dissonant opening to expect information that disagreed strongly with their favorable beliefs about Ford had actually become increasingly favorable to Ford in the interim. In other words, they showed a negative change in attitude (one contrary to the import of the message received). Those subjects who had been led by the consonant opening to anticipate information agreeing with their own belief about Ford showed attitudes growing increasingly less favorable to Ford at the end of the week. The positive change (one in line with the import of the message received) continued to grow with time. Furthermore, subjects led to expect information dissonant with their own beliefs later reported that the message was "biased," "illogical," "prejudiced," "unfair," and of "doubtful validity"; while those led to expect information consonant with their own beliefs reported later that the message was "unbiased," "unprejudiced," "fair," and "valid." Such evidence suggests that being led to expect information so incongruous with one's established beliefs and opinions that one must suddenly make large accommodative reorganizations of the information in the storage will evoke defenses which make it unnecessary to accommodate the dissonant information. It is this fact, that the opening phrases appear to be a factor of such great importance, which suggests that it may be the *rate* at which accommodative change is demanded that determines whether and how much emotional arousal will be detected. Just such a principle, of course, was implicitly recognized by Shakespeare when he had Marc Antony introduce his funeral oration to the Romans with the statement: "I come to bury Caesar, not to praise him."

Such a formulation suggests that studies of attitude change with subjects hooked up to a variety of physiological indicators such as the Russians have been using in their studies of the orienting reflex may be highly fruitful not only as evidence that emotional arousal is inherent in information processing but also as a basis for better understanding of the mechanisms of defense. A re-examination of Anna Freud's (1936) accounts of these mechanisms strongly suggests that many of them may be defenses against incongruous information or dissonance. In the meantime, the evidence summarized here clearly indicates that a cognitive, information-processing theory need not be "cold."

Incongruity, Arousal, and the Direction-Hedonic Question

Most intriguing is the role of intrinsic motivation in determining the direction of behavior and the hedonic value of situations, for incongruity appears to be a source of both avoidance and approach, of both negative, and positive hedonic value.

Withdrawal, Avoidance, and Negative Hedonic Valuation of Incongruity. The fearful withdrawal of chimpanzees from familiar objects in an unfamiliar guise already described in the work of Hebb (1946) illustrates the negative hedonic value of situations giving rise to incongruous inputs. Similarly, children fearfully avoid the dark and approach the light. In the strange setting of a summer camp, the homesick child asks to leave the strange camp situation to return to the familiar surroundings of his home. Similarly, Festinger (1957) cites experiments showing that once people have committed themselves by purchase of a given brand of automobile, they avoid stories extolling the qualities of other brands. And those subjects of the Ewing (1942) experiment, who were led by the opening phrase of a message to expect information dissonant with their favorable beliefs about Ford, later saw the message in a highly unfavorable light, and this unfavorable light served to discredit the credibility of the message and thereby made accommodative reorganization of information already in the storage unnecessary.

Similarly, in the domain of aesthetics, the dissonances of some modern music, the unfamiliarity of forms in some modern painting and statuary, and the irregularity of meter and rhyme of some modern poetry are hard to accept and enjoy when first encountered. In fact, appreciation comes as an acquired taste which many people fail to develop because the tendencies to withdraw from encounters with such aesthetic phenomena and to avoid them prevents their storing the residues of perceptions that might ultimately make these new forms pleasantly interesting and even beautiful. Thus, the common negative valuation of modern music and art appears to exemplify behavioral withdrawal from and avoidance of the sources of incongruous information just as does the three-year-old child's negative valuation of a reading of his favorite nursery rhymes with variations.

Approach and Positive Hedonic Valuation of Incongruity. A variety of facts attest that incongruous information may also have positive hedonic value which will serve as an incentive for approach responses in both animals and men. These facts include Berlyne's findings that both rats (1950) and human beings (1958a, 1958b) will remain oriented toward stimuli which are sources of greater incongruity than toward stimuli of lesser incongruity. The rats sniff longer at novel objects than familiar objects, and the human beings look longer at complex and novel objects than at simple or common objects. These facts include Harlow's (1950) observation that monkeys will show almost continual interest in a six-device puzzle through ten consecutive hours, the observation of Harlow, Harlow, and Meyer (1950) that monkeys will learn skill at disassembling puzzles when the activity affords them nothing but the opportunity, and the demonstration by McClearn (1954) that monkeys will learn discriminations for no other reward than the opportunity to manipulate objects as will also kittens (Miles, 1958), raccoons (Thackray and Michels, 1958), and human children (Terrell, 1959). They include Butler's (1953) finding that monkeys will not only learn to manipulate an apparatus that enables them to open a door giving them a peek at the scene outside the cage but will also learn discriminations (Butler and Harlow, 1957) for such peeks or for fresh auditory inputs (Butler, 1958). The monkeys will also peek more often at a changing scene, where the incongruity is relatively greater, than at an unchanging scene (Butler, 1954). They include Montgomery's (1952) finding that the spontaneous alternation of rats in a T-maze is a matter of the animal's choosing the relatively more novel (incongruous) goal box, and the finding of Jebb and Mahut (1955) that if hungry rats are given a choice between a short route to food without obstacles and a long route with obstacles, all will choose the long route with the relatively greater incongruity some of the time, and some will choose it more than half of the time. Finally, they include the findings of Bexton, Heron, and Scott (1954), Heron, Doane, and Scott (1956), and Lilly (1956) that after human beings have been faced with homeogenous, unchanging, and therefore completely congruous stimulation for a time, they seek the relative incongruity of new stimuli of almost any kind. The urgency of the positive incentive value of incongruity under such conditions may be dramatized by the behavior of a young man of such musical tastes that anything less than high-fidelity recordings of compositions by such men as Bartok and Stravinsky would be banal: during his third afternoon in the "stimulus-deprivation" chamber, he repeatedly pressed the key that brought him two minutes of "country music" from a scratchy record of originally low fidelity.[13]

It must be admitted that most of these facts have also suggested interpretations alternative to that of the intrinsic motivational desirability of incongruity, but these alternatives have been fairly well ruled out. One may doubt, for instance, whether longer inspection of incongruous, novel, and complex objects than of congruous, familiar, and simple objects means approach to what is hedonically positive, but such doubt is easily removed by the evidence from the study of Hebb and Mahut (1955) combined with Nissen's (1930) finding that rats not only will learn to run down an alley to explore one of the Dashiell (1925) checkerboard mazes containing a miscellany of objects but will endure the shock from an electrified grill in a Warden (1931) obstruction apparatus to get there. Or, Whiting and Mowrer (1943) have seen the exploratory behavior of rats as motivated by fear, i.e., as Mowrer has more recently put it, by wanting "to make sure they are safe" (1960, p. 175). In favor of this interpretation, Mowrer (1960) has noted also the tendency of novel stimuli to evoke both fear and exploration and has been led to assume that curiosity is motivated by fear. Such an interpretation is fairly ruled out also by the finding of Nissen (1930) and by the repetitions of his study with modifications by Montgomery (1953a, 1954) and Montgomery and Segall (1955) showing that rats will leave a highly familiar region, and endure pain to leave it, in favor of a region less familiar or unfamiliar. Moreover, the notion that curious exploration is motivated by fear is further weakened by the fact that Montgomery (1955) and Montgomery and Monkman (1955) have found exploratory behavior reduced by the presence of stimuli which have been associated with painful stimulation. Homeostatic needs may also hamper exploratory behavior (Montgomery, 1953b; Zimbardo and Montgomery, 1957), but the opposite has also been found (Dashiell, 1925; Alderstein and Fehrer, 1955; Fehrer, 1956), and what is found in a given experiment may be a function of the apparatus employed (Zimbardo and Miller, 1958). Such findings fairly eliminate the fear interpretation and imply a genuine preference for incongruous inputs over completely congruous inputs.

[13] Personal communication.

To continue, one may attribute exploratory and manipulative behavior to a need for activity, but this interpretation is weakened by the finding of Montgomery and Zimbardo (1957) that depriving rats of activity in very small cages for periods up to eight days has no effect upon the amount of exploratory behavior. This interpretation is further weakened for manipulation by the fact that Welker (1956a, 1956b) has found that one keeps a chimpanzee at his manipulation by continually giving him fresh materials. One can readily see a need for stimulation in the peeking of Butler's monkeys and in the stimulus seeking of the human subjects of the McGill studies of "sensory deprivation." Such an interpretation has been made by Nissen (1930, 1954) and others. Glanzer (1953a, 1953b) has made such an interpretation of the spontaneous alternation of rats in a T-maze and of their preference for relatively unfamiliar areas. This interpretation has been ruled out with findings of large significance from the Michigan laboratory. When Walker, Dember, et al. (1955) pre-exposed rats to either black or white by placing them in small black or white boxes outside the maze, the rats showed no tendency whatsoever to choose the arm of the T-maze opposite in color from that to which they had been pre-exposed. Even exposing rats for a period to one of the goal boxes of a T-maze failed to affect their subsequent choices, but when Kivy, Earl, and Walker (1956) noted that Glanzer had allowed his animals to come to the choice point during their pre-exposure, they devised an experiment in which the rats were allowed to explore the choice point of the T-maze during pre-exposure. Both the arms into which the animals could see through glass doors but could not enter were similar, i.e., black or white, but prior to the choice trial, one of them was changed. The rats chose preponderantly to enter the arm which had been changed. This finding, reinforced by studies by Dember (1956) and by Berlyne (1957c) with human subjects, lends support to the view that it is incongruity—defined as a change in the inputs from previous experience within a *given context*—that is sought rather than any mere need for stimulation. Such illustrations fall on the border between short-term and long-term incongruity, but they tend to confirm Hebb's (1949, p. 230) observation that "'interest' and 'motivation' are likely to be preoccupied by whatever is new in the [given] combination of familiar events," and they acquire generality when one extends the concept of "the combination of familiar events" to what Lewin (1935) called one's "life space." Then, what Hebb (1949) and Hebb and Thompson (1954) have seen as pleasurable interest in the strange sights and sounds of a circus, in the problems of bridge and other games, in the dangers of skis in preference to snowshoes, are all explained as incongruity seeking. Moreover, in view of the results from these studies prompted by alternative interpretations, the alternatives take on greatly weakened import.

Both Withdrawal and Approach to Given Situations in Given Organisms. The fact that situational sources of incongruity may evoke both fearful withdrawal and interested approach makes a puzzling issue for explanation. Whether the situation evokes fearful withdrawal or interested approach might be attributed to individual differences, but both directions of response have been observed in given rats (Berlyne, 1950), in given dogs (Melzak, 1954), in given chimpanzees (Welker, 1956c), and in given children to a single situation. In the case of human children, for instance, alternate tendencies of withdrawal and approach can be regularly observed as children get acquainted with a stranger. Welker's (1956c) description gives nearly the full picture. His method consisted of presenting chimpanzees with such novel stimuli as toys that move. The first reaction of chimps to such stimuli is typically fearful withdrawal such as Hebb (1946) observed in the Yerkes Laboratory. As the incongruous, novel stimulus-objects remain within the animal's view, or are presented repeatedly, alternating approach and withdrawal, reminiscent of the behavior of the rats that Miller (1944) had both fed and shocked at the same end of an alley maze, replaces the withdrawal. Such ambivalent alternation is then followed by approach and tentative manipulation of the novel stimulus-objects. Finally, the tentative manipulation gives way to full-fledged manipulation in which the chimpanzee shows its creative powers by disassembling the objects. Such results would appear to indicate that whether withdrawal or approach occurs is a function of the degree to which the organisms have got accustomed to (i.e., developed within the storage representative counterparts for) the novel or incongruous objects. There comes a time, however, when "familiarity breeds contempt" and something new must be added to maintain the pleasurable approach. The determination, thus, resides within the organism's relationship to the environmental situation.

The Optimum Hypothesis. The fact that incongruous stimulus situations can sometimes be attractive and pleasing and sometimes repelling and displeasing suggests that there must be an optimal level of something involved somehow in the organism's relationship with the environment which divides pleasure and attraction from displeasure and repulsion. The hypothesis of an optimum has been suggested by several theorists. One was implicit in Hebb's (1949) discussions of pleasure and fear, and was made explicit by Hebb and Thompson (1954, p. 551). Moreover, Helson's (1947, 1948, 1959) conception of the *adaptation level* (AL) is just such an optimum, and it is one based on past experience for it is defined quantitatively as a weighted log-mean of the stimuli of that sort which have impinged on the organism in the past or are impinging from the surrounding circumstances. But, an optimum of what? An AL of what?

OPTIMAL DISCREPANCY BETWEEN INPUT AND ADAPTATION LEVEL. One answer comes from an explicit attempt to synthesize Hebb's (1949) theory of pleasure and fear with Helson's (1947, 1948) theory of the AL (McClelland, Atkinson, Clark, and Lowell, 1953). According to McClelland and Clark, affective arousal is central in motivation, but affective arousal as conceived here is both subjective and directional; the direction is based on subjective pleasantness and unpleasantness. They assumed, moreover, that affective arousal is an innate consequence of the perception of the various characteristics of each modality of reception in relation to an experientially determined adaptation level (AL) (Helson, 1948). This notion of the AL had its origins in Helson's (1947) formulation of the principle of color conversion, was extended to lifted weights, and then generalized (see Helson, 1959). In their use of AL theory, McClelland and Clark came to see pleasurable affective arousal to be the consequence of small discrepancies between the intensity, or some other aspect of the modality of stimulation, and the AL of the organism for that intensity or aspect of stimulation. They also saw negative affective arousal as a consequence of large discrepancies between the impinging intensity or other aspect of stimulation and the AL. Haber (1958) has depicted this relationship in a bilaterally symmetrical curve (see Fig. 3–4).

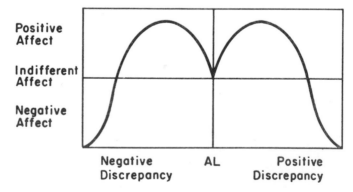

Fig. 3–4. A curve depicting the theoretical relationship between affective value and discrepancy of level of stimulation from the adaptation level (AL) (after Haber, 1958).

Haber's curve helps to explain why subjects will report any given intensity or quality of any modality of input as pleasant at one time and as unpleasant at another, for the affective arousal (perhaps a better term would be valuation) is conceived to be a function of the discrepancy between the characteristic of input and the AL for that characteristic, but the AL is not fixed. Rather, it is influenced by the inputs of the immediate past and even those of the surroundings of the present. Thus, immediate past experience becomes an important determiner of whether a given intensity (or other characteristic) of any modality of input will be pleasant or unpleasant.

The McClelland-Clark-Haber formulation is intriguing and it has been usefully suggestive. Inasmuch as it is concerned with all the specific aspects of all the various modalities of stimulation, however, it lacks a desirable degree of generality, a generality that hopefully can be achieved by dealing directly with informational meaning. Inasmuch as affective arousal is concerned with a comparison between the organism's immediate past experience with a given modality and the level of input at the present, moreover, the AL-input discrepancy can be seen to be a special case of what is here termed short-term incongruity. Furthermore, whether pleasure or displeasure will result must depend upon some implicit optimum of this discrepancy which is not defined in the theory. It is left to empirical outcome. In this sense, McClelland, Clark, and Haber all make an unusual use of the AL, for Helson (1959) conceives the AL itself to be the divider between the pleasant and the unpleasant.

There are two other limitations. First, as Hunt and Quay (1961) have pointed out, rearing animals on various kinds of stimuli which typically evoke withdrawal fails to make them positive incentives for approach responses or positive reinforcers. This fact suggests that various kinds of modalities of stimulation have innate, gene-determined negative (or positive) hedonic values. Becoming "used to" such stimulation only reduces the degree of its innate value, but it does not alter its directional or hedonic character. This is a point which McClelland and Clark have recognized, but one which was not incorporated in the bilaterally symmetrical, theoretical curve of Haber (1958). In view of these innate hedonic values of stimulation, the true relationship between hedonic value and discrepancy from the AL cannot be represented by a bilaterally symmetrical curve. Second, the crucial importance of context noted in the studies of Berlyne (1957c), Dember (1956), and Kivy, Earl, and Walker (1956) finds no place in this formulation. This factor of context is also alluded to implicitly in Hebb's statement that "those sensory conditions are called pleasant, then, which contribute to the *current* development in the cerebrum . . . [and motivate] the preoccupation with what is new and not too new" [italics mine] (1949, pp. 232–33). This factor of context which concerns the organism's process of building meaning out of its encounters with a given portion of the environment is of the essence.

While Hebb's intriguing observations and seminal formulations give full, if implicit, place to this factor of context, his preoccupation with neurophysiological mechanisms has had the unfortunate consequence of supplying the behavioral investigator with no handles for testing his formulation that organisms are pleasurably preoccupied "with what is new but not too new" in a given contest, no way of finding the optimum of newness (incongruity) is implicit in the statement. It was this defect which the McClelland-Clark-Haber formulation sought to overcome, but, beyond its empirical defects, and despite its suggestive use of the AL, it too has failed to define the optimum of discrepancy that divides approach and pleasure from withdrawal and displeasure.

OPTIMUM OF AROUSAL. A second answer to the optimum-of-what question has achieved generality by assuming that the direction-determining optimum is one of degree of physiological arousal assessed by means of some combination of the "expressive indicators" of emotion. This second formulation was made about simultaneously by Hebb (1955) and Leuba (1955).

Hebb (1955) apparently began by noting that the efficiency of "cue function" is maximal, as indicated by such evidence as reaction time (Lansing, Schwartz, and Lindsley, 1956), discrimination time (Fuster, 1957), and the capacity of the cortex to discriminate paired light flashed (Lindsley, 1957, p. 86) at a moderately high level of arousal (see Fig. 3–5). From this fact, Hebb apparently inferred that there must be an optimum level of arousal which is also the divider of approach from withdrawal and pleasure/displeasure. From the fact that the subjects of Bexton, Heron, and Scott (1954) exhibited, after some three days in an unchanging environment, EEG records indicating an abnormally low level of arousal in conjunction with their avidity for stimulation and their inability to tolerate the situation, Hebb was apparently convinced that the direction of behavior must be a function of the level of arousal. Thus, at times when the organism's level of arousal should happen, for any reason, to be below the optimum, the organism would be expected to approach and take pleasure in any circumstances that would increase the level of arousal; at times when the organism's level of arousal should happen to be above the optimum, the organism would be expected to withdraw in displeasure from any situation that would tend to increase arousal. Given the reaction demonstrated above between arousal and incongruity, this formulation leads to the expectation that when the organism's level of arousal happens to be below the optimum, it would prefer greater degrees of incongruity than it would prefer when the

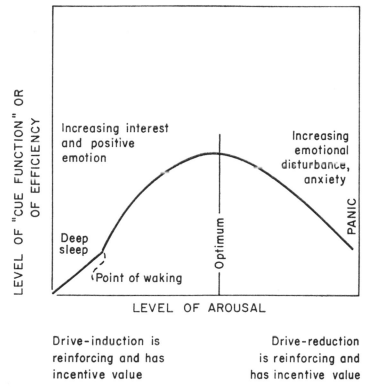

Fig. 3–5. Diagram of the theoretical relationships among arousal, "cue function," efficiency, and incentive or reinforcement value (after Hebb, 1955, with modifications).

level of arousal should happen to be above the optimum, and vice versa.

Leuba's (1955) formulation is similar, but it was based on somewhat different facts. Leuba noted what appears to be a curvilinear relationship between efficiency of such executive operations as reaction time (Freeman, 1940) and pursuit-performance (Schlosberg and Stanley, 1953), on one hand, and degree of arousal on the other hand (see Fig. 3–5). This is to say that maximal efficiency of executive operation, represented on the ordinate in Fig. 3–5, comes with a moderately high level of arousal, represented on the abscissa in Fig. 3–5. From this evidence of an optimal level for efficiency, Leuba, like Hebb, generalized this to account for the direction of behavior. Levels of arousal below the optimum were seen as the basis for the stimulus seeking that manifested itself in the peeking behavior. Contrariwise, Leuba conceived that at levels of arousal above the optimum, organisms would withdraw from stimulation and thereby manifest the traditionally conceived tendency to seek drive reduction. What Leuba meant by his term *stimulation* appears to have been its intensity, but, given the relationship between incongruity and arousal, this formulation would apply equally well to incongruity.

It is somewhat ironic that Hebb (1955), who appears to have been the first to formulate a version of the incongruity hypothesis (Hebb, 1946, 1949), should be led, by the results of the studies of so-called "stimulus deprivation," to abrogate it in favor of an hypothesis which makes arousal rather than incongruity the essential factor in answering the direction question.

OPTIMUM OF INCONGRUITY. A third answer to the optimum-of-what question may be derived from the formulation of Berlyne. Berlyne (1960) has also seen a need for assuming an optimum of something to answer the direction question. In an avowed effort to save drive-reduction theory, Berlyne notes but rejects the notion that unchanging stimulus conditions "will produce exceptionally low arousal and that low arousal, as well as high arousal, may therefore be aversive" (1960, pp. 188 ff.). Berlyne's interpretation appears to take its origin from one made earlier by Myers and Miller (1954). When these investigators found that well-satiated and comfortable rats will learn to press a bar or turn a wheel merely to get an opportunity to explore the opposite end of a Miller-Mowrer box, they interpreted their observation to mean that unvarying circumstances produce a monotony or "boredom drive" which can be reduced by increasing the variation in receptor inputs occurring through the changes in the animal's position that occur in exploratory behavior. With Myers and Miller, Berlyne has assumed that conditions of unchanging stimulus produce a boredom drive which implies an increase in arousal. Berlyne gets to the use of the optimum hypothesis by assuming what he calls an optimum of "arousal potential." Fig. 3–6 has been drawn here to depict the Berlyne position: In it, the ordinate and the abscissa get quite different labels from those they got in the Hebb-Leuba depiction in Fig. 3–5. Here, in Fig. 3–6, the ordinate represents arousal rather than efficiency of either cue function or executive function. Here, the abscissa represents "arousal potential," and also incongruity, as we shall see, rather than arousal.

According to Berlyne's argument, "arousal potential," an unfortunate term, inheres in the various "collative variables." As already noted above, these "collative variables" are composed of stimulus change, novelty, incongruity, and complexity. They are "collative variables" precisely because they derive from the relationship between the receptor inputs of the present and the residues of past receptor inputs. In Berlyne's formulation, these "collative variables" are presumed to have in common

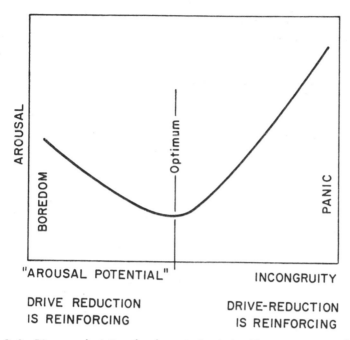

Fig. 3–6. Diagram depicting the theoretical relationships among arousal, "arousal potential," and reinforcement according to Berlyne (1960). From the standpoint of the Berlyne position, either too little or too much "arousal potential," based on the "collative variables," increases arousal, so that the amount of drive determines the direction of behavior, but drive-reduction is reinforcing. From the standpoint of the position to which I am inclined, arousal may be increased by either too little or too much incongruity, but it is incongruity that probably determines the direction of behavior. Arousal may commonly be associated with either too little or too much incongruity, but it is neither a necessary nor a sufficient basis for approach or avoidance.

some degree of conflict (Berlyne: 1957a; 1957b; 1960, chaps. 7 and 8). Because Berlyne appears not to be cognizant of the differing functions of the frontal and posterior intrinsic systems, he fails to distinguish frustration and conflict from incongruity and dissonance between incoming information and the information already in the storage of the posterior system. In view of these facts, however, Berlyne's "arousal potential" can be translated as an equivalent of *incongruity*. Thus, the abscissa of the graph in Fig. 3–6 can properly represent *incongruity* as well as "arousal potential." Furthermore, the curve in Fig. 3–6 may be seen to depict the theoretical relationship between arousal, represented on the ordinate, and incongruity, represented on the abscissa. Through these theoretical translations, a position is derived in which an optimum of incongruity determines the division of pleasant approach from unpleasant withdrawal. Although this formulation may be conceived to save the concept of drive reduction, it also has the ironic effect of making an optimum of incongruity the determiner of direction and the basis for an answer to the direction question.

In defending his position, Berlyne (1960) makes a very different use of the results of the study by Bexton, Heron, and Scott (1954) from Hebb's. He notes that Hebb based his conclusion that low arousal is intolerable upon the fact that the EEG records had indicated an average of low arousal in the subjects who remained for several days in the unchanging stimulation. Berlyne points out, however, that inasmuch as this is an average level of arousal, low arousal may not be the basis for the withdrawal of subjects from the Bexton-Heron-Scott experiment in spite of the $20 they were paid for each day of participation. Moreover, Berlyne cites personal correspondence with Heron for the fact that at times the subjects of this experiment appeared to show irritation; he suggests, therefore, that their withdrawal could well have been instigated by the heightened arousal of a boredom drive. Heron, Doane, and Scott (1956) note that, when their subjects were experiencing hallucinations, they also appeared to show fear. Such fear might also have instigated their withdrawal from the situation.

DIFFERENTIAL EMPIRICAL IMPLICATIONS. Fortunately, these two interpretations suggest quite different predictions concerning the behavior of organisms in various situations. If the Hebb-Leuba assumptions are true, i.e., that it is an optimum of arousal which determines the direction of behavior and that low arousal is aversive, then one would expect that monkeys in a Butler-type experiment would time their peeks when their level of arousal was lower than average. Contrariwise, if the hypothesis of optimal incongruity is correct, then one would expect the monkeys in such an experimental situation to time their peeking with higher than average levels of arousal. If one could make it feasible to record continuously the EEG and/or the palmar conductance of monkeys in a Butler-type situation, it should be possible to determine which of these two predictions holds. This might be very difficult with monkeys, but such an approach might be quite feasible with human subjects.

Another promising attack upon the issue of whether it is an optimum of arousal or an optimum of incongruity that is essential in determining the hedonic value of situations and the direction of behavior would consist of raising the level of arousal without altering the level of incongruity and so determining the effect of the increased arousal on the attractiveness of novel stimuli. Recent studies by Schachter and Singer (1962) have shown that injections of epinephrine will increase the vigor of either euphoric or angry reactions, but that the choice of reaction depends upon situational-cognitive factors. Such evidence suggests that a telling experiment might be based on giving subjects tests in which they have a choice of novel, and presumably exciting, stimuli, or familiar, and presumably unexciting, stimuli, both before and after injections of either epinephrine or Ringer's solution. One might assume that subjects free to operate about as they choose would come into such an experiment with the level of either arousal or incongruity near the optimum. Thus, if the Hebb-Leuba conception is correct, the increase in arousal produced by the injections of epinephrine should tend to reduce the proportion of novel stimuli chosen in the post-injection test as compared with the pre-injection test, and this reduction should be greater for those subjects injected with epinephrine than for those injected with Ringer's solution. If, on the other hand, it is incongruity rather than arousal which determines the hedonic value of stimuli and the direction of behavior, the injections of epinephrine might be expected to alter choices no more than injections of Ringer's solution.

One line of evidence, if it is reproducible, may imply that incongruity is more important than arousal in determining the direction of behavior. This is the work of McReynolds (1956), who has related novelty seeking to what he calls "anxiety." What he calls "anxiety" is assumed theoretically to derive from lack of assimilation, but may empirically derive from an accumulation of incompleted tasks. McReynolds makes here the kind of theoretical distinction between perception and apperception that Herbart (1816) made about a century and a half ago. Apperception or assimilation, thus conceived, is a kind of information processing, and it may be imagined to consist of a kind of reordering of information in the storage. In their experiment, what McReynolds and Bryan (1956) found was that schizophrenic patients showed less tendency to seek novel stimuli in preference to familiar stimuli after they had been exposed to a procedure theoretically calculated to leave them with a burden of unassimilated percepts. This procedure, however, consisted of presenting the subjects with a series of designs after telling them that they could expect a second sample of each. The experimental group got the initial test of novelty seeking, then a condition in which only a few of the designs were presented the second time before they got the second test of novelty seeking. The control group, on the other hand, got the initial test of novelty seeking, a series of designs in which each was presented twice, and the retest of novelty seeking. It was under these conditions that the schizophrenic subjects in the experimental group chose fewer of the novel stimuli than did those of the control group. On the basis of the procedure employed, what McReynolds and Bryan con-

ceived to be the result of unassimilated percepts could also be conceived
to be the result of a cumulative Zeigarnik (1927) effect following an accumulation of incompleted tasks. The reproducibility of these results
is in question; for example, when Haywood (1961) repeated the procedure with college students as subjects, he found an increase of palmar
sweating as indexed by the colorometric method but no reduction in
novelty seeking. In a later study, however, Haywood (1962) found that
interspersing a confusing message between two tests of novelty seeking
and two measures of palmar sweating both increases the palmar sweating
and decreases the tendency to choose the novel, rather than the familiar,
presentations in the test of novelty seeking. Such findings, in conjunction
with those of Schachter and Singer (1962), suggest that arousal per se
may have little to do with the direction of behavior, but may be a necessary aspect of the reorganizing of information in the storage called for by
encounters with situations emitting incongruous inputs, an optimum, or
adaptation level (AL), which divides pleasant approach from unpleasant
withdrawal. Increase in arousal may also be associated with below
optimal incongruity because either boredom or fear may ensue.

QUANTIFICATION OF INCONGRUITY. If the level of incongruity in relation to an optimum or an AL of incongruity is selected theoretically to
be the determiner of the hedonic value of stimuli and the direction of
behavior, it becomes highly important to quantify incongruity. Otherwise, this notion of an optimum or an AL can have relatively little meaning. Fortunately, it should be possible to quantify incongruity in terms
of information theory (see Attneave, 1959; Shannon and Weaver, 1949).
Here, incongruity would refer to the difference between the information
of a given domain to which the organism has been exposed, on the one
hand, and the information to which it is being exposed, on the other.
If such quantification does prove feasible, it should be possible also to
get one of Helson's (1959) adaptation levels for incongruity by assessing
the incongruity to which an organism is exposed in a number of contexts. If such a mode of attack can be made feasible, it should then be
possible to explore the possibilities of altering the adaptation level for
incongruity by means of forced encounters with circumstances in which
stimulation remains homogeneous for periods of varying duration. I
should also then become feasible to investigate the effects of any change.
in the AL for measures of arousal and for measures of efficiency.

While it is clear from the evidence summarized here that incongruity in information processing has something to do with the direction
of behavior, many questions remain unanswered. The optimum hypothesis is promising, and perhaps it is enough at this stage of history to
have available some testable hypotheses.

The Role of Intrinsic Motivation in the Answers
to the Other Questions

Space prohibits a full discussion of the role of the motivation inherent in information processing and action in answers to the other motivational questions, but it may be useful to give at least a synoptic account.

Intrinsic Motivation and Cathexis. It may seem radical to find a basis for cathexis in intrinsic motivation, but evidence indicates that one exists and that it is probably a very important one, especially during infancy. Part of this evidence comes from the observations which Piaget (1936) has made on the development of his own three children during their first two years of life. Although Piaget's attention was focused on the development of intellect, his observations indicate that there is an epigenesis of intrinsic motivation and that, in this epigenesis, recognition is one factor in the establishment of emotional attachments.

According to these observations of Piaget, the human child is essentially a responsive organism during the first two or three months of its extra-uterine life. It is responsive in that its various then relatively independent schemata are evoked by changes in the external stimuli. The Russians' "orienting reflex" to short-term incongruity is present at birth. In the course of being repeatedly evoked, the schemata become coordinated. Something heard becomes a conditional stimulus for looking and something to look at; something seen becomes a conditional stimulus for grasping and something to grasp; something grasped becomes a conditional stimulus for sucking and something to suck. Moreover, repeated encounters with various patterns of stimuli bring about *recognition*. Recognition and its hedonic value are manifest in the infant's smile and in his *intentional* attempts to hold on to the recognized patterns. This is the first transformation, the first epigenic landmark, in the development of intrinsic motivation. It occurs when the absence or withdrawal of recognized patterns begins to instigate striving to hold onto a given informational input. It appears to occur typically during the fourth or fifth month of life, but occasionally during the third. It is easy to see parallels between the effects of the repeated encounters that lead to recognition in the observations of Piaget with the "primary learning" of "cell assemblies" and "phase sequences" described by Hebb (1949). A second major transformation or epigenic landmark in the development of intrinsic motivation appears to occur typically at about the end of the first year when repeated encounters with already recognized patterns of stimulation lead gradually to positive interest in variations in the familiar patterns or to interest in novelty. This interest in novelty, or in mildly incongruous circumstances, appears to endure throughout the lives of organisms. It is presumably the motivation for the problem seeking remarked by Hebb and Thompson (1954) and even for curiosity and the ambivalent fascination of the scientific enterprise where incongruity between theory and observation continually "eggs the investigator on" to creative formulations of theory and to a search for new evidence.

The lines of evidence suggesting that recognition is a basis for cathexis are several. The first is the fact that the smile and other evidences of joy appear to come with the recognitive transition of a pattern from unfamiliarity to familiarity. The smile and these evidences of joy are typically manifest first in the child's recognition of a face. This has led Spitz (1946c) to see smiling as the basic social response, but Piaget's (1936) observations that the smile and these other signs of delight occur regularly with encounters with a wide variety of patterns which are known to have been encountered repeatedly before, even with the appearance of a newspaper taking a place on the covering-top of the child's bassinet, indicate that the smile and delight come with the development of recognition.

The second line of evidence comes from the fact that once the smile and the signs of joy have been observed in connection with encountering a given pattern, the child initiates actions to hold onto the "interesting spectacle" as it threatens to withdraw. Anyone who has ever jounced a child upon his knee, and stopped, will recall the intentional character of the child's jouncing in turn in an obvious effort to get the interesting jouncing to start again. In this sense, recognition would appear to be the motivational basis for such often-observed, autogenic activities as the hand- and foot-watching that typically make their appearance at about age four months (Bühler, Hetzer, and Mabel, 1928). Piaget (1936) watched his son smile at the appearance of his own hand and then gradually manage the skill of keeping it within view. It is probably through this recognition-motivated effort to keep the interesting sight of his hands in view that the child acquires his eye-hand coordination, the visual control of his hand-motions. It is also likely that recognition of given vocal patterns motivates their repetition in the babbling that Baldwin (1895), Allport (1924), and Holt (1931), as well as Piaget (1936), have termed a circular reaction.

A third point of interest, perhaps even a line of evidence, comes in the close parallels between such human phenomena and the phenomena of animal behavior included under the term "imprinting," which also appears to be a basis for emotional attachment. Heimroth (1910) noted that an incubator-hatched, gray-leg gosling will react to human beings, if it has encountered them a few times before encountering a goose or other moving animal or object, by following them. Lorenz (1935) has observed, moreover, that if the human being busies himself with gray-leg goslings which have been hatched in an incubator, the goslings will begin to peep as soon as the human being moves away, and after the peeping comes their following reaction, apparently designed to keep the human being within view. The parallel between these observations and those of Piaget on the human child is striking. The parallel has yet another merit. While in the case of human children one cannot rule out the possibility that it is the feeding of traditional drive-reduction theory and the warm soft contact, such as Harlow (1958) finds motivating the attachment of his young monkeys for their padded surrogate mothers, as the basis for cathexis, such motivational sources of cathexis are absent in the case of the following that occurs in the "imprinting" of goslings.

A fourth line of evidence that recognition is a basis for cathexis derives from the emotional disturbance that follows the separation of a child from recognized people and surroundings. This shows in the fact that what Anna Freud and Burlingham (1944) termed "separation anxiety" did not occur in the infants removed from their families during the London blitz of World War II who were less than seven or eight months of age. At this age, recognition of parents and even some degree of the "permanence of the representations of objects" have been established. Similarly, what Spitz (1946b) has termed "anaclitic depression" occurs only when a child is separated from his parents during the second half of his first year. Moreover, this emotional disturbance that occurs with separation from recognized persons and situations (an emotional disturbance which might better be termed grief than either anxiety or depression) increases during the second year and until the child has acquired sufficient language to enable parents to communicate that they will return. Similar phenomena occur in lower animals. A fear of strange persons or of familiar persons in unfamiliar guise appears in chimpanzees only after several weeks of contact with persons (Hebb and Riesen, 1943; Hebb, 1946). Moreover, the fact that this fear of the strange or of the "familiar in an unfamiliar guise" does not appear even at a much later age in chimpanzees reared in darkness strongly suggests that it is the factor of recognition that reinforces the attachment (Riesen, 1947).

It is interesting that such evidences of emotional attachment will occur in the newly hatched grayleg gosling after only a few encounters on the first day or two, but they require in the chimpanzee the many encounters of the first month.[14] Moreover, they appear to require in the human infant the even more numerous encounters of the first three or four months. This species comparison would seem to imply that the ac-

[14] Based on comments in a preliminary version of H. F. Harlow's Salmon Lectures.

quisition of recognition is more rapid lower in the phylogenetic scale than it is higher up. This may be a function of the relatively lower A/S ratio (after Hebb, 1949) in the gosling as compared with the infant chimp and in the infant chimp as compared with the infant human being.

Although the crucial experiments required to give the notion full empirical confirmation have not been made, the types of evidence outlined here appear to imply that recognition (the process of repeated encounters with situations whereby coded information supplies a representation within the storage to match the inputs from new encounters and thereby making those situations familiar and predictable) is at least one of the important bases for the emotional attachment which psychoanalysts have termed *cathexis*.

Intrinsic Motivation and the Choice Questions. Various investigators consider the choice questions to be central for motivational theory (e.g., Hebb, 1949; Maslow, 1954; Taylor, 1960). These questions are highly intricate, and it is only candid to admit that fully satisfactory answers do not exist. The traditionally dominant theory has attempted to answer them in terms of acquired drives and reinforcement, but as Brown (1943) has pointed out, this formulation results in both empirical and theoretical quandries. Fortunately, several other chapters in this book are either directly concerned with or contribute significantly toward answering the choice questions.

Although information processing undoubtedly makes a major contribution to the choices of both responses and goals, it is far from the only category of motivation participating in such choices. Maslow (1943, 1954) has long been calling attention to the existence of a hierarchy of needs which govern the organism's choice of responses and goals. In his conceptualization, the appearance of needs lower in the hierarchy demand that those higher in the hierarchy be satisfied. Thus when basic homeostatic needs are gratified, safety needs emerge. When these are gratified, the needs for love and esteem appear; and when these are gratified, the needs for self-actualization and the desire-to know appear. There is much truth in this conceptual scheme. In the conceptualization proposed here, however, there are but four gross categories of motivation: the withdrawal from painful stimulation, the seeking of gratification for homeostatic needs and sexual arousal, the plans and intentions which are independent of these, and the approach to and withdrawal from incongruity. There is a hierarchy of prepotence here. Escape from intensely painful stimulation typically takes precedence over all other forms of activity. In the absence of painful stimulation, homeostatic needs like hunger and thirst take precedence, even over sex. The sex system can often interfere with intentions and plans not tied with these other more prepotent systems, and it is likely that the pursuit of planned goals tends to predominate over concern with incongruity, positive or negative. But this typical order does not hold in all cases, for some men will endure hunger and thirst and considerable pain to achieve goals which have little relationship to these needs. Moreover, martyrdom is also a fact.

An epigenesis characterizes the choices of both responses and goals. In fact, various schemata may become goals. Following the coordination of the reflexive schemata during the first four or five months of the human infant, and following the development of intention that comes with recognition, as Piaget (1936, chap. 4) has noted, one of the child's schemata may become a goal while the others become means to that goal. A child may, for instance, seek to grasp something he has seen, and, in the pursuit of this grasping goal, he may utilize his creeping schema, his climbing schema, and perhaps others to achieve this goal. Once interest in novelty develops, the child rapidly increases both the differentiation and the mobility of his schemata as he discovers new means through his active groping for such goals. The interest in novelty also motivates the imitation of new patterns, especially new verbal patterns (see Piaget, 1945; Hunt, 1961, pp. 172 ff.). As the child develops verbal patterns, these gradually acquire the referents of the people from whom he imitates them. This appears to occur much after the fashion that Sherif (1936) has demonstrated in the development of "social norms." In the Sherif demonstration, people who discuss the distance that an autokinetic light is observed to move gradually come to see it moving within a similar range of distances. Thus, the child who has generalized his new-found garbling of the word "apple" to a potato hears the adults say something like the following: "That's not an 'apo,' that's a 'potato.'" In the course of millions of such corrections, the child's vocal schemata acquire the referents of those who correct him. When he gets the "learning set" that *things have names*, this process is greatly speeded, and the correcting comes at a new level, namely, at the level of concept organization, and what belongs to which categorical term. The child also learns how the words for action, the words for things, and the various kinds of modifiers are supposed to go together; he learns the syntax of his language. At this point, he is in a position to acquire information through language, and the conceptions thus acquired through linguistic communication must be tested against his concrete observation of reality. This is an endless, ongoing process of which all modern science is a part.

Through just such a process of communicative corrections, the child learns not only his language but what is important and what is not important if he is to be accepted as one of the group into which he is continually becoming. Every culture structures not only this acquisition of language but also the pattern of beliefs and values acquired through linguistic communication. The prepotence of painful stimulation and homeostatic need, being basically biological, is present in all cultures, and it can be utilized, after the fashion of acquired drives and acquired rewards, to give greater or less importance to various categories of symbols. They can be manipulated in one culture, like that of Alor (see Kardiner, 1945, p. 234), to give maximal importance to wealth and power. Moreover, since wealth and power afford access to freedom from pain and to the wherewithal to satisfy homeostatic and sexual needs, they are likely to be important in any culture, as Hobbes (1651) noted long ago. On the other hand, the corrective processes in child rearing can also be used in a culture to stress the value of friends and relatives, as in the case of the Arapesh (see Mead, 1935), and, it should be noted, having friends and relatives can also be a way of achieving freedom from painful stimulation and homeostatic need. The variations in the beliefs and values of people of the various social classes within a given culture are shaped in this same fashion (Davis, 1948). Moreover, within cultures and within classes, there are variations based upon neighborhood-differences and family-differences (Kluckhohn and Murray, 1954, chap. 1). Thus, for example, high valuation of achievement appears to be associated with having a mother who gives her approval chiefly to the development of competence in various areas and then allows her children freedom to use it, once the competence has been developed (Winterbottom, 1953).

The attitudes, beliefs, and values acquired during socialization supply the basis for choices of both responses (how things will be done) and goals (what things it is important to do). These attitudes, beliefs, and values supply the frames of reference or the adaptation levels that constitute the standards for the TOTE units with which intentions and plans are compared in the choice process. Whether a given plan is accepted or rejected may well follow the principles outlined in the section concerned with "intrinsic motivation and the direction-hedonic question." At any given stage of life, the values already established would presumably supply the standards by which the choices of both responses and goals are made (see, also, Taylor, 1960).

But there is another side, a social side, to this choice question. Just as the attitudes, beliefs, and values of the members of a group or culture supply the standard against which each individual measures his impulsive intentions or plans in the process of choosing among them, these same attitudes, beliefs, and values supply a standard against which he weighs his perceptions of the behavior of others. When their behavior differs from the standard enough to produce distressful incor gruity, it becomes a source of disapproval and hostility from the perceiver. Even from such a sketchy consideration of the issue, it can readily be seen that the motivation inherent in information processing and action integrates nicely with the role-theory of the social psychologists, and that it is probably the basis for most of the pressures for social conformity.

Intrinsic Motivation and Behavioral Change. The factor of incongruity between the information already in the storage and information coming through the receptors also provides a motivational mechanism for continual change in both conceptions and behavior. The principle that inputs too similar to the information in the storage come to be neglected, while interest concerns center on those in which an optimal degree of incongruity exists, means that interests continually change, and as they change, the information in the storage gradually alters the standard against which new inputs are matched. This is a conception of learning and behavioral or conceptual change which differs markedly from that in traditional learning theory. In traditional theory, behavior change is seen to be a function of frustration, and Melton (1941), for one, has explicitly asserted that all behavioral change results from frustration. While it is undoubtedly true that frustration and conflict will produce a change of means, and even a change of plans or goals, frustration of instrumental activities is certainly not the only basis for change in overt patterns of response or in attitudes, beliefs, and values.

The traditionally dominant theory has held drive reduction to be the reinforcement for all behaviors which persist. Inasmuch as all plans are presumably mediated by implicit central processes within the cerebrum which mediate the expectations present in the course of action, it is likely, as Miller, Galanter, and Pribram (1960) have suggested, that confirmation of these expectations inherent in these mediating central processes is a basis for reinforcement. Similarly, on the side of information processing, per se, confirmations of the standard of reference based upon information in the storage can be a basis for stability of conceptual schemes. While in many instances such confirmation may be based upon social communications and result in the "social norms" (see Sherif, 1936) discussed above, in many other cases it would appear that the confirmation of conceptions from direct observation of reality becomes so regular and consistent that these conceptions become interpersonally invariant. Such appears to be the case with the Platonic "reals" and with Kant's (1791) basic categories of reality. It has been the merit of Piaget (1937, pp. 311 ff.) to demonstrate that such Kantian categories as those of space, time, and motion are not "given" in the young child. They go through an epigenesis, but they finally achieve what Piaget terms an "equilibrium" which can be understood in the terms proposed here as a regular confirmation of conception with perceptual input. Thus, these basic categories of reality, which Kant conceived to be "a priori," can be seen to be a product of experience but of the experience which all human beings share. They are not, therefore, "social norms," because the confirmation comes directly from the perception of reality. Precisely because the confirmation comes regularly, such conceptions are taken for granted by all people, except those few like Poincaré (1906) who were concerned with fundamental questions of epistemology, or like Piaget (1937) who were concerned with the issue of the a priori character of such basic concepts. Except when men take a new view of these matters, they are "old stuff," and it is the novel in which there is that optimal level of incongruity that attracts their attention and concern. From this standpoint, behavioral and conceptual change can be seen to be both inevitable and fun.

Although experimental demonstrations of the intrinsic motivation of behavior change are extremely few, observational evidence comes from the joyous interest that children show in newly developed skills. Moreover, this same kind of motivation appears to carry over to the learning of reading with properly programed teaching machines in the work of O. K. Moore. I have personally seen these children leave their nursery-school play when their teacher wondered aloud if they wished their turn at, of all things, the teaching machine for reading. A little girl aged three years and seven months quickly put on her coat, skipped across a fifty-yard stretch in the zero-cold, opened the door to the "laboratory," put up her coat, skipped to the door of the cubicle housing the teaching machine, climbed into the chair, called for a change of the typed material she was to copy, and worked avidly for about eighteen minutes. After this, she began to make errors, and at twenty-four minutes she put her head down on the key-board of the electric typewriter. Finally, she responded to the speaker that repeated the letter she was to strike, worked another three-or-so minutes, then put her head down again. When the speaker continued to call out the letter every fifteen seconds, she grasped it in her little hands and said, "Aaa fo' today." She then got out of the high-chair before the typewriter, walked rather slowly to the coat rack, put her coat back on, and returned to the group in the nursery school. As she appeared, the teacher called out, "Johnny, do you want your turn?" Johnny, who had been finger-painting, immediately stopped. He stuck his hands under the faucet in the lavatory, wiped them on a towel, put on his coat, went out the door and ran across to the door of the "laboratory," hung up his coat, pushed his way through the group that had gathered at the door of the cubicle of the teaching machine and climbed into the high-chair.

Each of these children exhibited behavior implying that they were approaching something attractive. Anderson and Moore (1960) call such behavior "autotelic" because it contains its own goal, and they call attention to the fact that all cultures exhibit such autotelic folk models as puzzles, games, and aesthetic activities. The term, *autotelic*, has about the same import as my term, *intrinsic*. Moore's work appears to be a demonstration that the behavioral and conceptual change involved in learning to read can be fun if the teaching machine is programed so as to permit the child to choose his own rate of change, i.e., his own degree of incongruity. Moore's electric typewriter is equipped with a mechanism that counts the number of strokes per minute. The trick is to observe when this rate drops off. This is the signal that the program needs to be changed to maintain the child's interest. While this is not a truly experimental demonstration of the intrinsic motivation of behavioral change, it is a dramatic illustration of how such motivation can be utilized in the educational process.[15]

At least one truly experimental demonstration does exist. Dember, Earl, and Paradise (1957) have described one which is a paradigm deserving of imitation and extension. They presented rats with a choice between two levels of complexity in the form of a figure-8 maze where, in one case, the walls of one loop were painted a solid color and the walls of the other were painted in black and white horizontal stripes. In a second case, the walls of one loop were painted in black and white horizontal stripes and the walls of the other in black and white vertical stripes. In the first case, horizontal stripes are more complex than a solid color, and in the second, vertical stripes are more complex than horizontal stripes. On the basis of theorizing somewhat similar to that presented here, the experimenters could make no prediction about which loop would be preferred immediately by each of the rat subjects because they had no knowledge of the optimum of complexity that it might already have developed. They could, however, predict that those animals registering a change in choice of loop between a first and a second hour of exposure, by an increase in the proportion of time spent there, would make the change toward the more complex

[15] Moore (with Anderson) speaks for himself later in this volume, but note the shades of Montessori (1907, 1915). When this was written, she was to me only a name in the history of education, and I am indebted to Jan Smedslund for pointing out her utilization of intrinsic motivation in education. In "motivation inherent in information processing and action," behavioristic and physiological methods appear to be rediscovering, albeit in somewhat revised form, the spontaneity and the joy in learning upon which this "pedagogical anthropologist" (see Montessori, 1913) based the method of educating children that she devised more than half a century ago. Recently, Standing (1957) has reviewed Montessori's life and work, but the discussion of her work by the American novelist Dorothy Canfield Fisher (1912) remains the best introduction to it.

loop. This prediction was clearly confirmed. Of a total of thirteen animals making such spontaneous changes of choice, twelve made changes that were clearly in the predicted direction. This appears to be a demonstration of the "growth motivation" discussed by Dewey (1900), a concept that he appears to have borrowed from Forebel.

From such theoretical and empirical considerations, it would appear that the most important motivation in the process of educating the young is that inherent in information processing and action. Although Dewey (1900) may have been wrong in assuming that all values are relative in that they are based only on the confirmation that derives from social communication, he was certainly on the right tract in his attempts to reform the school curriculum (Dewey, 1902). Although various values, such as those which run through all the religions of mankind, may have a common basis in confirmation in direct contact with reality just as certain concepts have such confirmation, it is still true that the process of acquiring the information and skills of a culture involves an epigenesis in which the situation that the child encounters must be properly matched with the constructs he has already acquired if educational progress is to be both maximal and enjoyable (see Hunt, 1961, pp. 267–88).

Intrinsic Motivation and Persistence. Persistence has several aspects. When it concerns continuing to strive for goals against obstacles and momentary defeats, it is considered desirable. This is courage. When it concerns the tendency for behavioral patterns of beliefs and attitudes to persist in the face of evidence to the contrary, it is undesirable. This is rigidity. These two aspects of behavior are not as nicely separate as the language which describes them, and knowledge about their development is far from perfect.

A few things, however, can be said. From the standpoint of the incongruity principle, one would expect that a background standard based upon experiences of failure mixed with success, and a background of success which follows only after intensive striving would lead to courage. Such appears to be the case. Even in rats, getting food for every trip down a maze to the goal box results in a habit requiring fewer trials for extinction than does getting fed only after a portion of the runs through the maze. This phenomenon, often known as the Humphreys (1939) effect, after his demonstration of the effect with the eye-lid reflex, has been repeatedly demonstrated (see Jenkins and Stanley, 1950). The existence of the tragic persistence in the choice of goals, epitomized in Captain Ahab's quest for the Great White Whale in Herman Melville's *Moby Dick,* and the fixated persistence of various habits that lead to distress led Freud to postulate a "repetition compulsion" which he further, assumed to be motivated by a "death instinct." In an experiment that deserves amplification, Farber (1948) has shown that the tendency of rats to make one turn in a T-maze rather than another can be made very persistent by getting these turns timed appropriately with the painful stimulation of electric shock. Similarly, Akhtar (1962) has found that rats which have encountered a given number of electric shocks associated with pressing the level to get food during acquisition will persist in pressing the level during extinction, when it brings nothing, for more trials than will rats which have encountered merely an equal number of presses on which they got no food during the acquisition process. These laboratory phenomena are probably not unrelated to the finding that children who are reared in authoritarian fashion with a good deal of punishment are more persistent in their professions of affection for their parents than are children who have been reared more permissively and with less punishment (see Adorno et al., 1950; Rokeach, 1960). Frenkel-Brunswik (1949) attributed such evidences of rigidity to the inability of children to express their emotional ambivalence toward their parents, but perhaps the basic factor is the level of arousal at the time the beliefs, attitudes, and plans were laid down. If this level of arousal were high, it may take a high degree of incongruity to affect a rearrangement in the storage, and unadaptive rigidity may be the consequence.

Summary

In this paper, theories of motivation are seen as having attempted to answer eight questions: instigation, energization, direction-hedonic value, cathexis, choice of response, choice of goal, behavioral change, and persistence. In the theory dominant during the first half of this century, it has been assumed that *all* behavior is motivated by painful stimulation, by homeostatic need, or by innocuous stimuli which have become the conditioned stimuli for the emotional responses that are part of the pattern of response to painful stimulation and homeostatic need. This paper has reviewed the evidence, coming largely since World War II, which shows that play, manipulation, exploration, spontaneous alternation in mazes, and concern with novel stimuli all occur in the absence of homeostatic need and painful stimulation. Moreover, painful stimulation, homeostatic need, or innocuous stimuli which have been associated with them, tend, if anything, to inhibit these various forms of behavior. These suggest that there must be another kind of motivation, one inherent in information processing and action.

This paper has pointed out, moreover, that the concepts of drive naming, of spontaneous behavior, and of pointing to the adaptive, or telic, significance of behavior are all blind theoretical alleys in dealing with motivation. Furthermore, the change in the conception of the basic functional unit of the nervous system from the reflex to the feed-back-loop and the change in the conception of the cerebral function from that of an automatic but static telephone switchboard to a housing of active information processes like those built into electronic computers, have helped to suggest a mechanism for intrinsic motivation. The instigation question is answered in terms of an incongruity between inputs of the moment and some standard within the organism, either one fixed by the manner in which the organism is innately structured or one established by the past experience of the organism. The organism remains active until congruity appears. This paper describes evidence to show that emotional arousal is produced in the encountering of stimuli which produce incongruity. Furthermore, whether organisms approach incongruous stimuli or avoid them appears to be a function of an optimum, based on past experience, of either arousal or incongruity, which is a matter for further investigation.

This paper goes on to show that intrinsic motivation functions in the establishment of emotional cathexes in that recognition appears to be an important factor in the acquisition of emotional attachments. Response and goal choices are seen to be a function of values which go through a developmental epigenesis and which are derived from both social communication through language and direct contact with reality. The fact that organisms appear to seek an optimum of incongruity is shown to provide a continual ongoing basis for change in behavior and conceptions which can be of great importance in education. Courage as persistence in a response pattern or in striving for goals is seen tentatively to be a function of an experientially determined standard based upon having encountered failure and having succeeded only after intensive effort. Pathological persistence and the rigidity of concepts are attributed tentatively to the standard of excitement present when the concepts were acquired.

Chapter 4

Cognitive Aspects of Self and Motivation

O. J. HARVEY AND HAROLD M. SCHRODER

This chapter will focus on a treatment of the self as a motivational construct. Stemming from an S-O-R notion of psychology, self will be stressed as the significant O-variable that operates as the mediating linkage between environmental impingements and ultimate response evocation. It will be emphasized as a kind of cognitive framework in relation to which the environing world is broken down and compared, through which, in prism-like fashion, stimuli are passed and transformed into psychological relevance and meaning.

The manifold activities involved in these psychological processes cover such breadth and represent such diversity that objection might be raised as to the appropriateness of a single rubric to encompass them. A fitting response to such an objection might be that any definition, construct, or system approaches the best of all possible when it is simultaneously both most *inclusive* and most *exclusive,* shows ways in which the phenomenon under perusal is similar to all other related points of comparison and in what ways it is different from all others. Inescapably an adequate treatment of the self must be inclusive; its place in affecting psychological processes is indeed pervasive. Under the umbrella of this label one could enter into innumerable questions and issues that have plagued not only the psychologists but have concerned even more passionately the philosophers: what serves as the coordinating clearing house and gyroscope of all the energies, pressures, predilections, restraints, and interpretations that tend to keep the individual generally on a not too uneven keel in his transactions with the social and physical world about him. "The self," as Pillsbury wrote in 1907, "is merely all that we are and know . . . a growing vital unity that as a whole is effective in every experience. When it is directed toward the control of action, we know it as will; when choosing from among the many stimuli that offer, as attention; when interpreting the stimulus, as perception or judgment;

when constructing new forms from old experiences, as reason. But it is the same everywhere, always active, and active in very much the same way in every kind of mental process" (Pillsbury, 1907, p. 406).

Clearly, and defensibly, one could ride off in endless directions and sketch scenes and draw samples of activity that could be said to be self-related. No one yet has offered a set of criteria by means of which the bounding limits of the self can be drawn and the self from the not-self can be distinguished. Furthermore, it is quite improbable that anyone shall, unless the problem is approached only by artifically setting up and invoking the precepts derivable from a closed epistemological system. And closed systems, we know, while operating to prevent too much inclusion, may commit the equally grave error of stressing too much exclusion or specific differences.

We shall not presume to still this issue. Nonetheless, while the treatment deliberately will be at a rather genotypic level, the intent being to provide a skeleton of broadly applicable notions into which room is afforded for phenotypic variation, the need for specificity will not be altogether ignored. Following a general definition of the self, many of the characteristics that enter into it will be described, some of their more important cross-sectional effects on variations in self structure will be sketched, how such characteristics evolve will be outlined, and the application of these processes to several problem areas will be suggested.

Self Defined

Few are the constructs relating to human activity that have received attention from as wide a representation of disciplines as that of the self. The child of philosophy, it has since its birth received unbroken concern from these quarters, having today, for example, found its way as a core construct into that philosophical orientation that has come to be known as Existentialism. Psychology, on the other hand, has shown variable and sharply divided interest in the self, treating it with great respect in some circles and with even greater disdain in others. In those veins of psychology of certain philosophical heritages, especially of that Germanic vintage which found expression in such works as those of Kant, self, under one guise or another, has generally occupied a place of high theoretical stature. At the same time, this concept was cast into the realm of untouchable mysticism by those psychologists who felt that overt behavior, especially that accessible through some form of an S-R paradigm, comprised the only proper domain of endeavor to psychologists. Beginning with and following James (1890), social psychologists, of both the sociological and psychological varieties, have repeatedly turned to the notion of self as a kind of mediating linkage or theoretical bridge between individualistic and social determinants of behavior. They, along with philosophers, have felt the need to be concerned with those aspects of the individual which seem to find expression in selecting, synthesizing, and directing activities. It is to self or ego, which some use synonymously (e.g., Sherif and Cantril, 1947) and between which others differentiate (e.g., Allport, 1943; Murphy, 1947), that these activities are frequently assigned.

Without attempting a detailed history of the various definitions of the construct of self, which in simplest compendium would fill a sizeable volume,[1] *self, as it shall be employed in this chapter, will be synonymous with an individual's interrelated totality of modes of ordering of his psychological universe, with one's concatenation of more or less standardized cognitive tendencies or conceptual system(s).* Certainly there is nothing inherently valid or superior in the assignment of the label self to embody the totality of the cognitive or interpretive processes. One could treat of any isolated aspect of psychological functioning one chose and label it in whatever way suited one's purpose. But the assignment of the term self to those processes involved in discriminating and coding the motivationally relevant aspect of one's world is intended, as one thing, to focus attention on their central importance in one's reading of reality, indeed in one's definition and maintenance of his very essence and being. The possible accusation that we might be making of the self a homunculus will be unwarranted. If any genotypic construct can be dimensionalized into more phenotypic aspects and these can be shown to operate in specific ways, then movement is made toward that best of all possible theoretical states, that of concomitant inclusiveness and exclusiveness. We shall aim in this direction, toward both generality and specificity.

Self as Subject and Object (Cause or Effect)

From among the numerous approaches to the problem of the self, one of the most recurrent of the many issues that has fairly stably evolved is the question of whether the self can be treated more appropriately as the subject or the object; in slightly different languages: as the agent or the recipient; as the "cause" or the "effect" of the outcome of transaction of the individual with his environing world. In the tradition begun by James (1890), social psychologists often deal with this question in terms of the I and the Me, these referring respectively to the self as the agent or cause of action and the self as the recipient of an event.[2] As

---

[1] Treatments that present some of the major historical issues and usages surrounding the construct of the self are included in such works as: Allport, 1943; Sherif and Cantril, 1947; Chein, 1944; Sarbin, 1952; Hall and Lindzey, 1957.

[2] Some of the more important philosophical issues and problems relating to the I, or self as agent, have been sketched by MacMurray (1956).

equally prevalent is the use of the terms ego and self to refer to these same aspects of psychological activity. It would seem that the question of greater appropriateness is an unanswerable one, because any system, with the possible exception of a completely closed one, may be treated as *both cause and effect*. Yet one of the most consistent differences between social psychologists and personality theorists has appeared in their treatments of the self or its equivalent, the former treating it as effect and the latter as cause. Certainly one's concatenations of concepts, or self, represent the outgrowth or effect of interaction with the physical and social world. At the same time, however, it influences the course of this transaction, both modifying it and, in feedback fashion, being modified by it. Some of the processes and consequences of interaction with relevant aspects of one's social world are described picturesquely by Strauss:

> Face-to-face interaction is a fluid, moving, running process; during its course the participants take successive stances vis-a-vis each other. Sometimes they fence, sometimes they move in rhythmic psychological ballet, but always they move through successive phases of position. The initial reading of the other's identity merely sets the stage for action, gives each cues for his lines. Events may turn out as expected; nonetheless an astute observer can notice a ground-base of unwitting interplay and often witting by-play [Strauss, 1960, p. 55].

Even with the physical environment held constant, the very process of responding to it alters in some degree the conceptual system through which the impinging stimuli are filtered, so that at Response 2 the psychological value of the situation is different from what it was at Response 1, albeit infinitesimally so in many cases. As a consequence, the self is never completely fixed. It is always developing—becoming, to borrow from Allport (1955); changing, to borrow from James (1890). Very apropos is the oft quoted statement, perhaps lament, by James:

> . . . Often we are ourselves struck by the strange differences in our successive views of the same thing. We wonder how we ever could have opined as we did last month about a certain matter. . . . From one year to another we see things in new lights. What was unreal has grown real, and what was exciting is insipid. The friends we used to care the world for are shrunken to shadows; the women, once so divine, the stars, the woods, and the waters, how now, so dull and common; the young girls that brought an aura of infinity, at present hardly distinguishable existences; the pictures so empty; and as for the books, what *was* there to find so mysteriously significant in Goethe, or in John Mill so full of weight?
> But what here strikes us so forcibly on the flagrant scale exists on every scale, down to the imperceptible transition from one hour's outlook to that of the next. Experience is remoulding us every moment, and our mental reaction on every given thing is really a resultant of our experience of the whole world up to that date [James, 1890, Vol. 1, pp. 233–34].

Some Functions of Conceptual Systems

Definitional and Predictive Control. That an individual when facing a novel situation of relevance to him will structure it or make sense out of it in some way consonant with his extant motives and psychological makeup has become one of psychology's most worn truisms. While any number of labels could be—indeed have been—affixed to such more or less standardized evaluative predilections, we shall refer to them as *concepts.* (Concepts which evolve from interaction with and are shared by others are usually termed *group norms.*)

Concepts represent the relationship of a subject to differentiated aspects of his environment, the referents of which are as varied as are the objects of one's experience. Depending on whether the level of treatment is more phenotypic or more genotypic (Lewin, 1935), more matter or more form, to employ an Aristotelian distinction, a variety of functions served by one's conceptual matrix may be postulated. As schemata for evaluating impinging stimulus objects or events along some specifiable dimension, they serve as a kind of psychological yardstick to which the impinging world is compared, is differentiated and integrated; they operate as kinds of programs or cognitive metering systems through which reality is defined and read (Harvey, Hunt, and Schroder, 1961).

One might go so far as to postulate a need for structure, expressed in the "seeking after meaning" (Bartlett, 1958), and possibly in the so-called exploratory drive or curiosity motive (Berlyne, 1960). Whether or not making sense out of a situation is a biological imperative, certainly it is indispensably instrumental to the ability to predict recurrences in the world and to adapt to it. And without such an ability survival itself would in most cases be rendered impossible or at least markedly impaired. Concepts contribute to this assessment of the world; indeed they are perhaps the sole embodiment of it. As such, they provide one with a means of fate control, a vehicle through some sort of adaptive equilibrium is maintained between the inside and outside, to borrow from Herbert Spencer (1897); an avenue of accommodation and assimilation, to borrow from Piaget (1951). In this sense, one's system of concepts provides a nexus through which one anchors oneself in space and time; in terms of which one's very being is; without which one as a receiving and appropriately responding organism would not be. As Murphy has suggested, "Indeed, the self-picture [3] has all the strength of other per-

[3] From our point of view, the self picture or self concept is not equivalent to the total self, but is only a part, albeit a very important part. Self, as we have defined it, is the totality of one's concept—toward self, God, a flower, all the objects of experience. Some of these concepts are of greater centrality and as a consequence exercise greater effect on cognition and behavior. We assume that concepts having to do with self worth are at the top of the hierarchy of centrality. But we wish to caution self-concept theorists that this does not account for all the variance.

ceptual stereotypes and in addition serves as the chart by which the individual navigates. If it is lost, he can make only impulsive runs in fair weather; the ship drifts helplessly whenever storms arise" (Murphy, 1947, p. 715).

Self Maintenance. The essentialness of subject-object ties in self maintenance has received dramatic demonstration in such effects as brain-washing, sensory deprivation, and alienation. Common to all of these conditions is the threat to or severance of more central ties of the subject to relevant aspects of his environment, although the referents to which the cathexis or linkages exist may be different. It is quite probable that many of the American Army captives who died in the Chinese Communist prison camps were comprised largely of individuals whose basic anchorages to the world were completely obliterated. This need to relate in a consistent fashion to the environment, moreover, is not restricted to human beings. Paralleling many of the effects of "give-up-itis" manifested by these American captives seemingly are the behaviors of the adolescent elk observed by Altmann (1960). With their basic modes of evaluating and reacting to their world rendered inoperative through separation from their mother, through being kept from other adult elk—through being permitted to belong to no group—these young animals failed to clean themselves, their coats became unkept and ragged, they became more susceptible to disease, and they were more likely to fall victim to preying wolves and other pitfalls in their capricious and unfriendly environment.

While effects of self dissolution from severance of basic anchorages of the individual may be drawn from a wide variety of sources, less wide is the range of evidence revealing the effects of preventing formation of concepts in the first place. It appears, as would be expected, that one consequence of this type of a homogeneous or undifferentiated world, most typically effected by preventing the infant from establishing sufficient contact with his world to differentiate and integrate it, is the evolvement of only rudimentary self structures, if any at all. Seemingly illustrative of this are such findings as those of Harlow on "the need for contact" (1958), the suggestive results obtained by Spitz (1949), and the effects on young animals of being reared in aseptic environments observed in studies carried out at Notre Dame. It is possible that marasmus and childhood schizophrenia result from this same failure of the infant or young child to differentiate his environment stably and meaningfully relate himself to it. Evidence is beginning to converge from various sources, empirical as well as anecdotal, to suggest strongly the hypothesis that certain response potentials inherent in a species lie inert and unrealized until some appropriate environmental event or specific stimulus input activates them and starts their movement toward fruition. Hence it is quite probable that, for anything like an adequate self to evolve, a heterogeneous environment that provides both specific and diverse stimuli is necessary. Perhaps the most documented basis of this assumption has been offered in J. McV. Hunt's recent book *Intelligence and Experience* (1961). In Chapter 3 of this volume Hunt also makes this point clear.

Although intending to suggest the indispensability of conceptual ties for organismic adaptability, perhaps even survival, we would not want to imply that all organisms, certainly not even all human beings, must relate to the same things and in the same way. Indeed, the greater proportion of the remainder of this chapter shall be devoted, directly or indirectly, to showing basic ways in which individuals differ in both *how* and to *what* they relate for self definition and maintenance. To the extent that variation does exist in the how and what of subject-object ties, it would seem to follow that to that extent must the conditions that result in anomie and alienation, marginality, brain washing, and other threats to or severance of subject-environment tendrils also vary. Later we shall treat specifically, albeit briefly, some of these anomicizing conditions, in terms of differential effects resulting from variation in structures or organization of conceptual systems.

Events (Including Self as Object) Are Construed in Terms of Concepts. The importance of concepts in the definition of the situation has been clearly demonstrated in early studies on the effect of labeling and more recently by work carried out under the name of psycholinguistics. Experimental work by Carmichael, Hogan, and Walter (1932), Bartlett (1932), J. Gibson (1929), Brown and Lenneberg (1954), for example, and empirical observations by such anthropologists as Whorf (1956), Hoijer (1953), and Hallowell (1951) have shown that once an object is conceptually sorted into a particular evaluative category the tendency exists, especially under ambiguous conditions represented by an absence of the object through time, for the object to be made to fit the properties implied in the concept. Details and characteristics are both added and omitted in the transformation of the object into a fit for the cognitive mould embodied in the utilized concept, in ways described by Allport and Postman (1947) as leveling and sharpening.

The importance of concepts in definition of the self has repeatedly been pointed to by social psychologists. Their emphasis typically has been on those socially shared concepts embodied in roles and other normative prescriptions. Early and outstanding in this tradition are the works of James, Cooley, and Mead, all of whom stress the tendency of the individual to define and react to his self *as object* much in terms of the connotations derived from the definitive labels affixed to him by his primary group and significant other.[4] This position recently has been enriched and lucidly extended by Goffman (1959) and Strauss (1960).

Concepts of Status Affect Self Definition. Examples of rather specific effects of socially defined categories or concepts on self definition and related behavior are provided in several studies having to do with the relationship of group status—both standing within one's reference group and the standing of one's reference group in relation to other groups— to level of aspiration or expected attainment on group relevant tasks. Seemingly the norms defining appropriate performance levels for particular status positions become incorporated into one's self system where they operate to affect individuals' expected attainment.

Thus Chapman and Volkmann (1939) found that college sophomores tended to estimate their achievement on a literary task in terms of their standing in relation to the group whose attainment level was introduced as fictitious norms. Groups of subjects who were advised that W.P.A. workers had made a certain score on the test had a higher level of expected attainment for themselves than did subjects who had been advised that sophomores, graduate students, college professors, and literary critics had made the same score. Along the same line, Preston and Bayton (1941) found Negro college students lowered their level of expectancy when advised white students had achieved a certain score on a test and MacIntosh (1942) found white students tended to raise their expectancy when instructed of the achievement of Negro students on the same task.[5]

On the relationship of expectancy to status *within* the informal group, W. F. Whyte observed that predicted attainment in bowling bore a high correlation to the status hierarchy within the group (Whyte, 1943). Similarly, Harvey (1953) and Sherif, White, and Harvey (1955) found that group members tended to expect of both themselves and of other members in accordance with their status. Individuals of lower standing within the group both expected of themselves and were expected by other members to perform more poorly on group tasks while members of higher status expected and were expected by others to attain higher levels of performance. It may be of interest to add that within the num-

---

[4] The extensive literature relating to self concept is replete with examples of self construal following labels attached to the self. The high frequency of such work has precluded its detailed treatment in this chapter.

[5] In an unpublished study, carried out in the spring of 1958, aimed at tapping some of the effects of the changing social position of the Negro in the South, Harvey found that Negro students at a southern university not only failed to place their own expected attainment on a digit-symbol substitution task below a fictitious performance norm of white college students but actually expressed an expectancy that surpassed the white norm.

ber of trials sampled status was found to be highly related to expectancy while objective performance had no significant effect. This is not to imply, however, that over enough trials the actual performance levels of members would not come to affect expectancies held of them. With enough repetition, objective and subjective probability should come to bear a high relationship, except perhaps within completely autocratic and closed groups.

In summarizing one of our studies it was suggested, "Our findings seem to point to the conclusion that the expectations an occupant of a given status in a *well-defined* informal group holds of himself are largely determined by the expectations which have become defined by the group as appropriate to that status. As any group value or norm which is internalized may serve as an anchorage in determining judgments and perceptions of related situations, so it seems that the definitive labels and epithets attached to each status position, and thus to its occupant, by the group may serve as salient anchorages in determining one's judgments and perception of one's self as well as other group members" (Harvey, 1953, p. 366). This conclusion, no doubt, placed too much emphasis on social determinants of self-expectancy. In fact, as we shall indicate later, social psychologists typically have overweighted group and other social determinants of the self. While such social ingredients may characterize quite adequately the content of certain conceptual or self systems, they are much less applicable to others, as we have shown elsewhere (Harvey, Hunt, and Schroder, 1961) and shall show later in this chapter. Nonetheless, it is probably true that "Certainly, an outstanding problem for the whole area of ego-psychology is to determine to what extent our self-perceptions or conceptions, our very self-esteem, are a function of our group status and the definitive labels assigned it— in the family, play groups, adolescent cliques and adult reference groups. Such work would contribute immeasurably to the understanding of how broad cultural and social processes operate to influence the individual" (Harvey, 1953, p. 367).

Functional Blindness and Resistance to Change

Once formed, concepts seem to possess as an invariant characteristic some degree of resistance to change, irrespective apparently of the nature of the referent to which the concept relates—self-worth, distance between lights, or whatever (Harvey and Caldwell, 1959). This results in a kind of cognitive paradox, which in extreme form may impair veridical sensitization and adaptation to the world, especially under conditions of great complexity, change, and threat. Although the world would remain in a booming, buzzing confusion, even in a state of irrelevance and nothingness without concepts, once a way of ordering evolves, it tends to be perpetuated and to preclude seeking for or acceptance of other definitions of the situation (Harvey, Hunt, and Schroder, 1961). "Perceiving, thinking, judging and related activities are profoundly affected by—perhaps even wholly dependent upon—a pre-established system of ordering or conceptual placement . . . And yet this very dependence on a system of categories leads to a kind of conceptual closedness, reflected in a functional blindness to alternative evaluations that are not embodied in the conceptual framework employed at the moment" (Harvey and Beverly, 1961, p. 125).

Concern with the behavioral restrictions which result from limited conceptual alternatives is expressed clearly by James in his treatment of the "law of inhibition of instincts by habits."

When objects of a certain class elicit from an animal a certain sort of reaction, it often happens that the animal becomes partial to the first specimen of the class on which it has reacted, and will not afterward react on any other specimen.

The selection of a particular hole to live in, of a particular mate, of a particular feeding-ground, a particular variety of diet, a particular anything, in short, out of a possible multitude, is a very wide-spread tendency among animals, even those low down in the scale. . . . The rabbit will deposit its dung in the same corner; the bird makes its nest on the same bough. But each of these preferences carries with it an insensibility to *other* opportunities and occasions—an insensibility which can only be described physiologically as an inhibition of new impulses by the habit of old ones already formed. . . . Few of us are adventurous in the matter of food; in fact, most of us think there is something disgusting in a bill of fare to which we are unused. Strangers, we are apt to think, cannot be worth knowing, especially if they come from distant cities, etc. . . . And so it comes about that, witnessing this torpor, an observer of mankind might say that no *instinctive* propensity toward certain objects existed at all. It existed, but it existed *miscellaneously,* or as an instinct pure and simple, only before habit was formed. A habit, once grafted on an instinctive tendency, restricts the range of the tendency itself, and keeps us from reacting on any but the habitual object, although other objects might just as well have been chosen had they been the first-comers [James, 1890, Vol. 2, pp. 394–95].

Such "tunnel vision" and resistance to all but a limited band of environmental impingements are consistent with a host of early theoretical stances, including Herbart and the Gestalters. In keeping with a more current vogue, one might choose to say, in a kind of information theory language, that because of inherent structural limitations of the conceptual system an individual at any one time can delineate and consider only a finite and limited number of interpretive alternatives. Hence when the upper limits of the channel and coding capacities are reached, the individual becomes incapable of making further differentiations and integrations of his world. One could as theoretically fittingly postulate that an individual's need for structure and predictive control disposes toward maintenance, in varying degrees of absolutism, of the existent mode of reading the situation. Of course, the need for structure and control, which themselves probably interact, is not assumed to complete the list of determinants of conceptual closedness. Threat, ignorance— numerous other factors—no doubt affect this tendency toward restricting the acceptable or system-compatible inputs.

The Self and Motivational Arousal

One's interlocked matrix of concepts, operating as an evaluative base-line or cognitive metering system, serves, it is assumed, as the psychological referent points or internal standards in relation to which motivational arousal is effected and must be considered (Harvey, Hunt, and Schroder, 1961). This holds in relation to both so-called biogenic and sociogenic or primary and derived motives. In fact, there probably is no motive at the human level that operates independent of learning or conceptual components. As Cooley pointed out 60 years ago (1902), native predispositions and effects of experience become inextricably intermeshed so that any attempt at their separation is necessarily arbitrary and artificial. Also relevant is James' position on the inhibition of instinct by habit, to which reference was made earlier. Additionally, an instinct for James was transitory, operating as an energizing agent which changed into habit (concept, we would say) at that first instance where energy arousal became attached to or associated with a relevant object; or with an incentive, as some might say today. Hence, while the rabbit possesses the instinct of scurrying for a hole in the ground when pursued by the hound, such native predisposition remains only an untapped potential until the rabbit is chased and goes into the hole. At this moment of wedding between aroused instinct and the goal object habit is formed and pure instinct no longer exists.

Perhaps one would not be too far afield to assert that all, or at least most, of man's innate predispositions exist only as potentials, as kinds of seeds possessed of varying breadths of possible expressions whose ultimate fruition is contingent upon the appropriate interlocking of aroused state and object. This has already been demonstrated, it appears, in those restricted cases of imprinting. It appears quite probable that it may exist, but in a less readily provable fashion, in the cases of more complex states and practices. For example, Hunt (1960) has presented a compelling argument that this is the case for actualized intelligence. It would appear little is gained, therefore, by viewing conceptual components of motives as superstructures built upon more basic underpinnings. Like any marriage, it would be non-existent without both links of the chain. One eats, but not just anything. People partake of sex; but most not just indiscriminately. The goal object sought is not un-contaminated by what one learns as appropriate and fitting for his own aspiration and self image. Suicide and outright sacrifice of one's life for a believed cause represents those extremes where, paradoxically, one maintains certain central concepts at the expense of life. The cost of relinquishing existing values and conceptually generated strivings may be so high that one may be willing to pay the price of life itself to prevent it.

Confirmation and Refutation of Concepts. The quality and degree of motivational arousal, while dependent on a host of specific factors, is assumed to be the consequence of two genotypic phenomenological states, *confirmation* and *refutation* (Harvey, Hunt, and Schroder, 1961), both of which are consequences of the perceived relationship between impinging events and internal standards operative at the time. Every concept possesses as an inherent aspect of it a *directionality*, a course of action or predilection expressed generally in approach or avoidance tendencies toward the object to which the linkage exists.[6] It is this directional predilection toward a particular course that operates as the baseline for determining confirmation and refutation, which respectively is the evaluation of a situation as being compatible or incompatible with the directionality of the concept. In somewhat more typical language perhaps, confirmation represents the evaluation of a situation as facilita-tive of goal attainment, irrespective of the goal—object or incentive, whether it be a pellet of food or thinking positively of oneself. Refuta-tion is the interpreting of events as portending impediment of goal achievement.

Emphasis on the directionality of a concept as the more appropriate baseline for motivational arousal renders the present position different in certain important respects from other notions of motivation which in many ways are closely akin to our own, for example, that enunciated by McClelland and his associates in one of their earlier works (1953). These authors viewed *expectancy* as the appropriate baseline or adapta-tion level for determining whether a perceived stimulus discrepancy would result in positive or negative affect. The condition in which ex-

[6] The attribution of approach or avoidant tendencies to all concepts may prove to be an overgeneralization. It may be that with the engagement of any concept or matrix of concepts underlying brain organizations are simultaneously generated and that the basis of confirmation and refutation (along with their many consequences) will be the extent to which events are perceived as being congruent or incongruent with the existing neurological organization. Operationalizing such a possibility is a forbidding task, one which probably will have to wait for advances in knowledge of neurology.

pectancy was neither completely confirmed nor overly refuted was posited as the state conducive to maximal positive affect. Limitations of the applicability of this "butterfly curve" were, however, recognized by the authors themselves, for they pointed out the improbability of the prediction, which would follow from their theory, that if one expected to flunk out of school and almost did he would feel better than if he expected to flunk and did not even come close to it. From our position, that the directionality or striving of a concept or motive is the proper baseline for affective arousal, it would be predicted that the relationship between confirmation or refutation and affective arousal would be a linear one, with greater confirmation eliciting greater positive affect and greater refutation generating negative affect. This should hold, of course, only up to the point of ceiling, where further confirmation or refutation would have no effect. In all cases it would appear that expectancy must be considered against the backdrop of directional or volitional predilection, which in some cases will be compatible and in others will be incompatible with what is expected. This is indicated in the results of a study by Van Ostrand (1960) in which subjects low in self-esteem, and who presumably expected to be rated low by others, reacted more strongly and displayed greater negative affect when actually rated low by another person than did persons of high self-esteem. It might be pointed out parenthetically that the results of Van Ostrand are not in accord with predictions which Festinger would make from his consonance-dissonance model (1957), the reason being that Festinger, without making it explicit, also assumes that expectancy is the referent point of consonance-dissonance, conflict, or congruity.

The directionality embodied in a concept tends to channel the evaluative, affective, and behavioral tendencies toward the cathected object(s) so that the individual in his many aspects of functioning is rendered highly selective toward it, manifested in varied sensitization and altered thresholds toward the relevant objects. Sensitization may result in either lowered or heightened thresholds, lowered toward events portending confirmation and heightened toward situations portending refutation. (This is another way of saying that selectivity and differential sensitization may result in either perceptual vigilance offense or defense. Increased sensitization, toward either potential confirmation or refutation, can be inferred from at least three different kinds of behavior: (1) elicitation of a particular response at a lower threshold; (2) a more intense response with stimulus held constant; and (3) greater salience of a particular stimulus (it standing out more as figure) when included in a multiplicity of other, potentially competing, stimuli.

Selectivity operates, then, as a basic determinant of confirmation and refutation, in defining both the nature of the impinging event and its degree of compatibility or incompatibility with the conceptual standards operative at the time.

Some General Consequences of Confirmation and Refutation

Certainly many writers have been concerned with reactions to positive or negative incongruities, events which are either in accord with or incompatible with the yardstick embodied in the engaged concepts. In a general way, reactions to discrepant communications, deviant psychophysical anchors, and unexpected events can be conceived within this framework. This is not to imply, of course, that the strength of the responses to all discrepant inputs is equal. Presumably this would vary as a function of such things as direction and magnitude of the discrepancy as well as the centrality or strength of the concept being confirmed or refuted. It is our assumption, however, that confirmation and refutation tend to have certain common effects across concepts, although specific variations in the relevant concept will determine the specific outcomes. Some of the more important consequences of confirmation include (1) the generation of positive affect, to some degree, toward both the subject and the perceived causal agent of confirmation, and, correlatively, (2) approach tendencies, of some magnitude, toward the perceived causal agent. Refutation disposes toward the opposite consequences.

By approach is meant the tendency to decrease the psychological distance between subject and the relevant object and by avoidance the tendency to increase this distance, definitions which are broader than those typically given of these constructs. At the more concretistic levels of functioning these tendencies are more likely to take physical and motor expressions, such as the child's touching or taking into itself positively interpreted objects and trying to destroy or walk away from negatively evaluated situations. At the more abstract levels of functioning, on the other hand, approach and avoidance tendencies are more likely to find symbolic expression, in such ways as the attribution of positive or negative characteristics to the concept-relevant objects. Such behaviors are common consequences of interpersonal interaction and exposure to communications of either a confirming or refuting nature. The tendency for the source of a communication to be discredited and negative characteristics attributed to him as his message is construed as becoming more incompatible with the concepts of the recipient has been noted by several authors (e.g., Osgood and Tannenbaum, 1955; Hovland, Harvey, and Sherif, 1957). Under related conditions in interpersonal interactions, the tendency for subjects to lower their evaluation of another person when that person is perceived as being derogatory of them has also been noted (e.g., Harvey, Kelley, and Shapiro, 1955; Harvey, 1962). One of the more extensive documentations of these tendencies is provided in the recent work of Newcomb (1961) in which are demonstrated the effects of numerous varieties of system-milieu asynchrony or conflict in interpersonal relations.

The effect of a given stimulus discrepancy has to be considered in relation to the idiosyncratic baseline of the recipient. While certain inputs under certain conditions may have fairly consistent effects, in other instances the same input may produce a very different, even opposite, effect. Thus while Harvey, Kelley, and Shapiro (1957) found consistent effects between gradations of self-derogation, Harvey (1962) confirmed these effects and found in addition important personality differences in response to the same (stimulus defined) inputs. Further, an individual who is very pro-authority, for example, may respond just oppositely to a communication for a high authority source as compared to an individual who is strongly anti-authority (Harvey, Hunt, and Schroder, 1961). Comparable results have been obtained in relation to psychophysical stimuli, which most experimenters have seemed to assume were not affected by motivational or personality factors. In several of our own studies not only stimulus determinants of psychophysical judgments have been noted, but personality differences have also been found (e.g., Harvey and Caldwell, 1959; Harvey, 1963a).

The effect of variation in intra-organismic norms on various psychological criteria is amply demonstrated by Bevan in Chapter 2. Not only may the same stimulus input be judged differently, but its reinforcement value depends on the subjective baseline of the recipient.

Thus far we have written as if motivational and effective arousal results from the engagement of a single concept by a single event. This is far from reality, however, because generally more than one concept is triggered off by the situation; the operating adaptation level is multidimensional. Consequently, the attendant response tendencies vary in their degree of conflict or compatibility from complete coincidence, through orthogonality to complete opposition. All the effects may be confirmatory. All may be refutive. Or they may contain aspects of both. In the case of simultaneous confirmation and refutation, the individual is assumed to be faced with contradiction and conflict in his behavioral and affective predilections, a state of system dissonance or imbalance (Festinger, 1957; Harvey, Kelley, and Shapiro, 1957; Heider, 1958; Newcomb, 1961; Abelson and Rosenberg, 1958; Harvey, Hunt, and Schroder, 1961).

We assumed earlier that the individual is disposed toward keeping intact all of his existent concepts and toward behaving congruously with them. In those conflict situations represented by concomitant confirmation and refutation this might prove difficult, or even impossible. The situation could be so compelling that one interpretation or course of action is engaged at the expense of others. In a way reminiscent of Bentham's notion of felicific calculus, if we might forthrightly hazard such a confession, the individual is assumed to "calculate," at some level of awareness and rationality (from complete consciousness to unconsciousness and from complete irrationality to complete rationality) the psychological costs and credits of the various choices and courses of action available to him and to move in the direction of least affective cost. This probably means, when possible, following the direction implied in the most central of the activated concepts, the effect being that this "making the best of a bad situation" tends to protect or maintain with minimal alteration the more central aspects of the self. Yet under certain conditions it is possible that the behavioral predilections stemming from less central concepts are adhered to at the expense of the concept highest in the hierarchy of centrality. This could occur when the combined relevance or importance of several alternatives encompassed in less central concepts would outweigh that of the most central concept by itself. When pitted against each of the other concepts within the system singly, the more central concept should be favored. But when pitted against several of the others in combination, it might be sacrificed or modified in favor of the greater pooled significance of the others.

No attempt shall be made to deduce the full implications of the operation of conflicting conceptual predilections. Deductions can be made that would be relevant to, and in many cases parallel to, the principles of conflict treated by Lewin (1935), Miller (1944), Brown (1948), and more recently by the numerous cognitive theorists concerned with the effects of "dissonance," "discrepancies," "incongruities," and "imbalances." The specific outcomes of simultaneous arousal of incompatible concepts are, as are all reactions resulting from conflict, complicated by numerous defense or resolution mechanisms which are aimed at allowing the individual to have his cake and eat it too.

The specific interpretations and modes of psychological gerrymandering in which an individual engages in resolving conflicting tendencies are functions of numerous factors, more important among which are what we shall term structural properties of the conceptual or self system through which the events are being metered and evaluated (Harvey, 1958; Harvey, Hunt, and Schroder, 1961). Let us turn now to a consideration of the effects of structural differences of the conceptual or self system in defining the world and reacting to it.

Structural Properties of the Self System

By structure of the self is meant the relationship among the totality of component concepts which the individual at the particular time possesses. The simplest concept, the irreducible of psychological reality, is one involving only two points on some single dimension, which permits of only the rudimentary distinctions of sameness or difference. The more complex concepts are those involving multiple referent points and dimensions, interrelated in such a way that at the same time commonalities are abstracted from them and uniqueness is maintained between them. *In one sense, then, the self could be treated as one very complex, hierarchic, or superordinate concept into which more phenotypic concepts converge in form or streamlike fashion. Or it could be viewed as being constituted by an open-ended number of less inclusive concepts, which in their myriad of interdependencies and concatenations operate as one large system or, alternatively, as a series of less inclusive systems or subsystems.*

Any system then, self or otherwise, implies at least two or more parts of varying *articulateness* operating *interdependently* toward the fulfillment of some *common function* or *goal object* such that the contribution of one part not only affects the success of the function but also influences either directly or indirectly the activity and contribution of the other part(s). This could be expressed in various languages, the inseparableness of part-whole, phenotype-genotype, matter-form, and means-ends, the essential essence of structure being its membership as subordinate and integral parts of a more superordinate or embracing totality. As we have implied, what is form or superordinate to the included parts may in turn be subordinate or matter to a more encompassing set of interdependencies embodied in the conceptual system.

Stated differently, it might be said that by structure of concepts is meant *how* one ties to the differentiated aspects of his world as opposed to *what* he relates, which more appropriately would be considered as the *content* of the conceptual system. By virtue of membership in the human race we all make linkages to objects of some degree of commonality; to other people, for example. Also within a given culture the what or object-referents to which we anchor ourselves in approach or avoidant directions is quite common. But much greater variation occurs, it would seem, in the how or structure of one's ties to these relevant aspects of his world. Some may relate with closedness and avidity, for instance, while others might anchor themselves in less fixed ways. It is largely with structural variations and their consequences for self definition, maintenance, and reaction to incongruous events that the remainder of this chapter will be concerned. The role of structural differences may become more apparent if they are viewed in relation to certain developmental sequences or stages.

How Structural Variations Evolve

The world or some novel part of it when first faced by an individual is tantamount to psychological nothingness for him, a state in which it remains until the operation of some factor within the organism is activated at the proper moment, resulting in some type of adventitious wedding between the internal state and the object. This subject-object cathexis constitutes a concept. Itself the consequence of a concept, it in turn results in aspects of the world becoming psychologically relevant and a kind of boundedness being constructed around the limits of those things relevant. This probably is the stage of blooming, buzzing confusion portrayed by James (1890). From this state of gross boundedness, this high state of *inclusiveness,* the individual gradually begins to break his global concept into smaller or subordinate parts. He begins to employ the process of *exclusion* in which intraconcept differences are articulated. Ultimate progress and maximal information yield would be attained by a matrix of concepts in that hypothetical situation where the concepts simultaneously possessed maximal inclusiveness and maximal exclusiveness. This state would be the end product of all possible differentiations and all possible integrations, the latter in such a way that the autonomy or individuality of each differentiated subpart is maintained while all are simultaneously embodied in a superordinate or common fabric. Obviously such exhaustive inclusiveness and differences are impossible in an open-ended universe; so a system can be treated only as tending more or less in such a direction.

More straightforwardly, it might be said that concepts, in all their facets, evolve through the process of differentiation-integration in which the more undifferentiated and global parts are refined into more numerous and specific components and are then organized into interdependent systems.[7] In operating as the vehicle through which concepts come into being and are elaborated, differentiation and integration appear not to proceed at a steady or linear rate. Instead, this process, much like visual scanning, seems to move saccadicly (Carmichael and Dearhorn, 1948).

---

[7] The belief that the organism in both its biological and conceptual development advances through stages, from the simpler to the more complex or from the more undifferentiated and concrete to the more integrated and abstract, occupies a central position in some of the best known works in psychology and biology; in Murphy's treatment of personality (1947); in Piaget's many writings on the developmental aspects of behavior (1926, 1929, 1932, 1954); in Werner's comparative psychology of conceptual development (1957); and in Weiss' approach to biological structure and maturation (1939).

"The eyes when they scan the lines of a printed page, or in fact any scene, do so in a series of extremely rapid jerks (called saccades) between points of comparative rest (*fixation pauses*) at which they take in information (Cherry, 1957, pp. 122–23). As we have proposed elsewhere,

Conceptually, the saccades seem to operate much like "bracketing"—to borrow a term from artillery—in which defined referent points, sensory or more conceptual, are placed around the extreme limits of the target or phenomenon. With these end points at the extremes serving as anchorages from which to radiate, the subject begins to make finer differentiations in between these defining limits. In conceptual development, one seems first to form gross differentiations by cognitively cutting the ambiguous or undifferentiated into large chunks. This large chunk one might differentiate more before moving to break off another chunk, but generally one moves to the cutting of a second chunk before finely and clearly differentiating the first. In fact, it seems in most cases that it is with the aid of the differentiations and referent points gained from the latter gross segment that one is able to differentiate more finely—and even veridically—the facets of the first chunk [Harvey, Hunt, and Schroder, 1961, p. 18].

The hypothesis that concepts develop saccadically is underlaid by the further assumption that the end points or poles of a concept operate as a kind of opposites and, in a fashion akin to the Hegelian dialectic, exercise a force or energy that results in a conceptual outcome analogous to cell mitosis in which the grosser parts are divided into more precise and numerous ones.

Were a force of some nature not brought to bear on a phenomenon, if that phenomenon existed only in a cocooned vacuum, then presumably no modification of it, growth or otherwise, could occur. Hence for a grossly differentiated concept to attain a state of greater differentiation and refinement we assume that its two poles must exert sufficiently strong contradictory pulls for there to emerge evaluative alternatives other than the either-or categories existent at its earlier stage. The concept, in its less differentiated form could lead only to a bifurcated evaluation: something is all good or all bad. With further delineation of the concept into multiple facets through the reciprocal pull of the good-bad poles its engagement can, and tends to lead to more specific evaluations of gradations from good to bad [Harvey, Hunt, and Schroder, 1961, pp. 18–19].

Concreteness-Abstractness

Out of the saccadic process of differentiation and integration, of breaking down and interrelating, variations occur in important dimensions of the consequent systemic organization. One of the most important of these, at least of conceptual systems, is what we have come to refer to as *concreteness-abstractness* (Harvey, Hunt, and Schroder, 1961). The more concrete end of the dimension represents the state of minimal differentiation of the relevant situation while the more abstract end represents the state of maximal differentiation *and* integration.

In Fig. 4–1 are depicted the gross progressive sequences involved in the development of the self system from the more concrete to the more abstract. From this, some of the more important structural properties or within-system relationships which underlie the more molar dimension

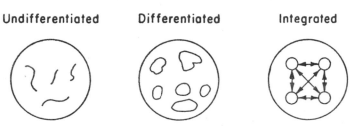

Fig. 4–1. Gross stages of system development from undifferentiation, through differentiation, to integration.

of concreteness-abstractness can be inferred:

(1) *Clarity-ambiguity* refers to the definitiveness of differentiation with which a concept has evolved. Low clarity disposes toward greater concreteness. At this stage of more global functioning the individual fails to make within-concept distinctions and as a consequence tends to react to many situations that contain basic differences as if they were similar. Learning theorists would probably speak of this as an instance of high stimulus generalization. We would feel, however, that such categorical and stereotyped behavior could be labeled more appropriately as lack of differentiation, with the term "generalization" being reserved for higher order functioning represented by concomitant abstraction of commonalities across situations and maintenance of differences between them, a state that necessitates both differentiation and integration.

(2) *Compartmentalization-interrelatedness* refers to the degree of connectedness among the parts following their individuation. Concepts may be differentiated and remain unintegrated or become interlinked to others. Differentiation without integration is less concrete than lack of differentiation, the "undifferentiated holism" described by Murphy in his treatment of personality (1947), but is less abstract than differentiation with integration.

Variation in either of these attributes could result from two quite different reasons: from neither differentiation nor integration having ever occurred; or from de-differentiation and de-integration, in which differentiation is lost and integration is abandoned. The former condition would be a more probable result of ignorance or lack of perceived relationship among the parts, whereas the latter state is more likely to represent an outgrowth of punishment and experienced fear of anxiety from making particular differentiations and integrations.[8]

(3) *Centrality-peripherality* refers to the degree of dependence of other concepts or parts of a system upon a given one. Given the case of four differentiated concepts or subparts A, B, C, and D, in one condition all four might be related in a reciprocal way with each of the others. In a second condition B, C, and D might be unrelated to each other but all three be related in a unilateral way to A. In the first case no concept would have as high centrality as A in the second case, but all of the concepts in the first case would have higher centrality than B, C, and D in the second case. *An optimal degree of centrality is necessary for more abstract functioning: All parts must contribute to the function, but none too heavily so.* Optimal centrality, coincident with high differentiation, allows for a higher *substitutability of parts,* whereas too high a centrality (placing too many of one's eggs in the same basket) would allow the entire function of a system to be impaired or destroyed by rendering inoperative the most central parts. High centrality disposes further toward defensiveness and closedness or a narrow latitude of acceptance and a wide latitude of rejection toward impinging events (Sherif and Sherif, 1956; Hovland, Harvey, and Sherif, 1957).

(4) *Openness-closedness* refers to the capacity of a system to admit in impingements from the outside. It is possible that this is an outgrowth of the preceding characteristics. Indeed it may best serve as an operational measure of some of the other attributes. Openness is meant to imply the capacity to entertain multiple alternatives and to base one's concept veridically on feedback from the environment rather than stereotypically imposing existing schemata on the impingements and molding them into this form. The excellent book by Rokeach (1960), in which the concept of openness-closedness occupies the key role, leads one to wonder if this dimension may not ultimately prove to be synonymous with concreteness-abstractness as we are using the notion here, and have used it elsewhere (Harvey, Hunt, and Schroder, 1961).

Behaviorally, more concrete functioning is represented by high stim-

---

[8] An issue with which social psychologists have long been concerned is the role and adequacy of information in changing such strong concepts as are embodied in prejudice. This distinction between the reasons for the absence of differentiation and integration might cast some possible light on this question. In cases where prejudice is due to ignorance, where differentiation or integration has never been made simply because such relationships have not occurred to the conceiver, imparting of information might suffice to reduce the prejudice. In the other instance, where differentiation and integration once existent have been relinquished because of adverse consequences, such as might occur, for example, when the child of anti-Negro parents attempts to apply the concept of equality of men and brothers' keeper to a Negro, information is not likely to be sufficient because of strong emotional involvement, closedness, and defensive distortions (Harvey, 1961).

ulus oughtness, the extreme of which could be illustrated by such 1:1 correspondence as that between the stimulus of a light and the taxic response of a moth. More abstract functioning, on the other hand, gives rise to less absolutism, greater relativism in thought and action. Variation in concreteness-abstractness is manifested in an almost endless number of ways. At a fairly genotypic level greater concreteness may be shown in such ways as

(1) a simpler cognitive structure, comprised of fewer differentiations and incomplete integration;

(2) a greater tendency toward bifurcated evaluations, viz., good-bad, right-wrong, black-white, etc.;

(3) a greater dependence on external or social definitions as criteria of validity and hence a greater dependency on authority, precedent, and other extrapersonal sources as guidelines to action;

(4) a greater intolerance of ambiguity, expressed in such ways as the tendency to standardize judgments more quickly of a novel situation, even at the expense of error and susceptibility of false but salient cues;

(5) a greater inability to change set and hence more stereotypy in the solution of more complex and changing problems;

(6) a greater resistance to change at low levels of stress, but a greater likelihood of collapsing or going to pieces under high stress;

(7) a poor delineation between means and ends and hence a paucity of different routes to the same goal and a greater disturbance of conceptual effectiveness from threat to or impairment of a set of means;

(8) a poorer capacity to "act as if," to assume the role of the other or to think and act in terms of a hypothetical situation;

(9) a less well-defined self and hence less entrance of the self as a perceived causal agent in effecting sought outcomes in one's environment (Harvey, 1961).

Greater abstractness, which on the other hand implies the opposite quantity on the above dimensions, rests upon a more highly differentiated *and* integrated conceptual system. A more abstract system might be analogized to a symphony orchestra which is comprised of both highly individuated (the capacity of autonomy or solo) and synchronously integrated parts, any or all of which can be volitionally controlled and engaged at the proper time. It would seem, in contradistinction to ideas of fusion, such as that of J. S. Mill, and the Gestalters to some extent, that in an abstract system the individuated parts *do not* lose their identity. Indeed, one of their striking characteristics seems to be the more nearly infinite number of reversible "compounds" or combinations into which they can be entered and withdrawn deliberately for different use.

Broad empirical and theoretical support of these propositions have been presented recently by Harvey, Hunt, and Schroder (1961). Additionally, from the assumption that concreteness-abstractness is a function of how one both differentiates and integrates relevant situations, we have subsequently devised several simple tasks which have yielded results that would be predicted from the present theoretical basis. Representative tests or tasks which we have employed to measure these abilities include having S: write stories involving single pictures and then put these more molecular stories together into one bigger story by only manipulating their order and the use of whatever conjunctions desired; express three wishes or goals of greatest relevance to him along with means of their attainment and then include both means and ends into more superordinate ones; indicate impressions of two persons conveyed by two sets of connotatively opposite adjectives under the assumption that the adjectives refer to two different people, following Asch (1952), and then under the instructions that the two sets of adjectives in reality apply only to a single person indicate their impressions of that single individual (Harvey, 1963b).

Some representative significant relationships obtained between these and other theoretically relevant measures, behavioral and test derived, include: negative correlation with authoritarianism; positive correlation with the Gottschaldt, in the direction of "field independence"; positive correlation with discriminations and proper use of relevant cues in a probability learning task; positive correlation with ability to extrapolate correctly to ultimate definitions of changing situations from minimal ones; positive correlation with what might be termed self-strength, as derived from subjects' reactions to highly negative information about them from an unexpected source, following the technique of Harvey, Kelley, and Shapiro (1955).

In an earlier work (Harvey, Hunt, and Schroder, 1961) we attempted to show that in the progressive development from the more concrete to the more abstract one's self or conceptual system tends to pass through certain plateaus or stages of varying time spans. If the self of a child, for example, is followed in the course of its evolvement, it tends to move in order from a stage of greater undifferentiatedness, where not even its physical limits are discriminated from the rest of the environment, through a kind of negativism and "self assertion," to the development of sympathy, role playing, and taking turns, on to a higher state of independence and relativism marked by greater self-sufficiency and adequacy of coping with a complex, changing environment. It is assumed that this same movement from absolutism to greater relativism applies to learning to cope with any new relevant situation, be the learner a child facing novelty, or an adult learning a new role or a new task. It may happen, of course, by virtue of certain circumstances springing from the interaction of the environment and person's native ability, that he progresses only minimally in his conceptual development; he may become arrested at any point along the way.

Levels of Concreteness-Abstractness. In the work of Harvey, Hunt, and Schroder (1961) are presented extensive theoretical and experimental bases from which we deduced four basically different levels of concreteness-abstractness (along with admixtures) which were treated as different conceptual systems. The four primary systems were treated as representing nodal points or ranges on a continuous dimension between the hypothetical extremes of greater concreteness and greater abstractness. In grossly oversimplified detail, descriptions of the four stages or systems are presented below, with no attempt made to describe the subtleties and complexities of the "in-between systems," that is, the points and gradations on the dimension of concreteness-abstractness that are not wholly bounded or included within the four major systems or modes of functioning. The functioning described may be viewed as resulting from arrestation at or attainment of a particular level. These systems, in a very real sense, may be viewed as approaches to fate control, the means which an individual under circumscribed conditions develops and comes to employ to gain rewards in the best way he can in that situation.[9]

Stage 1 represents the more concrete end of the continuum. This level of conceptual functioning, closely akin to high authoritarianism, seems to result from training conditions in which the training agent exercises complete (or near-complete) fate control over the trainee (child, student, any recipient). This investment of the agent with control over the rewards and punishments of the trainee allows him to define the nature of the reward and punishment as well as the means by which they are attained. Administration of this power takes the form of rewarding for highly specific performances and punishing for the much wider range of performances not compatible with the restrictive criteria of the training agent, standards which are justified to the trainee, when at all, as coming from some omniscient and omnipotent source, generally from such an extrapersonal force as God, the society, the organization, from "something bigger than all of us." The criteria are made known in such a piecemeal fashion that the trainee never gains an overview of their means-ends relations. He only comes to recognize that the route to rewards and avoidance of strong punishment lies in following the narrowly defined prescription of the training agent.

In omission of further elaboration of the etiological determinants of Stage 1 functioning, suffice it to suggest some of the more striking out

---

[9] The descriptions of the four stages that follow are not meant to imply typologies because any individual may possess in varying degrees characteristics representative of any of the four stages. These stages are to be viewed only as nodal points in the progressive development from the more concrete to the more abstract.

comes of these training conditions. Greater dependence on external authority and sources of causality results. The conceptual and self system remains fairly undifferentiated and poorly integrated. Evaluative schemata are categorical, either-or, good-bad, right-wrong, etc. Criteria of conduct are those gained from some authority: the parent, the teacher, God, the group, conventional norms, or the organization. Authority and status per se confer omniscience and omnipotence. Hence those who have it dominate; those who don't submit. The need for highly structured situations is great; the search for specific and absolutely correct answers follows. Positive self-worth becomes synonymous with conformity to the externally prescribed rules and codes of conduct. Violation of these engender feelings of guilt, sin, and unworthiness, accompanied by tendencies of self-denunciation and castigation. Defense of a rule is in the name of righteousness; punishment for deviation is in the name of morality. Acquiescence to the dictates of external authority offers the road to reward, to righteousness, to safety, and to unimpeachable validity. The search for multiple and realistic criteria is prevented. Stereotypy in approaching problems is one result. Resistance to change and environmental inputs is another; and further, the likelihood of "going to pieces" under high stress is increased.

Stage 2 arrested functioning seems to evolve from training conditions which, with the significant exception of greater capriciousness and unpredictability in the training agent's administration of rewards and punishments, are much like those that give rise to Level 1 functioning. Somewhat unlike the individuals who become arrested at Stage 1 functioning, the persons who evolve System 2 orientation as their most characteristic approach to situations are unable to delineate any clear routes to reward attainment because of the inconsistency of the training agent. One time the trainer will reward an act; the next time he will punish it; and the next he may, following punishment, overindulge the trainee for brief periods as a means of assuaging his feelings of guilt. Satisfaction by the trainee of what tenuously seemed to be one of the agent's predictable criterion results in the standard being changed, dropped, or shifted upward.

Out of these conditions of ambiguity, capriciousness, and vacillating expressions of authority no stable referents or positive guidelines to reward attainment emerge. As in System 1, but for different reasons, few avenues for acquisition of positive self-worth are open. Because of the forced necessity of relying more on their own resources than an unpredictable authority, representatives of System 2 functioning, however, are possessed of better differentiated selves than are persons at Stage 1 functioning as well as being somewhat more independent of external control. This greater freedom from external control and assertion of self characteristic of Stage 2 involves a high degree of negativism and rebellion in a strong attempt to avoid dependency, especially on authority and external control. Instead of acquiescence to authority and its perceived agents, a person operating at the level of Stage 2 tends more to move toward an avid denunciation of them: God, society, the group, and convention. As it turns out, however, in his blind drive to avoid dependence on and freedom from these agents of authority such an individual winds up being almost as dependent on them as is the representative of Stage 1. Hence the very beacons which the Stage 2 person decries afford him the crucial guidelines in defining his self and his world; instead of having approach tendencies toward them, as does the Stage 1 person, his inclinations toward them tend to be strongly avoidant in nature.

Thus, while representatives of conceptual Stages 1 and 2 are, *content-wise*, very dissimilar, the former possessed of approach and the latter of avoidance tendencies toward the same referents, *structurally* they are quite similar, both possessed of poorly differentiated conceptual systems, strong avidities, high stereotypy, and inability to delineate and try alternate approaches to complex problems. In political and social orientation one seemingly tilts heavily to the right while the other lists as stereotypically in the direction of the left.

Stage 3 functioning emerges out of conditions in which rules and other extrapersonal forces are not so influential. The assumed omnipotence and omniscience of the training agent, so characteristic of the conditions surrounding the preceding systems, are markedly reduced or even absent in Stage 3 training. Because of this, the trainee comes to articulate his self further and to perceive himself more as a causal agent in the control of his fate, the attainment of rewards, and avoidance of punishment. Extreme Stage 3 functioning comes from the situation where the trainee in crucial areas is overindulged and overprotected by the training agent. In the aforementioned conditions the line of influence was almost exclusively unilateral from the training agent to the recipient, with consistency in the case of Stage 1 and inconsistency in the case of Stage 2 outcomes. In Stage 3 training the lines of influence between agent and trainee become more reciprocal. In fact, in limited respects the influence is greater from the trainee to the trainer than in the reverse direction. This inordinate amount of influence by the trainee results from the agent's overreadiness, because of one reason or another, to get for the trainee "everything he wants." The wish of the trainee, expressed or in cases anticipated, is sufficient to trigger off activity of the agent aimed at satisfying it. Thus the trainee himself comes to be possessed of a degree of omnipotence in his own eyes because of his ability to manipulate the agent, who in turn effects certain ends upon the environment desired by the trainee. This very willingness, or in some instances eagerness, of the training agent to be so influenced by the trainee results in a symbiotic dependence of the trainee upon the agent. It means that in those areas of overprotection the trainee comes to have only minimal experience with the reality outside of his oversheltered environment. Because of failure to develop ways of coping with the outside world, a Stage 3 representative is fearful of facing the situation alone where his attainments would be dependent on his own task or performance skills rather than on his ability to get someone else to cope with the situation for him. Consequently such a person tends to seek dependency relationships with others so that he can rely on their help in defining and solving a situation. Expressive of his attempts to establish a mutual dependency is readiness to compromise his judgments in a conformity-type situation (Harvey, Hunt, and Schroder, 1961) and to disclose facets of his self to others (Cunat, 1960). Strong are the efforts of this individual to be liked and to establish mutual dependencies, but it is important to note that his dependency is on other finite people rather than on rules, etc., as is the case for Stages 1 and 2 individuals. Further, because of his experience in being a causal agent in transaction with his environment, inflated as it is, a System 3 representative has a more highly differentiated and integrated conceptual system than do persons of Levels 1 and 2 and is less categorical than they in his evaluative schemata.

Stage 4, characterized more by an information or task orientation to situations, represents the most abstract level of functioning which we shall describe here, although levels more abstract than this are theoretically possible. This level of functioning is assumed to grow out of training conditions in which the trainee gains rewards from exploration rather than from overt responses that match narrowly prescribed criteria of the training agent. Within the confines of health and general welfare, the trainee in this condition is rewarded for developing and exercising independence, much in keeping with the autotelic folk model depicted by Anderson and Moore (1959). Intrinsically valued by the agent, to use Ausubel's term (1952), he is treated as an individual in his own right, his demands and reasons for them are considered, but they are not met in the overindulgent fashion of Stage 3 practices. Hence, the training agent neither dominates nor is controlled by the trainee. A reciprocity develops such that each gets certain things from the other, but not at the expense of either's autonomy. The trainee is encouraged to seek his own solution to problems within his range of capacity; and his solution is treated with respect by the training agent but is not overextolled.

Because his positive self-worth is not dependent on some external criterion, the trainee in Stage 4 conditions is able to try alternate approaches to his environment without fear of rejection or punishment. His direct experience with the environment more than external dicta serves as the source of correction and reward. This self-correction through environmental feedbacks comes from an openness to the environment and lack of fear of it. The self or conceptual system that emerges from these conditions is more highly articulated and integrated, capable of coping with more varied conditions because of learning through understanding rather than from cathechismic reproduction of overt responses prescribed by an omnipotent and capricious agent. Mastery of the problem rather than of rules or of people is adapted under these conditions as the means of begetting rewards sought by the trainee. Information, as a legal tender, has high value in his marketplace. More than any of the previously described systems, the individual possessed of a Stage 4 capacity is more truly independent, an individual in his own right, committed neither negatively nor positively to particular external criteria; neither in control of others nor controlled by others. He is both autonomous and interdependent. His conclusions are made conditional upon relativistic premises. And his approach to problems is more varied and adaptive.

The remainder of this chapter will be devoted to an application of some of the notions thus far outlined to selected questions of more traditional concern to sociologists and psychologist. These implications will become more readily apparent from a brief recapitulation of our basic assumptions.

Synopsis

When facing a novel or problem situation of relevance to them, individuals will come to evolve more or less standardized ways of defining and reacting to it. Termed herein concepts, such evaluative predilections, possessed of an approach or avoidant orientation toward the relevant objects, serve as the cognitive baseline or mediating channel through which the individual makes sense of his environing world. The conceptual system(s), operating as an experiential filter or evaluative yardstick, comes to determine what is confirming and refuting, what will produce threat or its opposite, what will result in positive or negative affect, and what will arouse feelings of success or failure. But, because individuals vary in both the content and structure of their conceptual or self systems, the specific conditions that produce any of these psychological states for a given person must also vary. It is with a few of the theoretical consequences of variations in structural properties that the rest of this chapter shall be concerned.

Application to Theoretical Issues

Group Determinants of Self. Beginning a theoretical line that has remained fairly continuous, William James (1890) called attention to the importance of certain social referents in an individual's definition of his self, asserting that one has as many social selves as there are individuals and groups whose opinions are important to him. From a related rationale, Cooley (1902) stressed the importance of the primary group in the development of personality and the determination of the self, the "looking glass self" being in essence an individual's interpretation of his primary group's definition of him. Mead, in his theory of interactionism (1934), clarified greatly some of the processes through which "significant others" contribute heavily toward an individual's self development and conception. Today theoretical constructs related to these basic notions abound. Two of the most prevalent of these, in one dress or another, have to do with *reference group* and with *role*, the former tending to be the referent or significant other (individual or group) from which the prescription of concepts and behavior is drawn and role being the content of the prescription derived from the reference group or reference individual. Several very worthwhile works have emphasized the importance of social role in determining the self (Goffman, 1959; Newcomb, 1950; Sarbin, 1954; Sherif and Cantril, 1947; Strauss, 1960). In fact, some authors tend to go so far as to view the self as the totality of socially defined roles. Yet if our assumptions about consequences of differences in concreteness-abstractness are even partially valid, then it is probable that a postulation of a 1:1 correspondence between social norms or roles and the self is an overemphasis on social determinants. For individuals with certain self structures a perfect relationship between the self and such social norms as roles and status-linked behavior might possibly obtain, whereas for other individuals this relationship would be markedly reduced, although probably never completely nil. While the more concretely functioning persons, as we have characterized them, would tend to depend very heavily on social dicta and labels for derivation of their conceptual makeup, including even concepts toward themselves, the more abstract individuals would be much less dependent on these social sources, deriving their concepts instead from a more direct and personal experience with the object to which the concept relates. Individuals whom we have characterized as operating more at the Stage 4 level of functioning, for example, should be capable of assuming an even wider range of roles than representatives of the other less abstract conceptual levels, but at the same time they should be less committed to any of these social criteria as referents for their self definition.[10]

[10] We have recently completed one large scale experiment aimed at testing this assumption, the results of which are yet to be analyzed.

Roles, status positions, other norms and social regulations should be viewed more as means than as ends by the more abstractly functioning individuals and hence should occupy a far less central position in the hierarchy of self referents of such persons. Thus, while such notions as reference group and looking glass self might have high theoretical and heuristic utility for more concretely functioning individuals, their value in accounting for the assumed variance in conceptual properties probably becomes much less at higher levels of abstractness. These comments should not be construed as that we are arguing against the importance of social determinants of self. Far from it; because even the variations in the structural properties of concreteness-abstractness are assumed to be determined in no small degree by variations in the social environments, as we indicate more clearly in a later chapter. The point is that the outcomes of the numerous social environments are so diverse that important differences in self and behavior are masked out by the assumption that the self is coextensive with roles and norms for all individuals.

Anomie and Alienation. In keeping with the early definition by Durk-heim (1897), anomie has been considered to be a state of normlessness. The tendency has been to assume further that accompanying this social state were such psychological consequences as alienation and marginality, aloneness and insecurity. This assumption demands a further assump-tion, one that as far as we know seems never to be articulated, that existing social norms do in reality serve as basic anchorages of self con-tent and structure, so that as a consequence of "social disorganization" the individual finds himself in a psychological void and state of nothing-ness. Such a psychological condition might indeed prevail for extremely concrete individuals, those utterly dependent on norms, rules, and roles as guidelines to defining the world and responding to it. Such a state is far less likely to result, however, for the more abstract persons, whose self definitions transcend specific social referents.

If the Nettler (1957) and Srole (1956) scales of anomie may be pre-sumed to measure interiorization of and participation in the prevailing social motif, then individuals representing the four different stages of conceptual functioning described earlier should differ considerably in their scores on these scales. Representative of Stage 1, dependent heavily upon norms and traditions for their conceptual makeups, should score low on anomie as should individuals functioning in ways char-acteristic of Stage 3. At the same time persons at Stage 2 in their de-velopment should, because of rejecting social norms and being anchored stably to little or nothing else, score high on anomie. Stage 4 repre-sentatives should also score high, but for the reason presumably that they do not depend heavily, either positively or negatively, on norms for their identity. Results in line with these assumptions have been obtained in some of our recent research (Harvey, 1962c). A more traditional sociological approach would tend probably to assume a high degree of commonality in terms of alienation and lower self-esteem among the two groups higher in anomie (Stages 2 and 4), making no distinction between differences such as variation in concreteness-abstractness. We would assume, on the other hand, that while Stage 2 representatives might be characterized by rather high alienation and feelings of instability, persons at the Stage 4 level would be unlikely to show such conditions and instead to be possessed of higher self-esteem and regard. Since the self-worth and identity of the latter persons depend on a kind of perceived control of their own fate and less on existing rules and dicta, a high score on anomie should mean quite a different thing than a comparable score for Stage 2 persons. The results we have obtained support this hypothesis. By using a modified Q-sort technique of measuring the self concept, Stage 4 individuals were found, while being high in anomie as measured by both the Nettler and Srole scales, to be high in self-esteem as well (Harvey, 1963b).

It becomes apparent, then, that very significant differences occur among different individuals in their reaction to anomicizing conditions. This is readily seen in the results presented by Garfinkel in Chapter 7, although he makes no special point of it. Allport, Bruner, and Jandorf (1954) noted this several years ago in their article on differential responses of individuals to dispossession by the Nazis. This implies the necessity of one of two things: either that anomie be defined idiosyncratically as the threat to or severance of subject-object ties; or that anomie and alienation not be assumed to go hand in hand, because, as we can see, anomie, in terms of the rendering inoperative of a given set of norms, may or may not produce alienation within given persons. Alienation is the experience resulting from rendering inoperative basic self linkages one has in relation to differentiated aspects of his environment. To the extent one varies in the what and how of such ties, hence to that extent will the conditions producing alienation and related psychological outcomes also vary. The assumption that the self is no more than an interiorization of social norms, a prerequisite for expecting a 1:1 correspondence between threat to norms and threat to self, must be markedly revised. It might be stated more appropriately that the self is one's totality of ties, possessed of both content and structural aspects, and that for some individuals the dicta and other group-derived stimuli represent the most basic and essential kernels of the self system. In such an instance alienation would parallel impaired group norms. Development in a highly structural and closed environment, which could occur in either a "primitive" or "civilized" society, would be one major determinant of such a condition.

Homogeneity Versus Heterogeneity of the Self System. Throughout the history of psychology two streams of rather contradictory thought and theoretical emphasis have moved abreast. The focus of one has been on the attempt to understand human functioning through a kind of reductionism, by isolating and mapping out rather specific and finite faculties and activities. The main concern of the other has been to show the fallacy of such a "bundle hypothesis," to borrow Koffka's (1922) colorful phrase, that the "whole is qualitatively different from the sum of its parts" and consequently that concern with anything less than the organism-as-a-whole is artificial and doomed to failure. While this specific version of the argument evolved out of the reactions and counterreactions of the Gestalt psychologists to Titchenerian structuralism and Watsonian behaviorism, this general issue has been bandied about among psychologists of numerous concerns, reflected quite saliently, for example, in the division between the traditional experimentalists and clinicians and personality theorists.

The predominant thought among clinicians especially has seemed to be that not only do individuals tend to function as a whole but that such "integrated" activity bespeaks of a more adequate and better adjusted personality or self. This position is as characteristic of one school of clinical psychology or psychotherapy as of the other. The ideal in America, as Rosenman has pointed out, has been the personality of unity and integration. "The multiple personality, conceptually assimilated to this trend, has been regarded as invariably fragmented into unorganized parts. The shattered pieces were regarded as simply resonating differently with the demand of the individual's many social roles. The multiple personality was an unpleasant and confused cacophony" (Rosenman, 1954, p. 394).

Perhaps much of the confusion and argument surrounding this particular issue of reductionism versus holism springs from a lack of clarity about the meaning of holism. As was implied in earlier parts of this chapter, and as Murphy has clearly pointed out (1947), a marked difference exists between an undifferentiated and a differentiated and integrated holism. The former could be expressive of the global, unarticulated functioning of the infant, while the latter would be expressive only of an individual who conceptually had progressed through both exclusion and inclusion, the articulation of differences and the generation of conceptual commonalities. In our language, the first would be representative of more concrete, the latter of more abstract functioning. In both cases a kind of homogeneity, but a very different kind, would exist. Homogeneity stemming from lack of differentiation would tend to result in stereotypy, absolutism, and dependence upon and attribution of external causality. The homogeneity made possible through both differentiation and integration, on the other hand, allows for relativism of thought and action, entertainment of multiple alternatives, and the anchoring of the self to a wide variety of sources in more genotypic fashions. As Rosenman has suggested, "The multiply-structured individual," by which he meant a person whose self system was articulated and interrelated, "may use the existent personality structure as a base from which to launch new and better ways of relating to the world. Perhaps the psychologically dissociated personality has the greater chance of arising, not in the rationally multiple individual, but in one embarked upon the crusade to fulfill the ideology of single self-hood" (Rosenman, 1954, p. 398). An individual functioning in this latter, more concrete, fashion would distinguish minimally between means and ends, would tend to have his entire self cathected to a few, very central, referents. Threat to or severance of such central linkages is apt to result in extensive damage to the self, possibly even in collapse and disintegration. Although closed to environmental inputs at low levels of stress, the more concrete systems, because of lack of resiliency, appear more likely to become shattered when they change at all under conditions of high stress. As we proposed in another work (Harvey, Hunt, and Schroder, 1961), it may be that a large proportion of the American Army captives who died in Chinese prison camps did so as a result of dissolution of concrete self structures derived from commitment to referents readily vulnerable to destruction by the captors.

The individual whose self system is comprised of multiple facets, individuated and interlinked in such a way that the various parts may be engaged singly or in orchestrated totality under the volitional instigation of the possessor, seems not only to be more resilient to stress but to be more creative and more capable of adapting more or less veridically to complex and changing situations. Consistent with this possibility are the findings, to which reference was made earlier in this chapter, that the more abstract persons in contrast to the more concrete are more sensitive to minimal cues in the environment, are more likely to set their level of expectancy (subjective probability) to coincide with controlled feedback (objective probability) and to be more creative in the sense of being able to produce stories richer in both quality and quantity from a constant number of words.

Diversity of self referents and commitments are probably prerequisites for coping with adversity and adjusting to changing currents. In two provocative and insightful works (1960a, b) Bettleheim has indicated how an overcommitment of many European Jews to *things as they were at the moment* led to their deaths. Drawing a lesson from the case of Anne Frank, he points out,

> Little Anne, too, wanted only to go on with life as usual, and nobody can blame her. But hers was certainly not a necessary fate, much less a heroic one; it was a senseless fate. The Franks could have faced the facts as did many Jews living in Holland. Anne could have had a good chance to survive, as did many Jewish children in Holland. But for that she would have had to be separated from her own parents and gone to live with a Dutch family as their own child [1960a, p. 253].

"The Franks, with their excellent connections among Gentile Dutch families, should have had an easy time of hiding out singly, each with a different family. But instead of planning for this," continues Bettleheim, "the main principle of their planning was to continue as much as possible with the kind of family life they were accustomed to. Any other course would have meant not merely giving up their beloved family life, but also accepting the reality of man's inhumanity to man. Most of all it would have forced them to accept that going on with life as usual was not an absolute value, but can sometimes be the most destructive of all attitudes [1960a, p. 254].

When any means becomes too central, the resulting functional blindness prevents one from thinking about and preparing for other contingencies. This principle is well illustrated in the history of warfare where a good commander will feint, give off misleading cues or in some other way get the enemy committed to the high probability of one course of action and then pursue another. It would appear, in fact, that the definition of a good strategist is one who departs from an overly standardized expectancy of the opposition. If the focus is fixed on one part of the field only, the opponent is allowed a wide area through which he can make his way without surveillance or effective opposition [Harvey, 1961].

Bettleheim concludes from the case of Anne Frank that

> . . . the story of the extermination camps shows that even in such an overpowering environment, certain defenses do offer some protection. Surely the most important defense consists of understanding what goes on in oneself, and why. With enough understanding, the individual does not fool himself into believing that he protects himself with every adjustment he makes. He is able to recognize that an act which seems protective can actually be self-destructive [1960b, p. 50].

This means having some commitment, possessing ends, all right, but being able to distinguish them from means and to see all in a form and matter, superordinate and subordinate fashion. This the more abstract system is likely to attain, presumably be it individual or group. Even under ideal circumstances, of course, this is not an easy state to realize, given that it be a sought one, and some might question this. The very process of evolving systems of ordering and evaluation disposes toward a kind of adaptive paradox, as we suggested earlier. It means that certain selective discriminations and interpretations have been made, ones which at most represent only a few of the infinite possibilities. The evolvement of one system tends to preclude the evolution and use of others which might be much more effective than the one prematurely standardized. Hence to form systems, which serve as the prism through which reality is defined and read, is to be rendered partially blind to a wide range of potentially relevant events, although such boundedness may lead to increased discrimination within a narrow band. Yet not to have a way of ordering prevents even discrimination and results in the environing world being treated as irrelevant. It is to the one surrounded as if it did not exist. And this ignorance, blissful as it might at times be, may be just as maladaptive and costly, even more so, than ordering in a restrictive fashion. It seems then that some balance must be established and maintained between complete openness and complete closedness. Adapting, surviving itself, demands discrimination and differentiations that are inescapably selective as a consequence of limits both in the biological structure of the organism and in the ordering tendencies evolved through experience. Yet it is imperative that the structure through which reality is read be of enough facets that a wide range of the impinging world can be admitted into the system and can be interpreted and reacted to in diverse ways. We will return to this connection in relation to political systems in Chapter 5.

Knowledge of Self. To know oneself is man's greatest achievement, reasoned Socrates. Surely men vary in the extent of this attainment as well as in the deliberateness with which they set about to unravel their own being and functioning. Some yearn for and work actively for insight into their self makeup; others seemingly neither know nor seek information. Yet it would appear axiomatic that he who knows himself best stands a better chance of controlling his environment and his own fate, in the sense of recognizing more clearly means-ends relationships and being able to reach a desired goal by alternate routes.

Other characteristics may also be postulated that should distinguish the individual who has a high motive to know from the one who avoids knowing his self. Such a person would be more likely to profit from adversity; indeed to learn from any experience whether a specific end point was achieved or not. He might even seek adversity, at least place himself in potentially pressureful and stressful situations from the recognition that out of threat to one's basic subject-object ties one comes to know of his areas of commitment. His orientation might more aptly be termed an "ing" approach as contrasted to an "ed" orientation of the individual less motivated to become aware of his essence. An individual of the former predilection should be more likely to manifest exploratory behavior and curiosity, and to be inherently rewarded by the activities and consequences involved in look*ing*, search*ing*, do*ing*, rather than by the gaining of some terminal end point or external incentive. Possessed of a greater security in the foundations of the self, such an individual is less compelled to make the world fit into rigidly bounded and narrow conceptual moulds. He can afford, even seeks, to admit the world unfettered into his self system. Coming upon an unmarked trail in the forest, he may follow it; caught by the crest of the sea, he may allow himself to be borne by it; in neither case seeking to determine the destination, but hoping only to traverse the novel and to learn from his experience of the different. Thus Thomas Huxley was led to believe: "Sit down before a fact as a little child, be prepared to give up every preconceived notion, follow humbly wherever and whatever abysses nature leads, or you shall learn nothing. I have only begun to learn content and peace of mind since I have resolved at all risks to do this" (Thomas Huxley in a letter to Charles Kingsley, September 23, 1860. Reproduced in Schuster, 1940, p. 343). And Dostoevsky, partly as a consequence of the insight gained into his self makeup from his close brush with execution, came to write in a related vein,

. . . Man is essentially a constructive animal—an animal forever destined to strive towards a goal, and to apply himself to the pursuit of engineering, in the shape of ceaseless attempts to build a road which shall lead him to an unknown destination. But that is just why man so often *turns aside* from the road. He turns aside for the reason that he is *constrained* to attempt the journey; he turns aside because, being at once foolish and an independent agent, he sometimes takes it into his head that, though the road in question may eventually bring him to a destination of some sort, that destination always lies ahead of him. Consequently, as an irresponsible child, he is led at times to disregard his trade as an engineer, and to give himself up to that fatal indolence which, as we know, is the mother of all vices. Man loves to construct and to lay out roads—of that there can be no question; but why does he also love so passionately to bring about general ruin and chaos? Answer me that. First of all, however, I myself have a word or two to say about it. May not his passion for bringing about general disorder (a passion which, we must admit, allows of no dispute) arise from the fact that he has an instinctive dread of *completely* attaining his end, and so of finishing his building operations? May it not be the truth that only from a distance, and not close at hand, does he love the edifice which he is erecting? That is to say, may it not be that he loves to create it, but not to *live* in it—only to hand it over, when completed, to *les animaux domestiques*, in the shape of ants, sheep, and so forth? . . . On the other hand, man is a frivolous, a specious creature, and, like a chessplayer, cares more for the process of attaining his goal than for the goal itself. Besides, who knows (for it never does to be too sure) that the aim which man strives for upon earth may not be contained say, in the process which is comprised in the living of life rather than in the aim itself, which, of course, is contained in the formula that twice two make four? Yet, gentlemen, this formula is not life at all; it is only the beginning of death! At all events men have always been afraid to think that twice two make four, and I am afraid working to attain this formula, and though, in his search for it, he sails all the seas and sacrifices his whole life to the acquisition of his end, he fears *really* to succeed in the quest, for the reason that, if he were suddenly to come upon the formula, he would feel that he had nothing left to look for? [Dostoevsky, 1864, pp. 38–39].

Such attitudes of curiosity and exploration as those expressed by Huxley and Dostoevsky, we feel quite certain, are more likely to characterize the more abstractly than the more concretely functioning person. It is not improbable, in fact, that such relativism and openness can be attained only by that restricted population of persons who are able to progress to that level of functioning we have indicated as occurring at the fourth stage of development.

Reinforcement and the Law of Effect. Psychology has established few relationships that deserve to be called a principle; certain areas within it, such as learning theory, for example, even fewer. Yet, whatever the academic label one assigns oneself, whoever the drummer with whom one keeps step, the issues and phenomena encompassed in the principle of reinforcement, Thorndike's law of effect revamped, cannot be by-passed. In this, the final section of this chapter, we would like to suggest briefly some needed extensions of the principle of reinforcement if it is to have direct application to problems of the personality theorist and social psychologist.

Reinforcement has generally been defined operationally as an increment in response strength as a consequence of some controlled variation in the stimulus, which generally has meant allowing the subject to receive some external incentive or need-satisfying goal object following a particular performance. In his earlier thinking (1943), Hull argued that reinforcement resulted from tension reduction stemming from a lessening of a primary drive, one that could be shown to be underlaid by certain physiological bases, and that this was a necessary condition for acquisition of new responses. The work of Tolman and Honzig (1930) on latent learning necessitated a revision in the oversimplified Hull-like thinking. Learning was found to occur without the securing of food, drink, etc., by the rat which was allowed to explore his environment, leading the Tolman camp to conclude that reinforcement is not necessary for learning. If, however, the animal is posited as possessing an exploratory or curiosity motive (Myers and Miller, 1954), then Tolman's conclusion that latent learning resulted from the absence of reinforcement becomes unwarranted. But the conclusion that predilection toward exploration of the environment may serve as the basis of primary reinforcement at least makes necessary the added assumption that something other than simple extrinsic objects may serve as reinforcing agents. It is no longer heretical, even among those psychologists who would reserve "experimental" exclusively for their methods and approaches to questions, to speak of the need for contact or of the exploratory or curiosity drive.

Some would apply "intrinsic" to the curiosity motive, the implication being that, unlike other primary needs, it is not instrumental to the attainment of a goal object. True, it may not be instrumental in the same specific sense as are some of the other motives; a definite external incentive may not satisfy it. Yet the use of "instrumental" to apply only to a means of facilitating achievement of an external goal may indeed be too restrictive. If one maintains an open instead of a closed epistemological position, it can be argued in the fashion of infinite regression or progression that all things are either form or matter, ends or means, to something else. To what is curiosity instrumental or a means? To any number of possible ends: to seeking of information; to making sense out of the environment; to forming conceptual systems which allow for a way of reading reality, adapting to the world, even controlling it in a sense; to the evolvement of a self; and to the development of ties that provide anchorages in time and space. Whatever the language employed, whatever the level of analysis, there seems little doubt that curiosity and exploration are essential to the generation and use of veridical means of coping with the world, especially if that world is a complex and changing one. Whether or not this "seeking after meaning" (Bartlett, 1958) is innate or should be called a primary need perhaps is a meaningless question as far as its motivational significance is concerned. More relevant is the seeming fact that it occurs in all persons, that in the hierarchy of motives it occupies a position of centrality, and that, like other strivings and predilections, it may serve as the baseline for confirmation and refutation, with their attendant consequences. Any notions of reinforcement or the law of effect, if they are to have relevance to some of the more significant aspects of human functioning, must not ignore this.

Certainly not all individuals, as we have stressed, come to define the world in the same way, yet all do it in some way. Some, for example, do this more abstractly while others do it more concretely.[11] As a con-

---

[11] More authoritarian individuals and those functioning more concretely would be characterized by many writers as having a *greater need* for structure than the less authoritarian and more abstract persons. This probably is not quite correct. More valid perhaps would be the statement that all people have a need for structure, but that the form it takes varies among persons, some operating more consonantly and comfortably in a highly bounded and ordered environment and others gaining their structure and meaning of the world through a much more relativistic and unbounded conceptual system.

sequence of this structural variation in the self system, what is confirming to one individual might at the very same time be refuting to another. An individual functioning at the level of Stage 1, for instance, might be threatened, negative affect and avoidance tendencies generated within him by an event that favored an open-ended view of the world, whereas a person at Stage 4 functioning would experience the opposite consequences. The obvious point becomes, then, that reinforcement, along with all other motivational consequences, must be considered in relation to the idiosyncratic baseline of the receiving and responding individual. And the main message of this chapter is that the conceptual or self system, in its myriad of structural variation, is among the most crucial of such baselines, for it is the stream in which biology and experience have become wed.

Chapter 5

Conceptual Organization and Group Structure

HAROLD M. SCHRODER AND O. J. HARVEY

In Chapter 4 the self was presented as a system of interrelated concepts which, as a function of variation in organizational properties, varied in expression and reaction to common events. Self or conceptual systems possessed of *both* high differentiation and integration of component parts, referred to as being more abstract, were treated as disposing toward lower stereotypy and greater flexibility in the face of complex and changing problem situations, toward greater creativity, explorative behavior, tolerance of stress, and resiliency in response to alien environmental inputs as well as toward greater independence from social and authority dicta in judgments of a situation. A self system of a low state of differentiation and integration, referred to as being more concrete in structure, was depicted as disposing its possessor more in opposite directions; toward stereotypy; dependence on authority, absolutism, and intolerance; either-or definitions of the world, avoidance of the novel; and warding off as "bad" events or inputs that are only slightly discrepant from the holder's narrow latitude of acceptance.

Probably it is in reacting to complex and changing problem situations or environments that the differences between the more concrete and the more abstract systems are accentuated. While greater concreteness seems to impel toward threat and blindness in the face of changing environmental demands, greater abstractness seems to dispose toward greater sensitivity to and more proper use of the cues indicating change and toward an unthreatened willingness to relinquish past definitions and solutions in favor of the new task demands.

It is quite probable, on the other hand, that high environmental constancy and simplicity across time and tasks reduce the greater relative effectiveness of the more abstract system; indeed, such environmental conditions might even render concrete functioning more appropriate.

134

In the present chapter we wish to extend the discussion of structural determinants of system functioning to social systems. In doing this, we will be using dimensions and properties that are closely related linguistically and phenomenally to those employed in the discussion of conceptual systems in Chapter 4. This forces the assumption, which ultimately may or may not be warranted, that generalization can actually be made across levels of analysis, in this instance from individual to social systems. Precedent, especially in social psychology, argues against this, owing to the typically unquestioned tenet that the "whole is different from the sum of the parts" so that a phenomenon must be dealt with at its own level without an attempt at seeking parallels and generalities across other levels. But as we have suggested

it is not all improbable that certain structural aspects of systems dispose toward a particular kind of operation, irrespective of the specific content of the system. Hence as long as organizational or structural features of systems and *not content* are treated, then possibly the parallels may be more real than just analogous. Without making it explicit, perhaps even without recognizing it, the reason for the historical reluctance to attempt generalizations across levels may have been due to the heavy concentration of concern with content rather than with organizational aspects of system functioning [Harvey, 1961, p. 3].

General Sequences in Systems Development

In line with such writers as Spencer (1897), Piaget (1932), Weiss (1939), and Murphy (1947) we shall assume here, as we have elsewhere (Harvey, Hunt, and Schroder, 1961), that in evolving from the simpler to the more complex, from the more concrete to the more abstract in our language, a system passes through stages or phases of refined articulation of component parts and integration of them into a more superordinate framework. We have been led to posit four such stages of development, along with in-between transitional levels, which, *under optimal conditions,* are moved through in progressive sequence. This is to say that for the fourth or more abstract level to have been attained means that the system successfully passed in ascending fashion from the first, to the second, and through the third stages. But it is not to say, however, that progression to the more complex and abstract levels is inevitable. Far from it; any natural system, because of certain unfavorable environmental restrictions and obstacles, may become arrested at lower levels of development. Later in this chapter we will discuss those environmental attributes that appear to favor progression and those that seem to result in the arrested growth and development or differentiation and integration of systems.

In Fig. 5–1 is presented an oversimplified depiction of the phases in-

Order and Stage of System Development	Graphic Representation of Structure	System Characteristics
Stage I	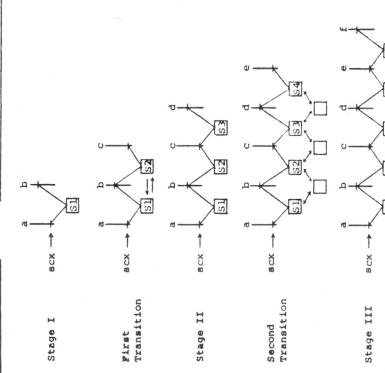	Absolutistic schema, conflict minimized, world maximally distorted to fit schema. Schema for self and other minimally differentiated.
First Transition		Conflict between single schema and its opposite. Initial emergence of opposition to absolutism.
Stage II		Emergence of many alternate independent differentiated schema. Minimum of integration of schemas. Problem of choice and probability ushered in.
Second Transition		Conflict between maintenance of independent schema and integration via compromise of alternatives. Initial emergence of simple integrative organization.
Stage III		Weak integration linkages emerge. Conflict present and resolved by compromise or weighting; multivariate approach. Schema for other and other's intentions differentiated from self.

136

Conflict between an empirical multi-variate orientation and the emergence of new supra-ordinate schemas as a basis for integration.

The emergence of new highly integrated schema for the resolution of conflict. A maximum of conflict in the system. Plus a maximum of potential for integration. Integration of alternatives for schema relevant to self and others.

Third Transition   SCX →

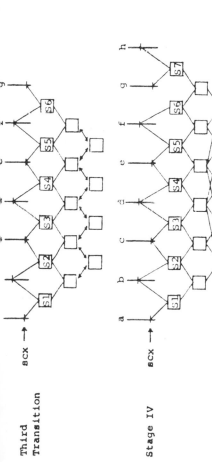

Stage IV   SCX →

SCX -- A particular stimulus configuration, e.g., a tone, a person, or a group.

a, b, c -- Concepts or dimensions along which the stimulus configuration is read or evaluated.

S1, S2 -- Conceptual schemas representing an organization of the single conceptual evaluations. Generates the interpretation of the event.

↓↑ -- Conflict between.

☐ -- Supraordinate schemas evolved through the integration of conflicting schemas.

Note: This figure indicates a direct relationship between the number of differentiated dimensions or concepts along which a stimulus configuration is read and the number of alternate integrated schema which they generate. While this relationship is positive—it is not necessarily perfect.

Fig. 5-1. Sequence of system development from the more concrete to the more abstract.

volved in the developmental progression from a more simple and concrete to a more complex and abstract system. Included here, in addition to the four nodal stages treated in Chapter 4, are the in-between or transitional phases of differentiation and integration along with some of their attendant effects.

We assume that individuals when faced with a novel situation of relevance to them will come to evolve a more or less standardized definition of the situation. *Such definitions evolved by single individuals are generally termed concepts. When the standardized evaluations result from interaction among individuals and come to be shared by most of the participants, they typically are labeled group norms.* Whether the concepts be shared or be only the private possession of a single person, it is our assumption that in the development from the more absolute and concrete to the more relativistic and abstract they follow common general paths. This is not to deny, however, that the total specific factors determining group development may be more numerous and complex than those influencing concept formation and refinement in single persons. With both viewed as systems, it seems meaningful nonetheless to apply similar structural dimensions to both and to ascertain the extent to which such organizational similarities result from common environmental determinants.

At the beginning, the initial definition, concept or norm, is generic and undifferentiated, resulting in its overgeneralized and absolute application. However, given the environmental conditions conducive to increased abstractness, alternate and more numerous possibilities for defining the situation begin to emerge; but at the onset of the second stage in only bifurcated and opposing form. Nonetheless, this is the beginning of relinquishment of the absolutism and tyranny stemming from a single schema representative of the first stage of functioning. Because of lack of conceptual integration in the early phases of the second stage, conflict and the problem of choice first arise. Out of this conflict between evaluative predilections there emerge additional and better articulated schemata which, under appropriate circumstances, become integrated components of a superordinate and more relativistically functioning system of reality definitions and rules. The first attempts at integration in this stage, however, follow a kind of juxtaposition in which the more or less compartmentalized differentiations are only loosely bonded together within only a rudimentary superstructure. Later in development, in the third transition and especially the fourth stage, a more complete integration occurs and truly superordinate schemata emerge which allow the parts simultaneously to operate both interdependently and independently, resulting in the more abstract capacity of perceiving simultaneously specific differences and generalized similarities. And, as we have indicated in Chapter 4, the most effective system of concepts or norms, in the sense of maximal information yield, sensitivity to differences, and flexibility, is the one characterized by both maximal exclusiveness and inclusiveness. This allows the individual employing the system to read a situation simultaneously in terms of differences and similarities.

Environmental Determinants of System Development

Even with heredity or group membership held constant, variations in crucial aspects of the environment with which a developing system is forced to cope in his experiential transactions may lead to wide differences in the level of concreteness-abstractness attained by a given system.

A prerequisite for progressive differentiation and integration, synonymous with increased abstractness, *is the openness of the system to diverse and conflicting inputs.* From the resulting opposing energies and forces new alternatives or component parts are generated and the groundwork is laid for the evolvement of a system possessed of the capacity to deal adequately with the changing, the different, and the adverse. Without exposure to heterogeneous and more enriched environments, a system presumably would remain largely in a homogeneous or differentiated state, able to deal with events only in terms of a paucity of different dimensions and alternatives.

Natural systems are assumed, however, to vary in the optimal degree of conflict and heterogeneity for maximal movement toward complexity and abstractness. The optimal for one system, because of letting in too many and too strong inputs, might be too demanding and too threatening for a simpler and more concrete one, or not challenging and demanding enough for a more complex and abstract one. The main factor on which the optimal would depend would be the existing level of abstractness of the particular system, be it conceptual or social.

If a developing system becomes overwhelmed by its environment, if, for some reason, exploration becomes too painful or threatening, the novel will be avoided and inputs which might demand modification of the existing schemata will be warded off. The "tried and true" is thus retained at the cost of markedly reducing the possibility of the emergence of new differentiations and more complete integrations.

Arrestation of the system at a more concrete level tends to result, giving rise to a wide range of related behaviors reflected in undue righteousness, bigotry, attribution of and dependence on external causality, fear and hostility toward persons and groups who define and behave toward the world differently. The intensity of affective involvement in the beliefs and ideologies that grow out of environments devoid of crosscurrents and pressures is likely to be much higher, a point recognized by Simmel (1956) and other sociologists. For example, Lipset points out, "Whenever the social structure operates so as to isolate naturally individuals or groups with the same political outlook from contact with those that hold different views, the isolated individuals or groups tend to back political extremists." He continues,

. . . Multiple and politically inconsistent affiliations, loyalties, and stimuli reduce the emotion and aggressiveness involved in political choice. . . . Where a man belongs to a variety of groups that all predispose him to the same political choice, he is in the situation of an isolated worker and is much less likely to be tolerant of others' opinion [Lipset, 1960, pp. 87–88].

A host of specific determinants may operate to isolate the individual and to produce within him the tendency toward concreteness and negative reaction to the different. Such geographical factors as oceans, mountains, distance, and other obstacles are among these. So are such social boundaries as intergroup antagonisms, castes, class, status, and restrictive role definitions. Generally mediating, adding to, or in some way modifying these forces is the behavior of the person's immediate training agent, or the agent that has the power to control important facets of the system's environment, including the means or instrumentalities of motive satisfaction and goal attainment. This is to say that broad social and geographical forces may operate toward certain boundaries and separations, but that within these the person who is more immediately in control of important aspects of one's fate serves as a crucial determinant of the system that evolves and level of abstractness attained. In a general way, the heart of the matter seems to be whether the developing individual and members of a system are encouraged to explore, to find their own solutions, to be their own reason and justification for action, or whether they are trained to accept as valid and absolute dicta and prescriptions passed on and embellished by a powerful training agent.

In an earlier work (Harvey, Hunt, and Schroder, 1961) we deduced and presented the effects on system growth and retardation of several environmental dimensions, largely as such dimensions are reflected in and mediated by the behavior of a training agent, the source of most immediate concern to the developing individual. We will follow a similar scheme in the subsequent pages as we depict training and other environmental factors which dispose systems toward differential concreteness-abstractness and varied openness to, even searching for, the novel and the challenging.

Unilateral Versus Interdependent Training Conditions. These two conditions are assumed to represent opposite poles on a generic training dimension. While the same cultural content can be transmitted by either major condition, the structure of the resulting systems and adaptive orientations are, in many important respects, opposites.

Unilateral conditions are those in which the training agent (parent, teacher, group, whoever) presents the trainee (child, student, social member) a set of dicta or criteria for evaluating and responding to situations without the latter's having had the opportunity to explore and generate definitive schemata for himself. In this situation the emphasis is upon the trainee's responses matching the external criteria handed to him. Attainment of rewards and punishments hinges upon the trainee's success or failure in doing this. In this sense, this method relies on *behavior control*, in which the trainee's behavior is moulded to fit absolute standards by the agent's rewarding or punishing it directly, rather than on *environmental control*, in which the trainee's environment is programed or arranged in such a way that he is allowed to explore it and experience it directly without its being mediated through the norms of the training agent.

The adaptive orientation that evolves out of a unilateral environment is one in which pleasing the training agent, the source of fate control, comes to occupy a position of centrality and the search for criteria which are independent of the agent's prescriptions comes to be highly negatively weighted. Because of the punishment connected with attempts at exploration and defining own criteria, and the rewards attached to conformity to authority dictates and definitions, a strict imposition of this condition results in the broad band of behaviors which we have characterized as being concretistic.

Interdependent conditions, on the other hand, are those in which the trainee is not presented with externally defined and fixed behavioral criteria by the training agent. He is instead allowed the freedom to participate in his own definitions. As we indicated in Chapter 4, he is rewarded for *looking* and *exploring* rather than for reaching specific end points and making particular responses. For the trainee not to be overwhelmed by a too powerful environment necessitates that the training agent arrange it or program it in such a way that the explorations of it and contact with it are not overly dangerous and threatening for the trainee's existent level of conceptual development. This method, then, involves *environmental control* (instead of behavior control), permitting the trainee to interact directly with his environment, to experience it through schemata he evolved for himself, and, as a consequence of direct feedback from it, to modify or maintain his definitions on the basis of environmental inputs instead of authority dicta.

The adaptive orientation that evolves from an interdependent environment hence is more likely to be veridical or environmentally appropriate and to be characterized by the exploration of alternatives, the tolerance and deliberate generation of conflict, the emergence of more superordinate and integrative concepts, and a heavy positive loading for information and searching.

This generic dimension of unilateral-interdependent training interacts with other properties of training methods in producing a particular system organization or variation in concreteness-abstractness. We have found it consistent with our purposes to treat unilateral conditions as being either more *reliable* or more *unreliable* and interdependent conditions as being either more *protective* or more *informational*. Further, the methods of learning control, which vary from behavior control in the unilateral condition, through minimal control, to environmental control in the interdependent condition, also vary in *acceleration* or "push" by the training agent. The situation of minimal behavior control is viewed as a condition of accelerated autonomy. The combination of the training dimensions which seem to relate more to variations in levels of concreteness-abstractness, our major concern, along with a summary of their presumed major effects on system development, is presented in Table 5-1. These will be elaborated in the following pages. First we will explore those conditions which are conducive to the toleration of conflict and diversity and hence which dispose toward openness to progression to the more abstract levels of functioning. Then we will consider those conditions which dispose toward excessive conflict, avoidance of the different, and arrestation of system development at the more concrete levels and closedness to progression to the more abstract levels.

Conditions Favorable to Openness and Progression to Structural Abstractness

Interdependent Training. We assume that under optimal environmental conditions a conceptual or social system will move from the absolutism of initial definitions of the situation toward greater relativism, reflected in a multiplicity and integration of alternatives. The sequence of structural change from the more concrete to the more abstract, from the simple to the complex, is thought to follow the course of development depicted in Fig. 5-1, p. 136. For the more abstract states, State 4, for example, to be attained, the system is assumed to have progressed in sequential steps from Stage 1 through the several transitions and nodal stages to Stage 4, with no intervening steps of development omitted. That is to say, for a system to have attained a higher level of development means that it necessarily passed successfully through the more concrete stages; it cannot have circumvented them. This assumption has important theoretical implications. It would be impossible, for ex-

TABLE 5-1

Training Conditions and System Effects

Conditions	Reliable unilateral	Accelerated unilateral	Unreliable unilateral	Accelerated autonomy	Protective interdependent	Informational interdependent
Their effect on development	Arrestation at Stage 1	Unique progression through Stage 1; arrestation at first transition	Unique progression to Stage 2; arrestation at Stage 3	Unique progression to second transition arrestation at second transition	Unique progression to Stage 3; arrestation at Stage 3	Optimal development through all stages to Stage 4
Character of system	Closed to opposition to absolute control	Compartmentalization of absolutism and opposition to absolute control	Closed to dependency and absolutism	Compartmentalization of assertive independence and need for support; isolation and comprise in conflict	Closed to autonomy	Open to differentiation and integration at all levels
Personality organization	Authoritarianism	Obsessive-compulsive	Negative independence	Assertive	Social accommodation	Interdependence
Group structure	Autocratic	Transitional autocratic	Anti-autocratic	Transitional anti-autocratic	Participant democratic	Interdependent democratic

* The third transition stage has been omitted.

143

ample, for a politically or organizationally backward nation which has just achieved independence from authoritative control immediately to evolve and effectively utilize a democratic organization. It would be equally impossible for a child who, throughout his development, had been prevented from exploring and exercising his own responsibility, to behave suddenly and effectively in terms of abstract criteria. Interdependent conditions are assumed to provide the appropriate environment for progressive differentiation and integration of a conceptual or social system and its successful development from the concreteness of Stage 1 to the abstractness of Stage 4.

This kind of environment fosters optimal diversity and conflict by: adhering to relativistic standards which allow exploration and idiosyncratic definitions; rewarding for exploration and attainment of new information instead of for responses which match external criteria; and, through proper control of the environment, allowing the individual or group to receive direct feedback from the environment, including the consequences of interaction with it. For this freedom to exist means that the cost of error is small enough to be tolerated by the training agent (individual or society) and not to overwhelm the trainee. Anderson and Moore suggest three characteristics of training methods, characteristics which we assume are inherent in interdependent training, which allow this freedom to the developing child and foster his progressive development.

1. They must "cut off," in some suitable sense, from the more serious aspects of the society's activity—those aspects connected with immediate problems of survival and well-being. If a child is learning the intricacies of interaction by experience, the activity in which he is experiencing or practicing interaction *must* allow him to make many mistakes without endangering the lives or futures of those around him. Similarly, such rewards as he receives from the activity must not be too expensive to those around him—or again the activity may have just those serious consequences which the teaching devices must avoid.

2. But in spite of the fact that the teaching device must avoid these serious consequences, some motivation must be built into the activity, else the learner may lose interest. If we rely on the distinction between activities that are *intrinsically* rewarding and those that are rewarding only as a means, or extrinsically rewarding, we may say that the rewards in the learner's activities must be intrinsic, or inherent in the activity itself. Such activities we call autotelic: they contain their own goals and source of motivation.

3. And finally, they must help a child to learn the relevant techniques [Anderson and Moore, 1959, p. 5].

While it seems reasonable and workable to institute such conditions in child training, it is infinitely more difficult to observe or create such conditions for group evolvement in natural social settings. Significant national groups, as well as subgroups within a nation, serve functions which to them are so critical and exist in such competitive in-out group environments that freedom to delineate and engage new alternatives is restricted, in some cases altogether prevented. So much importance is attached to existent group means and ends that pressures are brought to bear toward inculcating things as they are. For groups or nations to progress to the state of abstractness represented by Stage 4 functioning will necessitate marked reductions in intergroup fears, rivalries, and antagonisms. International tensions and cleavages today are such that even the newly born countries are not immune to the powerful pressures from East and West which restrict their freedom to explore, to make errors in their own way, to evolve and try out alternatives uniquely appropriate to their own people, geography, and circumstances. The optimal environment for developing nations can probably result only from effective safeguards from outside threats. The initial aim of the United Nations was the provision of such insurance. But now, because of its domination by two strong powers and lack of coherence among the others, this organization lacks the capacity to produce the optimal environment for the emergence of abstract national structures. Indeed, the rather dismal possibility exists that, as long as single nations are dedicated primarily to the maintenance of their unaltered sovereignty and pursuit of national self-interests, the conditions necessary for progression to the higher levels of abstract functioning will be prevented.

Stage 1 in development is concerned with the evolvement of a stable definition of the situation. This phase tends to be characterized by a paucity of alternate interpretations, greater absolutism of the existing definitions, greater avoidance of ambiguity, and increased dependence on external criteria, as well as the greater usage of either-or concepts and engagement of categorical cognitive functioning. These characteristics of the early phase of development have been observed in various areas of individual development by Eriksen (1950), members of the Gesell Institute (1955), Piaget (1932), and White (1960). In the initial phases of group development similar observations have been reported. Bennis and Shepard (1956) noted a preoccupation with authority and rules, Abrahams (1950) observed an orientation anchored to the past, Bion (1952) saw members as dependent on authority, and Martin and Hill (1957) interpreted the behavior of members in the early phases of group evolvement as being unshared and directed heavily toward the erection of structure and clear course of action.

Under interdependent conditions the behavior illustrative of Stage 1 functioning does not become fixated and the system, being open to progression producing factors, soon passes through transition on to Stage 2, where a variety of new and conflicting schemata emerge for defining and coping with the world. The transition from Stage 1 to 2 is characterized, in varying intensities, by a kind of rebellion against or opposition to the original definitions or readings of the situation, opening up the potential for the emergence of more superordinate schemata through increase differentiations and integration of the old and the new.

The phase of transition from Stage 1 to Stage 2 functioning is probably one of the most often observed and yet one of the most complex and least understood of the developmental landmarks of individuals and groups. Ilg and Ames (1955) as well as Eriksen (1950) and Levy (1955) confirm a period of negativism in children following a more obedient control period. Levy sees the phase as being characterized by the emergence of "self-will," "clash of wills," and a resulting "battle of the spoon." Bennis and Shepard (1956) described a phase of group development characterized by a preoccupation with rebellion following a stage of preoccupation with submission and control. Abrahams (1950), Hearn (1955), and Thelan and Dickerman (1949) have all reported observing this stage of resistance and opposition in group psychotherapy. Hearn treats this phase of development in terms of ideological conflict and polarization around issues following members' concern with structuring the unknown and defining their position in the group, while Thelan and Dickerman view it as one of frustration and conflict among stereotypes.

Interdependent training, in which the behavior of the parents "both promotes trust and gives permission and encouragement to develop assertiveness, opposition and age-appropriate independence" (Harvey, Hunt, and Schroder, 1961, p. 97), allows the developing individual to benefit from rebellion and trying out the new and hence to pass on to Stage 2. This stage is characterized by an openness to the original definitions against which rebellion occurred as well as to the alternatives which were generated by the opposition to them. The progression through Stage 2 is perhaps the most critical phase for the successful development of more abstract systems. Levy suggests that "without this resistant character the organism's response would be determined entirely by external stimuli . . . The capacity to resist external influence thus enables the organism to use and develop inner controls" (Levy, 1955, p. 213). The environmental conditions required for an effective transition through this stage, however, must not induce closedness but openness to the earlier conceptual schemata, allowing the simultaneous existence of conflicting possibilities. In discussing the transition from autocratic monarchies to democratic republics in nations, Lipset states,

> If . . . the status of major conservative groups and symbols is not threatened during this transitional period, even though they lose most of their power, democracy seems to be much more secure. And thus we have the absurd fact that ten out of the twelve stable European and English speaking democracies are monarchies. Great Britain, Sweden, Norway, Denmark, the Netherlands

Belgium, Luxemburg, Australia, Canada and New Zealand are kingdoms, or dominions of a monarch, while the only republics which meet the conditions of stable democratic procedures are the United States and Switzerland, plus Uruguay in Latin America.

The preservation of the monarchy has apparently retained for these nations the loyalty of the aristocratic, traditionalist, and clerical sectors of the population which resented increased democratization and equalitarianism. And by accepting the lower strata and not resisting to the point where revolution might be necessary, the conservative orders won or retained the loyalty of the "new" citizens, [Lipset, 1960, pp. 78-70].

The United States' Constitution is an example of a framework devoid of absolutism in which the forces of conflict were preserved.

Because of the strong desire for independence and self-assertion, Stage 2 functioning disposes toward the avoidance of commitments to, control by, and dependence upon other units. At the group level, we might expect to see the avoidant predilections expressed in such an anti-authority group structure as a loose confederation in which: (a) the units are defined in terms of members roles or territorially, not in terms of ideological differences; (b) the units contain within themselves conflicting ideologies; (c) members within the units do not force their ideology upon other members; and (d) the subunits are isolated from each other by means of control mechanisms which prevent their interference with others. At this stage the total group is relatively unintegrated and devoid of a superordinate structure. The major concern is with the rights and autonomy of each subunit. The results of this doubt, suspicion, and consequent jockeying were seen in America under the Articles of Confederation. It may be that a parallel development is now going on in the Congo.

Simmel (1956), Parsons (1959), and more recently Lipset (1960) have observed that proportional representation in an electoral system disposes toward cleavage and compartmentalization along ideological lines whereas territorial representation, which cuts across ideologies, includes conflicting orientations and increases the cohesion of effort toward common goals. "Federalism increases the opportunity for multiple sources of cleavage by adding regional interests and values to the other which crosscut the social structure" (Lipset, 1960, p. 91).

Open Stage 2 functioning is characterized, then, by diverse and conflicting schemata and components, each protected by a deliberate self-isolation, and an absence of an effective superordinate or integrating organization. As long as the parts are relevant to each other, however, the very presence of the diverse and conflicting creates pressures toward the evolvement of a more effective organization. The resulting conflict between the isolation and integration of the differentiated units marks the second transitional stage (i.e., between Stages 2 and 3). In individuals, this is a conflict between the independence of units and the emergence of superordinate concepts. Interdependent conditions induce openness to both poles of this conflict and result in the individual's ability to see, for the first time in his development, the equal plausibility of both sides. Yet he is not able to encompass these possibilities into a meaningful integrative framework. This hierarchical integration gets more underway in Stage 3 and reaches its height in Stage 4.

In open Stage 3 functioning individuals are open to both autonomy and mutual dependence. This increased freedom to entertain multiple alternatives allows greater choice and enhances the degree of self-articulation and awareness. The possession of alternative cognitive organizations increases sensitivity and openness to the decisions and perceptions of others (Newcomb, 1961; Driver, 1962). This is reflected in an increased ability and tendency to communicate and empathize with others, to read the world from another's premise, and in greater effort toward enlisting support from others for choice and action and avoiding rejection and isolation.

Observations of individual development at the Gesell Institute (Ilg and Ames, 1955) support the emergence of mutuality following a more oppositional stage. While not emphasizing the oppositional stage, Piaget (1932) eloquently describes the evolvement of moral concepts based on mutual responsibility from such concepts based on rituals and rules. He stresses the emergence of intentions as opposed to absolute rules, of cooperation as opposed to obedience. The social self (James, 1890), the "looking glass self" (Cooley, 1902), the conversation of gestures and specific "other" (G. H. Mead, 1934), and role taking (Sarbin, 1954; Kelly, 1955) are all illustrative of this stage.

Bennis and Shepard (1956) observed in group functioning that the power problem in groups was resolved by the emergence of member responsibility and that after a fighting phase the group's efforts were devoted to patching up differences and maintaining a harmonious atmosphere. Abrahams (1950) reports the development of a therapeutic attitude of mutality within therapy groups following a stage of resistance. Mann (1953) and Mann and Semerad (1948) report a stage of personal mutual analysis following a stage characterized by working through the intimacy problem and hostility. Martin and Hill (1957) observed an awareness of interrelationships following individual unshared behavior and the exploration of interpersonal potential in the group. Hearn (1955) noted attempts by group members to resolve conflict and restore harmony following a stage characterized by ideological conflict and polarization. Schutz (1958) depicted a period of affection following control. And Thelen and Dickerman (1949) reported a stage of attempt at consolidation of group harmony following a stage of "frustration" and "conflict among stereotypes."

Despite the variation in terminology, these independent observations lend support to the general contention that out of opposition to absolutes and the emergence of alternate schemata or divergent subunits emerges a stage in which the primary concern is with the principle of integration.

The structural characteristic which is most crucial during the third stage is that integration involves a compromise through interaction of the units. In groups this means that members interact in order to generate unity of purpose and action. Similarly in conceptual structure Stage 3 functioning is characterized by the emergence of more stable and autonomous internal referents (Wilkins and de Charms, 1961; Driver, 1962), a socially accommodating reaction, which involves conformity and an increased emphasis on affective components, and maintenance of personal relationships.

While tolerance of differences and diversity prevails in open Stage 3, the capacity to integrate the numerous parts into consistent and superordinate systems of thought and actions has not yet fully materialized. It is at Stage 4 that the ability to evolve superordinate schemata that both abstracts commonalities and maintains unique differences in the evaluative definitions reaches the greatest height. Here (Stage 4) the myriad of differentiated parts can be integrated in many ways depending on the task demands of the situation faced. Along with the greater capacity to combine the "elements" into more and different "wholes" goes the ability to maintain the identity of the elements and to withdraw them for recombinations in other superordinate organizations. This is why we earlier analogized this stage of functioning to a symphony orchestra, in which single parts may appropriately solo or the totality of components be brought together in one synchronized and interdependent expression.

Functioning at this highly abstract stage has been noted by several authors, although the language employed has been different from ours. Bennis and Shepard (1956) have observed that following the phase concerned with mutuality and reciprocal understanding among members the group moves on to a phase where conflict, undisturbingly existent, is generated from delineation of substantive issues instead of emotional clashes, and where consensus is a result of rational discussion rather than of a compulsive attempt at unanimity. Others have described this stage of functioning as personal mutual synthesis and the development of problem-solving skills and concerns and as a period in which the group acts as an affective integrative social instrument (Martin and Hill, 1957), as a stage of utilization of differences and collaboration on corporate tasks (Hearn, 1955), and as period of individual self-assessment, flexibility of group processes, and emphasis upon productivity in problem solving (Thelen and Dickerman, 1949). We also have stressed the task and information orientation of this mode of functioning (Harvey, Hunt, and Schroder, 1961).

From this state of greater differentiation *and* integration stems the ability to tolerate conflict. Indeed reality is defined as being possessed of multiple alternatives and hence diversity is sought as a means of enhancing validation. The system is actively sensitive and open to a more refined and wider band of the impinging world owing to the greater complexity and richness of the internal standards or schemata from which the environment is defined and read.

These more abstract and interdependent structures have been described as "democratic" groups and studied through the phenomenon of simultaneous autonomy and mutuality, of task orientation and affect, and of morale and productivity.

Numerous studies have focused on conditions affecting the democracy of organizations. We probably would not be stretching the point too far to say that conditions conducive to greater democracy parallel are perhaps even synonymous with those conditions inherent in interdependent training. If democracy is equated with greater and more numerous freedoms, then the kind of conditions that produce Stage 4 functioning are more democratic and free. While a strong value judgment no doubt lies at the heart of our assumption, it nonetheless appears to us that interdependent training methods and environments are absolutely essential for progression to the more abstract functioning represented by Stage 4 as well as to the accompanying freedoms and parallel personal responsibilities.

To attain an attitude of mutual responsibility, Piaget (1932) feels that children must be trained to act from the point of view of those around him, to learn to please rather than obey, both of which come from a feeling of equality with parents which prevents absolutism of parental suggestions and allows the child to operate in terms of intentions and underlying reasons rather than authority dicta. The work of Moore and Anderson at Yale has recently shown, and continues to demonstrate, the rapid learning, spontaneity, and creativity of very young children who are trained to read and write through the utilization of a "autotelic" environment, one that parallels in crucial respects the conditions we have termed interdependent. Starting with the study of Lewin, Lippit, and White (1939), several studies have found that American subjects are more satisfied, show less aggression and higher interest in "democratic" than in "autocratic" environments.

Related studies in other countries show the interaction of existing attitudes and values with what is preferred and influences. More than one study outside of America has failed to show the superiority of democratic atmospheres in relation to several behavioral variables. This is in line with a point we stressed earlier, that the optimal environment for a particular subject or group depends on the existent level of its abstractness or baseline. Interdependent environments are effective only when the proper base has been prepared for it. It would be meaningless to tell a person who all his life had been controlled by autocratic forces and outside influences to act with freedom all of a sudden. It is equally meaningless for Americans to expect newly evolving nations, whose history is one of domination and control by outside agents, to blossom immediately into effective democracies. Many foreign leaders are aware of this problem. India's Prime Minister Nehru is aiming at a "guided democracy" in which the proper base and experience among the Indian masses are established before the full impact of an interdependent environment is allowed to hit them. We might add that the foundations of such a base were begun by the British through their strong influence in India.

As the boundaries of groups expand to include more diversity, the problem of maintaining a balance between affective and instrumental goals becomes more central. That is, pressures toward mutuality and compromise may inhibit the effectiveness of the group in a "task orientation" sense. This problem also exists in autocratic groups (see later), in which equilibrium is restored by controls which result in a negation of directives or acceptance of the authority associated with increased tension between leader and followers (Lewin, Lippitt, and White, 1939). In groups that emerge out of interdependent environments, however, the position of the individual or subunit in the group, because of greater autonomy and self direction, is more secure, the affective component is accepted and achievement is no longer subordinate to relationships. In these groups morale emerges as an essential component, making the groups maximally resistant to stress and increasingly subject to mobilization and increased effort and productivity as a result of stress (Lowe, 1961).

The successful attainment simultaneously of the goals of task orientation and affective satisfaction has been observed in many studies of groups functioning in environments devoid of autocratic forces. Hemphill (1955) found that chairmen of college departments with the best reputations concerned themselves with organizing departmental activities and initiating new strategies alongside the development of warm participant relationships.

Since the goal of mutuality may conflict with instrumental goals, development from Stage 3 to Stage 4 involves the emergence of an organization capable of containing both. Initially, progression beyond Stage 2 is difficult if the degree of divergence between subunits is too great. Several nations in Europe have been unable to make a successful transition to the third or fourth stage politically, some perhaps (e.g., France) because of too many divergent ideological groups contained in their boundaries. In some nations, such as America and England, divergence and disagreement have been institutionalized into a few units, viz., the two-party system. This procedure is advantageous to development because it (a) legitimizes or normalizes opposition between units and (b) minimizes opposition to the superordinate units.

In regard to the latter point, it is perhaps essential that certain procedures and strategies develop the status of norms if developmental progression to participant groups and beyond is to be achieved. Verba (1961) discusses the role of norms in the resolution of the affective-instrumental conflict. Thibaut and Kelley (1959) observed that group norms decrease the tension and hostility between the more powerful and less powerful members of dyads. They report that this "impersonalization of expectations" makes the resolution of conflict and social influence more stable and less emotional. As integration proceeds in development, the emergence of norms and later a system of laws act as unifying forces which protect the autonomy of units and keep these forces in balance.

Conditions Disposing Toward Closedness and Arrestation at More Concrete Levels

In the preceding section we depicted interdependent conditions as those favorable to progression to Stage 4, the most abstract mode of functioning to be dealt with in this chapter. Our concern in this section will be with environmental conditions disposing toward closedness to progression and arrestation at more concrete levels. In synopsis, we will propose that *reliable unilateral* conditions will favor arrestation at Stage 1, where the guidelines to action are highly autocratic, absolutistic, and externally imposed. *Accelerated unilateral* training will be depicted as a major cause of arrestation at the transitional phase between Stages 1 and 2, where the conflict between the incompatible motive structures of Stages 1 and 2 operate in unresolved fashion, pushing the individual at one time toward submission to authority and at another time toward defiance and protest toward autocracy. *Unreliable unilateral* environments will be pictured as effecting arrestation at Stage 2, resulting in closed anti-authority concepts and group structures. *Accelerated autonomy* conditions will be hypothesized as disposing toward arrestation in the transitional phase between Stages 2 and 3 in which persons, unless they cognitively compartmentalize, teetertotter between assertive independence and need for interpersonal support and dependency. *Protective* training will be represented as disposing toward arrestation at Stage 3, characterized by fear of isolation and a strong tendency toward social accommodation and compromise.

Let us now treat each of these arresting conditions in more detail. The reader should keep in mind that, while reference will be made to modes of functioning described for the nodal conceptual stages in the preceding section, here we shall be talking about systems that are *arrested at a given stage* and are closed to inputs necessary for progression to more abstract systems. In the preceding section the systems we described were *open and progressive*, functioning only temporarily at lower levels before moving on to more abstract levels. The functioning now to be described is expressive of more fixed levels of development.

Unilateral Training and Autocracy. Unilateral training conditions are characterized by external control. Quite illustrative are the autocratic training practices treated by Baldwin (1955) and Lewin, Lippit, and White (1939); the close supervision described by Katz, Maccoby, and Morse (1950) and by Day and Hamblin (1961); and "Taylorism" in various industrial concerns.

Under unilateral environments punishment and reward are administered on the basis of whether or not the subject's overt response matches the specific requirements of the training agent. The trainee is presented with a ready-made, absolutistic set of authority defined dicta which, through reinforcement, he internalizes as concepts and employs as *the* valid criteria for reading and reacting to the world. Hence little latitude or likelihood exists for experiencing the consequences of direct contact with the environment. Because of failure in self-articulation and inability consequently to experience the self as a causal agent, the recipient avoids the novel and rejects the different. When forced to deal with ambiguity, he relies heavily upon definitions brought from past situations and, to escape the stress of the unstructured, closes inappropriately fast on a solution. And because of heavy dependence on authority-prescribed rules, such an individual submits to those of higher status or greater power and tries to dominate those of positions inferior to his own.

Unilateral conditions restrict contact, limit the quality and frequency of stimulus inputs, reduce the heterogeneity of differentiations and integrations, and, as a consequence, maximize the probability of fixation or arrestation at the concrete level of Stage 1. In the resulting conceptual system obedience to the dicta of the omnipotent and omniscient authority becomes an end in itself. Violations of these standards engender feelings of guilt, sin, and unworthiness, accompanied by tendencies toward self-denunciation and castigation. These rules, in the same way they are presented, come to be accepted and defended by the trainee in the name of righteousness while punishment for deviation is given and received in the name of morality. Out of this dearth of alternatives and unrealistic criteria evolves a brittle and closed conceptual structure, possessed of simplicity and aversion to alien inputs which, while keeping out the foreign, also increases the likelihood of "going to pieces" under high stress.

At the group level closed Stage 1 functioning finds expression in such things as: (a) a sharply peaked and clearly defined status hierarchy with a minimal number of persons occupying positions of greatest centrality; (b) a highly homogeneous ideology; (c) a narrow latitude of acceptance toward out-groups, accompanied by a marked tendency toward stereotypy and prejudice toward the out-groups; (d) a rigid and narrowly bounded set of norms which prescribe not only ends (what to do) but also means (how to do it); (e) and a more certain, stronger, and more punitive reaction to violation of the norms. "Great man" behavior, feudalistic social structure, divine right of kings, closed and unquestioned ideological assumptions such as those often advocated by religions and pursued in utopias, and various forms of fascism and totalitarianism exemplify structures and norms that are likely to evolve out of Stage 1 views of the world.

In autocratic groups interpersonal relations follow the channels of power and control, with submission to those in power and domination of the powerless as the normative response. Hence, as Maccoby (1959), Fromm (1941), and others have indicated, from the personality springing from unilateral environments issue simultaneously the tendencies toward domination and submission, the expression of which is determined by the relative power and status of the one toward whom reaction is directed. Control based on power, along with other attendant features of the structure, prevents fluidity of the structure, keeps members "in their place," stabilizes the existent, perpetuates the old, and minimizes the possibility of conflicting and divergent evaluations being generated.

Since self-worth of the individual is anchored to his confirmation of externally defined and authority mediated criteria, the resulting adaptive orientation is primarily geared toward making the world fit the socially packaged schemata. Because of the either-or nature of this orientation, its holder is compelled to see one of two alternatives as right and the other as wrong. And unless he be led to consider that *he* is wrong, a possibility precluded by the unimpeachable validity which he has been led to believe inherent in the beliefs handed him, he sets about convincing himself and others that *they are wrong and he is right*. Such attempts at convincing, which generally are accompanied by an avowed dedication to showing the misleds the light, have taken a multitude of forms. Attempts at domination and indoctrination of the non-believers, groups and individuals, attribution of negative characteristics toward those holding different views, and distorting or denying the conditions producing conceptual refutation are among the milder examples (Festinger, Riecken, and Schachter, 1956). More severe, but in no way less representative of such an orientation, are the various religious wars, inquisitions, exterminations, and destruction effected by the righteous zealot out to save mankind from perils he would encounter if he were but left free to pursue his own course of action.

Neumann (1932) has described such resulting groups as possessing a totally "integrated" ideology, by which he means a single dimension view of the world and not integration that results from multiple differentiations, as we have stressed the term. Such "integrationists" direct their efforts toward making the world fit a simple and undifferentiated mould, a mould which they appear to assume is the basic stepping stone toward the "best of all possible worlds." As Lipset (1960) indicates,

Neumann has suggested the need for a basic analytic distinction between parties of representation, which strengthen democracy, and parties of integration, which weaken it. The former are typified by most parties in the English-speaking democracies and Scandinavia, plus most centrist and conservative parties other than religious ones. These parties view their function as primarily one of securing votes around election time. The parties of integration, on the other hand, are concerned with making the world conform to their basic philosophy. They do not see themselves as contestants in a give-and-take game of pressure politics, but as partisans in a mighty struggle between divine or historic truth on one side and fundamental error on the other. Given this conception of the world, it becomes necessary to prevent their followers from being exposed to the cross-pressures flowing from contact with outsiders which will reduce their faith. (Lipset, 1960, p. 86)

Individuals who have grown out of reliable unilateral environments manifest higher morale and performance in subsequently constricted and authority controlled environments. The one boy in the Lewin, Lippit, and White study (1939) who preferred the autocratic environment was the son of an army officer. And similarly, it was been found that more authoritarian soldiers prefer more authoritarian officers (Crockett, 1958). For individuals who bring to the situation a broad background of freedom in exploring and defining the world for themselves the unilateral or autocratic environments tend to produce effects opposite to the above.

The effects and relative efficiency of autocratic structures, therefore, depend upon the past experience of the persons and the nature of the new environment or task to be solved. Fairly simple and unchanging task demands no doubt can be as well met by individuals or groups functioning at the level of Stage 1 as at Stage 4. On the other hand, the presence of situational complexity, need for exploration and delineation of new solutions, as well as instability and change, no doubt would favor individuals who had grown out of an interdependent and free environment. Concrete responses and approaches would suffice in the first case. But higher levels of abstractness would be essential for the latter. Thus Coch and French (1948) found that groups that were allowed to participate in decisions affecting company goals and policies as well as their own futures were able to adapt more efficiently to change than groups subjected to more autocratic environments. On the other side of the coin, Calvin, Hoffman, and Hardin (1957) observed dull children to perform better under more autocratic conditions while brighter ones did better and were happier under more democratic and permissive conditions.

In judging the merits of concreteness and abstractness, the criteria on which the evaluations are based must be kept clearly in mind. In addition to the preceding conditions that might favor greater concreteness, probably so does the practice of judging performance in terms of its degree of coincidence with externally imposed criteria. We have several bits of information from preliminary studies indicating that college subjects functioning at the level of Stage 1 tend to have higher grade averages and are more likely to be "overachievers" than those operating in terms of Stage 4 (Harvey, 1963b). It is our guess that this picture would be reversed if the emphasis and reward were more on creativity than on the ability to reproduce the words of the instructor, the state so characteristic of so many of our training institutions.

Accelerated Unilateral Conditions and Transitional Group Structures. An accelerated unilateral environment is one in which the trainee is pushed too hard and demands made on him are in excess of his capacity at the time of the demand. One consequence of the training agent's demands being a jump or two ahead of the ability of the trainee is the inability of the latter to gain consistent rewards, something possible only through a more invariant matching of behavior with the agent's requirements. However, owing to his ability to please the agent now and again through intense effort and realize some reward, the subject is often placed in a double approach-avoidant conflict situation. On the one hand, he is motivated to accept and abide by the external criteria and unilateral pressures in order to gain a modicum of reward. But at the same time he is disposed toward rejecting the overly demanding agent and his dictates because of the excess and his negative experience surrounding pursuit of them. A frequent outcome seems to be a fixated ambivalence disposing concomitantly toward rejection of authority and dependence upon it. Such conflict favors conceptual or cognitive compartmentalization, which in extreme form may actually result in "split personality" characterized by intense obsessive-compulsive conflict mirrored in an overdriven search of absolutistic structure and control and, at the same time, in rebellion against the source of this control. The resulting compartmentalization, even in its milder forms, restricts differentiations and sorely limits the integrations necessary for progressive development. Either of these opposing tendencies may, at different times, be of greater relative strength, giving rise to a kind of unresolved vacillation, doubt, guilt, and hostility.

This conflict is manifested at the group level by transitional autocratic groups, in which an authoritarian structure is shakily maintained over an unstable population torn by unresolved conflict and opposing ideologies. Often in such a setting individuals and group members lash out viciously against the seemingly capricious authority, expressing themselves in bloody and revengeful, but generally unsuccessful, revolts. Even if the rebels were organized and possessed of adequate physical resources, the ambivalence between loyalty and hostility, dependence and hate toward the target of revolt would hardly foster success. Further, as several aborted revolts in Latin America have shown, even dispossession of one authority tends to result in replacement by similar persons and practices. Perhaps even more illustrative have been the latent, hesitant, faltering, but finally explosive rebellions against feudal authority and structure with which history is replete.

Unreliable Unilateral Conditions and Closed Anti-Authority Group Structures. In one sense, unreliable unilateral conditions represent an extreme case of accelerated unilateral conditions. The main difference is greater capriciousness and unpredictability of the training agent's demands and response toward the trainee in the unreliable unilateral environment. The demands still tend to be made in the name of morality and external validity, however, as in the preceding unilateral conditions. (The word "unilateral" is meant to indicate a one-way line of influence: from agent to recipient.) In this situation, however, the agent will at one time reward for a response and at another punish for the same thing. Hence, even if he tried, there is no consistent route the trainee may traverse for motive satisfaction and authority approval. Whatever he does, punishment, neglect, and rejection are more likely to be the fruits of his efforts. This produces an effect very different from the other two unilateral conditions described. In the present case the concept toward authority becomes generally negative, with no counter tendencies. Strong becomes the trainee's drive to avoid dependence of any sort upon the untrustworthy and unfair agent. Hence authority dicta and cues come to have not a neutral weighting but a negative weighting. Basic social norms and methods of institutional control are viewed as shackles to be kicked off. The paradoxical consequence of this is that even while rejecting authority-related guidelines, the very negative dependence upon them gives them the power to guide the subject's behavior, even though it tends to be in the opposite direction.

Because of punishment received when doing his best, the trainee in this condition develops distrust of anyone who might affect his fate, along with a great resistance to self disclosure (Cunat, 1960) and a tendency toward giving off diffuse and misleading cues designed to prevent acquisition by another person of any information or means that might be used to control him. This drive to avoid control and absolutism tends to result in closedness and absolutism of the opposite sort. Because of the strong distrust and avoidance of commitment and dependency, interdependency with others is prevented and the possibility of mutuality and consensus as a means of revolving conflict between alternate schemata and views of the world is prohibited. Forced to rely upon his own resources and experiences as the only trustable guidelines, a person arrested at this stage of functioning is necessarily led into a great deal of exploration and generation of alternatives, even if much of this learning and related behavior concern ways of successfully defying the social pressures. But the subject is unable to integrate these differentiations into a reliable and effective set of constancies and criteria for consistent definition and action.

The lack of superordinate concepts and absence of commitment is, in extreme form, reflected in psychopathic tendencies. In degrees less than psychopathy this is also often mirrored in gang membership and behavior. The studies by Thrasher (1927), Whyte (1943), and others suggest that the motivation for joining antisocial gangs is often a feeling of rejection or inferiority, lack of social belongingness, and shared oppositional tendencies. We do not mean to imply, however, that all delinquency is an expression of arrested Stage 2 functioning.

Group structures likely to evolve out of unreliable unilateral conditions would be expected to have strong and clearly defined boundaries between subgroups or parts (little integration), to be differentiated on the basis of role or task boundaries rather than ideologies, to be arranged more in a wheel-like organization, with the leader having direct contact with members but little interdependence among them, and to engage in intercourse with other groups primarily through aggression and testing of the others' limits and integrity.

At the level of national groups some degree of closedness at Stage 2 is exemplified by extreme dedication to states' rights and an equally strong fear of any form of centralism or integration of group units. At one stage of American history there were strong forces directed toward the isolation of states. But enough of the units were amenable to superordinate inclusion that the federal system evolved. Resistance to integration and insistence on complete autonomy carried to its extreme would probably result in anarchy or a large number of endlessly feuding subunits. The prerevolutionary conflict between Bakunin and Marx over whether the goal of the new Russia should be one superordinate political structure or a multitude of semi-isolated small groups centered around this question, with Marx and autocratic centralism carrying the day.

Accelerated Autonomy Conditions and Transitional Anti-Authority Groups. Accelerated autonomy refers to conditions in which independence is stressed at the expense of mutuality or reciprocal interpersonal relationships, resulting in a subject's failure to learn to take other persons and their goals into account. In this condition the training agent vacillates between making environmental demands too easy on the trainee, often by solving the problem for him, and leaving him completely alone and on his own resources. While the agent may be somewhat unreliable in his demands, unlike the practices involved in the preceding unreliable conditions, he is fairly consistent in rewarding the trainee. In many cases rewarding almost becomes indiscriminate. The result is the evolvement of a conceptual system which contains strong predilections toward independence alongside the desire to rely heavily on the training agent for solution of the problem at hand.

This arrestation between Stages 2 and 3 should be distinguished from that occurring between Stages 1 and 2, which we discussed earlier. In the accelerated unilateral training, which disposes toward arrest between Systems 1 and 2, the subject is pushed beyond his capacity and only aperiodically achieves success and reward. Hence the drive toward independence that results in this instance involves strong avoidant tendencies and attempts to assert independence to escape the capricious control of the agent. In accelerated autonomy conditions, which we view as conducing toward arrestation between Stages 2 and 3, the trainee's predilections are more approach than avoidant toward both independence and dependency because of rewards associated with both kinds of behavior. This may be seen in those situations where the subject will enthusiastically tackle a new problem but will as quickly abandon it and call for support by the agent when it begins to get a bit tough. Instead of the agent being omnipotent, as in previously described conditions, the trainee in a sense exercises influence over the agent, being able to demand and get his help when in deep water. This accentuates the trainee's strong tendencies toward assertiveness and minimizes the change of learning real give-and-take, reciprocal influence, and influencibility in relation to others in an interactional situation. "The great paradox accounting for maturational failure in under-dominated children," suggests Ausubel (1952, p. 220), "is a super-abundance of the self-assertive aspects of volitional independence combined with a virtual absence of the personality traits that make implementation of this independence possible." A consequence of such training practices is to produce in the developing individual an unresolved conflict between assertive independence and individual success and the need for approval and acceptance.

The operation of the resulting motivational tendencies probably is more easily observed in personality and individual behavior than in group norms and structures because groups based on such orientations would find it difficult to survive over an extended period. The failure to develop a stable and effective superordinate structure and to pursue interdependent goals would weaken such groups and make them vulnerable to control by others. The problem in adaptation occurs when outside pressures are met. For example, a child arrested at this level of development may experience little threat or failure in the permissive family situation, but when the same child interacts with other children his quest for omnipotence and independence is likely to meet with ostracism and rejection.

Protective Conditions and Closed Participant Groups. This condition could perhaps be labeled more appropriately as overprotective. Here the training agent serves as a buffer between the trainee and the stresses and presses of the surrounding environment, preventing the developing person to make direct contact with his environment and to receive veridical feedback from it. While the trainee is not actually punished for exploring, as he is in Stage 1 training, he is effectively prevented from doing so because of anticipation of his needs by the agent. Only minimal experience is gained by the subject in reacting directly to and manipulating the physical world because of the "blocking" and "interference running" by the agent. However, the trainee has wide experience and develops rather effective skills in manipulating and pleasing people. In fact, this becomes his most salient mode of adjusting to his world. By gaining acceptance and approval of others he feels reassured and is able to gain their help in solving his problems.

The fear of isolation and rejection is a major concern of persons growing out of this environment. This is in keeping with the results obtained in a recent study by Harvey (1963b) in which it was found that college subjects classified as being arrested at Stage 3 development reported significantly more frequently than others that as children they were sent to their rooms and socially isolated by their parents as discipline measures. Being prevented from developing their own skills to cope with their physical environment, such individuals are rendered deeply anxious from the prospect of being left alone to cope with the situation singly.

Characteristic of the resulting orientation is the desire to avoid interpersonal disagreement and conflict, expressed in moves toward placating, compromising, and yielding to the evaluations of others (Harvey, Hunt, and Schroder, 1961). Harvey (1963b) has found that Stage 3 subjects show significantly less aggression and hostility toward a graduate student experimenter in a difficult task situation than do subjects representative of Stages 1 and 2. Unlike subjects from Stages 1 and 2, persons functioning at the level of arrested Stage 3 have also been found to be more willing to disclose about themselves, being seemingly eager to do so as a technique of establishing dependence on others (Cunat, 1960).

In attitude change and yielding studies Stage 3 individuals are found to be the more frequent conformers and yielders (Harvey, Hunt, and Schroder, 1961). In problem-solving tasks they fail to achieve a task orientation because of concentration on measures assuring reciprocal liking, harmony, and consensus. One could conjecture that in an industrial or any interdependent situation these persons would be more concerned with gaining social approval than production output. In such a case the conditions resulting in high morale might not coincide with high job performance. Morale would come from warm, supportive, and reassuring interpersonal environments which might or might not be compatible with the requirements for high production yield.

In an experimental study of four-man groups, Hemphill (1956) demonstrated that the more a member was sensitized to negative affective reactions of other group members the more reluctant he was to assume an instrumental directive role. Bales (1950) has concluded that instrumental role activity in the group requires a certain amount of "immunity to hostility," which arrested Stage 3 representatives would be expected not to have. Similarly, in referring to J. F. Kennedy's observations in *Profiles in Courage,* Verba (1961) says, "In a perceptive study of courageously 'maverick' senators, Senator John Kennedy suggests a similar point. Those senators who were highly motivated toward a particular goal and wanted to lead the rest of the Senate in that direction despite strong opposition had to have a certain immunity from the pressures to 'get along' with and obtain the 'comradeship and approval' of the other members of the Senate" (Verba, 1961, p. 158).

One might conjecture further that at the national scene an example of closed participant groups, resulting from overprotection, would be a welfare state characterized by a democratic structure in which members and subunits displaced responsibility onto a national government. Such an organization probably would be heavily concerned with compromise and less concerned with developing and assuming a task orientation that would cut across or be mainly independent of concern with fellowship and protection.

This completes the discussion of conditions assumed to produce arrestation in development at levels short of Stage 4. Interdependent environments, we proposed, favor openness to diversity and development to the more abstract height represented by Stage 4. The other conditions, reliable unilateral, accelerated unilateral, unreliable unilateral, accelerated autonomy, and protective interdependent, are assumed to dispose toward arrestation at levels more concrete than Stage 4.

Conceptual Properties as Cause and Social Environments as Effects

Throughout the history of social psychology, of both the psychological and sociological vintages, the focus of study has been on social factors (groups, societies, etc.) as cause of personality or conceptual outcomes. This emphasis is not wrong. It is just one-sided. Most theorists of social and individual focus concur that behavioral outcomes are an interactional product of situational and dispositional factors operative at the time. Despite such recognition, at the verbal level at least, the prevailing tendency still has been to look at existing social factors as "causing" personality and individual factors, with the reciprocal side of the coin ignored for the most part. While social norms and environments provide stimuli and affect individual definitions and conceptual systems, the determinants that produced a particular set of norms in the *first place* are also important. In this section we wish to call attention to this obvious but neglected fact by considering briefly some of the effects that differences in conceptual and personality makeups of the interacting members have on the resulting group products. Because of the historical legacies mentioned above, an extreme paucity of relevant experiments exists.

While it is no doubt true that a group norm or decision is not deducible by the simple addition of predilections members bring to the situation, this does not mean that the group outcome is independent of the component parts, the makeup of the individuals, comprising it. The parts affect the whole, the group, as well as reciprocally being affected by it. Depending on one's interest, either line of influence, from parts to whole or whole to parts, may be focused upon. But if the interest is in understanding all the variance, then *both must be considered.*

Haythorn *et al.* (1956) found that the behavior of individual group members could be predicted to some extent by personality measures, in this case the F Scale. They also found that members' behavior was affected by the personalities of other members. Subjects low in authoritarianism were more likely to choose leaders who were friendlier and less controlling than were individuals high in authoritarianism. The latter were more satisfied and performed better in a centralized and hierarchical power structure, a result that parallels Crockett's (1958) finding that more authoritarian paratroopers preferred more authoritarian officers and other leaders.

Assuming that different environments have operated to produce differences in conceptual or personality structures, our emphasis in the preceding section, it would be consistent with the side now under focus to view the cross-cultural difference obtained in environment and leadership preference as resulting from existing conceptual makeups. Hence Barschak (1951) found that German girls preferred rigid authoritarian control by parents and perceived this as an indicator of parental affection. Murphy (1953) obtained related results from group participants in India as well as finding that emotional and directive lectures were more effective in changing the attitudes of Indian boys toward the caste system than was a more democratic discussion technique. Also illustrative is a quote from Weiss, which we have borrowed from Verba (1961). In speculating on the outcome of an industrial psychologist's attempt to use a discussion method to arrive at vacation times in a German factory, Weiss is quoted as saying,

In the American factory there would be give and take, probably ending with a vote, and the agreement that the majority should rule. In the German factory, the first suggestion would be that the foreman decide. If the foreman said, "No, you men decide," the men would individually state the best period for them: "May," "Early August," and so on. If the foreman then said, "We can't shut down the plant all that time; you have to decide on one time," they would say "All right. You decide on the time. We have told you our preferences." Further insistence by the foreman on group decision would be met by increased opposition among the men. The difference is that Americans are able to see themselves as forming a group, aside from their working relationships. The Germans are a group only as they are led by their foreman. The informal group is a potentiality in America in a way it probably is not in Germany [quoted by Verba, 1961, p. 241].

Variations in group outcome as a function of personality and conceptual differences among members should be reflected in group performance as well as in member satisfaction. Several studies by the authors have found Stage 4 representatives to perform better on complex and changing tasks. For example, Stage 4 subjects working alone outperformed the others in a complex multiple probability learning task, on the Doodlebug problem described by Rokeach (1960), as well as on other tasks demanding the ability to change set and abandon stereotypy. Pairs of Stage 4 subjects working as a team were also found to outperform pairs of subjects representing Stages 1, 2, and 3 on a complex and interdependent task (Harvey, 1963b). Especially relevant are the studies carried out at Princeton by Davis (1962) and Driver (1962).

In the study by Davis three-person teams homogeneous in terms of

levels of concreteness-abstractness (as determined by sentence comple-
tion tests, dogmatism, and rigidity scales) competed in a simulated stock
market game, devised by John Kennedy at Princeton, in which the behavior of any group affected the market environment according to a
complex set of predetermined rules. After twelve two-hour sessions all
groups of the more abstract members performed better than the more
concretely constituted groups, even though the groups were matched in
intelligence and academic standing of the members.

In the most extensive study to date on the effects of conceptual structure on group functioning, Driver (1962), utilizing the Nation's Simulation Laboratory at Northwestern University (Guetzkow, 1959), observed
homogeneous groups of concrete and abstract subjects for ten runs of
seven groups per run. He found that: (a) the dimensional space (based
upon multidimensional scaling devices) of the more concrete groups
was simpler than that of the more abstractly constituted groups; (b) the
complexity of the dimensional space was reduced for all groups under
extreme stress (simulated internation war), but more so for the concrete
than the abstract groups; (c) after collapse of the dimensional space, the
remaining dimensions in terms of which members evaluated were more
complex and internally anchored for the abstract than for the concrete
groups; and (d) the more concretely comprised groups, owing to their
simpler and more primitive conceptual structure, reacted to frustration
with greater violence than did the more abstract groups.

Obviously, research along the preceding lines is only beginning. But
there seems little doubt that the conceptual makeup the interacting individuals bring to the situation they are to solve and standardize may
significantly affect the nature of the decision and norm that emerges. As
common group and social factors dispose toward related effects in conceptual outcome, so do related cognitive makeups dispose toward certain
group products. Thus, for example, if a social structure, of a nation or
smaller group, remains relatively autocratic as the conceptual structure
of the members evolve beyond this toward greater abstractness, members
could be expected to become dissatisfied and even to agitate for social
reform.

In urging a more balanced consideration of both sides of the per-
sonality-culture coin, we would concur in the highly germane statement
of Spiro:

Much of the research and theory in culture and personality, even that of
its pioneers—Mead, Hallowell, Henry, Kluckhohn, and others—exemplifies the
approach which is proposed in this chapter. This proposal, therefore, is intended not as a radical departure from, but rather as a strengthening of, a
trend which already has distinguished practitioners. But this trend must be
broadened as well as strengthened. Because, as comparative personality the-

orists, we have been primarily concerned with explaining personality, our studies have in general focused on those aspects of social systems and culture which putatively are determinants of personality. . . .

In suggesting that we abandon the Copernican revolution of culture-and-personality, I do not intend to imply that we abandon our concern for personality. On the contrary! . . . My suggestion implies, rather, that its conceptual status be changed from *explanandum* to *explanans*, from a concept to be explained to an exploratory concept [Spiro, 1961, pp. 469–70].

Some Implications

We have hypothesized that given optimal environments developing structures, conceptual and social, will, through the process of differentiation and integration, progress from primitive homogeneity and simplicity to integrated heterogeneity and abstractness. The absence of interdependent conditions, the environment optimal for such progression, is viewed as rendering likely arrestation of the system at the more concrete end of the scale. We have also called attention to the necessity of viewing both social and cognitive states as reciprocal cause and effect, that social factors dispose toward particular conceptual organizations but that also the effect of particular environmental condition depends on the existing conceptual state of the respondent. High task performance and satisfaction, therefore, depend on the degree of matching between the demands of the environment and the makeup of the respondents at the particular moment.

This would imply, among other things, that budding and underdeveloped national groups would be unable to institute an effective democracy immediately upon release from control of colonial nations. Notions of freedom, the tolerance of diversity and conflict, as well as their effective integration, cannot be solved simply by legislation or aspirations. These social products are compatible with, can only evolve from, persons whose history contains prior experience in exploration, self responsibility, and progressive development; in short, groups of people trained under interdependent conditions. Liberia, the oldest Negro republic, is a case in point. Founded by American philanthropists in the image of the American democracy for freed slaves from the United States, this small country remains today, with the possible exception of Ethiopia, as the most underdeveloped and malfunctioning of the African states. Inexperienced in freedom and self-determination, the people of Liberia find themselves presented with too much "freedom" instead of not enough. The early days of Reconstruction, following the American Civil War, in which former slaves were immediately invested with responsible position, showed graphically the adverse effects of a more interdependent environment on Stage 1 persons.

In line with this, perhaps a good leader, a good teacher, an effective communicator, would be one who always tried to make his message or behavior optimally consonant or congruent with the conceptual baselines of the recipients. Probably this would generally involve slightly discrepant inputs, by which the recipients would be challenged but not overwhelmed or utterly confused. This would conduce toward a balance between the forces of diversity and synthesis, enhancing the chance for development to the more abstract levels.

Training criteria or policy decisions which affect development and growth must be conceived and instituted in relation to the present characteristics of the individuals and social structure and to the end state sought. For example, a loose federation and opposition to external control in any form may represent the best prognosis at this time for an ultimate "democratic" or abstract outcome in many underdeveloped nations. The premature imposition of a democratic constitution in a country functioning at a more concrete and autocratic level would be expected not to work because of the absence of tolerance of diversity and the lack of machinery meaningfully to integrate disparate parts. Instead of a synchronized coherence, which also admits of solo performances, excessive conflict, possible anarchy, and firmer entrenchment in autocracy could well be the result.

The point we would make has been made concisely and clearly by Cantril:

All of this, of course, relates to an indispensable understanding of the concept of "freedom" which is basically a psychological, rather than a political, concept. "Freedom" if it is to be meaningful at all must be connected to some self-started action that brings about some desired results. This means, incidentally, that what one person regards as freedom is not necessarily freedom for someone else. One man's freedom is another man's bondage. Different people require different types and qualities of freedom according to their levels of development, their levels of social and political maturity. If an undisciplined, undeveloped people—like a young child—are given complete freedom, chaos and disillusionment are likely to result since they will not be in a position to recognize their own best interests and, even if they do, will not know how to go about pursuing them. If men are to enjoy the blessings of freedom, they must learn through experience to build up a set of constancies, a pattern of assumptions, which will produce a reality world within which flow can proceed from form [Cantril, 1961, p. 17].

Chapter 6

The Structure of Personality [1]

OMAR KHAYYAM MOORE AND ALAN ROSS ANDERSON

We would like to pretend in this paper, from time to time, that we are apprentices to Holmes and Watson (Doyle, 1886) faced with the following problem. We have just arrived on the earth and, though we have not yet encountered any earthlings, we *have* run across a number of libraries. Chief among the discoveries we have made are (a) Martin Gardner's book on puzzles (1956), (b) Cardano's study of probability (described by Ore, 1953), (c) Hoyle's rules for games (1748), and (d) Bach's *Wohltempierte Clavier* (1722). What could we deduce about the character of the "personalities" of living beings who make use of things described in books of this sort?

Of course it has always been recognized, in philosophical circles at least, that such deductions are at best plausible inferences, rather than species of logically valid inferences, and we will not pretend otherwise. Still, it seems interesting to consider the question: Why do people have puzzles, games of chance, games of strategy, and aesthetic objects, universally [2] in human societies?

Now of course we need not take such a light-hearted view of our task. We could assume a much deeper tone of voice, and write as if we had a *theory* about human behavior, to wit, functionalism. But we are essentially in agreement with criticisms of this view (as a *theory*), as

[1] This research was supported in part by the Office of Naval Research, Group Psychology Branch, Contract No. SAR/Nonr–609(16). We are grateful to Jon Barwise, Nuel D. Belnap, Jr., and Neil Gallagher for helpful comments on earlier drafts.

[2] We believe most anthropologists would agree that games and other autotelic cultural products are very ancient and widespread among human societies. Whether these cultural objects are "cultural universals" is partly a matter of definition. Some anthropologists have reported that there are some societies with no games at all (Roberts *et al.*, 1959; Roberts and Sutton-Smith, 1962a, 1962b). This seems to us hardly believable, though we cannot claim that we understand the classification of "games" used by the authors well enough to object. Of course, there *must* have been a time when there were no games (in the same sense that there *must* have been a time when there were no human beings). Games, as we understand them, are cultural products which must be developed.

presented by, for example, Hempel (1959) and Nagel (1957). Functionalism is not a theory of anything; it is rather a heuristic orientation which gives a point of view which makes us feel that we have some "explanation" of things, and (if we are lucky) will lead to rigorous theory construction and experiments.

Now, whence arises this feeling? We think that there are several things involved.

(1) We look at the events needing explanation as if they were a *system* of happenings, rather than simply a heap or congeries of events. There is some set of systematic interrelations among the events we watch, and we think we can pick out the parts that are relevant for an "explanation." Of course we may be wrong: We might think that the "function" of the front bumper, as we bend our rear bumper in the course of backing into another car, is to move the car backward. We ought to have *some* sensitivity in picking out the things to pay attention to. But the theoretical stance demands that we believe we have picked out the "right," or "important," things to pay attention to.

(2) We also require, for a functionalist heuristic, that we pursue things as far as possible: Given the categories in terms of which we intend to carry on the analysis, we go on as long as we can. Again no guarantee of the success of the "functionalist" approach is with us—but granted the point of view, we can still see how well it "functions." Sometimes it becomes trivial—as when archeologists find axes ("which function to cut down trees"), and saws ("which function to saw up wood"), and bone harpoons ("which function to harpoon fish"). And then they find some things which no one can figure out what to do with, and say that these things "were used for ritual purposes." So one might be in danger of trivializing the approach by making it analytic.

Still, recognizing all these dangers, we would like to apply this kind of analysis to the existence of autotelic folk-models [3] in the society in which *we* live. That is, we want to consider, from such a point of view, objects which have no immediate obvious connection with our real (healthy) welfare, like (a) puzzles, (b) games of chance, (c) games of strategy, (d) aesthetic objects.

One might, incidentally, be surprised that we should try to put the

[3] By autotelic we mean (if we may be permitted to quote ourselves) (Anderson and Moore, 1960):

> . . . those cultural products that contain their own goals and sources of motivation: puzzles, games, aesthetic objects; such activities are in a sense cut off from serious and immediate problems of survival and welfare. As a heuristic principle for the application of formal methods in sociology, these products may be viewed as *folk-models*—i.e., models in the pre-scientific culture, with the help of which members of a society learn about and play at the workings of their society.

objects talked about in the books mentioned above into these four classes. But the classification does seem to fit, in the sense that any of these items could probably be put unambiguously into one group or the other. What can this tell us of the nature of beings that create and use such things? It seems apparent that the objects under consideration are "useless," in the sense that it is hard to see how they help in acquisition of food or clothing, but their prevalence induces us to believe that they must be valued for some reason; and since their value seems not to be utilitarian, we assume that it must be intrinsic.

Such inferences are of course risky, as Holmes and Watson occasionally learned from Moriarity. We cite the following anecdote as a warning to ourselves and others who try to infer the "intrinsic values" held by people or organisms from the presence of things of a particular kind in the environment.

There is a story, possibly apocryphal, of the distinguished British biologist, J. B. S. Haldane, who found himself in the company of a group of theologians. On being asked what one could conclude as to the nature of the Creator from a study of his creation, Haldane is said to have answered, "An inordinate fondness for beetles." [4]

Of course we should pay attention not only to the quantity of beetles, but also to their quality, peculiar standards of excellence, and *structure*. It is the *structure* of puzzles, games of chance, games of strategy, and aesthetic objects, in relation to the concept "personality," which will occupy us for the remainder of this paper.

We consider puzzles first.

Puzzles

After examining hundreds of puzzles, crossword puzzles, magic squares, Chinese puzzle boxes, and so on, it becomes clear that all of them have a successful terminal state, or goal. So at the very least the beings that operate them must be sensitive to goals; i.e., be able to recognize when they "win." But an amoeba is capable of recognizing a bit of matter when it bumps into it, and of engulfing the bit; so this condition is not sufficient for puzzle-solving.

We seem to be required to suppose also that the puzzle-solvers be capable of making a search; they must be sensitive to goals, but in a position to take active steps toward them as well. But there is an additional condition on the steps they have to take: They may not be random.

---

[4] "There are at the present time supposed to be . . . about one million described species of animals. Of these about three quarters are insects, of which a quite disproportionately large number are members of a single order, the Coleoptera" (Hutchinson, 1959).

Random search procedures may sometimes be successful for *certain* types of problems—sometimes in fact as likely to succeed as any. But it seems clear that there are no puzzles of any merit for which this approach would be likely to lead to a solution, in any reasonable period of time.

So it would seem that something else is also required, namely that human beings have some analytic sense, which they use in the course of carrying out their search. Some of the steps they take must be guided by, or suggested by, the goal they have in mind. One, so to speak, works backward, conceptually or actually, from the goal, as well as forward from the starting point. And the complexity of some goals in some puzzles is such as to lead to the conclusion that problems are broken up into subpuzzles.

So our first inference from the existence of puzzles is that people must be capable of the kind of behavior described above, which we will call *goal-directed*.

Our reasonings up to this point have been rough and ready, and we would not necessarily expect anyone to join us in these free-wheeling inferences. But having arrived at this point, we now feel it incumbent on us to give some sort of precise indication of what we have in mind. Fortunately there are certain instances of *goal-directedness* which make the whole matter quite clear, if only by example. One of the more important of these is the idea of *natural deduction* in formal logic, originated by Gentzen (1934) and Jaskowski (1934), and elaborated by a large number of contemporary logicians. These ideas are well understood from a formal point of view, and we will have occasion to describe them in detail in a moment. But first we would like to make a methodological point.

It seems to us that the existence of *formal* analyses of games of chance and strategy, such as those by Cardano (Ore, 1953), Pascal (1819), and von Neumann (1928), is the one aspect of the matter that gives our heuristic considerations some force. It is fun to pretend to be apprentices to Holmes and Watson, but in the absence of formal techniques for analyzing the results, we would feel that we were on a sleeveless errand. So we shall give immediately as a paradigm case a clear and precise analysis of a certain kind of goal-directed behavior, adding only that we consider this simply as an example. (The reason for our describing the example at length is that this seems to be a fairly esoteric topic. Later on, when we consider games of chance and games of strategy, we will count on the reader to be familiar with probability theory and game theory.)

One of the more perspicuous formulations of the theory of "natural deduction" is that of Fitch (1952). The problem involved may be exemplified as follows. We all recognize that if the proposition q follows from the proposition p, then if the proposition r follows from q, then the proposition r also follows from p; i.e., we recognize that implication is transitive. We can put the matter also in the form (roughly): "Suppose that p implies q. Then if q implies r, p also implies r." And if we let an arrow stand for the "if . . . then—" relation, the matter might easily be symbolized as:

$$(p \to q) \to ((q \to r) \to (p \to r))$$

Our logical intuitions seem to guarantee that this statement is true, but what would be involved in giving a "proof" that it was true? One of the principal contributions of Gentzen and Jaskowski was to see that the problem ought to be broken up into subproblems. We are in a certain situation (i.e., we have as "given" that p implies q), and we want to reach a certain goal (i.e., that if q implies r, then p does also). In Fitch's formulation of natural deduction, this fact is made explicit: we set up a proof with "$p-q$" as a hypothesis, and "$(q \to r) \to (p \to r)$" as a conclusion:

(1) | $p \to q$ hypothesis

.
.
.

(n) | $(q \to r) \to (p \to r)$ (putative) conclusion

So the problem of proving

$$(p \to q) \to ((q \to r) \to (p \to r))$$

is "reduced" to the problem of proving the consequent of the implication, given the antecedent. What we need to do, then, is to fill in steps from (1) to (n), which will make the proof valid.

But now we notice that the problem can again be broken into a subproblem: the (n)-th step is itself an implication, so we wish to see that we can get validly from $(q \to r)$ to $(p \to R)$ (of course under the assumption that $(p \to q)$). So we again break up the problem as follows:

(1) | $p \to q$ hypothesis

(2) | | $q \to r$ subhypothesis

.
.
.

$(n-1)$ | | $p \to r$ subconclusion

(n) | $(q \to r) \to (p \to r)$ conclusion

That is, the problem has again been reduced, in the sense that we have turned it into solving a subproblem, paying attention *both* to the fact that certain premises are given, *and* to the fact that given these premises we have a certain goal to reach. But now it is obvious that we can again break up the problem into a subproblem, since the conclusion $(n-1)$ is again an implication; i.e., under conditions (1) and (2), we wish to see that we can validly infer r from p. So we reorganize the problem as follows:

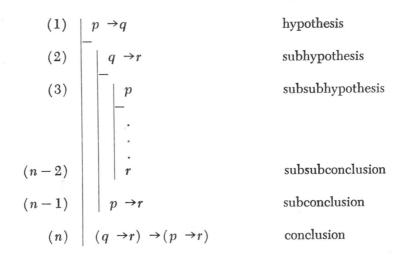

(1)	$p \to q$	hypothesis
(2)	$q \to r$	subhypothesis
(3)	p	subsubhypothesis
$(n-2)$	r	subsubconclusion
$(n-1)$	$p \to r$	subconclusion
(n)	$(q \to r) \to (p \to r)$	conclusion

The problem of getting from step (1) to step (n) has now been reduced to the problem of getting from steps (1)–(3) to step $(n-2)$ (and we remark, for later reference, that this reduction was effected by paying attention not only to where we were, but to where we were going: analysis of the goal was essential to performing the reduction). How are we to get, in the innermost proof, from p to r? In the system of Fitch (1952) (the pure implicational part of which is identical with Heyting's intuitionistic implicational calculus (1930), there is a rule called "reiteration," which allows us to import steps from outer proofs into inner ones. The intuitive idea is that once we have assumed (say) $p \to q$ (step (1)), then we can retain and use this assumption under any additional hypotheses we like; and the same would be true of step (2). Then importing steps (1) and (2) into the innermost proof by reiteration leads to:

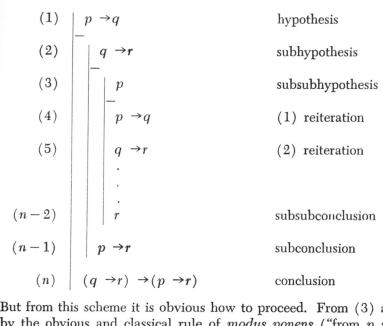

(1)	$p \to q$	hypothesis
(2)	$q \to r$	subhypothesis
(3)	p	subsubhypothesis
(4)	$p \to q$	(1) reiteration
(5)	$q \to r$	(2) reiteration
	.	
	.	
	.	
$(n-2)$	r	subsubconclusion
$(n-1)$	$p \to r$	subconclusion
(n)	$(q \to r) \to (p \to r)$	conclusion

But from this scheme it is obvious how to proceed. From (3) and (4), by the obvious and classical rule of *modus ponens* ("from p and if p and q, to infer q"), we reach q, and from q and step (5) we get r by the same rule; so that the final version of the proof is:

(1)	$p \to q$
(2)	$q \to r$
(3)	p
(4)	$p \to q$
(5)	$q \to r$
(6)	q
(7)	r
(8)	$p \to r$
(9)	$(q \to r) \to (p \to r)$
(10)	$(p \to q) \to ((q \to r) \to (p \to r))$

And the proof is completed.

This is not, needless to say, a full-scale exposition of Fitch's variant of natural deduction, for which we refer the reader to Fitch (1952). But examination of the example is probably sufficient for us to make a number of points about what we mean by *goal-directed* behavior.

As a summary of the points we feel this example *ought* to make clear, we cite the following from the experimental literature on problem solving (Carpenter, Moore, Snyder, and Lisansky, 1961):

A. Human beings frequently solve problems for which the likelihood of obtaining a solution by random or quasirandom trial and error is virtually zero.

B. Human beings frequently solve problems which satisfy A above without the aid of an algorithm. (An algorithm is a method which will produce solutions if they exist or, in the case of problems with no solutions, will indicate that there are none.)

C. Human beings are capable of behaving in a goal-directed way; i.e., they are able to guide their on-going activities in the light of the requirements imposed by the goal they seek.

D. Human beings, when faced with problems which satisfy A and B above and when behaving in a goal-directed way, are capable of elaborating an interrelated set of subgoals such that if the subgoals are achieved, the final goal can be reached.

E. Human beings, when faced with problems which satisfy A and B above and when behaving as stipulated in C and D above, can make use of resources immediately available to them (the "givens" of a problematic situation) in order to reason from the starting point to the goal.

And if any further evidence of the importance of *goal-directedness* (which involves the ability to work *backward,* in part, from the goal to be reached) is required, we offer the reader the following two mazes. The first is a simple Daedalian labyrinth, to be solved by the usual methods (and we suggest that the reader time himself):

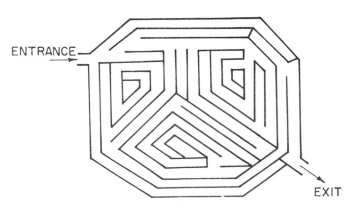

Fig. 6–1. Simple Daedalian labyrinth maze I.

We now suggest that the reader try the second maze (see Fig. 6–2, below), which is of the same sort; but before starting, please make a firm resolution to work *backward* from the exit as far as possible, while keeping the entrance in mind. Informal experiments with a variety of subjects indicate that the second procedure goes a good bit faster, and more pleasantly. This is somewhat like a very simple form of natural deduction—we work back from the goal to be achieved (again keeping in mind the starting point), and the problem (in this case) becomes completely trivial. One *could* easily get from entrance to exit by trial and error, and there would no doubt be some errors. But if one goes backward from exit to entrance, it seems to be *simply* a matter of trial, with no errors.

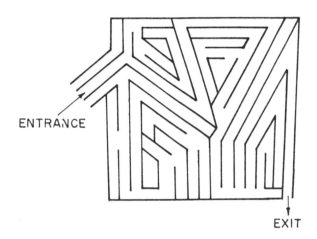

Fig. 6–2. Simple Daedalian labyrinth maze II.

We have tried in this section to explain what we mean by goal-directed behavior. Now this is in itself an interesting topic; one might spend a considerable amount of time getting clearer about the idea, and analyzing the formal properties of goal-directed activities. As we shall explain later, we think that many mathematicians have been involved in such analyses, for puzzles and other types of autotelic activities. But our purposes in this paper demand rather that we look for inferences which can be made about the "personalities" of beings which have such products as puzzles:

First, entities that can deal with puzzles must have at the very minimum something like a "data-tape." They must be able to take information in, process it, and have some output. But obviously this is not enough: They must also be able to recognize things in their environment. But machines and animals can do this, and neither machines nor animals have puzzles, in any significant social sense. So again this is not enough.

Another requirement is that the entities that deal with puzzles be able to envision themselves as *actors;* i.e., to think of themselves as being able to initiate chains of activity ("causal chains"). (This fact about human beings is perhaps at the bottom of "free-will" controversies.) But even this is not sufficient: They must also be able to envisage the consequences which such actions might have. In particular, they have to think about the consequences of such events as they might put into train, to *them.* That is, we would draw from the existence of puzzles the conclusion that earthlings must have some sense of *agency,* an ability to execute an action, or *do* something, together with some ability to evaluate the results for them (as successful or unsuccessful).

We now come (as promised) to games of chance.

Games of Chance

We begin by noticing that games of chance are universally (or almost universally) distributed, and that, in this sense, puzzles and games of chance are similar. And in the case of games of chance, we have a clear idea of the formal structure of the game: Every game of chance is a model of some part of probability theory. Indeed this is just how probability theory started; it was intended as a formal theory of games of chance. So we can now turn to another of our principal subjects of interest: What can we deduce about the nature of human personalities from the presence of games of chance?

One important difference between puzzles and games of chance is that in the latter case the causal nexus between input and output, at least for the players, is cut. This has nothing to do with questions about "determinism," or "free-will"; the point is not that there is *no* causal connection between the throw of the dice and the way in which they come up. The point is rather that the dice (or whatever) are designed in such a way that they lack means of control, so that the players are not *supposed* to be able to predict the outcome. It would be a pretty poor "game of chance" if it turned out that we could predict with accuracy how the dice were going to turn up.

It is clear that there are certain "chancy" elements in golf, but golf is not a game of chance. Similarly, we all recognize that there are "chancy" elements in craps, and craps *is* a game of chance. How do we decide whether or not to call a game a "game of chance"? Here is how we do it:

In the case of golf, it is clear that a practiced golfer has a large measure of control over what happens, partly because of the design of the equipment. He may miss the ball, or drive it into the water, but it is not a usual occurrence for him to hit it (by mistake) into the club-house. He can at least control matters so that, with a modicum of luck, the ball goes in the general direction of the green. But here the player has a lot of sensitivity (to the direction in which the green lies from him, the direction and force of the wind, and so on).

By contrast, with dice it would take an *enormous* amount of conscientious daily practice to throw sevens regularly, for human beings. We *could* imagine organisms with sufficient sensitivity and control to handle dice as well as human beings handle golf balls, but *we* can not do it, and judging from the general level of craftsmanship on earth, they can not do it either, or so the fact that craps is thought of as a game of chance would indicate. It would seem that shuffling cards, throwing dice, and spinning baccarat wheels are all sufficiently beyond the level of sensitivity and control of human beings, so that from *their* point of view, anyway, the causal connection between the actor and the outcome of his activity is cut. (At any rate, the last time we lost at a baccarat table, we did not feel that *we* had caused the outcome, and this is to be contrasted with the last time we flubbed *The New York Times* crossword puzzle.)

We mentioned earlier that in puzzle solving, a person had to think of himself in his capacity as an *agent,* and from that perspective to try to make things come out right. We also mentioned that he had to think of what the realization of the goal might mean to *him,* that is, he had to have some *value* in mind which would (or could) help him to assess the outcome of his activity.[5] We would now like to suggest that one of the "points" of games of chance, as opposed to puzzles, is that games of chance make clearer and more apparent the relation of agents to patients (adopting classical philosophical terminology). A "patient" is one to whom something is done: a recipient of an action. And we contend that in playing games of chance, we are setting afoot certain events of which the outcome to *us* is not known (though we do place a *value* on the outcome). In the same way that puzzles, as we have argued earlier, are models of problem solving, so games of chance are

---

[5] This point is hardly new. Santayana (1962) says: "Reason is as old as man and is prevalent as human nature; for we should not recognize an animal to be human unless his instincts were to some degree conscious of their *ends* and rendered his ideas in that measure relevant to conduct" (italics ours).

models of situations in which the outcomes to the patient are not predictable.[6]

Upshot: It is necessary for human beings, if they use both puzzles and games of chance, to be able to adopt at least two perspectives: that of *agent*, who might act, or set chains of events going; and that of *patient*, on whom actions initiated by themselves or others might impinge.

We therefore posit at least two systems of perspectives for human beings: (1) a system of *goals*, which are related to possibilities for action, and (2) a system of values, which are related to the possible outcomes of action for the actor. Each human being must be able to take both of these perspectives: goal-directed (or *actor*), and value-directed (or *patient*). These might coincide; we assume in some rat experiments that the goal is the food, and the value is eating it, so that rats eat the goal, with a result of value to the rat. But the existence of puzzles and games of chance may be an indication that human beings are a little more subtle, since one thinks of them as *reaching*, rather than eating, their goals.

Games of Strategy

So we are at least even with rats.

But so far as we know, rats have neither games of strategy, nor music, nor art, in any very significant sense. Since we have found both games of strategy and aesthetic objects on earth, we now pause to consider the differences between men and rats.

It is true that there are some psychological (we would prefer to say "philosophical") positions according to which there are no important differences between men and rats. Such we consider naive behaviorism to be (you give them some inputs; they give you some outputs). But we can tell men and rats apart very easily, and not *simply* because they do not look alike. There are, from the point of view we now wish to explain, more important differences. Being human requires not only goal

---

[6] The fact that we have, in games of chance, "cut off" the agent's efficacy, does not necessarily make it the case that the actor feels this to be true. We are all acquainted with the feeling on the part of dice players that, after the dice have been thrown, it somehow helps to "talk" to the dice. Even in the case of some games of skill, like billiards, or bowling, we are all acquainted with "body-English": the miraculous twist of the body that manages to get the last pin down, long after we have let go of the ball. And in the case of piano playing, the late Ernest Hutcheson (1907) used to advocate a kind of twisting movement of the elbow, after the key had been struck, and hence after anything the pianist did could affect the sound.

Our formal analyses of games of chance make it clear even to experienced crap players (who already half-suspected that it really does not help to talk to the dice) that psychokinesis is pretty implausible. But even when we are solely patients, we like to hope that we have *some* power as agents, and it seems to us that this feeling, or wish, accounts in part for "body-English."

sensitivity, together with goal directedness, but also some other abilities. So we move on to consider the third category of autotelic activities mentioned at the outset of this paper, namely, games of strategy.

We note first that nothing we have said so far is incompatible with a solipsistic stance. Even the silliest solipsist sees that *he* exists as an agent, and that things happen to *him* as a patient, even though he supposes that all the rest of us are figments of his imagination. But in the case of games of strategy, this attitude will not do. One *can* adopt it for games of strategy, but von Newmann's theory (1928) would indicate that one then would not be in the best position to win.

To play games of strategy seems to require that, in addition to the agent and patient perspectives, we must be able to "see ourselves as others see us" (Burns, 1786). That is, we must recognize that ladies, unlike lice, are analyzing us much as we are analyzing them. For lack of better terminology we entitle this third perspective the *reciprocal perspective*.

Implicit in the idea that I recognize, or take account of, the fact that there are other human beings who *also* have agent and patient perspectives, is the notion that they are looking at me as I am looking at them. I must be able to evaluate my own behavior, not only from my own agent-patient point of view, but also from the agent-patient points of view (as well as I can understand them) of others. When I act, I have to see (a) what possibilities are open for myself as agent, (b) what the consequences are likely to be for me as patient, and (c) what the consequences are likely to be for the other fellow as patient, and how he is likely to react to the situation as agent—and all this in the knowledge that he probably is doing the same thing to me. In this sense each of us is "represented" as a personality in each. We cannot get along socially without taking each other into account as *social* human beings.

At the very least it seems obvious that games of strategy give us opportunities for endless practice in viewing our actions from all three of these points of view, always recognizing the existence of other beings like ourselves. What the reciprocal perspective allows us to do is to reciprocate. In a play of the game of chess, for example, we reciprocate in just the sense that we take each other's actions into account, and guide our own behavior by considering not only what our knight can do, but what his queen can do, and what the outcome of the game will be.

It is hard to see how human beings could handle games of strategy, as we find them on earth, without being able to take account of the agent-patient perspectives of *others*. Some such ability would seem necessary for games of strategy. We might sometimes confuse the various "parts" of the personalities involved, or we may sometimes ignore a part of someone else—usually to our peril: If we do not sufficiently take into account another's role as agent or patient, we might lose a Knight which is pinned to the King. But unless we could keep these various perspectives "in perspective," it would seem difficult to understand how we could play at all.

It is said of certain Chinese philosophers that instead of arguing for the points they wish to make, they appeal incessantly to the authority of the Ancients. We hope that we will not be similarly accused if, in support of the distinction between Robinson Crusoe (*sans* Friday) (Defoe, 1719) and his puzzles, as against Adam (*cum* Eve) and social interaction, we quote von Neumann and Morgenstern (1952):

> Crusoe is given certain physical data (wants and commodities) and his task is to combine and apply them in such a fashion as to obtain a maximum resulting satisfaction. There can be no doubt that he controls exclusively all the variables upon which this result depends—say the allotting of resources, the determination of the uses of the same commodity for different wants, etc
>
> Thus Crusoe faces an ordinary maximum problem, the difficulties of which are of a purely technical—and not conceptual—nature, as pointed out.
>
> Consider now a participant in a social exchange economy. His problem has, of course, many elements in common with a maximum problem. But it also contains some very essential elements of an *entirely different nature*. He too tries to obtain an optimum result. But in order to achieve this, *he must enter into relations of exchange with others* . . .
>
> This kind of problem is nowhere dealt with in classical mathematics. We emphasize at the risk of being pedantic that this is *no conditional maximum problem*, no problem of the calculus of variations, of functional analysis, etc It arises in full clarity, even in the most "elementary" situations, e.g., when all variables can assume only a finite number of values [Italics ours].

The section from which we have just quoted seems to us to be one of the most perceptive discussions of the distinction between psycho logical and sociological questions in the literature; and the fact that *distinctively sociological* matters are under consideration was not over looked by the authors.

We have done our best to indicate why we believe that the agent patient ("output-input") way of viewing these curious beings we call "human," while *necessary* if we are thinking of puzzles and games of chance, is not *sufficient* if we are to imagine them as playing games of strategy. Games of strategy demand what we have called a "reciprocal perspective," namely, an ability to see our own behavior from the point of view of the agent and patient parts of the personalities of others.

But we may now ask again, as we have before: Are "human beings significantly different from rats in these respects? Do not animals also interact in the sense that they guide their own behavior in part by the behavior of their colleagues? Consider the following example of George Herbert Mead's (1934):

The act of each dog becomes the stimulus to the other dog for his response. There is then a relationship between these two; and as the act is responded to by the other dog, it, in turn, undergoes change. The very fact that the dog is ready to attack another becomes a stimulus to the other dog to change his own position or his own attitude. He has no sooner done this than the change of attitude in the second dog in turn causes the first dog to change his attitude. We have here a conversation of gestures. They are not, however, gestures in the sense that they are significant. We do not assume that the dog says to himself, "If the animal comes from this direction he is going to spring at my throat and I will turn in such a way." What does take place is an actual change in his own position due to the direction of the approach of the other dog [pp. 42–43].

Now it may be debatable whether or not a dog, in approaching a bone, actually *takes the role of* another dog doing the same. (We, along with Mead, think they do not, in any significant sense, but the matter hardly seems worth arguing, in view of the vagueness of the issues.) But one thing seems perfectly clear: One cannot imagine a dog saying, or even thinking, "Tut, tut, tut; that is not in accordance with the rules." We can of course imagine a dog being *surprised* by some unexpected event which "breaks rules" with which the dog is familiar; but the surprise is rather more like the surprise we feel at a sudden and unexpected earthquake, than the surprise we feel when a close friend suddenly slips a knife between our ribs. The former is a physical sort of surprise, and we are all partially prepared for those. But the latter are social surprises, and are available to dogs only in the same metaphorical sense that household pets are "people."

We have referred to the earthquake surprise as "physical," and the being-knifed-by-a-friend surprise as "social," and, though we are not very clear as to what this distinction involves, we will still try to give an account of it.

It does not make much sense to say that the earth "is not supposed to" (in the sense of "ought not") quake. We can all see that it would be nicer if the earth did not quake, or if volcanoes did not erupt; things like this hurt people. But if one were to say "volcanoes ought not erupt," in any sense which involved adherence to rules on the part of volcanoes, it would be hard to attach any sense to the utterance. It would be odd if, after the burial of Pompeii, someone were to shake a finger at Mt. Vesuvius and say in a severe voice, "Sceleste, sceleste, Vesuvius!"

It *would* be appropriate, however, to treat our treacherous ex-friend in this way. *All of us* can see what "Et tu, Brute," means, once the story and the Latin are explained. What it means is simply that friends are not supposed to do that kind of thing to one another. Which is to say that the notion of "friendship" involves conducting oneself according to certain *rules*. (We do not specify these for reasons which ought to be obvious: The problem is too difficult.)

Whatever feelings the treachery of our *own* friend in these circumstances might engender, it seems perfectly clear that all of us can see how Caesar might have felt—not about the wound, that is, but the treachery. And note that this understanding really has nothing to do with Caesar, Brutus, or ourselves (ourselves viewed as agents, patients, or from reciprocal perspective of anyone we know). We could substitute "Caesar" for "Brutus," and "Brutus" for "Caesar" throughout the whole play, without losing anything except such historical accuracy as the play has. We seem to be able to look at the matter, thinking not so much about Caesar or Brutus, or ourselves as individuals, but rather of the *role* of a friend, and the obligations it lays on anyone whatever, including ourselves. We are by such considerations led to postulate the existence of a fourth (and, we are happy to say, final) social human perspective, namely, that of an umpire—a detached standpoint from which we decide whether rules have or have not been broken.

It is important to see that the umpire's perspective can be applied to our own behavior as well as to that of others. When so applied, it goes under the name "conscience." When our conscience bothers us, it is, we claim, because we are able to look at our own actions, not only from the point of view of ourselves as agents, or patients, or from the reciprocal point of view of other individuals, but also from the point of view of a third party, who was really not there—namely, from the perspective of the umpire,[7] who is watching to see that the play goes fairly. (The fact that we *can* take this objective, impersonal, rule oriented attitude toward our *own* behavior as well as that of others, may have some connection with the traditional theological view that "God is watching us all the time." Cf., a delightful passage in Kaufmann (1957) in which there is a little girl who can accept this dogma as regards most moral matters, but feels on going to bed that He is a Peeping Tom.

Aesthetic Objects

We have said that among the four kinds of folk-models mentioned at the outset, puzzles tend to emphasize the role of an *agent*, games of chance tend to emphasize the role of a *patient*, and thus far games of strategy have suggested the *reciprocal perspective* and the *umpire* point of view. This would seem to leave our fourth category of folk

---

[7] The term "umpire" is of some interest. It derives from old French, *nompe* from *non* not, and *per* peer or equal. That is, the umpire's role is that of a third party and not that of a fellow interactor. (*Umpire*, without initial *n-*, arose through the incorrect division of *a numpire* as *an umpire*.)

models, namely aesthetics, dangling. What are we to say about aesthetics *vis-a-vis* the four perspectives we have been considering?

From a formal point of view, our speculations on this matter will be on much more shaky ground, we feel, than were those about the relations among puzzles, games of chance, and games of strategy (as folk-models) on the one hand, and serious matters on the other. Still, we would like to make some suggestions along similar lines for aesthetics as well. But we do want to emphasize that, except for certain highly specialized examples such as those of Schillinger (1948) and Kraehenbuhl and Coons (1959), we have nothing in the way of *formal* analyses to support our conjectures.

We are inclined to guess that all the elements required for games of strategy are present when we contemplate or enjoy aesthetic objects, but again that the emphasis is different. When we watch a performance of Sheridan's *The Rivals* (1775), two principal things seem to be involved: (1) our perspectives as patient to the spectacle, from which we feel enjoyment, or illumination, or any of the emotions appropriate to appreciation (or lack of it) of a play; and (2) our perspectives as referees, or umpires; i.e., as critics, who understand in an impersonal way the rules for enacting *The Rivals,* the rules for competent acting, and who can tell whether or not the affair is coming off properly—with the appropriate emotions of consternation, fright, or delight.

It seems clear, at any rate, that our perspectives as agents are involved in aesthetic responses in a very minimal way, unless we happen to be the performers, or we are on a showboat, where hissing the villain is good form. And it seems equally clear that the reciprocal perspective —looking at ourselves from the point of view of another person—is involved at best vicariously. But the way in which the performance is carried on (that is, the extent to which performers follow the rules, where rules are looked at from a referee's point of view) seems to be of much more importance in encounters with aesthetic objects.

Some Extrapolations

Before extending, let's recapitulate briefly: In addition to the "data-tape" mentioned earlier, we think there are four parts or pieces in each fully developed human personality, each part bearing an important relation to an autotelic folk-model. (1) Our perspective as *agent* is emphasized in puzzles; (2) our perspective as *patient* is emphasized in games of chance; (3) our *reciprocal perspective,* the ability to appreciate other human beings as "like us," is emphasized in games of strategy; and (4) our perspective as *umpire* is emphasized in aesthetic objects.[8] We also wish to make it clear that we do *not* believe that, e.g., no rules are involved in games of chance. Of course they are. And similarly with the other categories: Each is involved in each. But it does seem to make sense to try to see what distinguishes these various types of autotelic activity, and these differences of emphasis seem to us to be, if not the whole story, at least a partial account.

So, again as apprentices to Holmes and Watson, we now begin to fool around with the objects we have found. We begin, for example, by *playing* some games of strategy. And our first discovery in doing so is that there is one aspect of the matter which thus far has been left entirely out of account: to wit, our interest in winning the game.

What kinds of beings must these earthlings be, if they can care at all who wins? The notions of *caring*, or having feelings, or being *involved* (in the sense of many contemporary existentialists) presuppose some system of *affects* (in the sense of many contemporary psychologists). On this point we have three remarks to make:

(1) It is apparent that some system of feelings and emotions (hopes, wishes, strivings, disappointments) must be posited as an integral part of the structure of the personalities of these queer beings we are studying—at least it is hard to imagine how otherwise they would take any interest in folk-models at all. Why should one try to solve a puzzle, or play a game, or be able to enjoy an aesthetic experience, if only robots were involved? It would make no sense to suppose that our models would be of interest to beings incapable of joy, or anguish, or sorrow; these feelings and emotions require the agent, patient, and reciprocal perspectives at least. And since we have found these perspectives in the folk-models, we would hope that the requisite feelings and emotions would be available too.

And though we would not want to push the matter too far, it seems that many of the notions we use in considering sensibility and sentiment are closely related to one or another of the various perspectives we have been considering. Feelings of confidence, for example, or of frustration, seem to have to do primarily (though not exclusively) with the agent perspective. Fear and anxiety, on the other hand, seem more closely related to the patient perspective, from which I look at matters in the light of how they might affect me. Of course all these terms are slippery: We can *have confidence in* others (a matter belonging rather to the reciprocal perspective: "I can trust him not to hurt me or mine"), but

---

[8] We are pleased to note that the four perspectives which we have just distinguished correspond closely to the "I," "me," "significant other," and "generalized other," of Mead (1934). The fact that from a different point of departure we came out at about the same place that Mead did makes us feel better about Mead and ourselves.

this is clearly not the same as being confident of our own powers. Similarly, we can have fear for the well-being of others (again a matter of looking at the situation from the point of view of another person, namely our own reciprocal perspective), but again this is not the same as fearing for ourselves. We can also suffer embarrassment for others, realizing that someone else has made a *faux pas*, but tactfully affecting not to notice the fact.

Though the one-to-one correspondence between our vast variety of names for emotional states and the perspectives from which they are viewed (which one would like in a nice formal theory of the topic) obviously fails to hold as far as English is concerned, it still seems plausible to think that feelings are more or less closely connected with the perspectives we have been considering. (And we pause momentarily to point out that no one can prove us wrong in this conjecture; "more or less" leaves us too far up in the air to be shot down.)

We do not mean simply to be arguing, as one might think, that the various roles played by Pooh-Bah (Gilbert, 1885) could not be played by a robot. The point is rather that we *do* take serious things seriously, and that the emotions involved in serious social relations are really serious. But we also find occasions, as in the autotelic folk-models which suggested this classification to us in the first place, where the perspectives are scaled down to the point where we can play with them, and understand them better, without losing life, limb, or tempers.

(2) Now in view of the fact that so much of the literature on personality structure has been concerned with emotional attitudes, we can well imagine ourselves being attacked on the ground that we do not sufficiently recognize the emotional side of human beings. For this reason we are moved to make a second point about the emotional systems which we believe human beings have. *All* the perspectives are "run through" this emotional network in the course of deciding how to behave, or even in the course of acting "spontaneously" and without deliberation. As we hoped to make clear in the previous paragraphs, *each* of the perspectives is involved in our emotional reactions to events: We might even have *Angst*, for example, about whether the umpire may die, a matter which would affect our future actions as agents, our future passions as patients, and our relations with those whom we try to understand from our own reciprocal perspective.

(3) And if someone were to ask us what relation the feeling-emotion system bears to the more cognitive and "cold calculational" (or as we would prefer to say "nice warm logical") aspects of the folk-models we have been considering, we would reply by making three comments:

(a) We do not know, exactly.

(b) Still, there must be something like an adaptation-level system which enables us to scale down the emotions and feelings to the point where we can play poker without wanting to kill our fellow players in order to take away their money.

(c) In spite of any differences of detail that we may have with the paper by our colleague Professor William Bevan (also in this volume), we think something like a pooling mechanism is at the bottom of the relation mentioned under (3) above. Organisms have histories, and we can all recognize that a duchess might be as disappointed at a failure to receive an invitation to have tea with the queen as a chimney sweep might be at losing an opportunity to be the queen's sweep.

Summary

In this paper we have attempted to make some substantive points about what we take to be the structure of human personality. To re-capitulate, there are at least six parts to a fully developed human personality (i.e., *functional* parts, not physiological entities): a data-tape, four systems of perspectives, and a feeling-emotion system. In our view of the matter, incoming information is routed through each perspective and is continually checked against the system of emotions. We came to this view of the structure of human personality by reasoning backward from the properties of certain cultural objects—folk models—to characteristics of their users. We admit freely that this is a speculative adventure. We also admit that we have not dealt adequately with two notions of importance for us—the concept of a cultural object, and the idea of a model, especially a folk-model.

As regards the latter notion, we have in mind something closely analogous to the usage of the word "model" in the literature on logic, though we have not ourselves spelled the matter out in great detail. We do promise, however, to try to clarify the notion of culture in another article which belongs to the series (Anderson, 1958; Anderson, 1962; Anderson and Moore, 1957; Anderson and Moore, 1960; Anderson and Moore, 1962; Moore, 1961; Moore, 1962; Moore and Anderson, 1960a, 1960b, 1960c; Moore and Anderson, 1962), of which this paper is a member. In this series we have been trying to outline a point of view from which certain cultural aspects of human behavior can be understood; we, like Santayana, (1962), are trying to find the reason in common sense. The fact that we have been anticipated by Mean, Plato, and Simmel does not bother us much.

Chapter 7

A Conception of, and Experiments with, "Trust" as a Condition of Stable Concerted Actions [1]

In accounting for the persistence and continuity of the features of concerted actions, sociologists commonly select some set of stable features of an organization of activities and ask for the variables that contribute to their stability. An alternative procedure would appear to be more economical: to start with a system with stable features and ask what can be done to make for trouble. The operations that one would have to perform in order to produce and sustain anomic features of perceived environments and disorganized interaction should tell us something about how social structures are ordinarily and routinely being maintained.

The Point of View

Parsons' (1953) decision to incorporate the entirety of common culture into the superego has as its obvious interpretive consequence that the way a system of activities is organized means the same thing as the way its organizational characteristics are being produced and maintained. Structural phenomena such as income and occupational distributions, familial arrangements, class strata, and the statistical properties of language are emergent products of a vast amount of communicative, perceptual, judgmental, and other "accommodative" work whereby persons, in concert, and encountering "from within the society" the

[1] This investigation was supported by a Senior Research Fellowship SF-81 from the Public Health Service. Particular gratitude is due to Drs. Egon Bittner, Aaron V. Cicourel, Erving Goffman, Henry W. Riecken, Jr., Edward R. Rose, and Eleanor B. Sheldon for their generosity with criticisms and suggestions.

environments that the society confronts them with, establish, maintain, restore, and alter the social structures that are the assembled products of temporally extended courses of action directed to these environments as persons "know" them. Simultaneously these social structures are the conditions of persons' concerted management of these environments.[2]

This conception may be restated as several plausible assumptions upon which the program described here is predicated.

1. The organizational and operational features of concerted actions are importantly determined by whatever the personnel of the system treat as actual and potential displays of perceivedly normal events of their interpersonal environments and relationships of interaction.

2. A person responds not only to the perceived behavior, feelings, motives, relationships, and other socially organized features of life around him, but more relevantly for the purposes of this program, he is responsive as well to the perceived normality of these events. By the "perceived normality" of events I refer to the *perceived formal* features that environing events have for the perceiver as instances of a class of events, i.e., *typicality;* their "chances" of occurrence, i.e., *likelihood;* their *comparability* with past or future events; the conditions of their occurrences, i.e., *causal texture;* their place in a set of means-ends relationships, i.e., *instrumental efficacy;* and their necessity according to a natural or moral order, i.e., *moral requiredness.*

3. On the occasions of discrepancies between expected and actual events, persons engage in assorted perceptual and judgmental work whereby such discrepancies are "normalized." By "normalized" I mean that perceivedly normal values of typicality, comparability, likelihood, causal texture, instrumental efficacy, and moral requiredness are restored.

4. The occasions of "nasty surprise" as well as the work of normalizing do not occur either idiosyncratically or independent of the group's routinized social structures. Such occasions and such work not only are determined by but are determinative of routinized structures.

5. The persistence, continuity, reproducibility, standardization, uniformity of social structures—i.e., their "stability" over time and turnovers of acting personnel—are emergent products of the perceivedly normal values of interpersonal events that members of a group seek through their adjustive activities to maintain.

[2] This doctrine is illustrated in the delightful story by Robert M. Coates, "The Law" (1947). One fine spring evening the Manhattan entrance to the Triborough Bridge is jammed with cars for the length of Manhattan Island. Drivers consult each other to learn the reason for the jam but no one knows. Says Coates, that was the night "the law of averages failed." On that night every car owner in Manhattan decided it was a perfect night for a drive to Long Island.

6. The reconciliation of the stable features of social structures on the one hand with the treatment of interpersonal environments "seen from within" on the other is recommended with the use of two theorems that Parson's systematic theory (1961) explicates: (a) The social structures *consist* of institutionalized patterns of normative culture; (b) the stable features of the social structures as assemblies of concerted actions are guaranteed by motivated compliance with a legitimate order.

Our task is to learn what it takes to produce for members of a group that has stable features perceived environments of events that are "specifically senseless." This term, borrowed from Max Weber (1946), refers to events which are perceived by group members as being atypical, causally indeterminate, and arbitrary in occurrence, without a relevant history or future, means character, or moral necessity.

Ideally speaking, i.e., in terms consistent with such a theory of social organization as Durkheim's (1951), the behavorial states accompanying perceived environments with such properties would consist of the total cessation of activity. Short of this ideal terminal state, one should encounter the behaviors of bewilderment, uncertainty, internal conflict, massive incongruity, psychosocial isolation, acute general anxiety, loss of identity, and various symptoms of depersonalization. In short, one should encounter what Paul Schilder (1951), in a brilliant phrase, referred to as "an amnesia for social structure." Disorganized features of the social structures should vary accordingly. The severity of these effects should vary directly with the enforceable commitments of persons, i.e., with the conditions that guarantee motivated compliance to a legitimate order. Such a commitment appears from within as a grasp of and subscription to the "natural facts of life in society." Because such "natural facts of life," i.e., common culture, are described from a member's point of view as a world known and taken for granted in common with other members, the severity of these effects should vary independent of personality characteristics, as they are conceived and sought by most of the conventional personality assessment devices.

In pursuing the program on which this paper is based I have proceeded under the notion that in the course of routinized actions, anomic states are transient, of short duration, and are irregularly distributed through a person's biography of interactions as well as among social structures. I seek the operations that will increase and regularize the frequency and duration of such states so that their occurrence can be convincingly detected with the crude methods of immediate observation.

What can we do to a scene of events to produce for a person a situation in which he is unable to "grasp" what is going on?

Operating with the Concept of "Trust"

I shall exercise a theorist's preference and say that meaningful events are entirely and exclusively events in a person's behavioral environment, with this defined in accordance with Hallowell's (1955) usage. Hence there is no reason to look under the skull since nothing of interest is to be found there but brains. The "skin" of the person will be left intact. Instead questions will be confined to the operations that can be performed upon events that are "scenic" to the person. To aid in locating events that must be altered to produce anomic states, I have conceived the phenomenon of trust. I shall begin by consulting games. From an analysis of their rules, the concept of the "constitutive order of events" of a game will be developed. Compliance to this order will be developed as a general definition of the term "trust." I shall then support this concept by presenting some findings from the game of ticktacktoe. After some appropriate criticisms of the use of games, I shall extend what we learn about how trust is a condition for "grasping" the events of games to the case of how trust is a condition for "grasping" the events of daily life. Preliminary results will then be cited in support and criticism of this conception.

Basic Rules as Definitions of the Constituent Events of a Game. The stable situation I want to start with is a game. A game is selected because the basic rules of play serve each player as a scheme for recognizing and interpreting the other players' as well as his own behavioral displays as events of game conduct. The basic rules of a game define the situations and normal events of play for persons who seek to act in compliance with them (a *player*).

If the rules of any given game, e.g., baseball, chess, or any other described in a book of games, are examined, one set of rules of that game can be discriminated from all the others by the fact that they exhibit the following three properties.

(1) From the standpoint of a player, out of alternative territories of play, numbers of players, sequences of moves, and the like, they frame a set that the player expects to choose regardless of his desires, circumstances, plans, interests, or consequences of choice either to himself or to others.

(2) The player expects that the same set of required alternatives are binding upon the other player as are binding upon him.

(3) The player expects that, as he expects the above of the other person, the other person expects it of him.

Call these three properties *constitutive expectancies*.

Some Definitions and Remarks

1. These three properties constitute as a set the rules they are attached to. Call the set of such rules *basic rules*. Illustrative basic rules of ticktacktoe are: Play is conducted on a three by three matrix by two players who move alternatively. The first player makes a mark in one of the unoccupied cells. The second player, in his turn, places his mark in one of the remaining unoccupied cells. And so on. The term "ticktacktoe player" refers to a person who seeks to act in compliance with these possible events as constitutively expected ones.

2. It is possible to assign constitutive expectancies to any number of players, sequences of moves, territories of play, and the like. I shall refer to the fact that the three constitutive expectancies are assigned to some particular set of possible events and not assigned to others as the *constitutive accent* of the events to which they are assigned.

3. Call the *related* set of possible events to which the constitutive expectancies are assigned the *constitutive order of events* of the game.

4. Von Neumann and Morgenstern (1947) point out that a game is defined by listing its basic rules. In our terms, a game is defined by listing its basic rules to which constitutive expectancies are attached. In addition to the basic rule, there are at least three other features which are necessary to describe the game as a normative order or discipline: (a) an "et cetera" provision, (b) an enumerated set of rules of *preferred* play, and (c) an enumerated set of "game-finished" conditions. Beyond these, there are two further features which describe a game as people actually play it: (a) the "validity" of this discipline, i.e., the likelihood that persons will act in motivated compliance with the discipline, and (b) the non-game conditions which, whatsoever they consist of, determine the likelihood of motivated compliance.

5. The constitutive accent can be removed from one set of possible events and assigned to another. This operation produces a new game. For example, a basic rule of ticktacktoe provides that the first occurrence of "three in a row" is a win and terminates play. If this rule is changed to provide as a constitutive possibility that three in a row only on or after a player's *fourth* move is a win (and if provision is made that players use only three marks which they may erase one at a time to move to an unoccupied cell), the resulting game is known as "noughts and crosses." Similarly, in chess the constitutive accent is assigned to the possibility that the pieces retain their identical colors throughout play. By providing that at the time of a player's choosing a preselected combination of the opponent's pieces can be declared to have changed colors, F. R. Kling invented "Chess With Traitors" (1958).

6. The rules that remain after basic rules have been recognized are

exclusively either one or the other of two types. Either they are *rules of preferred play* or they are *game-furnished conditions*. Rules of preferred play are discriminated from basic rules by the feature that elections of alternative territories, sequences of play, number of pieces, number of players—i.e., *any* possibilities, including those that might in "another game" be constitutive of that game—are treated as within the player's discretion to comply with or not in accordance with whatever definitions of "correct procedure" he might invoke, as for example considerations of efficiency, efficacy, aesthetic preference, conventional play, precedented play, traditional play, and the rest. The possibilities that preference rules can deal with are provided by basic rules. For example, that any of the pawns or knights but no other pieces may be moved on White's first move in chess is provided by the basic rules of chess. But which among these alternatives the player can choose is a matter of the player's election. Apart from the fact that preference rules must deal with possibilities that basic rules provide, definitions of correct play provided by preference rules are in no way necessarily controlled by the basic rules.

While basic rules furnished the definitive criteria of legal play, rules of preferred play furnish the definitive criteria of effective, or aesthetic, or conventional, or for that part, poor play if the player seeks to play poorly. The decisions that the player makes *must* satisfy the basic rules and *will* satisfy *some* set of preference rules. It goes without saying that the set of preference rules may consist of very odd mixtures of efficacy, aesthetic correctness, conventionality, and the like. Basic and preference rules serve as conditions that a player's elections either must or will satisfy.

In addition to these conditions, there exist a number of further conditions that his decisions must satisfy. These additional conditions, however, are *not* criteria which define the correctness of a decision, nor are they provided for by the basic or preference rules. Nevertheless, it is the case that of necessity a player's decisions will be constrained by them. These conditions have the following features: (a) they describe characteristic features of play in the game; (b) they are independent of the chances of a player's success or failure in the game; (c) they are invariant to the changing states of the game in the sense that they hold as conditions for his decisions for every situation in which a decision is to be made; (d) they hold insofar but only insofar as the player treats the basic rules of the game as maxims of his own as well as his opponent's conduct, which is to say they hold insofar and only insofar as the person refers his and other players' actions for definition and interpretation to the normative order of possible events defined by the basic rules of the game.

A set of game-furnished conditions corresponds specifically to each set of basic rules of a game. Game-furnished conditions are illustrated in chess by the fact that every situation of play is one of perfect information or that every present state of the game is altered in an all or none fashion by an actual play and never by a supposed play. Kriegsspiel contrasts with chess in these and other respects, e.g., its situations of play are ones of imperfect information; a present state of the game can be altered by a supposed play.[3]

7. For the theorist, the interpretive rule is proposed that any and all game events are members of the set of constitutive or of preferential possibilities, or of the set of game-furnished conditions. To say that the constitutive accent is "removed" from one set of events is synonymous with the statement that the events have been moved to the set of preferential possibilities. Conversely, to say that events have been removed from the set of preferential possibilities necessarily entails that they have become members of the set of constitutive possibilities. The case where all possibilities are constitutive possibilities such that the set of preferential possibilities is an empty one defines a ceremonialized game.[4] To speak of the set of constitutive possibilities as an empty set and simultaneously to intend a game is formal nonsense.[5]

8. Say of persons, in that their treatments of interpersonal environments—whether they be game environments or otherwise—are governed by constitutive expectancies, that they *trust* each other.

9. The concept of trust is related to the concept of perceivedly normal environments as follows. To say that one person "trusts" another means that the person seeks to act in such a fashion as to produce through his action or to respect as conditions of play actual events that accord with normative orders of events depicted in the basic rules of play. Alterna-

[3] These contrasts are illustrative, not definitive. The topic of game-furnished conditions is treated definitively in a series of the author's unpublished works, e.g., Chapter 5 in *Parson's Primer* and Chapter 6 in *Essays in Ethnomethodology*.

[4] The conditions of a ceremonialized game of chess would be satisfied if two persons, A and B, agreed to play and played as follows. Prior to play A and B agree that when A moves, e.g., KP–K4, B will move QP–Q3; then A will move QP–Q4, to which B will reply KP–K4; after which A will move X, and B will reply Y; then A moves such and such and B in return moves so and so, and so on until a play of the game shall have been constructed by agreement. A and B then agree to treat the agreed program as a set of basic rules. The only contingency that would remain would consist of whether or not their actual play abided by the agreement. Responsive readings in church resemble a ceremonialized game.

[5] By formal nonsense is meant that one can speak of a game consisting of no constitutive rules, but the result is a juxtaposition of terms each of which has a meaning in its own right, but the object that is intended through these terms as specifications of the object cannot be grasped. One can speak similarly of a round square, or a triangle whose angles sum to more than three straight angles, or a refrigerator that has no capacity, or a sound that has intensity and amplitude but no duration with identical results.

tively stated, the player takes for granted the basic rules of the game as a definition of his situation, and that means of course as a definition of his relationships to others.

Perceivedly Normal Environments of Game Events

Several further features of basic rules must now be mentioned in order to show that the events depicted in the basic rules of play (i.e., the constitutive order of game events) provide the person who seeks to act in compliance with these basic rules the definition of normal events of game play.

1. The events depicted by the basic rules are categorical possibilities. As such, they define the environment of game events as a domain of possible observables which, in the same manner that the events of the idealized experiment, as Feller (1950) uses the concept in his discussion of a sample space, consist of rules of relevance whereby essential features of particular actual observations are recognized. The events that are provided by basic rules are intended events such that they delineate the essential uniformity in all actual observations that may be brought under the jurisdiction of intended events as particular cases of the intended events.

2. As categorical possibilities, the events provided by the basic rules have the property of remaining invariant to the changing actual states of the game.

3. Being invariant to actual courses of game play, these expected uniformities serve as standards, i.e., as definitions of correct play. Thereby they serve as the basis for recognizing the strange move, the move that is "outside the game."

4. The matter of bringing actual observations under the jurisdiction of intended observations provided by the basic rules consists of the procedures for justifying the claim that actual-observed-appearances-of-an-object and the-object-that-is-intended-by-the-particular-actual-appearances correspond. The problematic character of this correspondence consists in providing the rules whereby it may be decided for the two, standing as they do in a relation of signification, i.e., a sign relationship, what this relationship of signification consists of. For example, is the sign relationship one of mark, sign, symbol, index, icon, document, trope, gloss, analogy, or evidence? Or is the actual observation not an event "in the game" in the first place?

The basic rules provide the solution to the problem of jurisdiction by providing themselves the meaning of "adequate recognition" of actual appearances as recognized appearances-of-the-object. In that basic rules specify the domain of game-possible actions, they define the

domain of "game-possible actions" to which the variable of "mere behaviors" [6] can be assigned. Basic rules frame the set of possible events
of play that observed behaviors can signify.

To illustrate, bridge players respond to each other's actions as bridge
events, not behavioral events. They do not treat the fact that the other
player withdraws a card from his hand and places it on the table as the
event "putting down a pasteboard" or "effecting a translation of position
of a card." Instead, through the translation of the card's position the
player signalizes that "he has played the ace of spades as the first card
of the trick." From the player's point of view the question "What can
really happen?" is for him correctly decided in terms of basic rules.

5. Each different set of basic rules defines a different domain of possible game events that an otherwise identical behavioral appearance can
be set in correspondence to.

6. From the player's point of view, not only "What can happen?" but
"What happened?" is correctly decided as far as the player is concerned,
in terms of these rules. Basic rules serve as the terms in which the
character of the events of play not only *can* be recognized but as far as
players are concerned must *necessarily* be recognized. More generally
they serve as the set of presuppositions—termed by Schutz (1945) as a
player's "scheme of interpretation and expression"—whereby the player's
own behavior, as well as the behavior of the other person, is identified by
the player as a *datum of action*.

This property may be stated in its general form as the following
theorem. A sign correctly corresponds to a referent in terms of the
assumed constitutive order that itself defines "correct correspondence."

What holds for sign-referent relationships holds for the relationships
of term and word, term and concept, phoneme and lexeme, word and
meaning, behavior and action, sentence and proposition, appearance and
object. All of these pairs are formally equivalent. A behavior signifies
an action in terms of an assumed normative order.

The last several points may be summarized as follows: The basic
rules provide a behavior's *sense* as an action. They are the terms in
which a player decides whether or not he has correctly identified "What
happened?" "Subjective meaning" is "attached" to a behavior in terms
of these rules.

Insofar as a player refers for the correctness of his decisions about
the meanings of rules to other players as meanings known in common
with them, we may speak of the objective character of rules and thereby
of the *objective* character of game events. Insofar as a player refers

---

[6] By "mere behaviors" I refer to all events of overt conduct regarded under the
auspices of their definition as "translations of positions of an entity with respect to
a system of physical coordinates."

for the correctness of his decisions about the meanings of rules to his or
the other players' personal interpretations of the rules, we may, as Kaufman does (1944), speak of the *subjective* character of the rules and
thereby of the subjective character of game events.

7. For the person who seeks to comply with the constitutive order
of play, an action—and it need only be *one*—that breaches the basic
rules is incongruous in a particular way and its *occurrence violates the
game as an order of activities.*

(A) The action that occurs contrary to that prescribed by the basic
rules of the game is specifically senseless, i.e., it acquires the *perceived*
properties of unpredictability, arbitrary occurrence, indeterminateness,
lacking causal texture, means character, and moral necessity. We say
of the person whose behavioral environment of events shows these properties that he "is confused." Behaviorally, we should expect him to
act in the fashion described at the beginning of this chapter.

(B) It is a property of the action that breaches the constitutive
expectancy that the player cannot recognize the action without altering
the "constitutive accent" that is placed upon the events of play, i.e.,
without making them preferential. For example, consider that the
constitutive order of sequential play in ticktacktoe is A,B,A,B, . . .
Player B might move A,B,B,B. When the constitutive order provides
that players move in the sequence, A,B,A,B,A . . . , the expectancy is
provided that the normative sequence is followed and the actual sequence is produced irrespective of the player's motives, desires, calculations of self-interest and the like. The player who moves "out of turn,"
i.e., A,B,B . . . , presents to his opponent the incongruous possibility
that the sequence, A,B,A,B,A . . . , is within the player's discretion.

(C) The disorder consists in this: The action which breaches the
basic rule invites treatment as constitutive of the order of the game. But
assigning to it a constitutive accent is synonymous with transforming the
rules of the game. Sociologically speaking, it invites a redefinition of
"social reality" or, alternatively, of "normal play."

8. The physical stimulus field may be regular and definite, yet the
field of game events may be without sense.

A distinction between ambiguity and senselessness may help the
point. By saying that the field of *game events* becomes ambiguous, I
mean that the player's distribution of bets as to "what happened" over
the set of alternative possibilities becomes more equiprobable.

By the state of senselessness of the field of game events is meant that
the player is without a frame of possibilities to which the physical
stimulus field may be decided to correspond. In the case of an ambiguous field of game events, the person is unable to decide which among a
set of alternatives a person meant in a move or an utterance. In a sense-

less field, the person, although he hears an utterance that has been de-
livered in clear and correct English, does not recognize it as an English
sentence. What holds for an utterance holds for any behavior, since
the sign-referent relationship that holds for the relationship between
utterances and propositions holds as well for the relationship between
behavior and action.

The difference between ambiguity and senselessness may be illustrated
in the following procedure. Subjects were invited to play ticktacktoe.
After the subject made his move (X), the experimenter made his move
(O), thus:

In some cases the subjects responded by rebuking the experimenter:
"Don't be sloppy. Put your mark in the square." In other cases, however, the subjects responded with "What game are you playing?"

9. If the player adheres to the constitutive order of the game, the
anomic effects of breaching a basic rule are not attenuated by the
player's knowledge that a basic rule has been breached.

10. Regardless of what the rule specifically provide as possible events,
whether they specify nine cells in ticktacktoe, sixty-four positions in
chess, five cards to a poker hand, hidden boards in kriegspiel, etc., the
three definitive properties of basic rules are invariant to the actual content of the rules.

There are two important consequences of this feature. (a) With
respect to the question of what must be done to produce confusion, it
permits us to recognize in different fields of game events, i.e., in different games, those events whose breach will produce identical consequences, hopefully, confusion. (b) It is a condition of confusion that
the parties be reciprocally identified members of the same community,
that is, that they treat each other as persons presumably bound by the
same constitutive order of actions, i.e., "playing the same game."

11. The set, "All the basic rules," defines a game. This property yields
an important consequence as well as an important task. (a) The important consequence is that constitutive structures are integral to *all*
game events. (b) The important incomplete task is that of investigating
the logical properties of the set, "All the basic rules" of a game.

Further remarks are needed about each of these points.

(A) *The important consequence.* The conception that constitutive
structures are integral to all game events differs from currently used
sociological conceptions of the rules of action. According to current

sociological usage, the rules of action classify actions as disjunctive sets. For example, the events of conduct depicted in the incest rule are members of the "mores." The rules that prescribe allocations of duties in the household are members of the "folkways." The instructions that accompany a radio kit are technical rules. Emily Post has written the rules of etiquette.

As a consequence of such usage, current conceptions of the conditions of social order stress in common as a critical condition of a stable social order the extent to which rules are sacredly regarded. But should it turn out that the constitutive properties of events are not confined to games, one would then have to suppose that the uniformities of events depicted in the mores, the folkways, and the like are constituted through a set of "more fundamental" presuppositions in terms of which behavioral instances are attended by actors as instances of *intended* actions that a group member assumes "anyone can see." A line of reasoning then follows as an immediate consequence, and, because it is not reconcilable with current notions, presents the prospect of a crucial experiment. The alternative reasoning is this. If these constitutive properties extend to everyday events, then with respect to the problematic relationship between the normative regulation of action and the stability of concerted action, the critical phenomenon is not the "intensity of affect" with which the "rule" is "invested," or the respected or sacred or moral status of the rule, but the perceived normality of environmental events as this normality is a function of the presuppositions that define the possible events.

When the work with games was begun, we took for granted that the omnirelevance of normative regulation was peculiar to games, and that it was this feature that was frequently meant when scholars, e.g., Huizinga (1950), contrasted the well-regulated and orderly character of game events with those of "serious life." When, however, incongruity-inducing procedures were applied in "real life" situation, it was unnerving to find the seemingly endless variety of events that lent themselves to the production of really nasty surprises. These events ranged from those that, according to sociological commonsense, were "critical," like standing very, very close to a person while otherwise maintaining an innocuous conversation, to others that according to sociological commonsense were "trivial," like saying "hello" at the termination of a conversation. Both procedures elicited anxiety, indignation, strong feelings on the part of experimenter and subject alike of humiliation and regret, demands by the subjects for explanations, and so on. It was conjectured therefore that *all* actions as perceived events may have a constitutive structure, and that perhaps it is the threat to the normative order of events as such that is the critical variable in evoking indignation and not the breach of the "sacredness" of the rules. The conception is plausible, at least if one considers that the common factor to both the threat to the normative order of events as well as the breach of sacredness is the person's assumption that he, like his partner, is a competent member of the same community, which is a shorthand way of referring to the three definitive properties of the basic rules.

(B) *The incomplete task.* With respect to the set, "All the basic rules," one would like to know what the properties are of the boundaries of this set. More specifically, is the set a well-ordered or only a partially ordered one? And does it make any difference for the accomplishment by actual players of legitimate plays of recognizable games that the set is well ordered or not?

Several points seem to be worth putting into the record.

With regard to the well-ordered character, I have been unable to find any game whose acknowledged rules are sufficient to cover all the problematical possibilities that may arise, or that one cannot with only slight exercise of wit make arise within the domain of play. For example, although chess would seem to be immune to such manipulations, one can at one's move change pieces around on the board—so that, although the over-all positions are not changed, different pieces occupy the squares—and then move. On the several occasions in which I did this, my opponents were disconcerted, tried to stop me, demanded an explanation of what I was up to, were uncertain about the legality (but wanted to assert its illegality nevertheless), made it clear to me that I was spoiling the game for them, and at the next round of play made me promise that I would not "do anything this time." They were not satisfied when I asked that they point out where the rules prohibited what I had done. Nor were they satisfied when I pointed out that I had not altered the material positions and, further, that the maneuver did not affect my chances of winning. If they were not satisfied, neither could they say to *their* satisfaction what was wrong. Prominently in their attempts to come to terms, they would speak of the obscurity of my motives. One subject remarked that it reminded him of the way the Harlem Globetrotters played basketball, and that he had never considered that they played real basketball.

I suggest that one is in the area here of the game's version of the "unstated terms of contract," consisting perhaps of one more rule that completes every enumeration of basic rules by bringing them under the status of an agreement among persons to play in accordance with them, a rule which formulates the list as an agreement by the final "finely printed" acknowledgment, "et cetera."

With regard to the question of whether or not its well-ordered character makes a difference to the accomplishment of recognizable play,

I am struck by the fact that, while the rules of scientific inquiry are easily compared to the basic and preference rules in games, there operates in all scientific inquiries the inquirers' knowledge of the conditions under which they are permitted to relax the basic and preference rules and still claim for the product that it is an adequate scientific solution to the problem of inquiry. For games, one would have to find the conditions under which players could relax the basic and preference rules and still recognize their play as a legitimate play of the game. Thus far, at least, I have been unable to find a case of this, which is strange, given that the qualifying effect of the et cetera rule is easily discernible for every game that I have considered.

Finally, I have been unable to find any game that permits the time of occurrence, duration, and phasing of moves to be defined entirely as a matter of the player's preference.

Should it turn out that the boundaries of the set are essentially vague, that no matter how explicit the rules are, the set of them is essentially partially ordered, that every game contains its "unstated terms of contract," and that time is a parameter of the meaning of a move, then we have important grounds for optimism. These are precisely properties of those situations of events that sociologists have referred to as actors' "definitions of the situations" of "serious" life, and that inquiries have documented to the point where these properties may be safely assumed. It leaves open, too, the immensely important possibility that the constitutive accent is an integral feature of all events irrespective of whether they are events in the domain of games (referred by Schutz as the "finite province of meaning"), scientific theorizing, theater, play, dreaming, or whatever.

The Problem Again

Regardless of what the rules may provide as specifically possible events, whether they specify nine cells in ticktacktoe, sixty-four positions in chess, or five cards to a poker hand, the three constitutive expectancies are invariant to the actual content of the rules. They permit us to recognize in different games those events that are functionally the same with respect to the question of what must be done to produce confusion. Therefore, an operation that should produce confusion in one game holds for any game. If the constitutive expectancies operate in everyday situations, the operation that produces confusion in one concrete setting holds for any concrete setting. The operativeness of these constitutive expectancies in games or in everyday situations thereby serves as an important condition of stable features of concerted actions.

It is my purpose to show through experimental demonstrations that events that breach the constitutive expectancies multiply the anomic features of the environment of game events as well as the disorganized features of the structures of game interaction; that these effects vary directly with the extent of motivated compliance with the constitutive order of the game; that these effects occur independent of the personality characteristics of players; and that these statements hold not only for game interactions but for interactions of "serious life" as well.

We now ask:

1. Is the breach of a basic rule in a game a first-order determinant of anomic effects?

2. Is the breach of a basic rule in everyday life a similar first-order determinant?

Studying the Basic Rules Through the Use of Ticktacktoe

Sixty-seven liberal arts students in several of my classes served as experimenters. Each played ticktacktoe with three or more persons from among the 253 Ss, which included children, adolescents, young and older adults, of both sexes. The S, who was acquainted with E in varying degrees (from membership in the same family, through gradations of friendship to complete strangers), was asked, after his acceptance of E's invitation to play, to move first. After S made his mark, E erased the mark, moved it to another cell, and made his own mark while trying to avoid any indication to S that the play was in any way unusual. The Es were asked to report in behavioral detail what Ss did and said and to obtain from Ss, as well as to report for themselves, how they felt when invited to play, when the incorrect move was made, during the entire course of play and afterward. 67 Es reported on 253 instances of play.

Scoring Procedure. A standard reporting form was used by all Es, who were asked to report S's behavior immediately after E's own move.

If E reported that S

(1) Showed surprise, was startled, looked up, the account was scored "yes"; otherwise, "no."

(2) Showed or expressed bewilderment or was puzzled, the account was scored "yes"; otherwise, "no."

(3) Showed irritation, pain, or anger, the account was scored "yes"; otherwise, "no."

(4) Grinned, smiled, or laughed, the account was scored "yes"; otherwise, "no."

(5) Expressed suspicion or demanded an explanation, the account was scored "yes"; otherwise, "no."

(6) Showed some response but none of the above, the account was scored "yes."

Where the protocols did not contain sufficient information for a judgment, the account was scored as "No information."

The extent of S's disturbance was then scored as follows:

(1) If neither response nor laughter was noted and/or S showed surprise, was startled, or looked up but nothing more, the disturbance was classified as "None or mild."

(2) If the S showed responses (1) and any *two* others among the alternatives (2), (4) and (5), the disturbance was classified as "Moderate."

(3) If S showed responses (1), (2), (4), and (5), the disturbance was classified as "Severe."

Sometimes the sense that S made of E's move could be obtained from the subject's behavior and spontaneous remarks at the conclusion of play. Sometimes E had to elicit this by asking S "What do you make of it?" The Es varied in whether they asked this before or after the experimental intent had been disclosed.

The Ss' remarks were evaluated as follows:

(1) If the S: (a) acted as though nothing required an explanation or that there was no problem and/or (b) if he said that he felt that the E was trying a new way of playing, was a bug on ticktacktoe, or was playing or trying out a new game, this was scored as S's abandonment of tick tacktoe as an order and the election of a new order.

(2) If S said (a) that there was some undisclosed trick involved (e.g., that it was a gag, that E was acting like a character or a prankster that it was a test or an experiment of some sort) and/or (b) that E was playing an "unknown game" (e.g., E had mislead S or was not really playing ticktacktoe, there was some trick or joke being played on S, E was using this way of playing as a masked sexual pass or comment on S's stupidity, or E was acting like a wise guy), S was scored as perceiving E to be playing an unknown game. Both 2 (a) and (b) were regarded as S's abandonment of the order of ticktacktoe but without deciding an alternative order.

(3) If S said that E was playing ticktacktoe but cheating, this was scored as S's retention of the order of ticktacktoe.

The S could have continued to play; refused to continue to play; or played "no-game," i.e., retaliatory play or reciprocal spoiling (e.g., duplicating E's mode of play, or acting as if "you're playing any way yo like, I can play any way I like," "you're spoiling the game for me, I'll spoil the game for you," or "you think you can win that way so I'll put in all my marks now and win.")

Findings. Tables 7–1 through 7–7 report the results. The following gross findings showed up with sufficient prominence to invite at least an initial credence.

TABLE 7–1

What Difference Did the "Wrong" Move Make?

	Age grade								
	5–11		12–17		18–35		36–65		All subjects	
	N	%	N	%	N	%	N	%	N	%
Some response to the unusual character of the move reported	54	94.7	19	95.0	138	94.5	29	96.7	240	94.9
No response to the unusual character of the move reported	3	5.3	1	5.0	8	5.5	1	3.3	13	5.1
All subjects	57	100.0	20	100.0	146	100.0	30	100.0	253	100.0

TABLE 7–2

Did the Move Motivate an Immediate Attempt To Understand What Was Going On?

	Age grade								
	5–11		12–17		18–35		36–65		All subjects	
	N	%	N	%	N	%	N	%	N	%
Anything from request to demand for explanation	20	35.1	14	70.0	82	56.2	15	50.0	131	51.8
Makes charge; sees through the move; criticizes or rejects experimenter	29	51.0	0	0.0	28	19.2	9	30.0	66	26.1
Evidence of effect but neither of above	5	8.7	5	25.0	28	19.2	5	16.7	43	17.0
No immediate difference or response noted	3	5.2	1	5.0	8	5.4	1	3.3	13	5.1
All subjects	57	100.0	20	100.0	146	100.0	30	100.0	253	100.0
All subjects who made requests, demands, and charges	49	86.1	14	70.0	110	75.4	24	80.0	197	77.9

TABLE 7–3

Where Did the Subject Locate the Responsibility for the Character of the Game?

	Age grade									
	5–11		12–17		18–35		36–65		All subjects	
	N	%	N	%	N	%	N	%	N	%
You don't play correctly	43	75.5	14	70.0	101	69.2	26	86.6	184	72.7
I don't play correctly	6	10.5	2	10.0	12	8.2	0	0.0	20	7.9
We could both play correctly but we don't (spoiling play)	8	14.0	4	20.0	33	22.7	4	13.4	49	19.4
All subjects	57	100.0	20	100.0	146	100.0	30	100.0	253	100.0

TABLE 7–4

What Difference for the Extent of the Subject's Disturbance Was Made by the Nature of the Subject's Subscription to a Definite Normative Order?

Extent of subject's disturbance	Subject normalized the wrong move within the						All subjects	
	Election of a new order		Abandonment of ticktacktoe but without deciding an alternative		Retention of order of ticktacktoe			
	N	%	N	%	N	%	N	%
None or mild	26	86.7	36	30.8	20	19.4	81	32.8
Moderate	3	10.0	46	40.3	32	31.1	81	32.8
Severe	1	3.3	33	28.9	51	49.5	85	34.4
All subjects	30	100.0	114	100.0	103	100.0	247	100.0
No information							6	

$X^2 = 55.43$ at 6 d.f. $p < 001$ under the assumption that extent of disturbance and election of normative order varied independently.

TABLE 7–5

What Difference for the Extent of the Subject's Disturbance Was Made by the Subject's Age Group?

Extent of subject's disturbance	Age group									
	5–11		12–17		18–35		36–65		All subjects	
	N	%	N	%	N	%	N	%	N	%
None or mild	14	25.5	3	15.0	54	37.2	11	36.7	82	32.8
Moderate	14	25.5	8	40.0	51	35.2	9	30.0	82	32.8
Severe	27	49.0	9	45.0	40	27.6	10	33.3	86	34.4
All subjects	55	100.0	20	100.0	145	100.0	30	100.0	250	100.0
No information									3	

$X^2 = 11.39$ at 6 d.f. $.10 < p > .05$ under the assumption that age group and extent of disturbance varied independently.

TABLE 7–6

What Difference for the Extent of the Subject's Disturbance Was Made by the Degree
of Acquaintance Between the Subject and Experimenter?

Extent of subject's disturbance	Degree of acquaintance									
	Stranger		Acquaintance		Friend		Family		All subjects	
	N	%	N	%	N	%	N	%	N	%
None or mild	17	32.7	29	31.8	25	38.4	10	25.7	81	32.8
Moderate	18	34.6	27	29.7	21	32.3	16	41.0	82	33.2
Severe	17	32.7	35	38.5	19	29.2	13	33.3	84	34.0
All subjects	52	100.0	91	100.0	65	100.0	39	100.0	247	100.0
No information									6	

$X^2 = 3.89$ at 6 d.f. $.70 < p > .50$ under the assumption that degree of acquaintance and extent of disturbance varied independently.

TABLE 7–7

What Difference for the Extent of the Subject's Disturbance Was Made by the Fact
That Subjects and Experimenters Were Same or Different Sexes?

Extent of subject's disturbance	Sex of subject (S) and experimenter (E)									
	MS and ME		MS and FE		FS and ME		FS and FE		All subjects	
	N	%	N	%	N	%	N	%	N	%
None or mild	26	32.9	20	33.3	12	30.0	20	29.9	78	31.6
Moderate	27	34.2	18	30.0	13	32.5	24	35.8	82	33.4
Severe	26	32.9	22	36.7	15	37.5	23	34.3	86	35.0
All subjects	79	100.0	60	100.0	40	100.0	67	100.0	246	100.0
No information									7	

$X^2 = .67$ at 6 d.f. $p > .99$ under the assumption that sex of the subject and experimenter, and extent of disturbance varied independently.

1. That the "wrong" move had an effect on Ss' behavior is clear from Table 7–1.

2. Table 7–2 indicates that three quarters of the Ss were motivated immediately by the wrong move to try to understand what was going on.

3. Table 7–3 shows that three quarters of the players located the responsibility for the character of the game with E.

4. Tables 7–4 through 7–7 encourage us to proceed. Ideally, we would have wanted only the fact of the wrong move to produce the anomic effects within the condition that the person attempted to restore the normal character of the move within the normative order of tick-tacktoe.

Table 7–4 shows that persons who interpreted the move as a move in a new game showed little disturbance. Those who abandoned ticktacktoe but did not decide an alternative order showed more disturbance. Those who attempted to normalize within the order of ticktacktoe showed the most disturbance.

Tables 7–5 to 7–7 show that the extent of disturbance varied indepent of the S's age group, the degree of acquaintance between S and E, or the fact that the Ss and Es were of the same or different sexes.

The ticktacktoe findings supported two important theoretical points. First, a behavior that was at variance with the constitutive order of the game immediately motivated attempts to normalize the discrepancy, i.e., to treat the observed behavior as an instance of a legally possible event. Second, under the condition of a breach of legal play the discrepant event seemed best to produce a senseless situation if the player attempted to normalize the discrepancy while attempting to retain the constitutive order without alteration, i.e., without leaving the game or orienting a "new game."

We also found that the ticktacktoe produced a convincing and enduring bewilderment for children, particularly those from five to eleven years old. The procedure was less efficient in producing bewilderment for adults, though for them it was very efficient in producing an ambiguous situation of events. Protocols of both adults and children, however, were filled with expressions of distrust. This held across the board regardless of age, sex, or familiarity with the experimenter.

Limitation on the Further Use of Games

We are, after all, not interested in producing confusion in games, but in producing confusion in "serious" situations. Since constitutive expectancies proved useful in ticktacktoe, we now ask whether constitutive expectancies can be found for the events of everyday life.

They can be found, but to find them we must look to other situations than games.

We cannot consult games because game events are not structurally homologous with events of yesterday life. Several features of situations of game events contrast so markedly with situations of events of daily life that not only is the assumption of their structural equivalence difficult to justify, but the differences render any talk about norms of everyday situations as "rules of the game" mere figure of speech. If this were not enough, we would still be barred from using the findings on ticktacktoe to tell us how to multiply confusion in everyday situations because many adults were able to abandon the game without disrupting their relationship to the experimenter.

If we use Huizinga's (1950) analysis of situations of play as a point of departure, the following features of situations of games stand in marked contrast to those situations involving the routine social structuring of events of everyday life.

1. As compared with the events of everyday life, game events, both in process as well as in retrospect as accomplished products, have a peculiar time structure which consists in the fact that as of all present states of the game the time in which the game is played is essentially circumscribed. Over the set of all present states of the game, either in process or played, an integral sense of any present event is provided by an assumed future that consists of a definite time by which the game will have been completed, e.g., in a number of moves, or when the runners have reached the tape, or when sixty minutes of play have elapsed. Thereby an accomplished play of the game consists of an encapsulated episode. Basic rules and an actual accomplished course of play furnish the episode its entire character as a texture of relevances. Characteristically too, success and failure are clearly decidable so that one or the other outcome is very little subject to reinterpretation as having been something else. Nor are assessments of success or failure subject to waiting for later developments *outside* of the episode or the play of the game or the game itself in order to permit decisions as to what the episode "really amounted to." Finally, the knowledge that by a time the game will have been completed is actually and potentially available over every present state of the game to each player in identical fashion.

2. Any discrepancy between the "official" definition of the game and the person's private conceptions and reservations is of little moment in deciding the range of possible game events and outcomes. The game is for the players a public enterprise whose possibilities exist by reason of the person's motivated compliance to its basic rules, and these rules define a consensually understood domain. Basic rules are essentially objective rules, in the sense of Kaufman's (1944) definition of "objective." The events they provide are essentially objective events.

3. To be "in the game" involves by definition the suspension of the presuppositions and procedures of "serious" life. Many commentators on games have taken notice of this feature by speaking of the game as an "artificial world in microcosm."

4. Such a suspension is characteristically a matter of the person's preferences. It is essentially possible to exercise an option to "play the game." Characteristically, too, it is essentially possible, should things go badly, for example, for a person to "leave" the game or to change it into another one, and again as a matter of the person's preferences.

5. Characteristically, to "leave" the game is synonymous with reinstating the world of everyday life as an environment of events and the

attitude of daily life that constitutes this environment. The presuppositions of the game seem to be the product of certain modifications of the presuppositions of daily life which are provisionally and optionally suspended, i.e., made irrelevant, to the course of the game.

6. Although strategies may be highly improvised and the conditions of success and failure be unclear to the players over the course of play, the basic rules of play are known over the course of play, they are independent of the changing present state of the game and of the selection of strategies, and they are available for use by players and presumed by players to be available as required knowledge that players have prior to the occasions under which these rules might be consulted to decide among legal alternatives.

7. The basic rules of play are not altered by the actual course of play. For games, as ordinarily understood, players not only know the basic rules of play prior to undertaking the game, but they do not learn more about these rules as a function of their participation in the game. Clearly, such a situation has to be discriminated from one in which the basic rules are themselves learned by the player only in the course of play as a function of his playing and only insofar as he participates, i.e., that makes his actions subject to recognition, review, and correction according to an unknown set of basic rules.

8. With respect to basic rules of play, there is a practically perfect correspondence between the normative descriptions of game conduct and actual game conduct. Empirically this correspondence is found not only within a play of a game but between plays of that game. A similar correspondence between normative descriptions of everyday conduct and actual everyday conduct is exceptional.

9. Insofar as players are committed to compliance with the basic rules, these rules provide for players the definitions of rational, realistic, understandable actions in the environment of game events. Actions in compliance with basic rules define in games "fair play," while game-possible outcomes define "justice."

10. Within the basic rules that are presumed by each of the participants to be binding upon themselves and other participants in a more or less equivalent way, strategies that accord in the strictest fashion with norms of instrumental efficacy are in principle [7] adoptable by either

---

[7] It seems to me, although I am not able to prove it, that in games, but not in everyday activities, a player's wit or optional willingness alone limits the possibility that his strategies of play accord with strict considerations of instrumental efficacy. In games, the basic rules, and only the basic rules, impose the equivalent of "institutional constraints on rationality" that operate in "serious life" activities. The substantive rationality that Max Weber spoke of occurs in market transactions as an essential condition of stable calculations in and concerning such transactions. In such a "practical setting," attempts to establish and sanction activities in compliance

player. Further, it is essentially possible for each player to assume or insist upon this for himself or for his partner without impoverishing his grasp of the game that is being played.

The Constitutive Order of Events of Everyday Life

Can the "constitutive accent" be found for situations of events of "serious" life? I propose that the three properties that are definitive of the basic rules of a game are not particular to games but are found as features of the "assumptions" that Alfred Schutz, in his work on the constitutive phenomenology of situations of everyday life (1945, 1951), has called the "attitude of daily life."

Before listing the features imparted to events by this attitude, it is helpful to review the point that assumptions and rules may be translated into the language of expected events. To say, for example, that a player assumes the rule of ticktacktoe that players move alternately A,B,A,B. . . means the same thing as saying that his actions are governed in their course by the normative sequence of events, A,B,A,B. . . What a person is said to "assume" is equivalent to what he is said to "assume about the possible fall of events" which is equivalent again to saying that his actions are governed by a restricted way in which possible events can occur. What he is said to "assume" therefore consists of attributed features of events that are "scenic" to him. He attends their sense as a restricted frame of alternative specifications of the scene of events. The actor is therefore capable of experiencing "surprises" when actual events breach these expectancies.

The following formula defines the constitutive accent. It can be fitted to each of the features of the situation of events that Schutz talks about in his list of assumptions of the attitude of daily life. Each of the features carries the prefatory attribution: "Out of the alternative possibilities, the person (a) expects that. . . (insert the relevant feature); (b) expects that as it holds for him it holds for the other person as well; and (c) expects that as he expects it to hold for the other person, the other person expects it to hold for him."

---

with the ideal of formal rationality, as Weber speaks of it, would impoverish the person's grasp of his real situation, anomicize the perceived environment of actual and possible transactional events, and disorganize the interaction. In games, by contrast, substantive, as compared with formal, rationality occurs because players may opt for one or the other; or substantive rationality in game play may occur because the players may not know enough to play otherwise.

The Attitude of Daily Life

In a series of classical writings in sociological theory directed to the constitutive phenomenology of situations of daily life (1932, 1943, 1944, 1945(a), 1945(b), 1951, 1953, 1954, 1955), Schutz described those presuppositions whereby scenic occurrences were assigned by an actor the constituent meanings for him of the scene's feature, "known in common with others." In accordance with the program, attitude, and method of Husserlian phenomenology (Spiegelberg, 1960), Schutz looked for the presuppositions and the corresponding environmental features intended by them that were invariant to the specific contents of actions and their objects. The list is not exhaustive. Further research should reveal others. Like any product of observation they have the provisional status of "so until demonstrated to be otherwise."

1. Schutz found that in everyday situations the "practical theorist" achieves an ordering of events while seeking to retain and sanction the presupposition that the objects of the world are what they appear to be. The person coping with everyday affairs seeks an interpretation of these affairs while holding a line of "official" neutrality toward the view that one may exercise a *rule* of doubt about *any* objects of the world that they are as they appear to be. Instead the person's assumption consists in the expectation that a relationship of undoubted correspondence exists between the particular appearance-of-an-object and the intended-object that-appears-in-this-particular-manner. Out of the set of possible relationships between the actual appearances of the object and the intended object, as for example, a relationship of *doubtful* correspondence between the two, the person expects that the presupposed undoubted correspondence is the sanctionable one. He expects that the other person employs the same expectancy in a more or less identical fashion and expects that, just as he expects the relationship to hold for the other person, the other person expects it to hold for him.

2. Schutz refers to a second assumption as the person's practical interest in the events of the world. The relevant features of events that his interest in them selects carry along for the person as *their* invariant feature that they can actually and potentially affect the person's actions and can be affected by his actions. Under this presupposed feature of events the accuracy of his orderings of events is assumed by the person to be tested and testable without suspending the relevance of what he knows as fact, supposition, conjecture, fantasy, and the like by virtue of his bodily and social positions in the real world. Events, their relationships, their causal texture, are not for him matters of theoretic interest. He does not sanction the notion that in dealing with them it is correct to address them with the rule that he knows nothing, or that he can assume the

he knows nothing "just to see where it leads." In everyday situations, what he knows is an integral feature of his social competence. He assumes that what he knows in the way he knows it personifies himself as a social object to himself as well as to others as a bona fide member of the group. He sanctions his competence as a bona fide member of the group (i.e., he and other members take his competence for granted) as a condition for his being assured that his grasp of his everyday affairs is a realistic grasp.

3. Schutz describes the time perspective of daily life. In his everyday activities the person reifies the stream of experience into "time slices" with the use of a scheme of temporal relationships that he assumes he and other persons employ in an equivalent and standardized fashion. The conversation that he is having consists for him not only of the events of his stream of experience, but of what was, or may be said at a time that is designated by the successive positions of the hands of the clock. Not only is the "sense of the conversation" progressively realized through a succession of realized meanings of the thus-far accomplished course of the conversation but every "thus-far" is informed by *its* anticipations. Further, as of any here-and-now, as well as over the succession of here-and-nows, the conversation for him has both its retrospective and prospective significances. These include the as of here-and-now references to beginnings, duration, pacing, phasing, and termination. These determinations of the "inner time" of the stream of experiences he coordinates with a socially employed scheme of temporal determinations. He uses the scheme of standard time as a means of scheduling and coordinating his actions with those of others, of gearing his interests to those of others, and of pacing his actions to theirs. His interest in standard time is directed to the problems such specifications solve in scheduling and coordinating interaction. He assumes, too, that the scheme of standard time is entirely a public enterprise, a kind of "one big clock identical for all."

There are other and contrasting ways of temporally punctuating the stream of experience so as to produce a sensible and known-in-common array of events in the "outer world." For example, the person engaged in the activities of scientific theorizing uses standard time as a device for constructing one out of alternative empirically possible worlds (assuming of course that the theorizer is interested in matters of fact). Thus, what would, from his interests in the mastery of practical affairs, involve the person's use of time to gear his interests to the conduct of others, is, for his interests as a scientific problem which consists of clearly formulating such programs of coordinated actions in the fashion of relationships of cause and effect. Another contrasting example is found in attending the events in the theatre play. Interests in standard time are put aside as irrelevant. When he attends the social structures portrayed in a play like *Ethan Frome*, the playgoer allows the lovers' fate to come before, and as a condition for appreciating, the sequence of steps that led up to the lovers' fate.

4. Schutz describes the et cetera assumption. By this is meant the assumption that as events have occurred in the past, they will occur again in the future.

5. A closely related assumption is that the appearances of events can be intended again by the actor as an ensemble of constituent appearances. Thereby, the constancy of the intended object throughout variations in actual appearances consists in its temporal identicality. The person assumes that the intended object is the same object now as was intended in the past and can be intended again in the future despite the facts of time sampling, and changes of context, circumstances, and actual appearances.

6. The person assumes a commonly entertained scheme of communication. He is informed as to the sense of scenic events by a presupposed background of things that "Anyone like us knows." He assumes that such a background is used by himself and others in the manner of coding rules in terms of which the question of correct correspondence between the appearance of the object and the intended-object-that-appears-in-this particular-way is decided.

7. Schutz found the "thesis of the reciprocity of perspectives." This thesis consists of two assumptions: (a) the assumption of the "interchangeability of standpoints," and (b) the assumption of the "congruency of relevances."

(a) By the person's assumption of the interchangeability of standpoints is meant that the person takes for granted, assumes that the other person does the same, and assumes that as he assumes for the other the other assumes for him, that if they were to change places so that the other person's here-and-now became his, and his became the other person's, that the person would see events in the same typical way as does the other person, and the other person would see them in the same typical way as he does.

Stated in another way, the person attends a situation that has as its "background" feature that, given the specific actual appearances of scene, if each were to exchange places with the other, each would recognize the scene in a manner that was for all the practical purpose of their interaction more or less similar. As the person attends the scene the particular, actual here-and-now appearances of the scene are different for him than they are for the other. The person *knows* this. But even while knowing this, the scene has for him *at the same time* its char acteristic feature that what *actually* appears here-and-now is the-potential-appearance-it-has-for-the-other-person-if-the-two-were-to-exchange-positions. He assumes that what each actually sees can potentially be seen by both under an exchange of positions. Thus, Schutz found, the person assumes that there are different appearances but assumes too that these are due to different perspectival positions in a world that is identical for both. But this identical world, Schutz found, is the accomplishment of the assumed possibility of interchangeability of positions—physical and social—under which the presupposed interchangeability can be entertained with manageable incongruity. Hence, the feature of a scene for the actor that it is the identical scene for him and the other person can be modified by modifying this presupposition, e.g., by a change of interest, by ceremonial arrangement, by such instrumental manipulations as brain surgery, drugs, and the like. The identical world is guaranteed by the person's "ability" to retain this presupposition under the contingencies imposed by the factual world. This point will be discussed again later in the paper.

(b) By the assumption of the congruency of relevances is meant that the person assumes, assumes that the other person also assumes, and assumes that as he assumes it for the other the other assumes it for him, that differences in perspective that the person knows originate in his own and in the other person's particular biographical situations are irrelevant for the purposes at hand of either, and that both have selected and interpreted the actually and potentially common objects and their features in an "empirically identical" manner that is sufficient for all their practical purposes.

8. The person assumes a particular "form of sociality." Among other things, the form of sociality consists of the person's assumption that some characteristic disparity exists between the "image" of himself that he attributes to the other person as that person's knowledge of him, and the knowledge that he has of himself in the "eyes" of the other person. He assumes too that alterations of this characteristic disparity remain within his autonomous control. The assumption serves as a rule whereby the everyday theorist groups his experiences with regard to what goes properly with whom. Thereby there corresponds to the common intersubjective world of communication unpublicized knowledge which, in the eyes of the person, is distributed among persons as grounds of their actions, i.e., as their motives or, in the radical sense of the term, their interests" as constituent features of the social relationships of interaction. The person assumes that there are matters that one person knows that he assumes others do not know. The ignorance of one party consists in what another knows that is motivationally relevant to the first. Thereby,

matters that are known in common are informed in their sense by the personal reservations, the matters that are selectively withheld. Thus the events of everyday situations are informed by this integral background of "meanings held in reserve," of matters known about self and others that are none of somebody else's business: in a word, the private life.

The Definitive Features of Events Which Are Members of the Commonsense Environment

Each of the foregoing presuppositions assigns to a set of scenic event a feature that the members of that set share. A commonsense environment is defined by the feature, attached to all members of the set, "known in common with any bona fide member of the collectivity." Schutz findings explicate the compound character of the feature "known in common." This feature was analyzed by Schutz into several features that are the constituent meanings of "known in common."

Whatever an event may specifically consist of, whether its determinations are those of persons' motives, their life histories, distributions of income in the population, the conditions of advancement on the job kinship obligations, the organization of an industry, the layout of a city what ghosts do when night falls, and the thought that God thinks, *if and only if the event has for the witness the following additional determinations, is it an event in the commonsense environment.*

1. The determinations assigned to the event by the user are, from his point of view, assignments that he is required to make; the other person is required to make the same assignments; and just as the user requires the same assignments to hold for the other persons, he assumes that the other person requires the same of him.

2. From the user's point of view, a relationship of undoubted correspondence is the sanctioned relationship between the-presented-appearance-of-the-intended-object and the-intended-object-that-appears-in-this-presented-appearance.

3. From the user's point of view, the event that is known, in the manner that it is known, can actually and potentially affect the knower actions and circumstances and can be affected by his actions and circumstances.

4. From the user's point of view, the meanings of events are the products of a standardized process of naming, reification, and idealization of the user's stream of experiences, i.e., the products of the same language.

5. From the user's point of view, the present determinations of the events, whatever these may be, are determinations that were intended on

previous occasions and that may be again intended in identical fashion on an indefinite number of future occasions.

6. From the user's point of view, the intended event is retained as the temporally identical event throughout the stream of experience.

7. From the user's point of view, the event has as its contexts of interpretation:

(a) a commonly entertained scheme of communication consisting of a standardized system of signals and coding rules,

and

(b) "What anyone knows," i.e., a pre-established corpus of socially warranted knowledge.

8. From the user's point of view, the actual determinations that the event exhibits for him are the potential determinations that it would exhibit for the other person were they to exchange positions.

9. From the user's point of view, to each event there corresponds its determinations that originate in the user's and in the other person's particular biography. From the user's point of view, such determinations are irrelevant for the purposes at hand of either, and from the user's point of view both have selected and interpreted the actual and potential determinations of the event in an empirically identical manner that is sufficient for all their practical purposes.

10. From the user's point of view, there is a characteristic disparity between the publicly acknowledged determinations and the personal, withheld determinations of events, with this private knowledge held in reserve. From the user's point of view, the event means for both the user and the other more than the user can say.

11. From the user's point of view, alterations of this characteristic disparity remain within his own autonomous control.

The Commonsense Environment of Events

It is the case that what an event exhibits as its distinctive determinations is not a condition of membership in the commonsense environment, whereas its features would be seen by others if their positions were exchanged, that its features are not assigned as a matter of personal preference but are to be seen by anyone, and the rest, i.e., the constituent features of "known in common with others," are the conditions of membership.

The eleven features enumerated above, and these alone, define the commonsense character of an event. These eleven features are the critical conditions for the use by societal members of events as sanctionable grounds of further inferences and actions.[8] For members these features are constitutive of "actual events in a real and common world" irrespective of whatever other determinations these events may exhibit. Thus, if such events as "Husbands provide the primary support for their families," "If you jump in the water you'll get wet," "All Jews are rich," and "Christ will come a second time," are said to be members of the commonsense environment in general, then this is equivalent to saying that for the users they exhibit the above eleven features.

For users, these attributed features are necessarily relevant ones. That is, they are invariantly presupposed, or better, invariantly understood features of what the users are looking at and what they see. For example, the picture on the wall behind my fellow conversationalist which I see, but which he does not see as long as he is turned toward me, has for me as one of its features, along with the likeness of the scene it portrays, that it-would-be-seen-by-him-if-he-were-to-turn-his-head. In fact, I treat as an evidence of its "concrete" character, i.e., as a potentially testable specification of the picture, that it is the-picture-he-would-see-if-he-turned-his-head. But, for a multitude of situations in which I am involved, such a specification of the picture may be "merely taken for granted," a potentially testable feature by a variety of possible operations. The feature remains unproblematic, and not only beyond awareness but perhaps even beyond my inclination or ability to verbalize it. That it is nevertheless a matter that I am responsive to can under an appropriate operation (like an incongruity-inducing procedure) be demonstrated to be operative.

Such attributed features inform the user about any particular appearance of an interpersonal environment but without their necessarily being recognized in a conscious or deliberated fashion. Instead, these attributions are characteristically "seen without being noticed" features of socially structured environments. Although they are demonstrably relevant to the recognizable character of environing events for the person and, from his point of view, for others around him, they are rarely attended by him. As Schutz (1954b) points out, a "special motive" is required to bring them under review. The more the setting is institutionally regulated and routinized, the more does the user take for granted their feature "known in common with others." Hence such features are critical not only to the purposes of this paper but to sociological inquiries generally, for a perennial task of sociological inquiries is

---

[8] A common theme that runs through the many definitions that sociologists and anthropologists use for the term "common culture" is the reference to the socially sanctioned grounds of inferences and actions that persons, thought of as members of a society, use in the management of their everyday affairs and which they assume that other members use in the same way. Thus one may think of these eleven characteristics as constituent features of common culture, and may treat the various definitions as theoretical versions of commonsense knowledge of social structures.

to locate and define the features of their situations that persons, while unaware of, are nevertheless responsive to as *required* features.

The assumptions that make up the attitude of daily life are constitutive of a situation of events as a world known in common and taken for granted. This means that such an environment of events for the person includes these attributions as necessarily relevant ones, i.e., as invariantly presupposed, invariantly understood, in exactly the same way as the ticktacktoe player, throughout the alterations of the game, understands that the field of play consists of nine cells. These attributions to the field of events inform the ticktacktoe player about any particular event of play but without being a conscious part of his deliberations. Similarly for the person in everyday environments. And just as it holds for the game of ticktacktoe that such attributions are demonstrably relevant to the player's judgments but are rarely problematical, so does it hold for the events of everyday life. Such attributions are features of witnessed events that are "seen without being noticed." They are demonstrably relevant to the sense that the actor makes of what is going on about him but they are rarely attended to by him. In a person's situation of events such features are integral specifications of these events, and are essential to his recognition of an environment as consisting of real and understandable events and for his recognition of rational and reasonable actions occurring in and upon that environment.

These expected features of events that we have listed are conceived as features of domains of events about which the actor, even though he may be unaware of them, is capable of experiencing severe and nasty surprise. *Indeed, in proposing that they are features which receive the constitutive accent, the operation for multiplying the senseless character of his situation involves breaching them.* And in correspondence to the definition of "trust" in games, the constitutive accent placed upon these events provides us our general definition of "trust" in everyday situations.

What Conditions Must Be Established in Order To Induce Confusion?

Merely taking an action that breaches a constitutive expectancy will not by itself get us the results that we desire. To see that this is so consider once more the picture on the wall that my conversational partner does not see as long as he faces me but that he could see if he turned his head. Imagine that when I ask him, "How do you like the picture behind you?" he turns his head, scans the wall, turns back, and asks, "What picture?" Nothing is less obvious than that I must thereupon fall into bewilderment even though this is a procedure for breaching the constitutive expectancy of the interchangeability of standpoints. It is not obvious that confusion must result because nothing has been provided so far in this paper that would permit a decision as to which of my alternative responses to his remark are possible, let alone likely. I might suffer a disorientation, but I might take his remark as a rude comment on my taste in pictures, or I might ask him in a playful fashion how long he has been blind. As yet, no rule has been proposed that would restrict in any but an eclectic commonsense way the set of alternative responses. For example, for each alternative that I might select it is necessary that I assume something about the kind of relationship that I have with the person. If it is proposed that he is a status superior, then one might be inclined to "predict" a different reply on my part than if he is a close friend.

Some further decisions therefore are required in order to arrive at the conditions under which as a matter of logical necessity confusion must be predicted.

To help, I shall again borrow from Schutz (1945b) by accepting his findings that the situations of games, of play, of scientific theorizing, of dreaming, of staging in the theatre, of theatre going, are produced by modifying the presuppositions of the attitude of daily life. Just as one ceases to attend events in the "usual way" in favor of "getting into the play," in reverse one "leaves" the theatre, or one "puts aside" the scientific problem, or one "wakes" from dreaming, or one is "done" with the game, or one "stops" play-acting, only to return to the "everyday" events of the social order. The presuppositions that are constitutive of the feature of a situation of events "known-in-common-with-others-and-with-others-taken-for-granted" are "fundamental" in the sense that all alternative domains of events—of dreaming, of scientific theorizing, of play attending—are modifications of the attitude of daily life. For example, the presuppositions that constitute the sense for the playgoer of Caesar's death at the hands of the disaffected senators are produced by treating the time that it takes to put on a performance of Julius Caesar as a known but essentially irrelevant condition for "appreciating" the events of the play, e.g., for recognizing what Antonius is really telling the crowd about Caesar's assassins. But when the curtain comes down the presuppositions of the "mundane temporal order of things" is reinstated, i.e., "the play is over."

"Fundamental" and "derivative" accents upon an order of events are changed as one changes around between the attitude of daily life and alternative attitudes as modifications of it. The environmental product of each change, as the case varies, would be the domain of "the play," of the "scientific problem," of the "dream." Each of these is a "subdomain" of events whose sense is the product of a modification of the sense that events acquire through the attitude of everyday life.

To decide the conditions of confusion, we encounter first the fact that each of the possible modifications of the "sense of a situation" involves a particular suspension of the normative orders of events of everyday life. A person, therefore, who encounters a breach of the constitutive accent of everyday situations may cope with the "incongruity" by "leaving the field," e.g., by "making a game" of his situation or turning it into "an experiment" or "playful exchange" and the rest. But as we have just proposed, each involves the suspension by him of the relevance of ordinary structural constraints.

In the game of ticktacktoe we saw that confusion and bewilderment was most marked for those who sought to resolve "surprise" while retaining the order of the game, i.e., without leaving the game or attending a new game. Thereby a first condition is at least initially recommended. If we are going to confuse our subject, we have to prevent him from leaving the field. Concretely this means that, if we begin with a situation that is structured according to the presuppositions of everyday life, we must somehow prevent the person from turning the situation into a game, or treating it as an object of mere theoretic interest, or from "seeing" it as an experiment, and so on.

But, even if this condition is met, our subject would still have an important alternative open to him. If, however, we assume the "fundamental" character of the assumptions of everyday life, it would be the *only* other course open to him: He could place the constitutive accent of everyday life upon a new set of events. As was the case for games, this means exactly the same thing as redefining social reality.

But with respect to the possibility of a single person by himself achieving such a redefinition of social reality, there is much data to recommend that although such a process of redefinition can occur (a) it would seem that it is best done in concert with others; (b) it takes time; and (c) it has as its product the person's assumption of the consensual validity of the redefined reality.

We have arrived now at the conditions that would need to be established if we are to program a set of manipulations that will multiply the anomic features of a person's situation. If the person cannot leave the field, and if he cannot place the constitutive accent upon a new set of events because he must manage the redefinition by himself in insufficient time and without being able to assume that the new accent is a consensually supported one, then he should have no alternative except to normalize the breach of constitutive expectancies within the normative order of events of daily life. The result should be confusion.

Some Preliminary Trials and Findings

Since each of the presuppositions that make up the attitude of daily life assigns an expected feature to the actor's environment, it should be possible to induce experimentally a breach of these expectancies by deliberately modifying scenic events so as to disappoint these attributions. By definition, surprise is possible with respect to each of these expected features. The nastiness of surprise should vary directly with the extent to which the actor complies with the constitutive order of events of everyday life as a scheme for assigning witnessed appearances their status of events in a perceivedly normal environment.

Procedures were used to see if a breach of these presuppositions would produce anomic effects and increase disorganization. These procedures must be thought of as demonstrations rather than as experiments. "Experimenters" were upper division students in the author's courses. Their training consisted of little more than verbal instructions about how to proceed. The demonstrations were done as class assignments and were unsupervised. Students reported their results in anecdotal fashion with no controls beyond the fact that they were urged to avoid interpretation in favor of writing down what was actually said and done, staying as close as possible to a chronological account.

Because the procedures nevertheless produced massive effects, I feel they are worth reporting. Obviously, however, caution must be exercised in assessing the findings.

Demonstration 1: Breaching the Congruency of Relevances. This expectancy consists of the following. The person expects, expects that the other person does the same, and expects that as he expects it of the other the other expects the like of him that the differences in their perspectives that originate in their particular individual biographies are irrelevant for the purposes at hand of each and that both have selected and interpreted the actually and potentially common objects in an "empirically identical" manner that is sufficient for the purposes at hand. Thus, for example, in talking about "matters just known in common" persons will discuss them using a course of utterances that are governed by the expectation that the other person *will* understand. The speaker expects that the other person will assign to his remarks the sense intended by the speaker and expects that thereby the other person will permit the speaker the assumption that both know what he is talking about without any requirement of a check-out. Thus the sensible character of the matter that is being discussed is settled by a fiat assignment that each expects to make, and expects the other to make in reciprocal fashion, that as a condition of his right to decide without interference that he knows what he is talking about and that what he is talking about is so, each will have furnished whatever unstated understandings are required. Much therefore that is being talked about is not mentioned, although each expects that the adequate sense of the matter being talked about is settled. The more so is this the case, the more is the exchange one of commonplace remarks among persons who "know" each other.

Students were instructed to engage an acquaintance or friend in an ordinary conversation and, without indicating that what the experimenter was saying was in any way out of the ordinary, to insist that the person clarify the sense of his commonplace remarks. Twenty-three students reported twenty-five instances of such encounters. The following are typical excerpts from their accounts.

Case 1. The subject was telling the experimenter, a member of the subject's car pool, about having had a flat tire while going to work the previous day.

    (S) "I had a flat tire."
    (E) "What do you mean, you had a flat tire?"
        She appeared momentarily stunned. Then she answered in a hostile way: "What do you mean? What do you mean? A flat tire is a flat tire. That is what I meant. Nothing special. What a crazy question!"

Case 2. (S) "Hi, Ray. How is your girl friend feeling?"
    (E) "What do you mean, how is she feeling? Do you mean physical or mental?"
    (S) "I mean how is she feeling? What's the matter with you?" (He looked peeved.)
    (E) "Nothing. Just explain a little clearer, what do you mean?"
    (S) "Skip it. How are your Med School applications coming?"
    (E) "What do you mean, 'How are they?'"
    (S) "You know what I mean."
    (E) "I really don't."
    (S) "What's the matter with you? Are you sick?"

Case 3. On Friday night my husband and I were watching television. My husband remarked that he was tired. I asked, "How are you tired? Physically, mentally, or just bored?"

    (S) "I don't know, I guess physically, mainly."
    (E) "You mean that your muscles ache, or your bones?"
    (S) "I guess so. Don't be so technical."
    (S) (After more watching) "All these old movies have the same kind of old iron bedstead in them."
    (E) "What do you mean? Do you mean all old movies, or some of them, or just the ones you have seen?"
    (S) "What's the matter with you? You know what I mean."
    (E) "I wish you would be more specific."
    (S) "You know what I mean! Drop dead!"

Case 4. During a conversation (with the male E's fiancee) the E questioned the meaning of various words used by the subject. For the first minute and a half the subject responded to the questions as if they were legitimate inquiries. Then she responded with "Why are you asking me these questions?" and repeated this two or three times after each question. She became nervous and jittery, her face and hand movements . . . uncontrolled. She appeared bewildered and complained that I was making her nervous and demanded that I "Stop it!" . . . The subject picked up a magazine and covered her face. She put down the magazine and pretended to be engrossed. When asked why she was looking at the magazine, she closed her mouth and refused any further remarks.

Case 5. My friend said to me, "Hurry or we will be late." I asked him what did he mean by late and from what point of view did it have reference. There was a look of perplexity and cynicism on his face. "Why are you asking me such silly questions? Surely I don't have to explain such a statement. What is wrong with you today? Why should I have to stop to analyze such a statement. Everyone understands my statements and you should be no exception."

> *Case 6.* The victim waved his hand cheerily.
> (S) "How are you?"
> (E) "How am I in regard to what? My health, my finance, my school work, my peace of mind, my . . ."
> (S) (Red in the face and suddenly out of control.) "Look! I was just trying to be polite. Frankly, I don't give a damn how you are."

Case 7. My friend and I were talking about a man whose overbearing attitude annoyed us. My friend expressed his feeling.
> (S) "I'm sick of him."
> (E) "Would you explain what is wrong with you that you are sick?"
> (S) "Are you kidding me? You know what I mean."
> (E) "Please explain your ailment."
> (S) (He listened to me with a puzzled look.) "What came over you? We never talk this way, do we?"

Case 8. Apparently as a casual afterthought, my husband mentioned Friday night, "Did you remember to drop off my shirts today?"

Taking nothing for granted, I replied, "I remember that you said something about it this morning. What shirts did you mean, and what did you mean by having them 'dropped' off?" He looked puzzled, as though I must have answered some other question than the one asked.

Instead of making the explanation he seemed to be waiting for, I persisted, "I thought your shirts were all in pretty good shape; why not keep them a little longer?" I had the uncomfortable feeling I had overplayed the part.

He no longer looked puzzled, but indignant. He repeated, "A little longer! What do you mean, and what have you done with my shirts?"

I acted indignant too. I asked, "What shirts? You have sport shirts, plain shirts, wool shirts, regular shirts, and dirty shirts. I'm no mind reader. What exactly did you want?"

My husband again looked confused, as though he was trying to justify my behavior. He seemed simultaneously to be on the defensive and offensive. He assumed a very patient, tolerant air, and said, "Now, let's start all over again. Did you drop off my shirts today?"

I replied, "I heard you before. It's your meaning I wish was more clear."

As far as I am concerned dropping off your shirts—which ever shirts you mean —could mean giving them to the Goodwill, leaving them at the cleaners, at the laundromat, or throwing them out. I never know what you mean with those vague statements."

He reflected on what I said, then changed the entire perspective by acting as though we were playing a game, that it was all a joke. He seemed to enjoy the joke. He ruined my approach by assuming the role I thought was mine. He then said, "Well, let's take this step by step with 'yes' or 'no' answers: Did you see the dirty shirts I left on the kitchenette, yes or no?"

I could see no way to complicate his question, so felt forced to answer "Yes." In the same fashion, he asked if I picked up the shirts; if I put them in the car; if I left them at the laundry; and if I did all these things that day, Friday. My answers were "Yes."

The experiment, it seemed to me, had been cut short by his reducing all the parts of his previous question to their simplest terms, which were given to me as if I were a child unable to handle any complex questions, problems, or situations.

Demonstration 2: Breaching the Interchangeability of Standpoints. In order to breach the presupposed interchangeability of standpoints, students were asked to enter a store, to select a customer, and to treat the customer as a clerk while giving no recognition that the subject was any other person than the experimenter took him to be and without giving any indication that the experimenter's treatment was anything other than perfectly reasonable and legitimate.

Case 1. One evening, while shopping at Sears with a friend, I (male) found myself next to a woman shopping at the copper-clad pan section. The store was busy . . . and clerks were hard to find. The woman was just a couple of feet away and my friend was behind me. Pointing to a tea kettle, I asked the woman if she did not think the price was rather high. I asked in a friendly tone. . . . She looked at me and then at the kettle and said "yes." I then said I was going to take it anyway. She said, "Oh," and started to move sideways away from me. I quickly asked her if she was not going to wrap it for me and take my cash. Still moving slowly away and glancing first at me, then at the kettle, then at the other pans farther away from me, she said the clerk was "over there" pointing off somewhere. In a harsh tone, I asked if she was not going to wait on me. She said, "No, No, I'm not the saleslady. There she is." I said that I knew that the extra help was inexperienced, but that was no reason not to wait on a customer. "Just wait on me. I'll be patient." With that, she flushed with anger and walked rapidly away, looking back once as if to ask if it could really be true.

The following three protocols are the work of a forty-year-old female graduate student in clinical psychology.

Case 2. We went to V's book store, noted not so much for its fine merchandise and its wide range of stock as it is in certain circles for the fact that the clerks are male homosexuals. I approached a gentleman who was browsing at a table stacked neatly with books.

(E) "I'm in a hurry. Would you get a copy of *Sociopathic Behavior* by Lemert, please?"

(S) (Looked E up and down, drew himself very straight, slowly laid the book down, stepped back slightly, then leaned forward and in a low voice said) "I'm interested in sociopathic behavior, too. That's why I'm here. I study the fellows here by pretending to be . . ."

(E) (Interrupting) "I'm not particularly interested in whether you are or are only pretending to be. Please just get the book I asked for."

(S) (Looked shocked. More than surprised, believe me. Stepped around the display table, deliberately placed his hands on the books, leaned forward and shouted) "I don't have such a book. I'm not a clerk! I'm— Well!" (Stalked out of the store.)

Case 3. When we entered I. Magnin's there was one woman who was fingering a sweater, the only piece of merchandise to be seen in the shop. I surmised that the clerk must be in the stockroom.

(E) "That is a lovely shade, but I'm looking for one a little lighter. Do you have one in cashmere?"

(S) "I really don't know, you see I'm . . ."

(E) (*Interruping*) "Oh, you are new here? I don't mind waiting while you look for what I want."

(S) "Indeed I shall not!"

(E) "But aren't you here to *serve* customers?"

(S) "I'm not! I'm here to . . ."

(E) (Interrupts) "This is hardly the place for such an attitude. Now please show me a cashmere sweater a shade or two lighter than this one."

(The clerk entered.)

(S) (To clerk) "My dear, this—(pointed her face toward E)—*person* insists on being shown a sweater. Please take care of her while I compose myself. I want to be certain this (sweater) will do, and she (pointed her face again at E) is so *insistent.*" (S carried the sweater with her, walked haughtily to a large upholstered chair, sat in it, brushed her gloved hands free from imaginary dirt, jerked her shoulders, fluffed her suit jacket, and glared at E).

Case 4. While visiting with a friend in Pasadena, I told him about this being-taken-for-the-clerk-experiment. The friend is a Professor Emeritus of Mathematics at the California Institute of Technology and the successful author of many books, some technical, some fictional, and he is most satirical in his contemplations of his fellow man. He begged to be allowed to accompany me and to aid me in the selection of scenes . . . We went first to have luncheon at the Atheneum, which caters to the students, faculty and guests of Cal Tech. While we were still in the lobby, my host pointed out a gentleman who was standing in the large drawing room near the entrance to the dining room and said, "Go to it. There's a good subject for you." He stepped aside to watch. I walked toward the man very deliberately and proceeded as follows. (I will use E to designate myself; S, the subject.)

(E) "I should like a table on the west side, a quiet spot, if you please. And what is on the menu?"

(S) (Turned toward E but looked past and in the direction of the foyer) said, "Eh, ah, madam, I'm sure." (looked past E again, looked at a pocket watch, replaced it, and looked toward the dining room).

(E) "Surely luncheon hours are not over. What do you recommend I order today?"

(S) "I don't know. You see, I'm waiting . . ."

(E) (Interrupted with) "Please don't keep me standing here while you wait. Kindly show me to a table."

(S) "But Madam,—" (started to edge away from door, and back into the lounge in a lightly curving direction around E)

(E) "My good man—" (at this S's face flushed, his eyes rounded and opened wide)

(S) "But—you—I—oh dear!" (He seemed to wilt)

(E) (Took S's arm in hand and propelled him toward the dining room door, slightly ahead of herself.)

(S) (Walked slowly but stopped just within the room, turned around and for the first time looked directly and very appraisingly at E, took out the watch, looked at it, held it to his ear, replaced it, and muttered) "Oh dear."

(E) "It will take only a minute for you to show me to a table and take my order. Then you can return to wait for your customers. After all, I am a guest and a customer, too."

(S) (Stiffened slightly, walked jerkily toward the nearest empty table, held a chair for E to be seated, bowed slightly, muttered "My pleasure," hurried toward the door, stopped, turned, looked back at E with a blank facial expression.)

At this point E's host walked up to S, greeted him, shook hands, and propelled him toward E's table. S stopped a few steps from the table, looked directly at, then through E, and started to walk back toward the door. Host told him E was the young lady whom he had invited to join them at lunch, (then introduced me to one of the big names in the physics world, a pillar of the institution!). S seated himself reluctantly and perched rigidly on his chair, obviously uncomfortable. E smiled, made light and polite inquiries about his work, mentioned various functions attended which had honored him, then complacently remarked that it was a shame E had not met him personally before now, so that she should not have mistaken him for the maitre-d. The host chattered about his long-time friendship with me, while S fidgeted and looked again at his pocket watch, wiped his forehead with a table napkin, looked at E but avoided meeting her eyes. When the host mentioned that E is studying sociology at UCLA, S suddenly burst into loud laughter, realized that everyone in the room was looking in the direction of our table, abruptly became quiet, then said to E "You mistook me for the maitre-d, didn't you?"

(E) "Deliberately, sir."

(S) "Why deliberately?"

(E) "You have just been used as the unsuspecting subject in an experiment."

(S) "Diabolic. But clever, I must say, (To our host) I haven't been so shaken since —— denounced my theory of —— in 19—. And the wild thoughts that ran through my mind! Call the receptionist from the lobby, go to the men's room, turn this woman to the first person that comes along. Damn these early diners, there's nobody coming in at this time. Time is standing still, or my watch has stopped. I will talk to —— about this, make sure it doesn't happen to 'somebody.' Damn a persistent woman. I'm not her 'good man!' I'm Dr. _____, and not to be pushed around. This can't be happening. If I do take her to that damned table she wants, I can get away from her, and I'll just take it easy until I can. I remember _____ (hereditary psychopath, wife of one of the 'family' of the institution) maybe if I do what *this* one wants she will not make any more trouble than this. I wonder if she is 'off.' She certainly looks normal. Wonder how you can really tell?"

Demonstration 3: Breaching the Expectancy That a Knowledge of a Relationship of Interaction Is a Commonly Entertained Scheme of Communication. Schutz proposed that from the member's point of view, an event of conduct, like a move in a game, consists of an event-in-a-social-order. Thus, for the member, its recognizably real character is furnished by attending its occurrence with respect to a corpus of socially sanctioned knowledge of the social relationships that the member uses and assumes that others use as the same scheme of expression and interpretation.

It was decided to breach this expectancy by having students treat a situation as something that it "obviously" and "really" was not. Students were instructed to spend from fifteen minutes to an hour in their own homes acting as if they were boarders. They were instructed to conduct themselves in a circumspect and polite fashion: to avoid getting personal; to use formal address; to speak only when they were spoken to.

In nine of forty-nine cases students either refused to do the assignment (five cases) or the try was "unsuccessful" (four cases). Four of the "no try" students said they were afraid to do it; a fifth said she preferred to avoid the risk of exciting her mother who had a heart condition. In two of the "unsuccessful" cases the family treated it as a joke from the beginning and refused, despite the continuing actions of the student experimenter, to change. A third family took the view that something of an undisclosed sort was the matter, but what it might be was of no concern to them. In the fourth family the father and mother remarked that the daughter was being "extra nice" and undoubtedly wanted something that she would shortly reveal.

In the remaining four-fifths of the cases family members were stupefied, vigorously sought to make the strange actions intelligible, and to restore the situation to normal appearances. Reports were filled with accounts of astonishment, bewilderment, shock, anxiety, embarrassment, and anger as well as with charges by various family members that the student was mean, inconsiderate, selfish, nasty, and impolite. Family members demanded explanations: "What's the matter?" "What's gotten into you?" "Did you get fired?" "Are you sick?" "What are you being so superior about?" "Why are you mad?" "Are you out of your mind or are you just stupid?" One student acutely embarrassed his mother in front of her friends by asking if she minded if he had a snack from the refrigerator. "Mind if you have a little snack? You've been eating little snacks around here for years without asking me. What's gotten into you?!" One mother, infuriated when her daughter spoke to her only when she was spoken to, began to shriek in angry denunciation of the daughter for her disrespect and insubordination and refused to be calmed by the student's sister. A father berated his daughter for being insufficiently concerned for the welfare of others and of acting like a spoiled child.

Occasionally family members would first treat the student's action as a cue for a joint comedy routine which was soon replaced by irritation and exasperated anger at the student for not knowing "when enough was enough." Family members mocked the "politeness" of the students— "Certainly Mr. Dinerberg!"—or charged the student with acting like a wise guy and generally reproved the "politeness" with sarcasm.

Explanations were sought in terms of understandable and previous motives of the student: the accusation that the student was covering up something important that the family should know; that the student was working too hard in school; that the student was ill; that there had been "another fight" with a fiancee.

Unacknowledged explanations were followed by withdrawal of the offended member, attempted isolation of the culprit, retaliation, and denunciation. "Don't bother with him, he's in one of his moods again." "Pay no attention but just wait until he asks me for something." "You're cutting me, okay. I'll cut you and then some." "Why must you always create friction in our family harmony?" A father followed his son into the bedroom. "Your mother is right. You don't look well and you're not talking sense. You had better get another job that doesn't require such late hours." To this the student replied that he appreciated his consideration, but that he felt fine and only wanted a little privacy. The father responded in high rage, "I don't want any more of *that* out of *you*. And if you can't treat your mother decently, you'd better move out!"

There were no cases in which the situation was not restorable upon the student's explanation. Nevertheless, for the most part, family members were not amused and only rarely did they find the experience instructive, as the student argued that it was supposed to have been. After hearing the explanation, a sister replied coldly on behalf of a family of four, "Please, no more of these experiments. We're not rats you know." Occasionally an explanation was accepted and still it added offense. In several cases students reported that the explanation left them, their families, or both wondering how much of what the student had said was "in character" and how much the student "really meant."

Students found the assignment difficult to complete because of not being treated as if they were in the role that they are attempting to play and of being confronted with situations to which they did not know how a boarder would respond.

There were several entirely unexpected results. (1) Although many students reported extensive rehearsals in imagination, very few of those that did it mentioned anticipatory fears or embarrassment. (2) Although unanticipated and nasty developments frequently occurred, in only one case did a student report serious regrets. (3) Very few students reported heartfelt relief when the hour was over. They were much more likely to report a partial relief. They frequently reported that in response to the anger of others they became angry in return and slipped easily into subjectively recognizable feelings and actions.

Demonstration 4: Breaching the Grasp of "What Anyone Knows" To Be Correct Grounds of Action of a Real Social World. Among the possibilities that a premedical student could treat as correct grounds for his further inferences and actions about such matters as how a medical school intake interview is conducted or how an applicant's conduct is related to his chances of admission, certain ones (e.g., that deferring to the interviewer's interests is a condition for making a favorable impression) he treats as matters that he is required to know and act upon as a condition of his competence as a premedical candidate. He expects others like him to know and act upon the same things; and he expects that as he expects others to know and act upon them, the others in turn expect the like of him.

A procedure was designed to breach the constitutive expectancies attached to "what-any-competent-premedical-candidate-knows" while satisfying the three conditions under which their breach would presumably produce confusion.

Twenty-eight premedical students, of the University of California in Los Angeles, were run individually through a three-hour experimental interview. As part of the solicitation of subjects, as well as the beginning of the interview, E identified himself as a representative of an Eastern medical school who was attempting to learn why the medical school intake interview was such a stressful situation. It was hoped that identifying E as a person with medical school ties would minimize the chance that students would "leave the field" once the accent breaching procedure began. How the other two conditions of (a) managing a redefinition in insufficient time and (b) not being able to count on consensual support for an alternative definition of social reality were met will be apparent in the following description.

During the first hour of the interview, the student furnished the facts-of-life about interviews for admission to medical school by answering for the "representative" such questions as "What sources of information about a candidate are available to medical schools?" "What can a medical school learn about a candidate from these sources?" "What kind of a man are the medical schools looking for?" "What should a good candidate do in the interview?" "What should he avoid?" With this much completed, the student was told that the "representative's" research interests had been satisfied. The student was asked if he would care to hear a recording of an actual interview. All students wanted very much to hear the recording.

The recording was a faked one between a "medical school interviewer" and an "applicant." The applicant was depicted as being a boor; his language was ungrammatical and filled with colloquialisms; he was evasive; he contradicted the interviewer; he bragged; he ran down other schools and professions; he insisted on knowing how he had done in the interview and so on.[9]

Detailed assessments by the student of the recorded applicant were obtained immediately after the recording was finished. The following edited assessment is representative:

> I didn't like it. I didn't like his attitude. I didn't like anything about him. Everything he said grated the wrong way. I didn't like his smoking. The way he kept saying "Yeah-h!" He didn't show that he realized that the interviewer had his future in his hands. I didn't like the vague way he answered questions. I didn't like the way he pressed at the end of the interview. He was disrespectful. His motives were too obvious. He made a mess of it. He finished with a bang to say the least . . . His answers to questions were stupid. I felt that the interviewer was telling him that he wasn't going to get in. I didn't like the interview. I felt it was too informal. To a degree it's good if it's natural but . . . the interview is not something to breeze through. It's just not the place for chit-chat. He had fairly good grades but . . . he's not interested in things outside of school and didn't say what he did *in* school. Then he didn't *do* very much—outside of this lab. I didn't like the man at all. I never met an applicant like that! "My pal"—Just one of these little chats. I never met anybody *like* that. Wrong-way Corrigan.

The student was then given information from the applicant's "official record." This information was deliberately contrived to contradict the principal points in the student's assessment. For example, if the student said that the applicant must have come from a lower class family, he was told that the applicant's father was vice president of a firm that manufactured pneumatic doors for trains and buses. If the applicant had

[9] The actual script of the interview is available from the author upon request.

been thought to be ignorant, he was described as having excelled in courses like The Poetry of Milton and Dramas of Shakespeare. If the student said the applicant did not know how to get along with people, then the applicant was pictured as having worked as a voluntary solicitor for Sydenham Hospital in New York City and had raised $32,000 from thirty "big givers." The belief that the applicant was stupid and would not do well in a scientific field was met by citing A grades in organic and physical chemistry and graduate level performance in an undergraduate research course.

The Ss wanted very much to know what "the others" thought of the applicant, and had he been admitted? The "others" had been previously and casually identified by the "representative" as "Dr. Gardner, the medical school interviewer," "six psychiatrically trained members of the admissions committee who heard only the recorded interview," and "other students I talked to."

The S was told that the applicant had been admitted and was living up to the promise that the medical school interviewer and the "six psychiatrists" had found and expressed in the following recommendation of the applicant's characterological fitness.

Dr. Gardner, the medical school interviewer, wrote, "A well-bred, polite young man, poised, affable, and self-confident. Capable of independent thinking. Interests of a rather specialized character. Marked intellectual curiosity. Alert and free of emotional disturbances. Marked maturity of manner and outlook. Meets others easily. Strongly motivated toward a medical career. Definite ideas of what he wants to achieve which are held in good perspective. Unquestioned sincerity and integrity. Expressed himself easily and well. Recommend favorable consideration." The six psychiatric members of the admissions committee agreed in all essentials.

Concerning the views of "other students," S was told that he was, for example, the thirtieth student I had seen; that twenty-eight before him were in entire agreement with the medical school interviewer's assessment; and that the remaining two had been slightly uncertain but at the first bit of information had seen him just as the others had.

Following this, Ss were invited to listen to the record a second time, after which they were asked to assess the applicant again.

RESULTS. Twenty-five of the twenty-eight subjects were taken in. The following does not apply to the three who were convinced there was a deception. Two of these are discussed at the conclusion of this section.

Incongruous materials, presented to S in the order indicated, were performance information, and characterological information. Performance information dealt with the applicant's activities, grades, family background, courses, charity work, and the like. Characterological information consisted of character assessments of him by the "medical school interviewers," the "six psychiatrically trained members of the admissions committee," and the "other students."

Subjects managed incongruities of performance data with vigorous attempts to make it factually compatible with their original assessments. For example, when they said that the applicant sounded like a lower class person, they were told that his father was vice-president of a national corporation that manufactured pneumatic doors for trains and buses. Here are some typical replies:

"He should have made the point that he *could* count on money."

"That explains why he said he had to work. Probably his father made him work. That would make a lot of his moans unjustified in the sense that things were really not so bad."

"What does that have to do with values?!"

"You could tell from his answers. You could tell that he was used to having his own way."

"That's something the interviewer knew that *I* didn't know."

"Then he's an out and out liar!"

When Ss said that the applicant was selfish and could not get along with people, they were told that he had worked as a volunteer for Sydenham Hospital and had raised $32,000 from thirty "big givers."

"He seems to be a good salesman. So possibly he's missing his profession. I'd say *definitely* he's missing his profession!"

"They probably contributed because of the charity and not because they were solicited."

"Pretty good. Swell. Did he know them personally?"

"It's very fashionable to work, for example, during the war for Bundles for Britain. So that doesn't—definitely!—show altruistic motives at all. He is a person who is subject to fashion and I'm very critical of that sort of thing.

"He's so forceful he might have shamed them into giving."

"People who are wealthy—his father would naturally see those people —big contributions—they could give a lot of money and not know what they're giving it for."

That he had a straight A average in physical science courses began to draw bewilderment.

"He took quite a variety of courses . . . I'm baffled.—Probably the interview wasn't a very good mirror of his character."

"He did seem to take some odd courses. They seem to be fairly normal. Not normal—but—It doesn't strike me one way or the other."

"Well! I think you can analyze it this way. In psychological terms.

See—one possible way—now I may be all *wet* but this is the way I look at *that*. He probably suffered from an inferiority complex and that's an overcompensation for his inferiority complex. His *great* marks—his *good* marks are a compensation for his failure—in social dealings perhaps, I don't know."

"Woops! And only third alternate at Georgia. (Deep sigh) I can see why he'd feel resentment about not being admitted to Phi Bet."

(Long silence) "Well! From what—that leads me to think he's a grind or something like that."

Attempts to resolve the incongruities produced by the character assessment of "Gardner" and "the other six judges" were much less frequent than normalizing attempts with performance information. Open expressions of bewilderment and anxiety interspersed with silent ruminations were characteristic.

(Laugh) "Golly!" (Silence) "I'd think it would be the other way around."—(Very subdued) "Maybe I'm all wro—My orientation is all off. I'm completely baffled."

"Not polite. Self confident he certainly was. But not polite.—I don't know. Either the interviewer was a little crazy or else I am." (Long pause) "That's rather shocking. It makes me have doubts about my own thinking. Perhaps my values in life are wrong, I don't know."

(Whistles) "I—I didn't think he sounded well bred at all. That whole tone of voice!!—I—Perhaps you noticed though, when he said 'You should have said in the first place' before he took it with a smile.— But even so! No, no I can't see that. 'You should have said that before.' Maybe he was being funny though. Exercising a—No! To me it sounded impertinent!"

"Ugh—Well, that certainly puts a different slant on my conception of interviews. Gee—that—confuses me all the more."

"Well—(laugh)—Hhh!—Ugh! Well, maybe he looked like a nice boy. He did—he did get his point across.—Perhaps—seeing the person would make a big difference.—Or perhaps I would never make a good interviewer." (Reflectively and almost inaudibly) "They didn't mention any of the things I mentioned." (HG: Eh?) (Louder) "They didn't mention any of the things I mentioned and so I feel like a complete failure."

Soon after the performance data produced its consternation, an occasional request would be made: "What did the other students make of him?" Only after Gardner's assessment, and the responses to it had been made were the opinions of the "other students" given. In some cases the subject was told "34 out of 35 before you," in others 43 out of 45, 19 out of 20, 51 out of 52. All the numbers were large. For 18 of the 25 students the delivery hardly varied from the following verbatim protocols:

[34 out of 35] I don't know. —I still stick to my original convictions. I—I—Can you tell *me* what—I saw wrong. Maybe—I—I had the wrong idea—the wrong attitude all along. (Can you tell me? I'm interested that there should be such a disparity.) Definitely. —I—think—it would be definitely the other way—I can't make sense of it. I'm completely baffled, believe me. —I—I don't understand how I could have been so wrong. Maybe my ideas—my evaluations of people are—just twisted. I mean maybe I had the wrong—maybe my sense of values—is—off—or—different—from the other 33. But I don't think that's the case—because usually—and in all modesty I say this—I—I can judge people. I mean in class, in organizations I belong to—I usually judge them right. So therefore I don't understand at *all* how I could have been so wrong. I don't think I was under any stress or strain—here—tonight but—I don't understand it.

[43 out of 45] [Laugh] I don't know what to say now. —I'm troubled by my inability to judge the guy better than that. [Subdued] I shall sleep tonight, certainly—[Very subdued] but it certainly bothers me. —Sorry that I didn't—*Well!* One question that arises—I may be wrong—(Can you see how they might have seen him?) No. No, I can't see it, no. —Sure with all that background material, yes, but I don't see how Gardner did it without it. Well, I guess that makes Gardner, Gardner, and me, me. (The other 45 students didn't have the background material) Yeah, yeah, yeah. I mean I'm not denying it at all. I mean for myself, there's no sense saying—Of course! With their background they would be accepted, especially the second man, good God! —Okay, what else?

[23 out of 25] [Softly] Maybe I'm tired. (HG, "Eh?") [Burst of laughter.] Maybe I didn't get enough sleep last night. —Uhh! —Well—I might not have been looking for the things that the other men were looking for. —I wasn't—Huh! —It puts me at a loss, really.

[10 out of 10] So I'm alone in my judgment. I don't know sir! I don't know, sir!! —I can't explain it. It's senseless. —I tried to be impartial at the beginning. I admit I was prejudiced immediately.

[51 out of 52] You mean that 51 others stuck to their guns, too? (Stuck to their guns in the sense that they saw him just as the judges saw him.) Uh huh. [Deep sigh] I still don't—Yeah! I see. But just listening I don't think he was a—very good chance. But in light of his other things I feel that the interview was not—showing—the real—him. —Hhh!

[36 out of 37] I would go back on my former opinion but I wouldn't go back too far. I just don't see it. —Why should I have these different standards? Were my opinions more or less in agreement on the first man? (No.) That leads me to think. —That's funny. Unless you got 36 unusual people. I can't understand it. Maybe it's my personality. (Does it make any difference?) It *does* make a difference if I assume they're correct. What I consider is proper, they don't. —It's my attitude—Still in all a man of that sort would alienate me, A wise guy type to be avoided. Of course you can talk like that with other fellows—but in an interview? . . . Now I'm more con-

fused than I was at the beginning of the entire interview. I think I ought to
go home and look in the mirror and talk to myself. Do you have any ideas?
(Why? Does it disturb you?) Yes it *does* disturb me! It makes me think
my abilities to judge people and values are way off from normal. It's not a
healthy situation. (What difference does it make?) If I act the way I act it
seems to me that I'm just putting my head in the lion's mouth. I did have
preconceptions but they're shattered all to hell. It makes me wonder about
myself. Why should I have these different standards? It all points to me.

Of the twenty-five Ss who were taken in, seven were unable to resolve
the incongruity of having been wrong about such an obvious matter and
were unable to "see" the alternative. Their suffering was dramatic and
unrelieved. Five more resolved it with the view that the medical school
had accepted a good man; five others with the view that it had accepted
a boor. Although they changed, they nevertheless did not abandon their
former views. For them Gardner's view could be seen "in general," but
the grasp lacked convincingness. When attention was drawn to particulars, the general picture would evaporate. These Ss were willing to
entertain and use the "general" picture, but they suffered whenever in-
digestible particulars of the same portrait came into view. Subscription
to the "general" picture was accompanied by a recitation of characteristics
that were not only the opposite of those in the original view but were
intensified by superlative adjectives like "supremely" poised, "very" natural, "most" confident, "very" calm. Further, they saw the new features
through a new appreciation of the way the medical examiner had been
listening. They saw, for example, that the examiner was smiling when
the applicant had forgotten to offer him a cigarette.

Three more Ss were convinced that there was deception and acted
on the conviction through the interview. They showed no disturbance.
Two of these showed acute suffering as soon as it appeared that the interview was finished, and they were being dismissed with no acknowledge-
ment of a deception. Three others inadvertently suffered in silence and
confounded E. Without any indication to E, they regarded the interview as an experimental one in which they were being asked to solve
some problems and therefore were being asked to do as well as possible
and to make no changes in their opinions, for only then would they be
contributing to the study. They were difficult for me to understand during the interview because they displayed marked anxiety, yet their
remarks were bland and were not addressed to the matters that were
provoking it. Finally three more Ss contrasted with the others. One of
these insisted that the character assessments were semantically ambiguous
and because there was insufficient information a "high correlation opinion" was not possible. A second, and the only one in the entire series,
found, according to his account, the second portrait as convincing as the

original one. When the deception was revealed, he was disturbed that he could have been as convinced as he was. The third one, in the face of everything, showed only slight disturbance of very short duration. However, he alone among the subjects had already been interviewed for medical school, had excellent contacts, despite a grade point average of less than C he estimated his chances of admission as fair, and finally he expressed his preference for a career in the diplomatic service over a career in medicine.

As a final observation, twenty-two of the twenty-eight Ss expressed marked relief—ten of them with explosive expressions—when I disclosed the deception. Unanimously they said that the news of the deception permitted them to return to their former views. Seven Ss had to be convinced that there had been a deception. When the deception was revealed, they asked what they were to believe. Was I telling them that there had been a deception in order to make them feel better? No pains were spared, and whatever truth or lies that had to be told were told in order to establish the truth that there had been a deception.

Remarks on Some Modifications of the Attitude of Daily Life

The attitude of daily life furnishes a person's perceived environment its definition as an environment of social realities known in common. The sociologists gloss this environment with the term "common culture." The attitude of daily life is constitutive of the institutionalized common understandings of the practical everyday organization and workings of the society as seen "from within." Modifications of its presuppositions thereby modify the real environments of the society's members. Such modifications transform one socially defined environment of real objects into another environment of real objects.

One such modification includes its being learned. This involves for the neonate the growth of a world in Olds' (1958) and Parsons' (1955) sense of the growth of object systems, and the progressively enforced and enforceable compliance of the "developing member" to the attitude of daily life as a competent societal member's "way of looking at things."

A second modification consists of the ceremonial transformation of one environment of real objects into another. We mentioned before that such modifications occur in the cases of play, theatre going, religious conversion, "conventionalization," and scientific inquiry. If, for each of these cases, one asks where does the person "go" or where is he "called back to" when he "stops playing" or is admonished to "stop playing," or "leaves the theatre" or is admonished to "stop acting and be yourself," or "backslides" from his religious promises or is criticized for exaggerated virtue, or "puts aside his party disguise" or is warned that "the party is over," or "forgets his scientific problem for awhile" or is chided for his "absent mindedness," that in each case he returns to "life as usual" or is expected to give evidence of his grasp of the institutionalized common understandings of the organization and workings of the everyday society, i.e., of his "practical circumstances."

A third modification consists of the instrumental transformations of real environments of objects that occur in experimentally induced psychosis, extreme fatigue, acute sensory deprivation, the use of hallucinogenic drugs, brain injuries, and the like. To each of these there corresponds the modification of the presuppositions on the one hand and the social structures that are produced by actions oriented to these modified environments on the other. For example, subjects who were given Lysergic Acid at the U.C.L.A. Alcoholism Clinic frequently met the experimenter's inquiries about what they saw in the room with the rebuff that his questions were banal and indicated a stupid fellow who could never appreciate what they saw even if they were to trouble themselves to try to make it plain to him. An analysis of interaction using Bales' scoring procedures would have varied accordingly.

A fourth modification consists of the "discovery of culture" by anthropologists and sociologists. This discovery consists of the discovery from within the society of commonsense knowledge of social structures, and the attempt to treat commonsense action and commonsense knowledge as objects of mere theoretical social scientific interest. The modification of the attitude and objects of commonsense actions is detected in the attempts by sociologists to furnish in attitude and methods the procedures whereby commonsense attitude, actions, and knowledge of social structures are to be brought under the jurisdiction of sociological theory as a definition of their essential features. In their ideas, if not or perhaps not yet, in their actual practices, sociologists have thereby set for themselves the task of discovering an historically new and unprecedented definition of "real social structures." In that commonsense activities and environments are simultaneously the topic as well as the feature of sociological inquiries, a concern for describing the actual features of sociology's attitude and methods as possible modifications of the attitude and methods of commonsense, the "discovery of culture," reconstructs the problems of the sociology of knowledge and locates them at the heart of the sociological enterprise and with full seriousness.

In his essay, "The Stranger" (1944), Schutz spoke of a fifth modification which he described as the attitude's presuppositions "ceasing to stand the test." The stranger for Schutz was the person whose attempts to assign the attributions of the attitude of daily life to the intended sense of actual appearances produced situations of chronic "error." He becomes, says Schutz, the person who has to place in question nearly everything that seems to be unquestionable to the members of the group in which he seeks membership. His hitherto unquestioned schemes of interpretation become invalidated and cannot be used as a scheme of orientation with the new social surroundings. He uses with difficulty the in-group culture as a scheme of orientation for he is unable to trust it. The apparent unity of the cultural pattern for the in-group members does not exist for him. He has continually to realize his interests while having to reckon with fundamental discrepancies between his own and other's ways of seeing situations and handling them. Situations that in-group members see through in a glance, and who see too an appropriate recipe for its management, are specifically problematic and lacking in obviousness of sense or consequences. From the in-group member's view the stranger is a man without a history. Most importantly, too, his crisis is a personal crisis.

In the language of this paper, the perceivedly normal appearances of the stranger's scenes of interaction are for him specifically problematical. The stranger is the person whose rights to manage decisions of sensibility, objectivity, and warrant without interference from others, i.e., whose competence, neither he nor others are able to take for granted.

Since each of the presuppositions assigns a feature to the actor's environment, the user may suffer a nasty surprise with respect to each of them. Thus there is a sixth modification. It is possible to induce experimentally the breach of these suppositions by deliberately modifying scenic events so as to systematically disappoint these attributions. The attributer's environment should thereby be made strange to him and accordingly he should believe himself and act in the presence of others like a stranger.

A radical version of this modification consists of rendering the attitude's presuppositions inoperative. The procedure with premedical students was intended to produce such a modification. Despite the shortcomings of the demonstration, it nevertheless suggests a model for formulating the problematic phenomena of "alienation," "anomie," "deviance," and "disorganization" using the commonsensically ordered and ordering routines of everyday actions and their objects as the point of departure.

By way of brief explication, we may call to mind how considerable are the risks for persons whose appearances breach the attitude's attributions—whether they do it experimentally, or whether like the psychopath they manage it with habitual conduct. From the status of a perceived competent person in his own eyes and in the eyes of others, i.e., from the status of bona fide membership, he may prove or be moved by persons for whom these attributions continue to operate to any of those statuses that every society reserves for those who "lack commonsense."

Every mother tongue provides for a range of social types who do not appreciate these attributions or for whom it is believed that these attributions do not operate: characteristically, children, pre-adults, aged persons, outsiders, boors, fools, ignoramuses, and barbarians. The major institutionalized statuses for those who lack commonsense would seem to be the alternative ones of criminality, illness, immorality, or incompetence. Organizationally speaking, those who lack commonsense are not only not trusted, but themselves do not trust. Indeed, one might preliminarily think of the trustworthy and trusting person as someone who managed the discrepancies with respect to these attributions in such a fashion as to maintain a public show of respect for them.

The fact that its modifications include such possibilities as its being learned, of its ceremonial and instrumental transformations, of its being discovered, and of its being breached or made inoperative gives the attitude of daily life a critical place in any attempt to account for stable, persistent, continuing, uniform social interactions.

In reviewing the modifications of the attitude of daily life and its world one begins to sense why it is that the theme of commonsense thinking has been a major one in all major philosophies. One may begin to sense, too, why the phenomenon of commonsense thinking, activities, and knowledge is such an obstinate feature and is so strongly idealized and defended in all stable groups. Obviously, however, such a sense does no more than point to the attitude and environments of commonsense as problematic phenomena. It does not formulate the problem. Part of Schutz's great stature as a sociologist consists in having performed the fundamental work that makes it possible for sociologists to do so. This paper has attempted to get on with the task.

Chapter 8

Information Acquisition in Decision Making [1,2]

John T. Lanzetta

Empirical studies of decision making have typically utilized choice situations in which the alternatives, the possible consequences of a choice, and probabilistic data on the relationship between alternatives and outcomes are specified (e.g., Edwards, 1956; Davidson, Suppes, and Siegel, 1957; Scodel, Ratoosh, and Minas, 1959). The information gathering and processing activities preceding decision are assumed to have occurred, and, in essence, are simulated by the experimenter. The decision maker is not permitted the option of delaying a choice until additional information is available or while actively seeking further information regarding alternative courses of action, possible outcomes, or the probabilistic relationships between alternatives and outcomes.

The experimental paradigm embodies the boundary conditions on information which decision theory requires, and it is not surprising that the studies employing it have generally focused on testing one or another of the assumptions or predictions of the theory. As Simon (1957) has pointed out, however, a theory of decision making must eventually consider the activities of acquiring and processing information that precede decision; it cannot assume and thus leave unexplained the basis for the choice itself. The omnipotent rationality of economic man must eventually be replaced by a concept of rationality which considers the capacities of the organism for assimilating and organizing information and the information state of the organism at the time of decision (March and Simon, 1958).

[1] The research reported in this paper was supported in whole or in part by the United States Air Force under Contract No. AF 33(616)–5845, monitored by Aero-Space Medical Laboratory, Directorate of Research, Wright Air Development Center, Wright-Patterson Air Force Base, Ohio.

[2] Grateful acknowledgment is due Dr. Vera Kanareff for her active and invaluable collaboration during all phases of the work; to Mrs. Jo Ann Davis for her assistance in conducting several of the studies and analyzing the results; to Dr. Louis Miller, Mr. James Driscoll, and Mrs. Joan Sibol for their current stimulation and assistance.

Unfortunately, once the boundaries of decision studies are extended to include information acquisition and processing activities, a host of theoretical and empirical issues are raised. Under what conditions does an organism instigate a search for information? What variables control the direction and redirection of search activity? How does the organism utilize the information acquired, i.e., how are tentative decisions generated and modified as new information is obtained? What variables control the termination of search and lead to the commitment to decide? These are obviously important, far reaching, and difficult questions and, although research from a variety of disciplines has contributed to an understanding of the issues (e.g., Bruner, Goodnow, and Austin, 1956; Neimark, 1958; Irwin and Smith, 1957; Marschak, 1954; Tanner and Swets, 1954), we are, on the whole, still in the inchoate stages.

The empirical research directly addressed to problems of information processes in decision making has been fragmentary and limited in scope. For example, the studies by Pruitt (1961), Irwin and Smith (1957), Neimark (1958), and Bilodeau (1952) date back only ten years or so and, although excellent in conception and execution, do little more than scratch the surface. More comprehensive in scope has been the work of Tanner and Swets (1954) in the area of signal detection, but the full generality of this work has yet to be realized. Becker's study of sequential decision (1958) and Shuford's recent work (1960) have made important contributions by introducing statistical decision theory and Bayesian concepts into empirical studies, but the theoretical orientation has, of necessity, constrained the range and variety of decision tasks examined.

With respect to theory, several normative and descriptive models have been developed or revitalized in recent years which show promise for one or another aspect of the problem. Generally the normative theories have ignored the problem of motivation or direction and have focused upon the conditions under which a "rational" decision maker should acquire costly information (Marschak, 1954; Savage, 1954). In common with normative theories of the choice process itself they strike one as overly restrictive and "unrealistic" in the assumptions required. Descriptive theories, on the other hand, have addressed themselves only loosely to problems of decision making and have virtually ignored "rational" factors as determiners of information acquisition. They have primarily focused on the conditions which motivate and direct exploratory behavior with some little attention devoted to the variables which control the maintenance or reinforcement of search (Berlyne, 1960; Festinger, 1957). Normative and descriptive theories, in common, have sidestepped the most difficult problem of information processing and utilization, e.g., what happens to the information acquired, how does it interact with, modify, or supplant existing data in memory, although Festinger (1957), Abelson and Rosenberg (1958), and Miller, Galanter, and Pribram (1961) have recently suggested models of cognitive structure and dynamics which are provocative.

Fortunately there is a burgeoning interest in theory development and empirical research in the area and an increased awareness of the potential relevance of work ostensibly far removed from decision making. The present symposium is a concrete manifestation of this trend and we may hope that it serves to stimulate and possibly direct further work on predecisional information processes.

The work to be reported in this paper is modest in the extreme in view of the scope of the problems and the present state of empirical knowledge and theory development. The research focuses on one of the simplest of the variables subsumed under information processing— the amount of information acquired prior to decision. The spirit of the inquiry was frankly descriptive in conception and remains primarily so today though theoretical concerns have come to play a larger role in determining the selection of variables and experimental paradigms. The "theory," at this stage, is a rather loosely formulated set of propositions borrowed in part from other contexts and in part representing efforts to account for our empirical data and serves, primarily, a heuristic purpose. In the discussion to follow, empirical findings will be stressed but some brief attention will be directed to theoretical issues.

Empirical Findings

Our general approach is to place adult humans in choice situations in which the alternatives and outcomes of choice are specified but with varying amounts of initial information relevant to the assignment of a probability distribution to the alternatives. Additional information useful in identifying the "best" alternative is available by reference to an external display. Such additional data are not costless, however; time, effort, and/or a monetary cost are levied for information items. Subjects have no control over the type of information available and interest is focused only on the amount of information acquired prior to making a decision.

Using this general procedure we have examined the effects of variables such as the cost of information, time pressures, and uncertainty, on information acquisition behavior. In addition, the prominence of individual differences in information acquisition has stimulated some exploratory work on personality and ability correlates of search behavior.

Information Acquisition Under Varying Cost-Payoff Schedules, Level of Aspiration, and Time Pressures. The earliest studies, though descriptive in intent, focused primarily upon variables which normative models suggested were important: costs, payoffs, and utility of outcomes. In addition, an effort was made to control the expected utility of acquiring information since normative decision models suggest maximization of expected utility as a reasonable criterion of choice. The expected utility was controlled by controlling the contingency between probability of payoff and amount of information acquisition, and by judicious selection of cost-payoff schedules. However, Ss were not informed of the probabilities of payoff or the contingency between probability of payoff and the number of information queries. From Ss' point of view, they were faced with the necessity of making a difficult choice, the probability of being "correct" presumably improved with additional information not because of an experimenter controlled contingency but because the information was relevant to selecting an alternative. Problems were carefully pretested to ensure that Ss, in fact, perceived the information as relevant.

In brief the experimental procedure was as follows: S is presented with a series of decision problems. Each problem requires a choice to be made among six possible alternatives and consists of an information base (a statement of the problem, some facts or observations which may aid in selecting an alternative, and a statement of the six alternatives) plus five additional information items. S is presented the information base and provided the option of making an immediate decision or obtaining one of the additional information items. This same option is available for a maximum of five information items at which time S must make a choice among the six alternatives. If correct, S receives a chip redeemable for money at the end of the session.

The problem materials are on slides and are projected on a ground glass screen. A movable opaque screen masks all but the "information base" of the problem. S "purchases" additional information by inserting a poker chip into a slot in a "query box"; the chip activates a circuit which drops the opaque screen to reveal an additional portion of the projected image. S makes a choice by depressing one of six appropriately labeled spring loaded switches located on a response unit. Depressing one of the switches automatically changes the slide presenting a new problem on the ground glass screen, and automatically returns the masking screen to its maximum height so that only the information base of the new problem is visible (slide 1).

Ss sit at a table facing the ground glass screen. The response box, "query" box, and chips are placed on the table in front of him. The number of queries made by S, the time delay between queries, and Ss choices are automatically recorded on an Esterline-Angus Operations Recorder.

Although the information S obtains by making a query is phenomenally relevant to reducing uncertainty (as determined by pretests), it in fact has no bearing on the probability of obtaining a payoff. The probability of payoff is programed by E and is a linear function of the number of information-seeking responses (queries) made by S. The schedule employed is as follows:

Query	0	1	2	3	4	5
Probability of payoff	0	.2	.4	.6	.8	1.0

Thus, an S who makes all five queries is assured of a payoff irrespective of his actual choice whereas one who makes no queries can receive no payoff whatever his choice. Intermediate numbers of queries are associated with intermediate probabilities of payoff. Thus, information-seeking and not effective decision making or information processing is instrumental to obtaining a payoff.

The major independent variables in the two studies were the information cost-payoff schedule, the level of aspiration for being correct, and time pressures. The conditions of information cost-payoff employed were equated for expected profit which varied with the number of queries in the following way:

No. of Query	Probability of Payoff	Expected Profit [3]
0	0	$ 0
1	.20	.01
2	.40	.02
3	.60	.03
4	.80	.04
5	1.00	.05

In the first study we examined two cost-payoff schedules, no cost for an information query with a $.05 payoff (0–5) and $.05 per query with a $.30 payoff (0–30), and three levels of aspiration. The level of aspiration was manipulated by the presentation of fictitious group norms. The three levels were introduced by reporting to S before the beginning of the session that either 25, 50, or 75 per cent of the problems were correctly solved by previous Ss. In addition two orders of problem presentation were used. The twenty-five problems were twice randomly ordered providing some check on sequence effects.

The two cost-payoff schedules, three levels of aspiration, and two problem sequences formed a two by three by two orthogonal design.

[3] Expected profit $= p \, \$ - qc$

where $p =$ probability of payoff
$\$ =$ amount of payoff
$q =$ number of queries
$c =$ cost of a query

Four male and four female Ss were randomly assigned to each cell of the design. Ss were summer school students at the University of Delaware.

In the second study there were five conditions of information cost-payoff used: no cost/query—no payoff (0–0), no cost/query—$.05 payoff (0–5), $.01/query—$.10 payoff (1–10), $.05/query—$.30 payoff (5–30), and $.10/query—$.55 payoff (10–55). For example, under the 5–30 schedule Ss "purchased" each additional information item at $.05 per item and won $.30 if they made a "correct" choice. In addition, two conditions of pacing were examined, one minute thirty seconds or two minutes fifteen seconds. This refers to the total time available for each problem. Ss were informed of the time constraints and given two practice problems to familiarize them with the pacing requirement. Pretesting indicated that both pacing conditions allowed sufficient time for obtaining and reading all of the information avaiable, although, as expected, Ss reported feeling "rushed" at the faster pace.

The five cost-payoff schedules and two pacing conditions formed a five by two orthogonal design. Ten male Ss were randomly assigned to each cell of the design. The one hundred Ss were freshman and sophomore undergraduates at the University of Delaware. In addition, fifty female Ss were run under the fast pace condition, ten each being randomly assigned to the five cost-payoff conditions.

Figures 8–1, 8–2, and 8–3 present the average number of queries per trial for the two cost-payoff schedules and the three level of aspiration

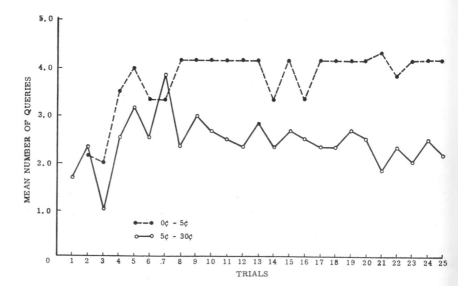

Fig. 8–1. Twenty-five per cent level of aspiration.

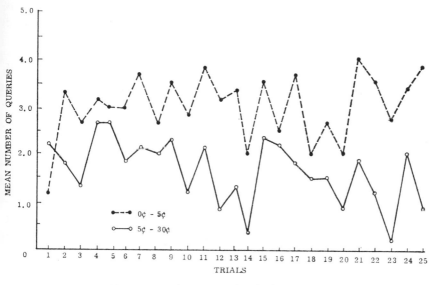

Fig. 8–2. Fifty per cent level of aspiration.

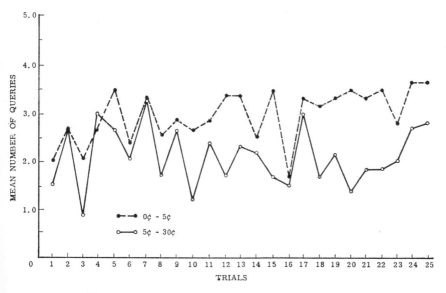

Fig. 8–3. Seventy-five per cent level of aspiration.

conditions used in the first experiment. In general, the over-all level of information seeking is not very high even when information is cost-less, and there is an unexpected slow rate of acquisition of information seeking, considering the instrumental value of a query. The lower cost-payoff schedule elicits a greater number of queries under all level of aspiration conditions, and there appears to be some inhibition of search for the higher levels of aspiration.

The effect of the cost-payoff schedule is seen more clearly in Figure 8–4, as is the change in information seeking over trials for the two cost conditions. Although there is an increase in queries under the 0–$.05 schedule, the average number of information-seeking responses never exceeds four queries per trial. For the $.05–$.30 schedule there is some indication of a decrease in queries over trials.

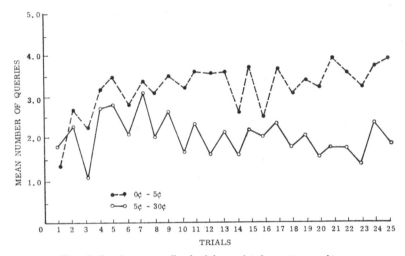

Fig. 8–4. Cost-pay off schedule and information seeking.

As noted earlier, in addition to the "search" measure, we obtained records of time devoted to various aspects of the task. The total time per problem could be naturally divided into three periods: the time from the initial presentation of the problem to the first query (problem time or PT), the time from the first query to the last query (total query time or QT), and the time from the last query to a decision (decision time o DT). It is assumed that PT reflects time spent in reading the problem and formulating an initial hypothesis as to the correct decision; QT reflects time devoted to acquiring, assimilating, and organizing addi tional information; and DT reflects time spent in evaluating the alterna tives and making a choice. The time measures, of course, can be con sidered only approximate indicators of the allocations of time to such functions since E had no control over Ss' cognitive activity. For example Ss may very well have delayed reading new information until after th last query, resulting in a short QT and long DT. At any rate, the assump tions bear mainly on the interpretation of results; the measures themselves are unambiguous.

Analyses of variance of the data on total time, problem time, average time per query, and decision time indicated the following: Subjects within conditions and trials contribute significant variance for all time measures whereas none of the experimental variables contribute significant variance. In considering the difference between cost-payoff schedules in average number of queries the failure to find time differences between schedules is surprising. Apparently Ss take as long to handle a problem under $.05–$.30 conditions as under 0–$.05 conditions even though they seek less information.

Although characterized by marked fluctuation, total time, average time per query, and decision time decrease somewhat over trials. Some of this variation almost certainly reflects a "problem" effect and effects contributed by the interaction between problems and experimental conditions. We return to a consideration of this problem effect below.

Figures 8–5 and 8–6 present the average number of queries per trial for the five cost-payoff conditions and two pacing rates used in experiment 2. The average number of queries per trial is consistently higher

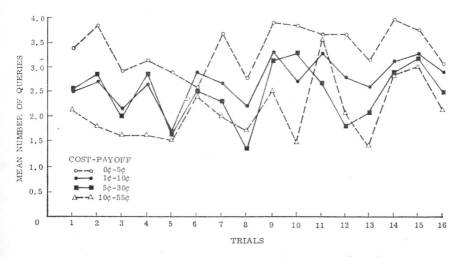

Fig. 8–5. Mean number of queries for the fine cost-payoff conditions.

for the slow pace condition and relatively uniform for both conditions. On the other hand, there is great variability over trials and much overlap between conditions for the various cost-payoff schedules. Figure 8–7 presents the mean number of queries for the cost-payoff and pacing conditions. In general, there is a decrease in information acquisition under higher cost payoff for both pacing conditions, although the addi-

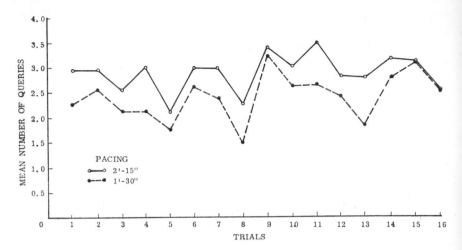

Fig. 8–6. Mean number of queries for the two pacing rates.

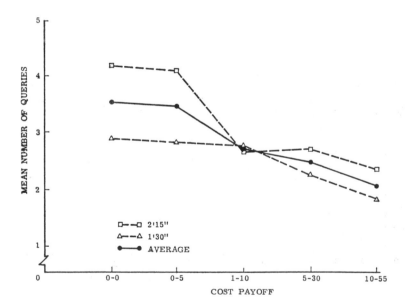

Fig. 8–7. Mean number of queries for the cost pay-off and pacing conditions.

tion of any cost for information is much more pronounced for the slow pace than the fast pace condition.

As in the first study, there were no significant differences for any of the time measures attributable to the cost-payoff variable. However, as expected, there was less time spent in reading the problems, making queries, and in making a decision under the faster pace condition. The greatest change occurs in the average time spent per query, i.e., when time is limited, Ss speed up information processing more than deliberation over the choice of an alternative. Also, Ss spend less time in all phases of the problem with increasing experience. Once again, the greatest change occurs in the average time per query—Ss spend about 25 per cent less time per query on the last four trials than on the first four trials.

In summary, the major results for the search and time measures are as follows:

(1) For none of the experimental conditions did a majority of subjects obtain all of the information available to them. This result is especially surprising for the zero cost conditions.

(2) The mean number of queries per trial decreased as the cost-payoff schedule increased. Ss made their decisions on the basis of less information when information was costly even though, in terms of expected profit, the risks were the same for all cost conditions.[4]

Uncertainty, Uncertainty Reduction, and Information Acquisition. As was noted above, there were pronounced differences in information acquisition and time allocation for the various problems used. The differences could result from a variety of factors intrinsic and extrinsic to the problems, e.g., length of problem, previous experience with certain types of material, extent of knowledge in specific areas covered by the problems. Such factors would presumably contribute to differences in the amount of perceived initial uncertainty concerning the best decision alternative. There is reason to expect that differences in uncertainty would result in differences in decision time (Cartwright, 1941a, 1941b; Festinger, 1943) and possible also in the amount of information seeking.

In an attempt to determine whether problems could be categorized according to degree of initial uncertainty two samples of twelve and

[4] In view of earlier findings by Edwards and others with respect to probability preferences, it was considered possible that such differences between conditions might be due merely to specific preferences for certain cost-probability-payoff combinations over others. Accordingly, Dr. Louis Miller of our Center conducted a study in which three of the cost-payoff conditions were presented to seventy-two Ss in the form of four alternative gambling situation, in which the costs, probabilities of win, and pay-offs were all clearly made known to S. S was required, on each of eighty trials, to choose one of these four alternatives to bet on.

In contrast to the findings reported above, choice behavior was not found to differ significantly between conditions, either in terms of an over-all index of average choice behavior, or in terms of the specific distribution of choices among the four alternatives. It thus appears inappropriate to attribute the differences between conditions in mean number of queries observed in the above reported studies to preferences for certain cost-probability-payoff combinations. The decrease in information-seeking behavior which accompanied increase in monetary level of play remains to be accounted for.

twenty-six Ss, respectively, were presented the problems with and without the information available from queries. Ss were students in two separate extension courses and, in each case, the entire class responded during a two-hour period of a class session. The problem material was projected, using an overhead projector, and Ss after reading each problem responded to the following three questions:

a. Decide which of the six alternatives is the correct answer. Circle the number of your selection. 1) 2) . . . . . . 6)

b. Indicate your degree of confidence in the answer you selected by placing an X on the scale below.

```
    .        .     .      .     .     .     .      .              .
_____
    0        25           50          75          100
   No                                          complete
 confidence                                    confidence
```

c. Which of the remaining alternatives can be disregarded in the consideration of the correct answer? Circle the number(s). 1) 2) . . . . . . 6) The instructions were amplified upon by E and Ss' questions were answered before beginning the session.

Two indices of uncertainty were developed. The uncertainty measure (UM) for each problem was determined from the following equation:

$$H = - \sum_{i=1}^{6} p(i) \log_2 p(i) \qquad \text{(Attneave, 1959)}$$

Three types of alternatives were distinguished and probabilities assigned as follows: $p(i_c) - \dfrac{1}{100} x$ confidence score for the alternative i chosen as correct; $p(i_d) = 0$ for the alternative(s) which was discarded; and $p(i_r) = 1 - p(i_c)$ for the remaining alternatives.

$$\overline{\text{No. of remaining}} \atop \text{alternatives}$$

Thus

$$\text{UM} = - p(i_c) \log_2 p(i_c) + \sum_{i=1}^{5} p(i_r) \log_2 p(i_r)$$

The prominence measure (PM) for each problem was based on the same equation, but $p(i)$ was estimated from the proportion of Ss choosing alternative i. It was assumed that the degree of initial uncertainty associated with a problem would be reflected in the distribution of choices of the most likely alternative: the lower the initial uncertainty the greater the likelihood that there would be a "prominent" choice. The average correlation between the uncertainty measure and the prominence measure for both samples is .245, which is not significant at the .05 level.

Based on the distribution of UM scores and on PM scores the problems were categorized as either high, medium, or low in degree of perceived initial uncertainty. One problem was discarded and cut-off points were selected so that eight problems were placed in each of the three categories. Separate analyses of variance for the number of information-seeking responses and total time for completing a problem were performed for the two bases of categorization.

Degree of initial uncertainty, as measured by UM, is positively associated with number of information-seeking responses and time per problem, but only the former difference is significant (at the .01 level). An examination of the means for information-seeking responses for the three uncertainty categories suggests a slight curvilinear relationship: the largest numbers of queries for problems of medium uncertainty and the smallest number of queries for problems of low uncertainty. For the prominence index (PM) there is also evident an association between uncertainty and the number of queries and time per problem, with only the latter difference significant (at the .01 level). Again the greatest number of queries is obtained for problems of medium uncertainty, but the lowest number of queries now occurs for problems of high uncertainty. Total time, as with the UM measure, increases monotonically with increasing uncertainty.

Considering the crudity of the scaling operation the results are only suggestive. Degree of perceived initial uncertainty appears to be curvilinearly related to the number of information-seeking responses and monotonically related to total time per problem, but does not interact with any of the experimental variables to a significant extent.

A third study explored further the relationships between problem uncertainty and information acquisition behavior. The earlier work suggested that information search was elicited by a response conflict engendered by response uncertainty; the greater the degree of uncertainty, the stronger the conflict and the stronger the instigation to search. However, the relationship obtained between information cost and amount of information acquisition also suggested that search was maintained only when the rate of uncertainty reduction exceeded an expected rate, the latter being a function of the cost of information. Thus Ss would initiate a search for information whenever a choice represented a response conflict, but they would maintain the search only so long as the amount of uncertainty reduction was commensurate with the cost of information, i.e., as long as information acquisition "paid off."

In the study Ss were presented with a concept attainment task, again with the option of delaying a choice until further data were gathered.

Six groups of Ss were run under varying conditions of degree of initial uncertainty, rate of uncertainty reduction, and level of monetary play. The primary dependent variable, as before, was the number of information-seeking responses prior to decision.

The tasks were modeled after those used by Bruner (1956) in his concept-attainment research. The task material consisted of an array of cards each containing a geometric pattern. The pattern on a card could vary in respect to four attributes; form, color, number of borders, and number of objects, each with three values.

Ss were to identify a "concept" held by the experimenter, the concept being defined in terms of one value of each of two different attributes, e.g., red-square. The Ss were given an answer sheet for each problem consisting of groups of "concepts"; their task was to choose the group containing the correct concept. They could eliminate concepts by requesting cards showing *positive examples* of the concept, i.e., examples containing one *or* both of the attribute values of the correct concept. The elimination strategies were fully explained to Ss and several practice examples were used to ensure that Ss completely understood the procedure.

The details of the construction of the problems to obtain varying rates of uncertainty reduction need not be elaborated upon here. We experienced considerable difficulty in controlling the rate of uncertainty reduction as a function of queries and found it impossible to obtain the range of variation desired in degree of initial uncertainty, rate of uncertainty reduction, number of possible queries, and terminal uncertainty level, while at the same time exercising reasonable control over the difficulty of the problem. Problems were constructed which varied with respect to level of initial uncertainty and rate of uncertainty reduction. Whatever the initial uncertainty and rate of uncertainty reduction, all problems had approximately the same terminal uncertainty level (.9 bit). That is to say, Ss could eliminate *almost all* of the alternatives if he asked for all the available information, but he could not reduce to zero his uncertainty regarding the correct alternative. Two levels of initial uncertainty, 3 and 2 bits, were obtained by varying the number of response categories from which S had to make a choice. Two rates of uncertainty reduction, approximately .2 and .4 bits per query, were obtained by varying the number of concepts eliminated by the particular card shown S. In addition to the above variations, two cost-payoff schedules were employed; $0–$.05 and $.03–$.45.

In order to have a reasonable possible range of search responses, it was not feasible to employ a high rate of uncertainty reduction with a low level of initial uncertainty. Thus three conditions of initial uncertainty–rate of uncertainty reduction were run: high initial uncertainty

(HIU—3 bits)–high rate of uncertainty reduction (HUR = .42 bit per query); HIU (3 bits)–LUR (.26 bit); LIU (2 bits)–LUR (.21 bit). All three conditions were run under both cost-payoff schedules.

The mean number of queries, averaged over subjects and trials, for all conditions is shown in Table 8–1. An analysis of variance of this data supports, in part, our expectations. Ss obtain more information when initial uncertainty is high. However, the expected greater amount of information acquisition with a higher rate of uncertainty reduction did not occur; in fact, the opposite effect was obtained. Also, in contrast to our earlier results there is little effect on search behavior of increasing the cost for information.

TABLE 8–1

Mean Number of Queries, Averaged over Subjects and Trials,
for the Experimental Conditions

	High uncertainty–high uncertainty reduction rate	High uncertainty–low rate	Low uncertainty–low rate
Cost			
High	4.52	5.32	3.67
Low	4.10	6.55	3.70

Since both the initial level of uncertainty and average rate of uncertainty reduction were controlled, it was possible to determine the average residual uncertainty remaining at the time of decision. Table 8–2 presents the means of the residual uncertainty at decision for the various conditions. It appears that the uncertainty level at decision

TABLE 8–2

Means for Residual Uncertainty at Decision for the Experimental Conditions

	High uncertainty–high uncertainty reduction rate	High uncertainty–low rate	Low uncertainty–low rate
Cost			
High	1.15	1.61	1.23
Low	1.32	1.29	1.22

is relatively constant for all conditions. Residual uncertainty is slightly greater for the higher level of initial uncertainty and slightly lower for the higher rate of uncertainty reduction, but neither of these differences is significant. Ss vary their acquisition strategy depending on the initial conditions of uncertainty and the rate of uncertainty reduction so that the final level of uncertainty is relatively constant. It should be pointed out that this residual uncertainty level is higher than the terminal uncertainty level, i.e., the level of uncertainty remaining if *all* queries were made. This can be seen most clearly in Figure 8–8.

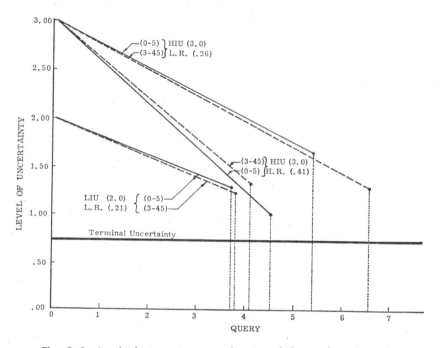

Fig. 8–8. Level of uncertainty as a function of the number of queries.

This finding suggests that there exists a "commitment threshold" for decision; Ss require information until they reach this uncertainty threshold at which point they make a decision. There is also some suggestion that commitment threshold is a function of the level of initial uncertainty and rate of uncertainty reduction, although further research on the determinants of commitment thresholds is obviously required.

Individual Differences in Information Acquisition. As noted above, E had informally observed large individual differences in approach to the problems. The large and significant variance contributed by Ss for the time measures and for the information-seeking response supports this observation. Table 8–3 and Table 8–4 present the correlations between averages of the time and query measures across problems, by subjects, for the first and second studies, respectively. Although there are differences in the pattern of obtained correlations, the similarities permit some license in generalizing across the experiments. The positive correlations between total time and the other indexes are to be expected since total time is the sum of problem time, average time per query times the number of queries, and decision time. The significance of the correlations between average time per query and total time is, however, surprising. Ss who are slow and deliberate over queries as compared to those more rapid information gatherers make more queries and tend to be slower in reading the problem and in making decisions.

TABLE 8–3

Intercorrelations Between Number of Queries and Time Measures (Experiment 1)

	S	TT	PT	Av. T/Q	DT
Search (S)	X	.46†	−.57†	.17	−.36*
Total time (TT)		X	.40*	.73†	.34*
Problem time (PT)			X	−.32	.70†
Average time/query (Av. T/Q)				X	−.22
Decision time (DT)					X

* Significant at .05.
† Significant at .01.

TABLE 8–4

Intercorrelations Between Number of Queries and Time Measures (Experiment 2)

	S	TT	PT	Av. T/Q	DT
Search (S)	X	.33†	−.44†	.53†	−.52†
Total time (TT)		X	.18	.27*	.11
Problem time (PT)			X	−.69†	.58†
Average time/query (Av. T/Q)				X	−.46†
Decision time (DT)					X

* Significant at .05.
† Significant at .01.

The amount of information seeking is negatively correlated with decision time; the more queries the more rapid the decision, hardly a surprising result. More difficult to explain are the high negative correlation between problem time and number of queries and the high positive correlation between problem time and decision time.

The intercorrelations between average number of queries and the time measures indicate that the descriptors of decision behavior are not independent. But what assumptions can account for the pattern of obtained correlations? Without presuming too much regarding the nature of the processes involved, it seems reasonable to assume that the total available time for decision making is partitionable into two components—time spent in information processing and time devoted to information acquisition. In a forced paced task, time spent in acquiring information must of necessity reduce the time available for processing it, e.g., reading, selecting, comparing. As the pool of available information increases, the value of acquiring further information would presumably decrease while the value of processing time would increase. Thus, in general, one would predict less time devoted to information acquisition the greater the amount of information currently available, with the termination point of information seeking being a function of the difficulty of processing the information. Thus, if Ss differ in their ability to process information, they should differ in the relative amounts of time allocated to processing and acquisition. The table of intercorrelations indirectly supports this assumption: Those Ss who take more time in reading the initial problem make fewer queries and spend more time in evaluating the available information before decision. Presumably, for slow processors the value of processing time is greater than the utility of time spent in acquisition and thus fewer queries are made.

Pruitt (1957) in a study of the personality correlates of the amount of information acquisition before decision found relatively high correlation between information seeking and a measure of confidence. The more confident individual required less information before making a decision. The present results, however, indicate that low information seekers spend more time in processing initial data and in making a decision—hardly consistent with the usual conception of a "confident" decision maker. Pruitt's data also indicate that anxiety level and risk preferences were related to search behavior. To check on whether the relationship between confidence and information acquisition does obtain in our task and to explore the relationship between other suggested indexes and information acquisition, we administered a number of tests and questionnaires to the one hundred males and fifty females used in Experiment II. The measures obtained were based on Pruitt's procedures (1960) and consisted of the following:

a. Sequential decision: Ss were presented the task of guessing whether a red or green light was programed to flash 60 per cent of the time.

b. Betting preferences: Two measures were obtained, probability preferences and variance preferences. In both cases Ss were presented with a questionnaire in which pairs of bets were listed. The bets were of equal expected value but differed in probability of winning (with variance held constant) or in variance (with probability of winning held constant). Preference for high or low probability of winning and high or low variance bets was assessed by counting the number of choices of high probability bets and high variance bets.

c. Anxiety: A seventeen-item true-false scale adapted from the MMPI was used to assess anxiety level.

d. Academic achievement: The cumulative index of each S was obtained from official university records.

Table 8–5 presents the correlations between the first four measures and between these indexes and the information search and time scores. As can be seen the correlations are generally low and not significant. In a replication of this study with fifty females Ss even those correlations which are significant fail to hold up. However, rather consistently

TABLE 8–5

Correlations Between Search and Time Scores and Selected Indexes

	Sequential dec.	Preference for low probabilities	Preference for high variance	Anxiety
Amount of search	.23*	.17	—.05	.03
Total time	—.19	.24*	.75†	—.20
Problem time	.11	—.01	.11	—.28*
Av. time/query	.15	.01	.10	—.08
Decision time	—.10	—.04	.17	—.22
Probability preference	.02			
Variance preference	—.00	.08		
Anxiety	—.35†	—.02	—.13	

* Significant at .05.
† Significant at .01.

the anxiety scores correlate negatively with the time measures—highly anxious Ss take less time in all phases of the decision task.

With regard to academic achievement, when Ss were divided at approximately the median on cumulative index, there was a significant difference between high and low achievers in average number of information acquisition responses in favor of the high achievers. Various explanations may be advanced to account for this relationship: High achievers may have stronger information acquisition habits; may be more cautious and less impetuous, generally; or may place a higher value on being "correct" than on maximizing profit. Further data to check and clarify this relationship will soon be obtained.

Theoretical Comments

Several issues have rather persistently intruded themselves throughout the course of our investigations of information acquisition behavior. Not surprisingly, they are the same questions one may pose with respect to any response or behavior sequence of interest. What are the conditions that elicit the behavior? Under what conditions is the response maintained? And, related to both, what variables determine the cessation or termination of the particular response or behavior sequence?

One form of normative decision theory suggests a deceptively simple hypothesis to account for the instigation, maintenance, and cessation of search activity. In choice situations characterized by risk or uncertainty a decision maker will (or should) instigate a search for information when the expected gain of basing a decision on the additional information exceeds the cost of the search and/or information, and he should continue to search until this inequality reaches equality or reverses itself. When precise knowledge is available of the probabilities of outcomes associated with the choice of particular alternatives with and without additional information, a decision maker should base his search decision on this knowledge.

In sequential decision situations it is reasonable to assume a distinction between decisions leading to environmental consequences of value or profit, and decisions leading to the acquisition of information on which decisions of the former type may be based (Kochen and Galanter, 1958). Information of potential relevance to decision may be directly available to the decision maker, requiring a minimal "search" effort, or may require active acquisition behavior and be relatively costly in terms of time, money, or effort. In the latter case, the decision to seek information has implications for the profit that can ultimately be obtained since the "cost" of the information must enter into a calculation of profit. A "rational" decision maker would presumably be guided by the value of the information as well as its cost in choosing whether to invest in information acquisition or not.

But how should a value be assigned to information? Several alternatives are available; the one suggested here as a reasonable and simple assumption is that information has value to the extent that it increases the probability of choosing the alternative which yields the most favorable outcome. If the outcomes are being correct and receiving a prize or being incorrect and receiving nothing, then information has value to the extent that it increases the probability of choosing a correct alternative. In terms of the assumption the decision to acquire information may be treated in the same manner as the ultimate decision; in Coombs' terms (Thrall, Coombs, and Davis, 1954) as a pay to play decision situation. Some probability of achieving a payoff exists prior to obtaining any information and new information may or may not increase this probability. The expected "value of any inquiry" (Marschak, 1954) is then assumed to be a direct function of the change in probability of choosing the correct alternative, the utility of the prize, and the utility of the cost of the information or

$$\text{EV} = U(z) \ [p_a - p_b] - U(c)$$

where z = prize, in dollars
$\quad U(z)$ = utility of the prize
$\quad p_a, p_b$ = probability of success after and before the new information, respectively
$\quad c$ = cost of information, in dollars
$\quad U(c)$ = utility of the cost of the information
A "rational" rule would be to acquire the additional information when $U(z) \ [p_a - p_b] \ U(c)$ and to make a decision in terms of the present information base when $U(z) \ [p_a - p_b] \ U(c)$.

This result assumes that information is acquired in discrete "packets" and that a probability of payoff can be associated with each information level resulting from the acquisition of a new packet. In the usual case the probability of payoff will be an increasing monotonic function of the number of information packets since information generally assists in the selection of a correct alternative. The association of a probability of payoff with every information level allows the computation of an expected value for each level:

$$\text{EV} = p_q \ U(z) - \ _qU(c)$$

where p_q = probability of payoff with q information packets
$\quad U(z)$ = utility of payoff
$\quad U(c)$ = utility of the cost of each information packet
$\quad q$ = number of information packets
A reasonable rule would be to acquire that amount of information which yields the maximum expected value. This rule would yield a result identical with that obtained by successive application of the criterion previously mentioned for all situations in which probability of payoff is a monotonic function of the number of information packets.

When the decision maker does not have precise knowledge of the probability of a successful outcome at each information level, the "rationality" criteria is difficult to apply. One may reasonably assume, however, that under such circumstances Ss will expect the probability of successful choice to increase with the amount of information available at the time of decision and that this prior expectation will be reinforced, since in most decision situations "better" decisions are made when information is available. Thus Ss' subjective probability of success, initially, would be a monotonic increasing function of the amount of information acquisition and, with experience, should approach the "true" probability of success. Of necessity, such subjective estimates of the relevant probabilities would have to be utilized in applying the "rational" criteria suggested.

In some respects our empirical data are consistent with predictions from such a normative model. The results on information-seeking responses (queries) do not support an expected value maximization assumption if the experimenter-controlled objective probabilities of payoff are used since, for all cost-payoff conditions, expected profit is greatest when the maximum number of queries are made. This is clearly not in accord with the findings: Ss do not make the maximum number of queries even under the most favorable condition of zero cost for additional information and the average number of queries decreases as cost-payoff values increase.

However, as was noted earlier, Ss were not informed of the linear increase in the objective probability of payoff with increasing number of queries. Since there were few trials and thus little opportunity to assess the "true" probabilities, Ss' expectations of payoff may have been quite at variance with the experimenter controlled objective probabilities. A check on this may be obtained from questionnaire data obtained in experiments 1 and 2 which provides an estimate of Ss' subjective probability-query function. Table 8–6 shows the subjective probabilities and the expected profit functions obtained when subjective probabilities are substituted for the objective probabilities. The expected profit function for the $.05 condition remains monotonic increasing, but for the

TABLE 8–6

Approximate Average Subjective Probability Estimates and Expected Profit-Query Function Based on These Estimates

Queries	Subj. prob.	0–5	1–10	5–30	10–55
0	.20	$.01	$.02	$ .06	$.11
1	.30	.15	.02	.04	.065
2	.40	.020	.02	.02	.02
3	.50	.025	.02	0	−.025
4	.70	.035	.03	.01	−.015
5	.75	.038	.025	−.025	−.087

other cost-payoff combinations there is a transition from higher to lower expected profit occurring at progressively lower information levels.

In terms of these functions and a maximization of expected profit assumption, a decrease in search should be evident over the increasing cost-payoff combinations, a prediction clearly consonant with the obtained results. However, for none of the cost-payoff conditions does the average number of queries equal the information level of maximum subjective expected profit. Thus, in only a limited sense, is Ss' behavior consistent with the "rational" criteria proposed.

The results are encouraging and would support further refinement and development of the model if it had greater predictive and heuristic value for understanding the effects of other variables, e.g., uncertainty level and uncertainty reduction rate, and also if it provided a better conceptual apparatus for handling the problem of individual differences in search and time allocation. Within the framework of the theory, variables exert their effect on search by modifying either expectations, the utility of the cost of information, or the utility of payoffs. Individuals presumably differ in their estimation of probabilities, in the value they attach to the effort, time, or money involved in information acquisition, and in the value attached to the consequences of a decision. In addition, various situational factors, such as time pressure, would be expected to influence these variables. However, until more efficient procedures are devised for measuring such factors, it is hard to take seriously the task of developing a comprehensive model encompassing the variables demonstrated to have an effect on search behavior.

The above considerations provide one basis for prediction in multistage decision situations which include a decision to acquire additional information or not. With some equivocation predictions can also be made from drive reduction theory, although not so precisely or easily since the application requires identification of the drive-evoking stimuli, response habit hierarchies, and the conditions which serve to reduce drive and thus reinforce the behavior. With respect to cognitive processes there is considerable disagreement and confusion on all of these points.

Most "cognitive" theorists would probably agree with the statement that some form of dissonance, or incongruity, is a sufficient condition for eliciting search behavior either directly (Festinger, 1957) or through the mediation of emotional distress or arousal (Berlyne, 1960). Dissonance and/or incongruity may arise from a discrepancy between a self concept and concrete perceptions of self-other interactions, an incompatibilty between stored information and present inputs, or a discrepancy between stored cognitive elements such as beliefs.

Whatever its source, dissonance functions as a drive in eliciting responses that conduce to the mitigation of the dissonance. One possible course of action that may be instrumental in reducing an incongruity is information acquisition. For example, a discrepancy between our memory of an event and someone's report may be removed by checking an objective record, discordance between a conception of oneself as nonaggressive and an accusation of aggression may be reduced by checking the reactions of observers other than the accuser. Thus, information seeking, being often instrumental in reducing incongruities, should have a high probability of evocation when incongruities occur. Some theorists insert an intervening event, emotional distress or arousal, between the evocation of incongruity and the elicitation of a search response. Arousal and emotional excitement are assumed to constitute the basic factor in a conception of generalized drive and additions to, or reorganizations of, information in memory are postulated as drive reducing.

A similar line of reasoning may be followed when the stimulus conditions elicit response conflict and/or uncertainty. Presumably "uncertain" decision situations evoke response conflict since the choice of a "best" alternative is equivocal. In such situations the subjective probability of a desired outcome occurring if, say, alternative A is selected, is one determinant of the strength of the tendency to select A, and similarly for alternatives B, C, . . . N. If one assumes that this anticipatory response strength directly determines the probability of the response, then an information measure of response uncertainty can be derived from the decision makers' subjective probability distribution relating alternatives to outcomes. More important, one would expect such a measure to be directly related to the degree of induced conflict and thus to various indicators of emotional distress and arousal. There is evidence to support the contention that arousal is a concomitant of conflict (Pavlov, 1927; Polezhaev, 1958, 1959) and uncertainty (Sharpless and Jasper, 1956; Papov, 1953, Berlyne, 1961) and that such arousal functions as generalized drive.

Thus, increases in response uncertainty should result in increases in arousal, which constitute basic determinants of generalized drive level. The strength of responses previously instrumental in reducing uncertainty should then be increased, as reflected in higher probabilities of response evocation. Since information seeking presumably has a long and successful history in reducing uncertainty, the probability of information-seeking responses should increase with increases in uncertainty. If one assumes that increases in disjunctive reaction time reflect, in part, more "search" activity, then the large number of studies demonstrating a positive relationship between uncertainty and disjunctive reaction time would support the assumption that increasing uncertainty results in increasing search behavior (e.g., Hyman, 1953; Alluisi, Muller, and Fitts, 1957).

Our results on information acquisition are partially in accord with the assumption that increases in uncertainty result in increases in search behavior. An increase in objective response uncertainty did result in more queries as did an increase in subjective uncertainty over part of the range. However, in the latter case, further increases in subjective uncertainty were associated with a decrease in information acquisition. The obtained curvilinear relationship between information acquisition and subjective uncertainty can be accounted for within the "drive" framework by assuming that other responses, incompatible with search, are also strengthened as uncertainty, and thus motivation arousal, increases. For example, it is conceivable that "internal" information search and symbolic information-processing acts are also "aroused" by uncertainty and may, in fact, be dominant. When faced with uncertainty the organism may first search in memory for information which can provide a basis for choice and attempt to evaluate and integrate such data to assess its implication for the problem at hand. Only when these processes are completed and only if they fail to produce data of relevance will the organism seek to acquire further information. Even then, since new information is rarely coded in a form suitable for direct application to a specific problem, these symbolic processing activities may again be evoked. Thus, at any stage in the sequential decision process the organism may be faced with a conflict between choosing on the basis of present information, seeking new information, and conducting a more intensive and extensive search and processing of recently acquired or stored data.

The development of a model to predict the transient dominance of one or another of these responses is obviously beyond the scope of this paper, but one can suggest some of the variables that may be important. The amount of relevant information in immediate memory, the similarity between the present situation and others experienced, the difficulty of understanding and synthesizing new information available, ability to process data and search memory, all should effect the relative priority the organism places on acquisition of additional data versus the processing of stored data. Thus, for example, one would predict less time devoted to information acquisition the greater the amount of information currently available, with the termination of information seeking being a function of the difficulty of processing the information.

The correlations between the search and time allocation measures may be reflecting the operation of such factors. If Ss differ in their ability to process information, they should differ in the relative amounts of time allocated to processing and acquisition. The correlations presented in Tables 8–3 and 8–4 indirectly support this assumption since Ss who take more time in reading the problem and spend more time in evaluating the available information before decision make fewer queries. In addition, we find that higher academic achievers (fast processors) make more queries than lower achievers (slow processors). Presumably, for "slow processors" the value of processing time is greater than the utility of time spent in acquisition and thus fewer queries are made.

Indirectly implied in the above formulation is the assumption that information search would not occur under conditions of certainty. As Berlyne (1960) and others (Leuba, 1955; Glanzer, 1958a) have noted, however, there is some evidence that organisms tend to maintain a rather specific amount of "arousal tonus" and thus, by inference, would prefer situations of some uncertainty. This suggests that information seeking would not be initiated at zero uncertainty but at that level of uncertainty which produces arousal greater than a preferred level of "arousal tonus." The probability of search should then increase with increasing discrepancy between a preferred uncertainty level and the level of uncertainty induced by the choice task and should terminate when the preferred uncertainty level is reached. Our results on residual uncertainty suggest the existence of an "uncertainty-commitment" threshold for decision. This may be a manifestation of an attempt on the part of our Ss to maintain a preferred level of "arousal tonus."

So far, we have avoided confronting the issue of "what is the reinforcement" for information search. Two possibilities exist, the occurrence of a desired outcome, e.g., a payoff, or subjective uncertainty reduction.

In the studies reported the two factors are somewhat confounded as they probably are in most complex decision tasks. However, in the procedure employed the probability of payoff increased more rapidly than subjective uncertainty reduction (Table 8–6) and, thus, the assumption that uncertainty reduction serves as a reinforcer could account for the generally low level of information acquisition by our Ss. The assumption could not in itself, however, account for the differences between cost-payoff conditions in information seeking.

If the expectation of uncertainty reduction were a function of the cost of information, i.e., the higher the cost the greater the expectation of uncertainty reduction, and if a positive discrepancy between obtained and expected uncertainty reduction served as the reinforcer for search, the cost-payoff results could be explained. The higher the cost of information the greater the expectation of uncertainty reduction and the greater the likelihood that the obtained reduction will be less than the expected. Reinforcement for information search would then be less likely the higher the cost of information and the asymptotic level of queries would be lower the greater the information cost.

It is apparent that the collection of concepts and propositions discussed constitute the bare beginnings of a theory of "search" behavior. The "theory" is neither an S-R nor a consistently need-reduction one but borrows freely from both traditions. It is based largely on the concepts advanced by Berlyne (1960) and thus focuses on "arousal" as the intervening variable representing the common motivational effects of uncertainty, dissonance, and incongruity. For all organisms there is some optimum level of arousal greater than zero, and displacements from this level elicit responses which have been instrumental in the past in restoring equilibrium. Information acquisition and symbolic information processing activities are two responses assumed to have high habit strength under conditions of uncertainty and thus have a high probability of being elicited. Since such responses tend to restore the organism to its preferred arousal level, they are reinforced.

To account for the obvious importance of "cost" variables the concept of an expectation for uncertainty reduction is introduced. Information search is reinforced only if the uncertainty reduction which results from search exceeds the expected rate of uncertainty reduction. The latter variable is assumed to be a positive function of information cost, importance of the problem, and initial level of uncertainty.

The major appeal of the "conflict-arousal" theory is its ability to handle affective states which have been sorely neglected by investigators in the study of decision making. Its major deficiency is the relative neglect of "rational" factors in choice behavior. Organisms are neither computers that impartially weigh and evaluate costs, payoffs, and probabilities, nor irrational, impetuous seekers of equilibrium in drive states, whatever the costs. Presumably, they exhibit some facets of both idealizations in their decision-making behavior; the task is to determine the nature of the compromise.

Chapter 9

Conceptualizing and Measuring Structural Properties of Cognition

William A. Scott

Much of the discussion in this conference reflects a mutual interest in formulating descriptions of personality by means of structural concepts. A structural property may be designated tentatively as one which refers to the relations among components of content, conceived in quasisystemic fashion, rather than to the elements of content themselves. For example, the strength of an achievement motive is a variable referring to the content of personality, while the degree of compatibility or conflict between this motive and some other represents a structural variable. At the level of cognitive processes, the phenomenal object, India, constitutes an element of content, while the perceived conflict of interest between India and China represents a relation between two phenomenal objects and, hence, a rudimentary structural property of cognition.

The proposed distinction between content and structure is not as neat as it may appear, for what is one and what the other depends on the level of analysis. Though a structure constitutes a relation among elements, it may itself form an element in some superordinate structure; conversely, the elements of any designated structure may themselves be conceived as complex structures consisting of their own units and interrelations. For the notion of structure to be meaningful, therefore, one must designate explicitly those elements which constitute the structure referred to.

A number of psycholgists (e.g., Bieri, 1955; Harvey, Hunt, and Schroder, 1961; Kelly, 1955; Rosenberg, 1956; Scott, 1962; Zajonc, 1960) have recently proposed some more or less systematically defined structural properties at a cognitive level of analysis. By cognitive structures I mean those whose elements consist of ideas consciously entertained by the person in his phenomenal view of the world. This concern for structural properties of cognition is commonly based on beliefs such as:

(a) The content of experience is organized into structural assemblies from which any element of content derives its significance. (b) The way in which any new experience is received, processed, and interpreted depends on the capabilities and characteristics of the pre-existing cognitive structure into which it is read. (c) While the contents of cognition may be endlessly varied, structural properties can be described in a limited number of genotypic terms, thereby permitting a more parimonious formulation of psychological processes. (d) The contents of cognition develop from social norms and other fortuitous experience which cannot be well predicted from personality theory; they may be widely shared by different individuals for different reasons, and they may fluctuate markedly within a single individual over time. By contrast, the structure of cognition is regarded as more enduring, organism-specific, and invariant over situations; hence structural variables provide better description of the person as conceived in most psychological theories.

The alleged essential, genotypic, characteristic, and causative nature of the proposed structural properties has hardly been established empirically; rather these beliefs have, at the moment, the status of assumptions which are tentatively used to justify our focus on structural variables.

No one, I trust, will object to the use of structural concepts simply because they do not correspond to anything in the body. No psychological construct resides in the person, conceived as a biological organism; all theoretical constructs reside in theories; some of them may be attributed to the psychological person, which is itself a complex theoretical construct. Direct translatability into neurophysiological events is not something we demand of our structural concepts. Certain other characteristics, however, can be reasonably expected of them: (1) Structural properties should be conceptualized differently from properties of content; otherwise there is no point in distinguishing the two classes. (2) For each property the elements of the structure should be specified, so that one can know what level of analysis is referred to. (3) The designated structural properties should have different implications for behavior from some more simply formulated content properties; otherwise use of the former is uneconomical or redundant. (4) Any structural property should be empirically assessable; that is, one should be able to elicit behaviors which are epistemically coordinated to the presence or absence, or the magnitude, of the theoretically defined property. (5) The measuring procedures for assessing psychological structure should be distinct from those used to assess psychological content; otherwise any conceptual distinction between content and structure is operationally meaningless.

Methodological Considerations

This paper will deal mostly with problems of assessing a few structural concepts encountered in the recent literature. In order to clarify the basis for the critique, it will be worthwhile first to set forth some general methodological considerations relating to the assessment of any psychological variable. These deal with (1) the need for assessment, (2) isomorphism between construct and measure, (3) reliance on the subject's self report, (4) objectivication of measures, (5) multiple measures of a single construct, (6) controls for contamination, and (7) the compromise between instrument refinement and ease of administration.

The Need for Assessment. Structural properties of cognition are ordinarily designated in an attempt to account for some observed individual differences in thinking or overt behavior. Conceivably, they might have the status of purely logical constructs whose validity is entirely a matter of their usefulness in predicting the relevant behaviors. Most often, though, the logic is not so explicit as to provide complete definition of the construct, and some substantive meaning is added through less formal imagery. The very word chosen to designate the property generally has both theoretical and commonsense meaning derived from the common culture. "Complexity," "dissonance," "balance"—all carry substantive meanings which give an idea of what sort of psychological phenomenon is involved and help tell the researcher what to do next in studying it. When an explanatory label is attached, it implies at least a tentative suggestion of some presumed underlying state.

It would seem appropriate, therefore, to devise a method of assessing the hypothetical state as directly as possible. Unless this is done, the surplus meaning of the label attached to it goes to waste and the theoretical designation is purely arbitrary. Some other word, and some other presumed substantive state, might just as well have been used in place of those which were chosen. If, for example, a change in attitude following induced behavior that is inconsistent with it is attributed to "cognitive dissonance" (e.g., Festinger, 1957), this implies some intrapsychic state of disequilibrium that produced the change in any particular subject. If so, the state should be measurable more directly, and its reduction should accompany the change in attitude that is attributed to it. Most research relating to this theory does not include an attempt to assess "dissonance" directly; rather it is alleged to occur in all subjects, under the experimental conditions, on the basis of implicit assumptions about what is dissonance producing in their culture. Without some attempt to designate responses which can be more directly coordinated to the dissonant or consonant state, it is hard to tell whether the essential psychological process underlying the attitude change has been appropriately identified.

An attempt to measure directly some presumed essential intervening variable, rather than simply to assume it from the manipulated stimulus conditions, is well illustrated in Schachter's (1951) study of communication in small groups. In addition to manipulating the cohesiveness variable by experimental instructions, the researchers quizzed the subjects afterward to obtain more direct evidence of differential attraction to the group. They did not simply regard the outcome on the dependent variables (differences in group pressures and conformity) as sufficient evidence that the cohesiveness variable had operated in the theoretically required manner.

In similar fashion, it may be suggested that whenever some property of cognitive structure is proposed, even implicitly, as a substantive, explanatory construct, rather than simply as a logical linkage between stimuli and responses, some means should be found to assess the property directly, instead of just inferring it either from the stimulus conditions or from the responses it is used to explain.

Isomorphism Between Construct and Measure. In order for an operation to have even face validity in representing a theoretical construct, it would seem important that it bear some structural similarity to that notion at which it is aimed. In the assessment of cognition, for example, a construct referring to content should be assessed by a content instrument, whereas a construct referring to structure should be assessed by a structural instrument. The content property "information" can be directly measured by finding out what a subject knows about the domain; the content property "motive" can be assessed, either directly or indirectly, by determining what the person wants or, more specifically, by counting the number of statements he endorses relevant to a specified motive type.

In order for a measuring procedure to bear an isomorphic relation to a cognitive structural property, at least two things would seems to be required: that the subject perform a task which is structurally similar to that theoretically defined property, and that the researcher analyze the data in such a way that the structural characteristic is preserved in his measure. Just what sorts of tasks and analysis procedures fit these requirements is by no means completely clear. In regard to the task, either structural or content properties of cognition have to be inferred from performance, verbal or behavioral. Structure must be inferred from function, just as content is. However, some kinds of performance seems more structural than others. Tentatively, let us say that a structural task is one which requires S to arrange elements that are theoretically included in the structure to be assessed. (It was proposed earlier that the definition of a structure is incomplete unless it specifies the elements included.)

As an example, the rudimentary structural concept, "similarity," might be appropriately represented by a task in which S used elements A and B in a comparable manner, or by a semantic differential test in which he responded to A and B similarly. The quicker method of just asking S whether A and B are similar would appear less adequate for the desired structural concept, since the word "similar" may not carry the same meaning for S as it does for the investigator. If the investigator means something specific, like functionally equivalent or close together in semantic space, then he should elicit responses which permit direct assessment of this property.

Initial theory of the "authoritarian personality" (Adorno *et al.*, 1950) suggested that cognitive rigidity was one of its components, and subsequent studies (see Mischel and Schopler, 1959; Titus and Hollander, 1957) have demonstrated correlations between scores on the F Scale and certain external measures of rigidity. These considerations have tempted some researchers to use the F Scale itself as a simple and direct measure of rigidity. But the items on the scale reflect not resistance to change but the contents of certain beliefs (together with a characteristic mode of expressing them). Just because one can demonstrate an empirical correlation between a content variable and a structural variable, this gives no ground for using the former as a *measure* of the latter. Rigidity needs to be assessed more directly, by ascertaining subjects' resistance to change under appropriate conditions. An instrument measuring content will contain many extraneous features irrelevant to the structural property of interest, and hence may yield misleading relationships with other variables.

The procedure for analyzing data should also be structurally appropriate to the property being assessed. For instance, in measuring some characteristic of an individual's cognitive structure, it is the relations among elements for this particular person that have to be treated, not the relations which are abstracted from group data. Osgood's Semantic Differential (Osgood, Suci, and Tannenbaum, 1957) has been widely used to establish a dimensional space for assessing similarities among the meanings of words. But if these dimensions are established through the usual procedure of factor analysis across subjects, then they represent not the cognitive space for any particular individual but a sort of cultural space which the group of subjects share in common. An individual's private semantic space would more appropriately be assessed through a factor analysis based on his own ratings of the concepts.

Reliance on Introspective Data. Since the content of cognition consists of phenomenological material, it is difficult to assess cognitive structure without introspective data from the subject. Yet most people, particularly in dealing with familiar objects, are not accustomed to analyzing their phenomenal properties in terms useful to the researcher. Some subjects would probably find it difficult even to describe systematically the difference between such common objects as a rock and a tree. In order to meet this problem, the researcher can take the Tichenerian approach of using only subjects highly trained in his special set of introspective categories; alternatively he can try to devise tasks which won't put too much burden on the average subject's introspective capacity. The latter approach would seem preferable, since it places less severe restrictions on the population to be studied and seems less likely to introduce artifacts of the method of study into the phenomenon being observed.

Some kinds of subjective report can probably be relied upon—indeed are often necessary to tap cognitive processes at all. The subject may be required to provide his own list of phenomenal objects in the cognitive domain being studied. This can be done, for example, by asking him to name the nations that he regards as important in world affairs, and then performing the required structural tasks with his own list (Scott, 1961b). An alternative procedure would be to present all subjects with the same standard list of objects to be classified. This affords only superficial standardization, however, for the common list content may not be that which is most central for any particular person; hence it may not call forth characteristic features of his cognitive structure. The important structural characteristics of cognition are presumably those which one habitually uses. These can perhaps be better assessed on his own private sample of objects than on a standardized sample selected at random from the total domain.

Since cognitive content is treated as manifest, it is reasonable to assume that S means the same things as E by the words he uses in referring to it. If he names Canada, England, and Brazil among his list of countries, these items of content may legitimately be treated at face value. But to the degree that structural properties of cognition are latent, one cannot assume that the subject's introspections concerning them will necessarily be valid. Even in assessing the simple relation of similarity or dissimilarity between two attributes, S's judgment may be faulty. Zajonc's (1960) method for assessing dependency between two elements is to ask S, essentially, "If characteristic A changed, what other characteristics would change along with it?" Under these instructions, S might report a particular dependency which actually did not obtain in his normal treatment of the objects; or he might fail to report one which did. A more searching measure of dependency would presumably induce S to deal with the objects under different degrees of characteristic A, and determine directly what other attributes changed too. For more complex measures of cognitive structure—such as differentiation, integration, and the like—it is even clearer that S is in no position to report directly his own status with respect to them.

In defining the content of cognition, it would thus seem advantageous to rely heavily on S's introspection, for this offers less chance of contributing material that is not normally present. But in assessing structure, the researcher would probably do well to avoid direct introspective reports, substituting instead structural tasks from which the relevant properties can be reliably inferred.

Judgmental Versus Objective Assessment. Structural properties can be assessed judgmentally in various ways. Subjects might be required to write essays or to work with objects, and then the researcher judge the product according to the attributes in which he is interested—such as unity, organization, etc. Under an objective assessment procedure, one would abstract from the manner of task performance or from its product some features that can be directly counted, or otherwise quantified, so that there is little ambiguity as to how a given response is to be scored.

From what we know about psychometrics, the latter approach seems definitely preferable, both for assessing the variable reliably and for avoiding bias. There are enough opportunities for the investigator's own preconceptions to creep into the interpretation of research data, without having the very measurement of the variables themselves depend heavily upon subjective judgment. Desmond Cartwright (personal communication) has obtained some intriguing data in his study of change in psychotherapy. Among the measures of change was a set of global ratings (pre- and post-therapy) by a diagnostician, based on TAT protocols. The rated characteristics included "adequacy of psychological comfort with own thoughts, feelings, and impulses," "adequacy of relationships with other people," "adequacy of decision making," "insight into own disturbances," and so forth. In the factor analysis of these and numerous other change scores, all of the TAT-based ratings loaded heavily on the same factor, which was almost entirely independent of all the other criteria, including the changes in therapist's judgment concerning the same variables. This was a skilled diagnostician working with a type of protocol which is widely used. Nevertheless halo effect seems to have far outweighted differential validity. At least reliable and distinct measures could have been obtained from a more objective assessment technique.

Of course, there is still the matter of instrument validity. If it is impossible to develop an objective measure which is as valid for the particular purpose as a judgmental one, then the choice must fall to the latter. One suspects, though, that in the end such issues will resolve in about the same manner as that concerning clinical versus statistical prediction (Meehl, 1954), namely that when biases and contaminating features are eliminated from the criteria, objective indexes will predict at least as well as judgmental ones—even for presumably subtle characteristics. In addition, there is the advantage that objective measurements can be made by less highly skilled labor.

Convergent Validity. Before any postulated structural property can be empirically useful, there must be some way of assessing it—either objectively or judgmentally, through introspection or by means of a structured task. Furthermore, before one can have any degree of confidence that a particular assessment technique is getting at the intended construct, he must show that it correlates quite highly with some other technique aimed at the same property. Unless this can be done, then the measure is instrument-specific, and may just as well reflect characteristics of the measuring device as the intended psychological property (see Scott and Wertheimer, 1962, pp. 137–38).

In other words, without at least two different measures of a property that correlate appreciably, one cannot assume that the concept is useful. This is, of course, an insufficient condition for validity, for two different instruments might have the same extraneous factors built into them and thus correlate highly, without getting at the intended variable. Nevertheless, this requirement of convergent validity sets an initial task for the coiner of structural concepts—namely, devise two or more independent measures for each one. Failure to find a substantial correlation between them would suggest (1) that there is too much error in the measures, (2) that each is getting at a somewhat different attribute, or (3) that the *methods of measurement* themselves contribute too much to subjects' scores on the variable. The first and third of these possible explanations point to deficiencies in the instruments which may require considerable effort to repair. The second interpretation has different implications. It may suggest to the investigator that, where he had formulated a single structural concept, he should really have considered two (or more). The measuring problem still remains, however, for it is now necessary to clarify the separate concepts sufficiently to permit the development of yet another measure for each. Then the convergent validity of the new instruments is assessed anew. An assertion, on the basis of poor convergence between instruments, that they are "really measuring different things" must be substantiated further by finding other ways of measuring those things. Otherwise, explanations (1) and (3) are not precluded.

Discriminant Validity. Since many different characteristics of an instrument can spuriously inflate its correlation with a particular criterion, it is important to build into the validation research some checks against contamination from extraneous sources. One straightforward way of doing this is provided by Campbell and Fiske's (1959) "multitrait-multimethod matrix," though the techniques of factor analysis and partial correlation are also useful in this context. These involve relating measures of the structural property not only to variables which are theoretically relevant, but also to variables which are theoretically irrelevant, so that the magnitudes of the former correlations can be compared with the magnitudes of the latter. The logic here is that one should be able to say not only what his instrument *does* measure, but also what its does *not*. The particular structural concept should be empirically distinguishable from others which the researcher does not intend to be tapping.

A classical example of instrument contamination is provided by the F-scale. Initial correlations between this instrument and measures of certain other variables were startlingly high (*Adorno et al.*, 1950; Levinson, 1957; Gilbert and Levinson, 1956)—until it was noted that all instruments had in common a scoring procedure which gave high scores to people who said "yes" to all the items (Chapman and Bock, 1958; Christie *et al.*, 1959; Jackson and Messick, 1958). When the effect of acquiescence set is eliminated by including an equal number of reverse-scored items as well, correlations may drop appreciably (Chapman and Campbell, 1959; Howard and Sommer, 1958). F-scale enthusiasts may object that, acquiescence to this kind of statement being an essential component of authoritarianism, a measure which deliberately eliminates it cannot tap the intended trait. If this be so, then perhaps the F-scale should have been named and interpreted differently. The meaning of whatever it measures is commonly understood by reference to the item content; but if response style and item wording are equally important in affecting scores (Couch and Kenistan, 1960; Jackson and Messick, 1958), then this requires a rather different interpretation of the underlying trait. If, in its initial validation, the F-scale had been related to a sample of theoretically non-relevant variables, all measured by instruments with a common style of wording and a common scoring bias, then both the concept and the measure might have been clarified through noting that it correlated in some instances where it theoretically should not have.

Measures of cognitive structure are apt to be particularly vulnerable to contamination by general or specific intelligence factors—if only because proficient performance on them may require understanding of com plicated instructions. If, therefore, the theorist wishes to distinguish his concepts from general intelligence (presumably he does; otherwise he would be simply proliferating terminolgy needlessly), he should include the relevant measures of intelligence in his validating studies. Then he can, if necessary, control these latter variables statistically in relating the structural measure to its criterion.

Fortunately, present-day high-speed computers permit exploration of a wider band of potential correlates than was formerly feasible. If subjects can be induced to take a sufficiently large battery of instruments, one can try out a range of variables which should *not* correlate with the structural measure, along with those that should. If the former correlations turn out embarrassingly high, this will suggest either (1) that the intended structural property has not been conceptualized clearly enough to distinguish it from something else or (2) that the instrument is not measuring precisely what was intended (because it includes something that was not intended).

Instrument Refinement Versus General Applicability. Increasing objectification of structural measures may result, unintentionally, in cumbersome assessment procedures, which place undue demand on subjects' time and attention. In the extreme, one might find his instruments applicable only to captive college students, motivated, attentive, and trained in the required procedures. Kelly's (1955) Role Constructs Repertory Test, for example, is a searching technique which, individually administered, can probably be quite successful with subjects who are well motivated. But reduced to standard questionnaire form, it becomes quite formidable (see, e.g., Campbell, 1960), and one would hesitate to confront either a streetcleaner or a busy executive with such an instrument.

The disadvantage of overly complicated assessment techniques lies in the corresponding limit on their utility for studying structural characteristics in a wide population of subjects. There is even a danger that exclusive testing of precious, captive, specialized populations may yield results which are highly artificial, even for this group, for the measuring procedures may force variables and relationships which are insignificant or nonexistent in the people's normal functioning.

It is inappropriate to prescribe in general just what compromise to make between refinement of technique and ease of administration; in any specific case one may wish now to emphasize one direction, now the other. Lest all of the preceding recommendations concerning well-structured, objective, reliable, and valid testing procedures be pursued to the extreme, however, it is important to remember the people who are to be tested; the level of rapport with them sets a limit on the validity of data obtained.

Some Structural Properties of Cognition

With this extended preamble on methodological problems, the reader should now be prepared for an extremely tentative discussion of specific structural properties. Each of them is tied to some formal model which bears only a remote and exceedingly abstract correspondence with the psychological domain to which it is coordinated. If any systematic way of measuring the construct has been developed, it is at best crude, and only one of many that might be proposed. Also, one cannot be sure in most cases whether the alleged structural property is empirically distinguishable from some content variable which it is not intended to duplicate, for the validating studies have generally omitted variables which were not of immediate theoretical relevance. Nevertheless, some of the notions, and the preliminary data, seem sufficiently compelling to encourage further exploration that would take into account the considerations offered above.

Structural Models. We are indebted to Kurt Lewin (1936) for his compelling suggestions of many structural properties that are conceptualized more precisely today. Another important feature of Lewin's theory was the distinction between two levels of theoretical discourse—the formal and the content. Lewin used topology (or hodology) as a formal model whose components he coordinated to psychological constructs, which were then coordinated to observable phenomena. In this way, the abstract, formal model often served as a guide to the construction of content theory, while the latter served as a guide to the measurement and prediction of empirical events. True, in order for the model to be useful in the formulation of content theory, it had to bear some ultimate resemblance to the event domain which was to be comprehended. But, given preliminary grounds for suspecting such a correspondence, one could go ahead on the formal level and elaborate quite economically and precisely relationships which might not have been noticed or which might have been unduly cumbersome to formulate at the level of psychological content theory.

A given formal model can be coordinated to different content theories —dealing, for instance, with cognition or group processes or cultural events—which require different sorts of data for their application. Some of the models used in cognitive theories can potentially serve such multiple functions. Lewin's topology could be applied not only to personality theory, but also to theory of social structure. (The latter was especially developed by J. F. Brown in his *Psychology and the Social Order*, 1936.) The graph theory, which has been elaborated and transmitted to psychologists by Harary and Norman (1953), finds application at both the psychological and social levels.

A model uniquely appropriate for cognitive structure has been proposed by Abelson and Rosenburg (1958); it is a kind of matrix algebra by which cognitive balance and processes associated with it may be described. Scott (1961b, 1963) suggests a geometrical model of cognition, consisting of a set of points and the lines intersecting them in multidimensional Euclidean space. These elements are coordinated in psychological theory to a person's concepts of objects (called *images*) and his concepts of the attributes which inhere in the phenomenal objects. An object-image is represented by the intersection of multiple dimensions, while an attribute is coordinated to a locus of points representing cognitive objects which embody the attribute to varying degrees. A simple image may be visualized as a point which is intersected by only one or two dimensional lines, whereas a complex image is seen as the intersection of many lines, representing a multitude of attributes. A complexly conceived attribute may be correspondingly represented in the formal model as one which runs through a large number of points that stand for the images that contain the attribute to varying, finely shaded, degrees. A barren attribute, by contrast, runs through few points or else permits few quantitative distinctions by lumping many object-images together in gross categories.

Certain structural concepts of cognition may be formulated within the framework of this model, employing the geometrized notions concerning relations among image-concepts and among attribute-concepts.

Differentiation. Basic to any concept of structure is the notion of differentiation, or distinctiveness of the elements which constitute the set. Psychologically this involves an articulation of concepts, an isolability of one idea from another. Without an initial distinction between two cognitive elements, it is meaningless to speak of their relationship. This very word, differentiation, was used by Vera French (1947, 1948) in her discussion of sentiments. Krech and Crutchfield (1948) spoke of the precision of an attitude, defining this in terms of clarity and differentiation. Zajonc's (1960) research on cognitive tuning made use of both the concept and an empirical measure of cognitive differentiation. Harvey, Hunt, and Schroder (1961) referred to "clarity vs. ambiguity" as an important characteristic of concepts. This property depends on the "articulation of component parts," so it is appropriate to equate their notion with that of differentiation.

It is not so immediately apparent that differentiation of object concepts is intimately connected with the structural property which has been designated as "complexity of the attribute concepts." Bieri (1955) has noted this, and Scott (1960, 1961b) has developed the same point, as follows: In order for two object-images to be distinguished, they must be seen as embodying different attributes; for attributes to be phenomenally different, they must order the object-images in different ways. The degree of differentness in the ordering of objects along two attributes can be represented (inversely) by a correlation coefficient and, correspondingly, by the angle between the attribute-vectors. The greater the difference, the more nearly orthogonal are the vectors; hence the more dimensional space utilized by the pair of attributes. Considering the cognitive domain as a whole, the greater the differentiation among object-images, the greater must be the distinctiveness among the attributes embodied in the objects. So the degree of distinctiveness among elements of either class—images or attributes—amounts to the same thing.

Bieri (1955) used a measure of cognitive complexity which was a simplified analysis of Kelly's (1955) Rep Test. Campbell (1960) applied a non-parametric factor analysis to the same instrument, using the strength of the first factor as a measure of cognitive simplicity—the direct obverse of complexity. Ulehla (1961) developed quite a different measure aimed at the same construct (which he referred to as "channel capacity"); this consisted of an index of multidimensional information yield adopted from information theory (Attneave, 1959). Scott (1963) has developed yet another measure of dimensional complexity, which is simpler than Kelly's (1955) Rep Test to administer and score. It is based on an object sorting task, which is quite generally acceptable to all kinds of subjects. The measure of complexity represents the information yield from S's category system, or the number of groups-worth of information which S's sorts produce. It has been found to correlate with certain other structural and dynamic characteristics of cognition that will be mentioned presently.

There are deficiencies in all these measures. Both the Kelly and the Scott techniques are designed solely for dichotomous attributes. It is quite probable that one characteristic of an increasingly complex cognitive structure is the conversion of dichotomous judgments into more refined discriminations. Ulehla's measure permits such refined discriminations, but requires a huge sample of objects in order to obtain a stable measure of complexity. All of these measures require either that a standard sample of objects be presented to S, or that he list a relatively small number of objects for classification. Thus the index of complexity derived from such a task reflects the question "Does S conceive these attributes as distinct when applied to this particular sample of objects?" Perhaps a more relevant question in assessing dimensional complexity would be "Is S capable of distinguishing these attributes, given any conceivable sample of objects?"

Even in an articulated structure, the elements within it can vary in degrees of distinctiveness. A basic cognitive attribute which is found in all structures and seems to develop very early is the affective attribute, involving a liking or disliking of objects—or, in more sophisticated form, assessing them as good or bad in a moral sense. The distinctiveness of any other attribute is in large part, then, a matter of how independent it is of the affective attribute. Probably cognitive development consists to a great extent of learning to comprehend frames of reference which are not directly related to self-gratification.

According to Osgood et al.'s (1957) group factor analysis of data from the Semantic Differential, two attributes which are commonly distinguished from affectivity are those which these authors label "activity" and "potency." It must be noted, however, that these represent culturally shared attributes applied to a domain consisting of adjectives and nouns. It is reasonable to expect that the particular dimensions which become distinguished from the primary affective attribute will differ depending on the individual and depending also on the cognitive domain referred to by Ossorio (1961). Probably the more sophistication acquired by a person with regard to a particular area of cognition, the greater his dimensional complexity—in other words, the more he tends to comprehend it in terms of attributes independent of "good" and "bad." Nevertheless, it is noteworthy how salient this evaluative attribute is even for presumably sophisticated psychologists. Much research on personality seems to be generated from an ideological vantage point in which it is predicted that all good traits will go together, and all the bad traits likewise: Authoritarianism is associated with narrow-mindedness, ethnic prejudice, intolerance of ambiguity, nationalism, conservatism, autocratic child-rearing practices, fascism, anality, etc. Without judging the validity or invalidity of such generalizations, one can simply note that they are among the most frequently found in present-day social science writings. As a matter of fact, we generally do not have enough empirical data, with potential contaminating factors controlled, to assess their validity. If psychologists look for only one class of correlates (i.e., evaluated attributes), they miss the opportunity to discover others and compare their relative potencies.

If the degree of cognitive differentiation is to be a useful structural concept, it must permit prediction of certain behaviors which cannot be understood on the basis of some simpler, more readily assessable property. It is almost a tautology that differentiation should correlate with analytic capacity, for a person can dispassionately dissect a phenomenon only if he has the cognitive categories to do so. Some data recently reported by

Scott (1961b) indicate that people with relatively high cognitive complexity concerning the domain of foreign nations showed a greater than average capacity for cognitive reorganization as well—that is, they were better able than Ss of low complexity to conceive new attributes in the phenomenal objects. Moreover, the greater a subject's cognitive complexity, the more likely was he to gain, rather than lose, information in the reorganization process; in a complex structure, reorganization consists not in indiscriminate breakdown of the category system but in selective modification of attributes. Both of these correlates of cognitive complexity—ability to reorganize and ability to gain information from reorganization—were independent of Ss' level of information about world affairs.

These findings suggest that cognitive differentiation is associated with a particular kind of modifiability that is neither rigid nor brittle. Of course, the capacity to entertain alternative perspectives is not necessarily a virtue; it may quite conceivably be incompatible with a zealous moral fervor that can aid the relentless pursuit of ideological goals. To the extent that one's cognitive structures are well differentiated in areas of dominant cultural values, he may be deemed morally weak—a vacillating, indecisive character.

Relatedness. Once two cognitive elements can be distinguished, the question "In what manner are they related?" becomes meaningful. The relationship between two elements may be treated as a primary structural characteristic which forms the basis for more complex structural properties. The relation of "similarity" has already been treated in the discussion of differentiation. Other terms for this are association, spatial proximity, covariance, and likelihood of simultaneous (or consequent) arousal. All of these similarity relationships may be formally represented either as the angle between two attribute-vectors or as the distance between two object-images in attribute-space.

Another kind of relatedness is of greater interest here. It is what Zajonc (1960) has called dependency—or its obverse, determinance. This refers to the phenomenal influence of one element upon another (see above). There remains the problem of determining from S's response whether the phenomenally dependent element, B, is really distinct from, but causally connected with A, or whether it has simply not been differentiated from A. It would probably be helpful to devise some task which would permit S to show that, though A and B tend to co-vary empirically, they can be separated in some hypothetical circumstance.

The *salience* of a particular attribute refers to the likelihood of its being triggered off by environmental cues. Structurally, this may be represented as the number of other concepts with which it is associated in a dependent fashion. As previously noted, there is a tendency for the evaluative dimension to be salient in the cognitive functioning of many people. This may be due either to the failure of other attributes to be distinguished from it or to their being phenomenally connected in a causal fashion.

Other concepts besides evaluation may be salient as well, appearing psychologically as dominant concerns in the person's relation to his environment or in his view of objects. Some people are vigilant with regard to Communism and sedition, others with regard to restriction of individual freedom. When any such characteristic of one's world is repeatedly highlighted and sought where others ignore it, we speak of an obsession with the attribute in question. There is a more general structural notion within which this trait can be framed: It may be called the *dispersion among saliences*. If only one or two attributes appear in equal degrees of salience, there is low dispersion; if many attributes appear in equal degrees of salience, there is high dispersion. In the latter case, the attribute that is aroused will presumably depend more on the environmental cues than on internally generated obsessions. Kluckhohn and Murray (1955) used an apt term when they spoke of the "regnancy" of a psychological process, referring to possession of one's behavior by a particular determining tendency. In the normal case, any regnancy is of moderate duration, reflecting a structural condition somewhere between maximum and minimum dispersion of saliences. An exceedingly transitory regnancy of all a person's determining tendencies would be manifest as scattered attention and sporadic pursuit of any goal. A particularly long-enduring regnancy, on the other hand, would presumably lead to overly focused concern and to a limitation on free exploration of the environment. Harvey, Hunt, and Schroder's (1961) notion of openness-closedness, defined as the degree of receptivity to external events, appears quite related to this structural concept, dispersion of saliences, with its consequent effect on the duration of regnancies.

Integration. While the various terms relating to the differentiation of a psychological structure can all be fairly well reduced to a common meaning, the single term *integration* appears to have a variety of meanings which will probably have to be distinguished before convergent operations are devised. The most common meaning—still rather imprecise in most cases—refers to the connectedness among parts of the structure, a state in which the relations among the various attributes (or concepts) are known and manipulable by the person, so that he can shift as necessary from one to another. Zajonc's (1960) measure of cognitive unity explicitly equals the sum of the dependencies in ratio to the maximum number possible, given the number of cognitive elements to be related. Krech and Crutchfield (1948) had previously defined a property of an attitude or belief which they called "specificity" or isolation from other belief systems, in contrast to the property of connectedness with other attitudes and beliefs. Harvey, Hunt, and Schroder (1961) present the idea of "compartmentalization vs. interrelatedness" among concepts; in the latter state all parts of the concept system can be activated in unison, or each part can be activated solo. It would also seem that Vera French's (1947, 1948) designation of the degree of unconscious component of a sentiment is a closely related notion; for "unconscious" may be interpreted as unverbalizable, inaccessible to awareness, unconnected with other cognitive concepts—the opposite of integration in the present sense.

I am not aware of any very satisfactory objective measure of integration in this general sense of interconnectedness among parts. Zajonc's (1960) assessment of cognitive unity, though not dependent on the researcher's judgment, nevertheless relies heavily on S's introspection concerning the component dependencies. A somewhat more objective measure might be proposed within the framework of the sorting task used by Scott (1961b) to assess cognitive differentiation: Following assignment of the objects to groups, S might be asked, "Suppose group A did not exist, would that affect any of the other groups? How? What objects would be added to (or subtracted from) group B?" Alternatively one could inquire, "Which object in group A is the main (defining) object? Suppose it were not in A, would that make it belong in any of the other groups? Which ones?" The intent of such questioning would be to get S actually to manipulate the objects on other attributes as a consequence of their change on the focal one; from his manipulation the researcher could infer the phenomenally causal relations involved. Since the procedure has not yet been tried at this writing, it is impossible to report its actual usefulness, but the features of objectivity and coordination with other structural measures have a priori advantages.

Once a satisfactory method (or series of methods) for assessing psychological interconnectedness has been developed, then it will be possible to characterize any given element according to its degree of centrality or peripherality in the structure—i.e., the number of other concepts to which it is connected. These properties can be formally represented by means of graph theory (Harary and Norman, 1953). Harvey, Hunt, and Schroder (1961) have supplied psychological content by suggesting that centrality refers to the "essentialness" of a concept to the self or to a constellation of concepts. Of course, this characteristic could be assessed indirectly (in fact, they suggest it) by attempting to refute the concept and observing the degree of resistance encountered; but the methodological considerations reviewed above lend preference to a structural measure which would reflect centrality directly, rather than indirectly through its consequences.

In order for Zajonc (1960) to develop his measure of cognitive unity, it was necessary to specify a particular kind of connectedness among the elements, namely "dependency." Very likely this will be necessary for any other measure of integration as well, for the general notion of "connectedness" is probably too vague to suggest any specific operations. It may well be, therefore, that each different variety of connectedness among elements will lead to a different meaning of the concept "integration." Two or three relevant notions can be found in current discussions of cognitive structure.

Perhaps the most familiar is that which Heider (1946) called "structural balance." Originally he defined this property as follows: "A balanced state exists if all parts of a unit have the same dynamic character (i.e., if all are positive, or all are negative), and if entities with different dynamic character are segregated from each other" (p. 107). By "dynamic character" Heider meant affective sign (like or dislike), and by "unit" he referred to a set of cognitive elements related by "similarity, proximity, causality, membership, possession, or belonging." Subsequent interpreters have, however, focused on more restricted meanings of "unit," such as "other people who are seen as liking each other."

In a restricted sense, therefore, a balanced state of interpersonal perception exists if one sees his friends as liking each other, his enemies as liking each other, and the two groups as mutually antagonistic. This may appear as one mode of integration—i.e., having elements of like affective sign grouped together. Another perspective, however, suggests that cognitive balance consists essentially of a perfect correspondence between the affective attribute and whatever other cognitive attribute is used as a basis for grouping the elements. In the restricted sense, mutual friendship is the second attribute, while in the original, more general meaning the basis of "belonging together" constitutes the second attribute. To the extent that any other attribute is highly correlated with the affective dimension, the cognitive structure is thereby simplified, or poorly differentiated. Hence, one would expected to find balanced structures most predominantly in people of low dimensional complexity. Essentially, this is what was found by Campbell (1960) and Scott (1961a) in two quite different attacks on the problem. One might say, then, that structural balance constitutes a simplistic mode of cognitive integration.

Another kind of integration is suggested by the notion *cognitive consistency* (Scott, 1959). When applied to a single attitude, this refers to the degree to which it is "embedded" in a structure of related values and expectancies. When applied to the structure itself, cognitive consistency suggests that the object of an attitude is perceived in relation to the person's values in such a fashion that its positive and negative features exactly balance at the point on the affective continuum at which his attitude falls. An objective method for measuring varying degrees of cognitive consistency was proposed, based on Rosenberg's (1956) procedure for assessing the cognitive components of an attitude. The major deficiency of the measure lies in its inability to tap what, for any particular subject, constitute all the major values and expectancies relevant to his attitude. Nevertheless, an important consequence of this structural property has been repeatedly found: Cognitively consistent attitudes are less subject to change under persuasive attempts than are cognitively inconsistent attitudes. This result is independent of initial attitude strength. The implication of these studies is that that particular kind of integration specified here—namely, consistency of an attitude with its cognitive surround—serves to stabilize the attitude in the face of pressures to change.

Neither of these modes of integration, balance or consistency, carries any implication of logical appropriateness or empirical validity. They are entirely subjective and subject-specific. If S sees two of his friends as getting along, this constitutes a balanced state, regardless of the facts of the case. If S favors both segregation and the value of human rights and sees no connection between the two notions, his attitude toward segregation may still be quite cognitively consistent (with other values) in the above sense. If the researcher wishes to apply standards of validity or logic to the relations among cognitive elements, these can provide another basis for defining integration: "Integration" among a set of elements consists in their being related in a manner specified by the externally defined criterion. Some research on attitudes (e.g., Henle and Michael, 1956; Morgan and Norton, 1944) is explicitly based on such a definition, and one suspects that it underlies a good deal of thinking about cognitive integration (e.g., the notions of dissonance and consonance, Festinger, 1957). Such an approach, however, requires an explicit external standard of "proper" integration that may be more or less arbitrary and culture-bound; even though a cognitive structure is not integrated in this sense, it may still be integrated in another sense, as discussed previously.

Yet another kind of integration is suggested by the property *hierarchic organization,* indicating the degree to which a cognitive domain is dominated by a small number of concepts to which the others are subsidiary. In a highly organized structure, information about one attribute of an object would be sufficient for the person to determine all of its other essential properties. Zajonc's (1960) measure of organization indicates the degree to which the unity of the entire structure depends on a single element; other measures might be devised to represent more segmented organizations in which two or three elements share dominant positions.

Though this property of hierarchic organization seems, on the face of it, formally and psychologically distinguishable from the concept of differentiation, operationally the two may be difficult to separate. Complete and uniform dependence of all attributes on a single one may simply mean that the former set is not well differentiated from the dominant element; hence the cognitive structure is simple in the sense described previously. Until research is performed assessing complexity and organization independently, their degree of empirical covariation cannot be determined. It is not even clear whether they can be assessed independently. This is an instance in which we probably need better conceptual clarification, followed by the development of precise measures, before much can be said about this particular kind of cognitive integration.

The Generality of Structural Properties

All of the above characteristics of cognitive structure have been described with respect to a single domain of cognition. Operationally one is restricted, at best, to assessing the degree of differentiation, balance, unity, etc., pertaining to a given set of phenomenal objects that constitute considerably less than the totality of any person's life space. So it seems preferable, at least in the beginning, to restrict the structural notions to a scope that can be encompassed empirically.

There is an even better reason for talking about just one domain of cognition at a time. It is that there is little empirical assurance at present of any generality of these structural properties across cognitive domains. Psychologists are used to assuming a functional unity within a person and within his cognitive processes. This leads them to expect that a structural characteristic encountered in one domain of cognition will be duplicated elsewhere. Yet empirical work to date does not generally support this expectation with respect to the structural attributes referred to here. In Ulehla's (1961) study, the cognitive complexity of nurses in dealing with schizophrenic symptoms was not correlated with their cognitive complexity in defining the nurse's role. Among a group of college students Scott (unpublished data) found no correlation between the cognitive complexity of concepts about nations and of those about people. With respect to the property of cognitive consistency, neither Gochman (1960) nor Scott (unpublished data) has found much consistency of high or low scores across a sample of attitudinal domains. The only study at hand which reports a correlation between structural measures applied to two different areas is that of Bieri and Blacker (1956) concerning the perception of people and of inkblots. However, their operations reflect variability of response, which they relate theoretically to cognitive complexity, rather than measuring the structural property more directly; therefore it is not certain that structural generality has been demonstrated. In any case, one can hardly say that there is overwhelming evidence for the generality of these structural attributes from one domain of cognition to another.

If the results of further studies continue in the same vein, they will pose a problem. Either we must discard our measures in favor of some that are more reliable; or we must suspect that what they are tapping is an ephemeral product of the instruments rather than an inherent quality of cognition; or we must revise our assumptions about the functional unity of cognition which have led us to expect generality in the structural attributes. Since most critics would presumably be prepared to follow the first two lines of attack, let us pursue the third. In the first place, one need not think of total cognitive activity as particularly unified, and in the second place it is not necessarily true that such structural unities as there are will show up in the domains that have been assessed so far.

When one considers past difficulties encountered in developing the traits of "logical reasoning ability" and "precise thinking" via the study of Latin and geometry, he may become less sanguine about the prospects of nurturing a particular cognitive style which will be manifest in a wide range of applications. Moreover, to the extent that one takes an empiricist, rather than a nativist, approach to the origins of cognition, he will be reluctant to believe that people are born with ready-made cognitive styles that are quite generally manifest. This is not to deny some striking individual differences in organization and approach to central areas of the life space. But it is quite likely that these modes of organization, and the cognitive structures associated with them, have been built up through specific experiences with the object domains—the way a person is introduced to an area, the amount of time he spends thinking about it, the way in which he uses his knowledge, etc. It would seem altogether possible to maintain a conceptual framework concerning professional activities that is structurally quite different from that relating to family or social life—mainly because the situations in which they are developed and expressed pose quite different functional demands. It would seem unproductive, therefore, to go looking for "types" of people identifiable by their over-all cognitive structures—the differentiated and undifferentiated, the integrated and unintegrated, and so forth. Maybe extreme cases exist in which all cognitive functioning is of a piece, but they would be so few in number that the typology would have little utility; more likely such people would be found in mental institutions, since the very consistency of their functioning across all domains would severely impede their adaptation.

At present, the appropriate unit of analysis in the study of cognitive styles would seem to be not the total person, but a particular area of his functioning that is associated with an identifiable event-domain. It is, of course, possible that in central areas of a person' life he will tend to develop similar modes of cognitive organization—particularly if those areas are experienced close together in time, space, and interpersonal surround. However, the instruments for assessing cognitive structure used so far do not generally tap central features of any particular subject's life. Rather they deal with nations in the world, or a general sample of people that he has encountered, or topics of opinion that are not necessarily of major concern. Perhaps one could assume that it is in these relatively peripheral areas of a person's life space that he will most likely manifest any dominant and central cognitive style (c.f., Smith, Bruner, White, 1956). But the opposite assumption seems more compelling at the moment—namely, that dominant, pervasive styles gain expression more readily in the familiar, well-used areas of one's life space. They are likely to differ for different people, so that a single standardized instrument with completely preformed content will not pick up the central content areas nor, therefore, any structural commonalities among them. It will be necessary, rather, to discover for each subject what are his central domains, then proceed to examine them structurally with a generalized instrument that is not tied to any particular content.

It is, of course, not certain that this approach will turn up structural commonalities across different areas of cognition, for the various other sources of differences mentioned above may dominate over any tendency toward similarities. At least for the present there is little ground for distinguishing "classes of people" by their types of cognitive structure, but only for describing different ways of structuring any selected cognitive domain. Doubts concerning the prospects of wide generalization are raised by past experience with typologies which used the individual as the unit of analysis: Usually correlations among the component characteristics are so low that nothing approaching a multimodal distribution of persons can be generated; hence those falling in the "pure types" constitute such a small sample of the total as to be trivial.

Conclusion

This paper has provided a rather oblique focus on the central problem of dealing with structural properties of cognition. In its emphasis on methodological issues it has ignored many more intriguing matters, such as the theoretical and empirical relations among structural properties, the relation between structure and content, the genesis of structural properties in the individual's life history, and the structure of the social environment within which a given cognitive style is likely to emerge. If there is any justification for this concern with preliminaries, it is that dependable results demand dependable measures. Perhaps our measures can be improved by greater attention to some of the problems raised here.

Chapter 10

Concluding Comments on the Current Status of the Incongruity Hypothesis

O. J. HARVEY

This volume has focused heavily on the effects of negative incongruities upon various aspects of motivation and social behavior. Brief attention was also given to consequences of positive discrepancies.

The labels "negative" and "positive" imply necessarily that the receiving individual has been led to construe the stimulus situation as either in accord with or deviant from the evaluative schemata he more or less customarily employs as a psychological yardstick in the interpretation of a particular class of events. Because of marked variation in the internal standards through which the external world is filtered and defined, variously referred to as "conceptual systems," "adaptation levels," "plans," "cognitive structures," and "data tapes" by different ones of us, the same objective input or occurrence may be evaluated entirely differently by different persons and consequently effect markedly different outcomes.

The implications of this tenet of stimulus relativity for many of the traditional questions of psychology were sketched in the preceding chapters. The presentation of a series of papers between the same covers obviously does not ensure integration, whether the writings be those of single or of multiple authors. We would hope, however, that despite different terminologies we have at least succeeded in making clear, substantively and not just analogously, that many issues that are typically treated from seemingly disparate and unrelated bases may be of a highly common fabric; and certainly so when treated at a somewhat genotypic level. Important issues surrounding the discrepancy hypotheses not only were not solved but many were left completely untouched. Such a shortcoming, however, is not unique to this volume. It is characteristic of the burgeoning work in the area. But there are broad bands of agreement, both by the present authors and other writers, on this problem. First we shall offer a brief synopsis of the points of general consensus and then sketch a few of the more basic unresolved issues.

Some Common Assumptions

Concern with reactions to baseline-event incongruities represents a salient development in psychology during the last few years. Psychophysicists, neurophysiologists, social psychologists, and personality theorists are among the different area representatives who have found such concern of importance to their theorizing and psychological points of view. Despite the diversity in points of departure and terminology, there seem, nevertheless, to be a number of basic assumptions held in common by the majority of workers in the area.

With the possible exception of some psychophysicists, it appears to be generally assumed, at least tacitly, that the perception of an event as being markedly different from the way it is ordinarily interpreted generates tension, arousal, some kind of psychological discomfort, and leads consequently to activity aimed at reducing the mismatch between the input and the evaluative standards. Attitude change, decision making, communication, interpersonal relations, and problem solving have been interpreted as outcomes of attempts at maintaining some optimal level of congruity between one's concatenation of definitional predilections or choices and the external environment. Effects of sensory deprivation have been treated by some as failure to maintain some optimum, either in terms of magnitude of stimulation or in getting meaning from the situation.

Much of the supportive theorizing surrounding the effects of baseline-situation incongruities involves assumptions of drive reduction. Such notions are different from Hull's, however, owing to the insertion of one important qualification: the idea of an optimal that is somewhere between the extremes of high drive arousal and complete absence of such arousal. Striving to maintain this optimal level of arousal may mean that in cases where the arousal surpasses the optimum the organism may take active steps to reduce the stimulation. In those cases where arousal is too low, on the other hand, the organism may engage in activity aimed at increasing the tension or arousal level. It is this latter assumption that sets such thinking apart from the related theorizing of Hull.

More and more, curiosity, exploratory behavior, and human creativity are being viewed as an expression of self-initiated drive toward keeping an amount of diversity, novelty, and complexity sufficient to maintain the arousal level at some theoretical optimum. Because repeated presentation of a pattern of stimulus events results in satiation, reduced stimulus effectiveness, and boredom, the organism may move toward seeking new and often more intense inputs in order to keep the arousal level up to the optimum.

Some Unresolved Issues

Within this broad realm of agreement, the bases of which are still more theoretical than empirical, issues exist which remain fairly untouched or on which there is divided opinion. At least five of these include: (1) the nature of the evaluative schemata or baseline from which incongruities are detected, defined, and responded to; (2) the magnitude of the baseline-event incongruity; (3) the direction of the deviant event from the baseline; (4) the effects of such idiosyncratic factors as personal histories and conceptual differences; and (5) the question of whether or not the evaluative yardstick can adequately be represented by a single value, as many assume it can.

The Nature of the Baseline (What Is Being Maintained?). Since Hebb's early writing (1949), neurophysiologically inclined psychologists have come more and more to assume that the organism seeks that amount of varied stimulation necessary for the maintenance of an optimal level of cortical activity. Too much or too little stimulation is thought to induce behavior aimed at making the magnitude of stimulation conform to the optimum. Sensory deprivation, exploratory behavior, curiosity, and the manipulatory drive have all been treated within this theoretical paradigm (e.g., Bexton, Heron, and Scott, 1954; Leuba, 1955; Hebb, 1955; Glanzer, 1958; Berlyne, 1960).

Seeking the stimulation necessary to keep the level of cortical arousal high enough is hypothesized by Hebb (1955) as explaining much of the positive attraction of risk taking and problem solving in which the individual deliberately exposes himself to fear-inducing and frustrating situations of mild intensities. "When you stop to think of it," avers Hebb, "it is nothing short of extraordinary what trouble people will go to in order to get into more trouble at the bridge table, or on the golf course; and the fascination of the murder story, or thriller, and the newspaper account of real-life adventure or tragedy, is no less extraordinary. This taste for excitement *must* not be forgotten when we are dealing with human motivation. It appears that, up to a certain point, threat and puzzle have positive motivating value, beyond that point negative value" (Hebb, 1955, p. 250). This formulation leaves problems, as Hebb himself has stressed. "It is not *any* mild threat, *any* form of problem, that is rewarding; we still have to work out the rules for this formulation" (1955, p. 250).

It would seem, to this writer at least, that one set of variables that have to be included in any such set of adequate rules would be that having to do with *meaning* or *relevance*. By this is meant that it is not just magnitude of stimulation *per se* that is important but variation of events that are integrally related to the goals, the desires, the motives, the hopes, and wishes of the receiving individual. A high level of stimulation could be maintained by any number of techniques that would not at the same time convey usable information or meaning to the subject. Intense and homogeneous noise, intense and homogeneous light, intense and homogeneous stimulation of any modality could suffice to keep the level of arousal high, at least for awhile, until possibly the subject gave up trying to make any particular sense out of it. But this kind of increased stimulation would be unlikely to prevent some of the effects found in acute sensory deprivation. In fact, it probably would increase the likelihood of some of the more dramatic effects occurring. Thus would seem that instead of the individual in such situations having too little stimulation he has too much; *too much meaningless* bombardment *and not enough meaningful* or motive-relevant stimulation.

What motive or internal state is such stimulation incompatible with? We would say to the seeking of information; to the seeking of structure through which reliable and stable predictive schemata of the world can be built up; to the striving of the individual to be in command of his own fate, to have control in some way over the means and instrumentalities of his own need satisfaction and goal attainment. An overabundance of homogeneous and undifferentiable bombardment yields no meaning. It even renders inoperative pre-established ways of ordering and defining the situation. It creates situations of stress, renders the individual helpless, reduces his competence (White, 1959) to cope with his world. The point we have tried repeatedly to make in this connection is well made by Bruner:

> What is this maintenance problem? I would like to suggest that it perhaps relates to a kind of continuing feedback-evaluation process by which organisms guide their correction strategies in perceiving, cognizing, and manipulating their environments. Let me suggest that the unhampered operation of this evaluation process is critical in the continuing adaptation of the organism, both in the development of adequate cognitive functioning . . . and also in moment-to-moment functioning. Consider the massive effects that occur when the evaluation process is interfered with by various means. Distort auditory feedback in speech by the conventional technique of delaying the rerun of the speech pattern to the speaker's ear by a fraction of a second, and the effect is highly disruptive. Stuttering occurs and the speaker reports a lively discomfort, sometimes bordering on panic. So, too, with the discomfort of a visual Ganzfeld, where virtually all orienting cues are removed and only a white unstructured space remains. Distorting spectacles have the same effect of disrupting and preoccupying the organism, setting him off on a battle for adequate feedback that makes all else seem trivial. One may suggest that one of the prime sources of anxiety is a state in which one's conception or perception of the environment with which one must deal does not "fit" or predict that

environment in a manner that makes action possible. If there is anything to this view of anxiety, then it follows that when one prevents an organism from monitoring the fittingness of his precepts and his cognitive structures, one is cutting him off from one of his principle sources of maintaining adjustment [Bruner, 1961, pp. 205–6].

In the same symposium in which Bruner made the above statement, Goldberger and Holt (1961) and Cohen et al. (1961) offered kindred explanatory bases for the effects of sensory deprivation. Ten years earlier Sherif and Harvey (1952) employed a related rationale in their study of induced anxiety or self-disorganization through elimination of environmental referent points and cues. These kinds of assumptions would imply that much of the time spent in sleep, instead of stemming from low levels of arousal, as many would maintain, may actually have occurred as a kind of defense, a kind of tuning out of the disturbing ambiguity which defies attempts at structuring it and making it meaningful.

Perhaps the comparative effects of reward, punishment, and no feedback on rate and quality of learning are also illustrative of the importance of motive-relevant information in the development of veridical concepts of the situation. It has been shown repeatedly that both reward and punishment are superior to no feedback as conditions of learning, reward being the most effective of the three treatments. This, of course, is not incompatible with the Hebbian hypothesis. Reward and punishment presumably more nearly effect the optimal level of stimulation than does no feedback. But the hypothesis of optimal stimulation, with all traces of the law of effect removed, would not predict the superiority of reward over punishment because theoretically the magnitude of negative and positive feedback could be equated. It would seem then that the notion of optimal stimulation still has to deal with qualitative aspects of stimulation as well as magnitude. And, as we have repeatedly stressed, quality of a stimulus is at least partially dependent on the internal standards operative at the time of impingement. They operate to determine what kinds of stimuli have positive and negative quality.

Magnitude of Stimulation. The effects of a given magnitude of stimulus discrepancy are also dependent on the baseline from which the impingement is construed. Hence this question is inextricably bound to the preceding one.

Many writers today assume the butterfly curve posited by McClelland et al. (1953) depicts accurately the effects of different magnitudes of stimulus discrepancy. Small deviations in either direction from the internal standard are assumed to produce positive affects and attendant

consequences. Zero discrepancy is generally assumed to produce boredom and some discomfort, while large discrepancies in either direction
are assumed to cause negative effect, high tension, and more acute discomfort. There are, however, alternative positions on this question
which would lead to different predictions on the effects of varied magnitudes of discrepancy.

Two related theoretical premises would predict that extreme discrepancies would have negative consequences only up to a point, beyond
which the negativity would begin to dissipate. One might assume from
a purely psychophysical and non-motivational basis that an event too
deviant from its customary definitional baseline would be evaluated as
being irrelevant to the dimension at hand or at least representative of
some concept other than what the perceiver had in mind. Parallel conclusions might also be reached from a motivational arousal point of view.
When the discrepancy gets too great and the tension and negative arousal
become too high, the subject might invoke some kind of dissociation or
redefinition process in which he neutralizes the deviant event. Increased
discrepancies beyond this point would produce no further effects; if anything, a further disposition toward dissociation and redefinition.

The picture here, however, is very unclear. The results seem to
indicate that even extreme discrepancies continue to exercise effects.
In several communication studies in which the message of the source has
been made to deviate in graded amounts from the position of the recipient, larger discrepancies have continued to produce greater effects,
although not in a linear progression (Hovland and Pritzker, 1957; Goldberg, 1954; Harvey, Kelley, and Shapiro, 1957; Harvey, 1962). This
picture is complicated by the fact that increased discrepancies dispose
toward their source being discredited, a probable manifestation of the
tendency to preserve one's view of relevant situations as intact as possible. Related results have been obtained in psychophysical studies in
which deviant inputs in the form of extreme anchors have been studied.
In a preliminary and unpublished study Bevan found extreme anchors
continued to affect the scale. Some evidence indicates that in the case
of well-established scales or concepts, however, the tendency toward
distorting the anchor away from the scale increases with increased discrepancies (Harvey and Caldwell, 1959; Harvey and Campbell, 1962).
This might prove to be an expression of the same determinant that results in distorting communications away from one's own stand when
they are too discrepant from it (Hovland, Harvey, and Sherif, 1957).

Despite the absence of a complete picture, it still seems safe to conclude that, even though extreme discrepancies continue to produce negative effects, new effects such as discrediting, distortion, and attribution
of blame to the source also get generated. Thus extremely deviant in-

puts, particularly from baselines to which the individual is highly committed, seem to produce qualitiative changes as well as variation in effects induced at lower discrepancies.

Directionality of Discrepancy. Whether or not events equally deviant from the evaluative baseline in either direction produce identical effects is a question that has received almost no experimental examination. Most writers concerned with dissonance, balance, and incongruity fail to consider this problem, and those who do tend to assume that magnitude of discrepancy is the crucial factor, with directionality making no difference for similar magnitudes. Commonsense would suggest, however, that the answer to this question depends heavily upon the nature of the baseline from which the incongruity is perceived. If the baseline implies *directionality*, i.e., a predisposition or desire to perceive or behave in one direction, such as toward the "desirable," then it would seem that the direction of the discrepancy from the baseline might be a very weighty determinant of the effects of an input.

McClelland *et al.* (1953), among the first to point to the importance of the present question, proposed that the simplest assumption, although not necessarily the best one, would be that equivalent magnitudes of discrepancy in either direction would have the same effects. But what these writers treated as the baseline, or adaptation level as they termed it, was a person's expectancy toward a particular event. If expectancy is the baseline and if the expectancy is not also tied up with a preferred outcome or a directional striving, then equal deviations in either direction might produce comparable effects. Most of our evaluative schemata that serve as a psychological yardstick, however, do involve valued ends and hence preferred directions. In such an instance the further the event departed from the sought end state the more negative the effect, and the more the event conformed to the hopes the more positive the effect and related consequences. For example, one might deeply love another person, want very much to be loved in return, but perceive oneself as not being. This probably would lead to hoping for one kind of information, that indicating reciprocal love, and expecting the reverse. In such a case refutation of expectancy would produce positive affect, for while expectancy was being refuted a valued end state (desire to be loved) was being confirmed.

In a study carried out at the University of Colorado, Van Ostrand (1960) experimented with a closely related situation. It might be assumed, as Festinger does (1957), for example, that if a person thought poorly of himself he would be likely to expect negative appraisals of himself from others and consequently would not experience dissonance or be upset when actually presented with unfavorable evaluations from another. Van Ostrand tested this possibility by exposing subjects who were both low and high in self-esteem to others' ratings of them which were either more or less positive than their own initial ratings by a controlled amount. The low self-esteem subjects were more influenced by both the favorable and unfavorable ratings than were the persons high in self-esteem. In relation to high self-esteem subjects, they became more positive toward both themselves and the source from receipt of positive evaluations and more negative toward both self and source when they were recipients of negative evaluations. If the low self-esteem subjects could be assumed to expect unfavorable appraisals of themselves, the effects produced by the positive and negative ratings should be equivalent since they were equidistant (in physical units) above and below initial self ratings. Such was not the case, however, suggesting that in instances of commitment and preferred ends hope is the more appropriate baseline.

Results compatible with the preceding ones have recently been obtained in one of our pilot studies. Subjects were asked to indicate both their hope and expectancy for a term grade in a psychology course. In several cases the hope was higher than expectancy, which allowed for the two to be confirmed and refuted independently. Confirmation and refutation of hope produced significantly greater effects, positive and negative, respectively, than did the same treatment of expectancy.

Where value, commitment, and ego-involvement come in, as they do in so many of our evaluations of the world, directionality of discrepancies seems to be of major importance in the effects produced.

Personal History and Conceptual Makeup. To the extent that individuals differ in their histories of contact with relevant environmental and training dimensions they should, at least theoretically, vary in both the structure and content of their conceptual and personality makeups. Such variations would mean necessarily that the evaluative baseline or psychological yardstick would be slightly colored or in some way affected by idiosyncratic differences. The world would consequently be construed somewhat differently and accordingly effect different behavioral outcomes. While several of the chapters in this volume stressed this point, a few additional comments aimed at tying this in with the issues sketched in the present chapter are appropriate.

Variations in life histories may produce marked difference in the directional effects of discrepancies. Discrepancies toward the negative end of one's scale, the end associated with negative affect and avoidance behavior, would have effects different from the same magnitude of deviation toward the positive end, the end of one's scale associated with positive affect and approach tendencies. Assume that on a scale of alcoholism the subject's own position was that which favored the use of alcohol in moderation. If the subject had reached the position of moderation after strong rebellion against his previous dedication to complete abstinence, which had come to be associated with intensely unpleasant experiences, then it is likely that he would react more negatively to discrepancies toward "teetotalism" than to equally deviant stimulus events toward increased "wetness." The same picture would hold true, perhaps even more strikingly, for the person who had had extremely unhappy experiences with alcohol and moved away from favoring its use in large amounts toward the dryer position of moderation.

Differences in personal histories are reflected in variations in cognitive or conceptual structure. One of the clearest ways in which conceptual structure affects reactions to input is through influence upon the openness or closedness of the metering system, the number of alternatives that can be simultaneously entertained, and hence the magnitude of discrepancy that is tolerated before certain effects are produced. More concrete individuals, those possessed of simpler cognitive structures, have been found to be more authoritarian, more intolerant of ambiguity and difference (Harvey, 1963b), more disposed to viewing the world in good-bad dimensions (Campbell, 1960) and to displaying a stronger tendency toward sociometric symmetry (Campbell, 1960) and cognitive balance (Scott, 1962). This would imply that more abstract individuals would tolerate large stimulus discrepancies before being aroused and instituting techniques at neutralizing the deviations. It might mean even that such a person could be exposed to experimenter-defined conditions of dissonance and incongruity without experiencing them as such.

There is at least one other way in which cognitive structure might operate to prevent the experience of dissonance from logically inconsistent inputs or behavior. If the cognitive elements or concepts were compartmentalized, an individual could subscribe to contradictory premises without experiencing conflict, strain, or inconsistency. Highly prejudiced persons and schizophrenics have often been noted to manifest marked discontinuities in behavior, pursuing logically inconsistent courses of action without apparent awareness. One might say that by definition dissonance is the experience of conflicting evaluative or choice predilections. This, however, makes dissonance a phenomenological construct and one not anchored to experimental operations. Festinger maintains that "two elements are in a dissonant relation if, considering these two alone, the obverse of one element would follow from another" (1957, p. 13). If this definition of dissonance is based on the external observer's point of view, then it would seem that either cognitive compartmentalization, which prevents the inconsistencies from being noted, or high cognitive complexity, which allows the person to experience an event as deviant but not be upset by it, would reduce or even prevent the occurrence of dissonance-reducing behavior that is supposed to result from incongruous situations.

Variations in personal histories and conceptual structure seem also to affect reactions to sensory deprivation. In a preliminary study we have found more concrete and more abstract subjects, those depicted in Chapters 4 and 5 of this volume and in Harvey, Hunt, and Schroder (1961), as representative of Stages 1 and 4 functioning, to be affected differentially by a sensory-depriving environment. Subjects made their way through a maze in a large dark room to a slowly revolving table on which they lay while they did division problems in their heads, reproduced lists of digits, and responded to tone discrimination tests. In relation to their pre-experimental performances on these tests, the more concrete individuals were more adversely affected by the ambiguous and confusing environment than were the more abstract subjects.

Not all these results were significant at the generally accepted .05 level, although all were below .10. If, however, these results are replicated by a better designed environment, currently being pretested, they would have important implications for much of the current theorizing concerning sensory deprivation. Unpublished research carried out during the past two years by my colleagues Dave Hunt and Harry Schroder and me makes it quite clear that the more abstract Stage 4 representatives tend to come from training environments in which they were rewarded for exploring, for seeking information, for being their own causal agents. The more concrete Stage 1 individuals seem quite clearly to come from more controlled environments in which they were forced to depend heavily on the dictates and controls of authority and social prescriptions. In several studies Stage 4 subjects have been found to be more informational and task oriented, to be more tolerant of ambiguity, to be less stereotyped and rigid, and in general to look more favorably upon novelty and diversity than the more concrete individuals. This means that the level of stimulation habitually sought by Stage 4 persons should be, and clearly seems to be, higher than that sought by Stage 1 representatives.

According to Hebb's (1949), Leuba's (1955), and Glanzer's (1958) formulations the individual who has developed an habitually higher level of stimulation and arousal should be the one most affected by sensory deprivation because in relation to his higher baseline homogeneous and ambiguous environments should produce a greater paucity of stimulation. Those persons who have standardized lower levels of stimulation should be less affected. This seems to be just the reverse of our tentative findings. The more abstract persons, who presumably have higher stimulation or cortical activity levels, were less adversely influenced by an unstructured environment than were the more concrete individuals, who should be expected to have much lower needs for stimulation and arousal.

These findings are consistent, however, with the hypothesis of a need for structure and meaning. The more concrete individuals, with their heavy reliance upon external referent points as guidelines to behavior, should be more impaired in their functioning when such cues are removed or rendered inoperative. The more abstract persons, possessed of more differentiated and integrated conceptual systems, more autonomous self structures, are less dependent upon physical and external cues and hence should be less upset by conditions of ambiguity in which such cues are absent.

Two things should be kept in mind: Our results are tentative; and in our experimental conditions we sought deliberately to disorient the subject whereas in the McGill-type experiment subjects are maintained in a fairly confined space in which they can orient themselves to key referent points, such as the source of food supply and the toilet, fairly accurately. But even in the latter type environments it would still be our prediction that more abstract subjects would be less negatively affected than the more concrete ones. In fact, it would not be surprising if Stage 4 subjects actually enjoyed the experience. This would present novelty and diversity, would allow them to introspect and to pursue understanding of self. How this would be reflected in frequency and nature of hallucinations and other such experiences, however, would be difficult to predict.

If our above speculations prove to hold up, this would be an instance where the inclusion of such an idiosyncratic factor as cognitive structure might lead to an opposite prediction from what would be made if one relied on the stimulus environment alone. In the present case such an inclusion might provide a clear test of the relative validities of cognitive-self theory and of the neo-neurological hypothesis of optimal stimulation, represented by the average level of stimulation in one's history, according to Glanzer (1958).

Can Evaluative Baselines Be Summarized in a Single Value? Experimental work stemming from the conceptualizations of Helson (1947, 1948, 1959) has provided the most widespread investigation of this question. Numerous studies in psychophysics, such as those described by Bevan in Chapter 2, have found that strikingly accurate predictions can be made from the adaptation level, the weighted geometric mean of present and past stimuli.

Yet it may still be meaningful to ask if important parameters other than that represented by a pooled single value may not significantly influence the cognitive baseline. A study by Harvey and Campbell (1963) was addressed to a facet of this question. Subjects first formed a scale of two sets of stimulus weights which varied in range but were calculated to yield comparable adaptation levels. The narrow range consisted of weights 3, 4, 5, 6, and 7, separated by equal log-gram intervals. The wide scale consisted of weights 1, 3, 5, 7, and 9, meaning that the distance between the weights was twice that in the narrow scale. In both scales, however, weight 5 represented approximately the common adaptation level value. Following controlled exposure to the two ranges of weights, subjects then judged the heaviness of anchor weights which exceeded the upper limits of the scale by fixed amounts. One of the hypotheses was that the anchors would be judged lighter in relation to the wide than the narrow scale owing to less distance between them and the upper limit of the wider range. This, as well as other predicted range effects, was borne out. Even with Helson's "d-factor" included to correct for differences in stimulus intervals, the adaptation range was a better predictor of responses than was the adaptation level. In fact, some of the obtained results were contradictory to what adaptation level theory, based upon a pooled, single-value concept, would have predicted.

Bibliography

ABELSON, R. P., and ROSENBERG, M. J. 1958. Symbolic psychologic: A model of attitude cognition. *Behav. Sci., 3,* 1–13.

ABRAHAMS, I. 1950. Group psychotherapy: Implications for direction and supervision of mentally ill patients. In THERESA MULLEN, *Mental health in nursing.* Washington, D. C.: Catholic University.

ADAMSON, R., BEVAN, W., and MAIER, BARBARA. 1961. Shifts in bar pressing as a function of alternating extinction and reinforcement. *J. gen. Psychol., 64,* 147–52.

ADORNO, T. W., FRENKEL-BRUNSWIK, ELSE, LEVINSON, D. J., and SANFORD, R. N. 1950. *The authoritarian personality.* New York: Harper.

AKHTAR, M. 1962. The role of counterconditioning in intermittent reinforcement. Unpublished Ph.D. dissertation, University of Illinois.

ALDERSTEIN, A., and FEHRER, E. 1955. The effect of food deprivation on exploratory behavior in a complex maze. *J. comp. physiol. Psychol., 48,* 250–53.

ALLPORT, F. H. 1924. *Social psychology.* Boston: Houghton Mifflin.

ALLPORT, G. W. 1943. The ego in contemporary psychology. *Psychol. Rev., 50,* 451–78.

———. 1955. *Becoming: Basic considerations for a psychology of personality.* New Haven: Yale University Press.

ALLPORT, G. W., BRUNER, J. S., and JANDORF, E. M. Personality under social catastrophe. Life histories of the Nazi revolution, ed. M. C. KLUCKHOLM, H. MURRAY, and SCHNEIDER. 1954. *Personality in Nature, Society and Culture* (rev. ed.). New York: Knopf.

ALLPORT, G. W., and POSTMAN, L. 1947. *The psychology of rumor.* New York: Holt.

ALLUISI, E. A., MULLER, P. F., and FITTS, P. M. 1955. Rate of handling information presentation. USAF WADC Tech. Note, No. 55-745.

ALTMANN, M. 1960. Adjustment problems in the adolescent moose and elk. Unpublished manuscript, University of Colorado.

AMSEL, A. 1958. The role of frustrative nonreward in non-continuous reward situations. *Psychol. Bull., 55,* 102–19.

AMSEL, A., and ROUSSEL, J. 1952. Motivational properties of frustration: I, effect on running response of the addition of frustration to the motivational complex. *J. exp. Psychol., 43,* 363–68.

ANDERSON, A. R. 1958. A reduction of deontic logic to alethic modal logic. *Mind, 67,* 100–03.

———. 1962. What do symbols symbolize: Platonism. In B. BAUMRIN (ed.), *Proceedings of the Delaware Conferences on the Philosophy of Science.* Newark, Del.: University of Delaware Press.

ANDERSON, A. R., and MOORE, O. K. 1957. The formal analysis of normative concepts. *Amer. Sociological Review, 22,* 11–17.

———. 1959. Autotelic folk-models, ONR Technical Report, No. 8.

———. 1960. Autotelic folk-models. *The Sociological Quarterly, 1,* 203–16.

———. 1962. The formal analysis of cultural objects. *Synthese, 14,* 144–70.

APPLETON, L. E. 1910. *A comparative study of the play activities of adult savages and civilized children.* Chicago: University of Chicago Press.

ASCH, S. E. 1952. *Social psychology.* New York: Prentice-Hall.
ASHBY, W. R. 1952. *Design for a brain.* New York: Wiley.
ATTNEAVE, F. 1954. Some informational aspects of visual perception. *Psychol. Rev.,* 61, 183–93.
————. 1959. *Applications of information theory to psychology.* New York: Holt.
AUSUBEL, D. P. 1952. *Ego development and personality disorders.* New York: Grune.
BACH, J. S. 1722. *Das Wohltempierte Clavier.* Zurich.
BALDWIN, A. 1955. *Behavior and development in childhood.* New York: Dryden.
BALDWIN, J. M. 1895. *Mental development in the child and in the race.* New York: Macmillan.
BALES, R. F. 1950. *Interaction process analysis.* Cambridge, Mass.: Harvard University Press.
BANDURA, A., and WALTERS, R. H. 1959. *Adolescent aggression.* New York: Ronald Press.
BARSCHAK, E. 1951. A study of happiness and unhappiness in the childhood and adolescence of girls in different cultures. *J. Psychol.,* 32, 173–215.
BARTLETT, F. C 1932. *Remembering: A study in experimental and social psychology.* London: Cambridge University Press.
————. 1958. *Thinking.* New York: Basic Books.
BEACH, F. A. 1945. Current concepts of play in animals. *Amer. Natur.,* 79, 523–41.
————. 1955. The descent of instinct. *Psychol. Rev.,* 62, 401–10.
BECK, A. 1890. Die Bestimmung der Lacalisation der Gehirn und Rüchenmarks-funktionen vermittelst der elektrischen Erscheinunger. *Centralbl. Physiol.,* 4, 473.
BECKER, G. M. 1958. Sequential decision making. Wald's model and estimates of parameters. *J. exp. Psychol.,* 55, #6.
BECHER, W. C. 1962. Developmental psychology. *Annu. Rev. Psychol.,* 13, 1–34.
BELL, C. 1811. Idea of a new anatomy of the brain submitted for the observation of his friends. In J. F. FULTON (ed.), *Selected readings in the history of physiology.* Springfield, Ill.: Charles C Thomas, 1931. Pp. 251 ff.
BENNIS, E. G., and SHEPARD, H. A. 1956. A theory of group development. *Hum. Rel.,* 9, 415–37.
BERGER, H. 1929. Ueber das Elektrenkephalogramm des Menschen. *Archiv. Psychiat.,* 87, 527 (cited by BRAZIER, 1959).
BERLYNE, D. E. 1950. Novelty and curiosity as determinants of exploratory behavior. *Brit. J. Psychol.,* 41, 68–80.
————. 1957a. Conflict and information-theory variables as determinants of human perceptual curiosity. *J. exp. Psychol.,* 53, 399–404.
————. 1957b. Uncertainty and conflict: a point of contact between information theory and behavior-theory concepts. *Psychol. Rev.,* 64, 329–39.
————. 1957c. Attention to change, conditioned inhibition (SIr) and stimulus satiation. *Brit. J. Psychol.,* 48, 138–40.
————. 1958a. The influence of complexity and novelty in visual figures on orienting responses. *J. exp. Psychol.,* 55, 289–96.
————. 1958b. Supplementary report: complexity and orienting responses with longer exposures. *J. exp. Psychol.,* 56, 183.
————. 1960. *Conflict, arousal, and curiosity.* New York: McGraw-Hill.
————. 1961. Conflict and the orientation reaction. *J. exp. Psychol.,* 42, 476–83.
BERNARD, C. 1859. *Lecons sur les proprietes physiologiques et les alterations pathologique des liquides de l'organisms.* 2 vols. Paris: Balliere.
BERTALANFFY, L. V. 1951. Theoretical models in biology and psychology. *J. person.,* 20, 24–38.
BETTELHEIM, B. 1960a. *The informed heart.* Glencoe, Ill.: Free Press.
————. 1960b. The lesson of Anne Frank. *Harper's Magazine.*
BEVAN, W., and ADAMSON, R. 1958. Internal referents and the concept of reinforcement. AFOSR TN-58-1101, AF 49 (638) 33.

————. 1960. Reinforcers and reinforcement: their relation to maze performance. *J. exp. Psychol.*, *59*, 226–32.

————. 1961. Internal referents and the concept of reinforcement. In N. F. WASHBURNE (ed.), *Decisions, Values and Groups.* Vol. II. New York: Pergamon, 453–72.

BEVAN, W., and DARBY, C. L. 1955. Patterns of experience and the constancy of an indifferent point for perceived weight. *Amer. J. Psychol.*, *68*, 575–84.

BEXTON, W. A., HERON, W., and SCOTT, T. H. 1954. Effects of decreased variation in the sensory environment. *Canad. J. Psychol.*, *8*, 70–76.

BIERI, J. 1955. Cognitive complexity-simplicity and predictive behavior. *J. abnorm. Soc. Psychol.*, *51*, 263–68.

BIERI, J., and BLACKER, E. 1956. The generality of cognitive complexity in the perception of people and inkblots. *J. abnorm. soc. Psychol.*, *53*, 112–17.

BILODEAU, E. A. 1952. Statistical vs. intuitive confidence. *Amer. J. Psy.*, *65*, 271–77.

BINDRA, D. 1955. Organization in emotional and motivated behavior. *Canad. J. Psychol.*, *9*, 161 67.

————. 1959. *Motivation: a systematic reinterpretation.* New York: Ronald Press.

BION, W. R. 1952. Group dynamics: A re-view. *Int. J. Psychoanalysis*, *33*, 235–47.

BLACK, R., ADAMSON, R., and BEVAN, W. 1961. Runway behavior as a function of apparent intensity of shock. *J. comp. physiol. Psychol.*, *54*, 270–74.

BLOOM, J. M., and CAPALDI, E. J. 1961. The behavior of rats in relation to complex patterns of partial reinforcement. *J. comp. physiol. Psychol.*, *54*, 261–65.

BOWERS, G. H. 1960. Partial and correlated reward in escape learning. *J. exp. Psychol.*, *59*, 126–30.

————. 1961. A contrast effect in differential conditioning. *J. exp. Psychol.*, *62*, 196–99.

BRAZIER, MARY A. B. 1959. The historical development of neurophysiology. In H. W. MAGOUN (ed.), *Neurophysiology* [in JOHN FIELD (Ed. in Chief), *The Handbook of Physiology*, Sec. 1, Vol. 1]. Washington, D. C.: American Physiological Society. Chap. 1.

BROWN, J. F. 1936. *Psychology and the social order.* New York: McGraw-Hill.

BROWN, J. G. 1948. Gradients of approach and avoidance responses and their relation to motivation. *J. comp. physiol. Psychol.*, *41*, 450–65.

BROWN, J. S. 1953. Problems presented by the concept of acquired drives. In M. R. JONES (ed.), *Current theory and research in motivation: a symposium.* Lincoln, Neb.: University of Nebraska Press.

————. 1961. *The motivation of behavior.* New York: McGraw-Hill.

BROWN, J. S., and FARBER, I. E. 1951. Emotions conceptualized as intervening variables—with suggestions toward a theory of frustration. *Psychol. Bull.*, *48*, 465–95.

BROWN, R. W., and LENNEBERG, E. H. 1954. A study in language and cognition. *J. abnorm. soc. Psychol.*, *49*, 454–62.

BRUNER, J. S. 1961. The cognitive consequences of early sensory deprivation. In P. SOLOMON et al. (eds.), *Sensory deprivation.* Cambridge, Mass.: Harvard University Press.

————. 1957. On perceptual readiness. *Psychol. Rev.*, *64*, 123–52.

BRUNER, J. S., GOODNOW, J. J., and AUSTIN, G. A. 1956. *A study of thinking.* New York: Wiley.

BÜHLER, CHARLOTTE, HETZER, HILDEGARD, and MABEL, F. 1928. Die Affektwirksamkeit von Fremheitseindrücken im ersten Lebensjahr. *Z. Psychol.*, Abt. 1, *107*, 30–49.

BÜHLER, K. 1918. Die geistige Entwicklung des Kindes. Jena: Fischer.

————. 1928. Displeasure and pleasure in relation to activity. In M. L. REYMERT (ed.), *Feelings and emotions: the Wittenberg symposium.* Worcester, Mass.: Clark University Press. Chap. 14.

BURNS, B. D. 1958. *The mammalian cerebral cortex.* London: Edward Arnold & Co.

BURNS, R. 1786. To a louse. *Poems chiefly in the Scottish dialect.* Kilmarnock.

BUTLER, R. A. 1953. Discrimination learning by rhesus monkeys to visual exploration motivation. *J. comp. physiol. Psychol., 46,* 95–98.

———. 1954. Incentive conditions which influence visual exploration. *J. exp. Psychol., 48,* 19–23.

———. 1958. The differential effect of visual and auditory incentives on the performance of monkeys. *Amer. J. Psychol., 71,* 591–93.

BUTLER, R. A., and HARLOW, H. F. 1957. Discrimination learning and learning sets to visual exploration incentives. *J. gen. Psychol., 57,* 257–64.

CALVIN, A. D., HOFFMAN, F. K., and HARDEN, E. L. 1957. The effect of intelligence and social atmosphere on group problem solving behavior. *J. soc. Psychol., 45,* 61–74.

CAMPBELL, D. T., and FISKE, D. W. 1959. Convergent and discriminant validation by the multitrait-multimethod matrix. *Psychol. Bull., 56,* 81–105.

CAMPBELL, V. N. 1960. Assumed similarity, perceived sociometric balance, and social influence. Unpublished Ph.D. dissertation, University of Colorado.

CANNON, W. B. 1915. *Bodily changes in pain, hunger, fear and rage* (rev. ed.). New York: Appleton, 1929.

———. 1932. *The wisdom of the body.* New York: Norton.

CANTRIL, H. 1961. *Human nature and political systems.* New Brunswick, N. J.: Rutgers University Press.

CARMICHAEL, L., and DEARBORN, W. F. 1948. *Reading and visual fatigue.* London: Harrap.

CARMICHAEL, L., HOGAN, H. P., and WALTER, A. A. 1932. An experimental study of the effect of language on the reproduction of visually perceived form. *J. exp. Psychol., 15,* 73–86.

CARPENTER, J. A., MOORE, O. K., LISANSKY, E., and SNYDER, C. 1961. Alcohol and higher-order problem solving. *Quarterly J. of Studies in Alcohol, 22,* 183–222.

CARR, H. A. 1925. *Psychology, a study of mental activity.* New York: Longmans, Green.

CARTWRIGHT, D. 1941a. Relation of decision-time to categories of response. *Amer. J. Psychol., 54,* 174–96.

———. 1941b. Decision-time in relation to the differentiation of the phenomenal field. *Psychol. Rev., 48,* 425–42.

CATON, R. 1875. The electric currents of the brain. *Brit. med. J., 2,* 278.

CHAPMAN, D. W., and VOLKMANN, J. 1939. A social determinant of the level of aspiratrin. *J. abnorm. soc. Psychol., 34,* 225–38.

CHAPMAN, L. J., and BOCK, R. D. 1958. Components of variance due to acquiescence and content in the F-scale measure of authoritarianism. *Psychol. Bull., 55,* 328–33.

CHAPMAN, L. J., and CAMPBELL, D. T. 1959. The effect of acquiescence response-set upon relationships among the F-scale, ethnocentrism, and intelligence. *Sociometry, 22,* 153–61.

CHEIN, I. 1944. The awareness of self and the structure of the ego. *Psychol. Rev., 51,* 304–14.

CHERRY, C. 1957. *On human communication: A review, a survey and a criticism.* Published jointly by the Technology Press of the Massachusetts Institute of Technology, John Wiley & Sons, New York, and Chapman & Hall, Ltd., London.

CHOW, K. L. 1952. Further studies on selective ablation of associative cortex in relation to visual mediated behavior. *J. comp. physiol. Psychol., 45,* 109–18.

CHRISTIE, R., HAVEL, JOAN, and SEIDENBERG, B. 1959. Is the F-scale reversible? *J. abnorm. soc. Psychol., 56,* 143–59.

COATES, R. M. 1947. The law, *The New Yorker Magazine,* November 29, 23, 41–43.

COCH, LESTER, and FRENCH, J. R. P., JR. 1948. Overcoming resistance to change. *Hum. Rel., 1,* 512–32. Reprinted in D. CARTWRIGHT and A. ZANDER (eds.), *Group Dynamics.*

COHEN, S. I., SILVERMAN, A. J., BRESSLER, B., and SHMAVONIAN, B. 1961. Problems in isolation studies. In P. SOLOMON *et al.* (eds.), *Sensory deprivation.* Cambridge: Harvard University Press.

CONANT, J. B. 1947. *On understanding science.* New Haven, Conn.: Yale University Press.

COOLEY, C. H. 1902. *Human nature and the social order.* New York: Scribner.

COOMBS, C. H., and BEARDSLEE, D. On decision making under uncertainty. In R. M. THRALL, C. H. COOMBS, and R. L. DAVIS (eds.), 1954. *Decision processes.* New York: Wiley.

COTTON, J. W., and LEWIS, D. J. 1957. Effect of intertrial interval on acquisition and extinction of a running response. *J. exp. Psychol., 54,* 15–20.

COUCH, A., and KENISTON, K. 1960. Yeasayers and naysayers: agreeing response set as a personality variable. *J. abnorm. soc. Psychol., 60,* 151–74.

COURTS, R. A. 1959. Relations between experimentally produced muscular tension and memorization. *J. exp. Psychol., 25,* 235–56.

CRESPI, L. P. 1942. Quantitative variation of incentive and performance in the white rat. *Amer. J. Psychol., 55,* 467–517.

CROCKETT, E. P. 1958. Authoritarianism and leader acceptance. *ONR Technical Report, No. 8,* Vanderbilt University. Contract Nonr 2149(02).

CUNAT, R. 1960. Self disclosure and personality. Unpublished Master's thesis, University of Colorado.

DASHIELL, J. F. 1925. A quantitative demonstration of animal drive. *J. comp. Psychol., 5,* 205–8.

———. 1928. *Fundamentals of objective psychology.* New York: Houghton Mifflin.

DAVIDSON, D., and SUPPES, P., in collaboration with S. SIEGEL. 1957. *Decision-making, an experimental approach.* Stanford, Calif.: Stanford University Press.

DAVIS, K. 1962. The effects of group composition in a simulated business game. Unpublished manuscript, Princeton University, Princeton, N. J.

DAVIS, W. A. 1948. *Social-class influence upon learning.* Cambridge, Mass.: Harvard University Press.

DAY, R. C., and HAMBLIN, R. L. 1961. Some effects of close and positive styles of expression. *ONR Technical Report, No. 8,* Contract NONR 816(11).

DEESE, J. 1953. *Psychology of learning* (2d ed.). New York: McGraw-Hill.

DEFOE, D. 1719. *Robinson Crusoe.* London: printed for W. TAYLOR at the Ship in Pater-Noster-Row.

DELL, P. C. 1956. Les systèmes réticulaires du tronc cérébral et L'adrènaline circulante. In *Progress in neurobiology, Proc. First Internat. Meeting on Neurobiology* (cited by BERLYNE, 1960).

DEMBER, W. N. 1956. Response by the rat to environmental change. *J. comp. physiol. Psychol., 49,* 93–95.

DEMBER, W. N., EARL, R. W., and PARADISE, N. 1957. Response by rats to differential stimulus complexity. *J. comp. physiol. Psychol., 50,* 514–18.

DENNIS, W. 1955. Early recognition of the manipulative drive in monkeys. *Brit. J. anim. Behav., 3,* 71–72.

DESCARTES, RENÉ. 1649. *Passions de l'Aime.* Amsterdam (cited by BRAZIER, 1959).

DEWEY, J. 1894. The theory of emotion. *Psychol. Rev., 1,* 553–69, and continued as 1895, 2, 13–22.

———. 1896. The reflex arc concept in psychology. *Psychol. Rev., 3,* 357–70.

———. 1900. *The school and society.* Chicago: University of Chicago Press (Phoenix Books, P3), 1960.

DOLLARD, J., DOOB, L. W., MILLER, N. E., and SEARS, R. R. 1939. *Frustration and aggression.* New Haven, Conn.: Yale University Press.

DOLLARD, J., and MILLER, N. E. 1950. *Personality and psychotherapy.* New York: McGraw-Hill.

DOSTOEVSKY, F. 1864. *Letters from the underworld.* (Translated by C. J. HOGARTH. New York: Dutton.

DOYLE, A. C. 1866. *A stndy in scarlet.* London.

DRIVER, M. J. 1962. The perception of simulated nations: A multidimensional analysis of social perception as affected by situational stress and characteristic levels of cognitive complexity in perceivers. Unpublished Ph.D. dissertation, Princeton University, Princeton, N. J.

DUFFY, ELIZABETH. 1934. Emotion: an example of the need for reorientation in psychology. *Psychol. Rev., 41,* 184–98.

———. 1941. An explanation of "emotional" phenomena without the use of the concept "emotion." *J. gen. Psychol., 25,* 283–93.

———. 1951. The concept of energy mobilization. *Psychol. Rev., 58,* 30–40.

———. 1957. The psychological significance of the concept of "arousal" or "activation." *Psychol. Rev., 64,* 265–75.

DUNLAP, K. 1919. Are there any instincts? *J. abnorm. soc. Psychol., 14,* 307–11.

DURKHEIM, E. 1897. *Suicide.* Translated by J. A. SPAULDING and G. SIMPSON. London: Routledge and Kegan Paul, 1952.

———. 1951. *Suicide.* Glencoe, Ill.: Free Press.

EDWARDS, W. 1956. Reward probability, amount, and information as determiners of sequential two-alternative decisions. *J. exp. Psychol., 52,* 177–87.

ERIKSON, E. H. 1950. *Childhood and society.* New York: Norton.

EWING, T. 1942. A study of certain factors involved in changes of opinion. *J. soc. Psychol., 16,* 63–88.

FARBER, I. E. 1948. Response fixation under anxiety and non-anxiety conditions. *J. exp. Psychol., 38,* 111–31.

———. 1954. Anxiety as a drive state. In M. R. JONES (ed.), *Nebraska Symposium on motivation.* Lincoln, Neb.: University of Nebraska Press.

FEHRER, E. 1956. The effects of hunger and familiarity of locale on exploration. *J. comp. physiol. Psychol., 49,* 549–52.

FELLER, W. 1950. *An introduction to probability theory and its applications.* New York: Wiley.

FESTINGER, L. 1943. Studies in decision: I. Decision-time, relative frequency of judgment and subjective confidence as related to physical stimulus difference. *J. exp. Psychol., 32,* 291–306.

———. 1957. *A theory of cognitive dissonance.* Evanston, Ill.: Row, Peterson.

FESTINGER, L., RIECHEN, H. W., and SCHACHTER, S. 1956. *When prophecy fails.* Minneapolis: University of Minnesota Press.

FISHER, DOROTHY CANFIELD. 1912. *Montessori Mother.* New York: Holt.

FISKE, D. W., and MADDI, S. R. (eds.). 1961. *Functions of varied experience.* Homewood, Ill.: Dorsey Press.

FITCH, F. B. 1952. *Symbolic logic.* New York: Ronald.

FONBERG, ELZBIETA. 1956. On the manifestation of conditioned defensive reactions in stress. *Bull. Soc. Sci. et Lett. de Lodz, 7,* 7–8.

FREEMAN, G. L. 1934. *Introduction to physiological psychology.* New York: Ronald Press.

———. 1940. The relationship between performance level and bodily activity level. *J. exp. Psychol., 26,* 602–8.

———. 1948. *Energetics of human behavior.* Ithaca, N. Y.: Cornell University Press.

FRENCH, VERA. 1947. The structure of sentiments. *J. Pers., 15,* 247–82; 1948, *16,* 78–100, 209–44.

FRENKEL-BRUNSWIK, ELSE. 1949. Intolerance of ambiguity as an emotional and perceptual personality variable. *J. Pers., 18,* 108–43.

FREUD, ANNA. 1936. *The ego and the mechanisms of defense.* Translated by CECIL BAINES. New York: International Universities Press, 1946.

FREUD, ANNA, and BURLINGHAM, DOROTHY. 1944. *Infants without families.* New York: International Universities Press.

FREUD, S. 1894. The justification for detaching from neurasthenia a particular syndrome: the anxiety-neurosis. In *Collected Papers.* Vol. 1. London: Hogarth, 1950. Pp. 76–106.

————. 1898. Sexuality in the aetiology of the neuroses. In *Collected Papers*. Vol. 1. London: Hogarth, 1950. Pp. 220–48.

————. 1900. The interpretation of dreams. Translated and edited by A. A. BRILL. *The basic writings of Sigmund Freud*. New York: Modern Library, 1938.

————. 1905. Three contributions to the theory of sex. Translated and edited by A. A. BRILL. *The basic writings of Sigmund Freud*. New York: Modern Library, 1938.

————. 1915. Instincts and their vicissitudes. In *Collected Papers*. Vol. 4. London: Hogarth, 1950.

————. 1917. *Introductory lectures on psychoanalysis* (2d ed.). Translated by JOAN RIVIERE. London: Allen & Unwin, 1940.

————. 1920. *Beyond the pleasure principle*. New York: Boni & Liveright, 1922.

————. 1923. *The ego and the id*. London: Hogarth, 1927.

————. 1926. *Hemmung, Symptom und Angst*. Translated as *The problem of anxiety* by H. A. BUNKER. New York: Norton, 1936.

————. 1932. *New introductory lectures on psychoanalysis*. Translated by W. J. H. SPROTT. New York: Norton, 1933.

FRITSCH, G. H., and HITZIG, E. 1870. Ueber die elektrische Erregbarkeit des Cross hirns. *Arch. Anat. Physiol. wiss. Med.* (Leipzig), 37, 300 (cited by BRAZIER, 1959).

FROMM, E. 1941. *Escape from freedom*. New York: Rinehart.

FUSTER, J. M. 1957. Tachistoscopic perception in monkeys. *Fed. Proc.*, 16, 43.

GAGNE, R. M., and PARADISE, N. E. 1961. Abilities and learning sets in knowledge acquisition. *Psychol. Monogr.*, 75, No. 14 (whole No. 518).

GARDNER, M. 1956. *Math, Magic and Mystery*. New York: McGraw-Hill.

GENTZEN, G. 1934. Untersuchurger über das logische Schliessen. *Mathematische Zeitschrift*, 39, 172–210, 405–31.

GIBSON, ELEANOR J. 1952. The role of shock in reinforcement. *J. comp. physiol. Psychol.*, 45, 18–30.

GIBSON, J. J. 1929. The reproduction of visually perceived form. *J. exp. Psychol.*, 12, 1–39.

GILBERT, DORIS C., and LEVINSON, D. J. 1956. Ideology, personality, and institutional policy in the mental hospital. *J. abnorm. soc. Psychol.*, 53, 263–71.

GILBERT, W. S. 1885. *The Mikado*.

GLANZER, M. 1953a. Stimulus satiation: an explanation of spontaneous alternation and related phenomena. *Psychol. Rev.*, 60, 257–68.

————. 1953b. The role of stimulus satiation in spontaneous alternation. *J. exp. Psychol.*, 45, 387–93.

————. 1958. Curiosity, exploratory drive and stimulus satiation. *Psychol. Bull.*, 55, 302–15.

GOCHMAN, D. S. 1960. Ego-tension, cognitive consistency, and attitude change. Unpublished Master's thesis, University of Colorado.

GOFFMAN, E. 1959. *The presentation of self in everyday life*. Garden City, N. Y.: Doubleday Anchor Books.

GOLDBERG, S. C. 1954. Three situational determinants of conformity to social norms. *J. abnorm. soc. Psychol.*, 49, 325–29.

GOLDBERGER, L., and HOLT, R. R. 1961. Experimental interference with reality contact: Individual differences. In P. SOLOMON *et al.* (eds.), *Sensory deprivation*. Cambridge, Mass.: Harvard University Press.

GRANIT, R. 1955. *Receptors and sensory perception*. New Haven, Conn.: Yale University Press.

GRANT, D. A., and SCHIPPER, L. M. 1952. The acquisition and extinction of conditioned eyelid responses as a function of the percentage of fixed-ratio random reinforcement. *J. exp. Psychol.*, 43, 313–20.

GROOS, K. 1896. *The play of man*. Translated by ELIZABETH L. BALDWIN. New York: Appleton, 1905.

GUETZKOW, H. 1959. A use of simulation in inter-nation relations. *Behav. Sci., 4,* 183–91.

GUTHRIE, E. R. 1938. *The psychology of human conflict: the clash of motives within the individual.* New York: Harper.

HABER, R. N. 1958. Discrepancy from adaptation level as a source of affect. *J. exp. Psychol., 56,* 370–75.

HALL, C. S., and LINDZEY, G. 1957. *Theories of personality.* New York: Wiley.

HALL, M. 1843. *New memoire on the nervous system.* London: Sherwood, Gilbert and Piper (cited by BRAZIER, 1959).

HALLOWELL, A. I. Cultural factors in structuralization of perception. In J. H. ROHRER and M. SHERIF (eds.), 1951. *Social psychology at the crossroads.* New York: Harper.

————. 1955. The self and its behavioral environment, in *Culture and experience.* Philadelphia: University of Pennsylvania Press. Pp. 75–110.

HARARY, F., and NORMAN, R. Z. 1953. *Graph theory as a mathematical model in social science.* Ann Arbor, Mich.: Institute for Social Research.

HARLOW, H. F. 1950. Learning and satiation of response in intrinsically motivated complex puzzle performance by monkeys. *J. comp. physiol. Psychol., 43,* 289–94.

————. 1953. Mice, monkey, men and motives. *Psychol. Rev., 60,* 23–32.

————. 1958. The nature of love. *Amer. Psychologist, 13,* 673–85.

HARLOW, H. F., HARLOW, M. K., and MEYER, D. R. 1950. Learning motivated by a manipulation drive. *J. exp. Psychol., 40,* 228–34.

HARLOW, H. F., and McCLEARN, G. E. 1954. Object discrimination learned by monkeys on the basis of manipulation motives. *J. comp. physiol. Psychol., 47,* 73–76.

HARVEY, O. J. 1953. An experimental approach to the study of status relations in informal groups. *Amer. Sociol. Rev., 18,* 357–67.

————. 1961. System structure and adaptability. Paper presented to symposium of the American Psychological Association.

————. 1962. Personality factors in resolution of conceptual incongruities. *Sociometry, 25,* 336–52.

————. 1963a. Authoritarianism and conceptual functioning and change across situations. *J. abnorm. soc. Psychol.* (in press).

————. 1963b. *Conceptual structure and generalized behavior* (forthcoming).

HARVEY, O. J., and BEVERLY, G. D. 1961. Some personality correlates of concept change through role playing. *J. abnorm. soc. Psychol., 63,* 125–30.

HARVEY, O. J., and CALDWELL, D. F. 1959. Assimilative and contrast phenomena in response to environmental variation. *J. Pers., 27,* 125–35.

HARVEY, O. J., and CAMPBELL, D. T. 1963. Judgments of weight as affected by adaptation range, adaptation duration, magnitude of unlabeled anchor and judgmental language. *J. exp. Psychol., 65,* 12–21.

HARVEY, O. J., HUNT, D. E., and SCHRODER, H. M. 1961. *Conceptual systems and personality development.* New York: Wiley.

HARVEY, O. J., KELLEY, H. H., and SHAPIRO, M. 1957. Reactions to unfavorable evaluations of the self made by other persons. *J. Pers., 25,* 393–411.

HAYTHORN, W., COUCH, A., HAEFNER, D., LANGHAM, P., and CARTER, L. F. 1956. The behavior of authoritarian and equalitarian personalities in groups. *Hum. Rel., 9,* 57–74.

HAYWOOD, H. C. 1961. Novelty-seeking behavior as a function of manifest anxiety and physiological arousal. Unpublished Ph.D. dissertation, University of Illinois.

————. 1962. Relationships among anxiety, seeking of novel stimuli, and level of unassimilated percepts. *J. Pers., 29,* 105–14.

HEARN, G. 1955. The process of group development. Cassidy Lecture, University of Toronto (mimeograph).

HEBB, D. O. 1946. On the nature of fear. *Psychol. Rev., 53,* 259–76.

————. 1949. *The organization of behavior.* New York: Wiley.

————. 1955. Drives and the C. N. S. (conceptual nervous system). *Psychol. Rev.*, 62, 243–54.

HEBB, D. O., and MAHUT, HELEN. 1955. Motivation et recherche du changement perceptif chez le rat et chez l'homme. *J. Psychol. norm. path.*, 48, 209–20.

HEBB, D. O., and RIESEN, A. H. 1943. The genesis of irrational fears. *Bull. Canad. Psychol. Assoc.*, 3, 49–50.

HEBB, D. O., and THOMPSON, W. R. 1954. The social significance of animal studies. In G. LINDZEY (ed.), *Handbook of social psychology*. Cambridge, Mass.: Addison-Wesley. Chap. 15.

HEIDER, F. 1946. Attitudes and cognitive organization. *J. Psychol.*, 21, 107–12.

————. 1958. *The psychology of interpersonal relations*. New York: Wiley.

HEINROTH, O. 1910. Beitrage zur Biologie, namentlich Ethologie und Physiologic der Anatiden. *Verh. Internat. Orn. Kongr.*, 5, 589–702 (cited by THORPE, 1956).

HELSON, H. 1938. Fundamental problems in color vision. I. The principle governing changes in hue, saturation, and lightness of nonselective samples in chromatic illumination. *J. exp. Psychol.*, 23, 439–76.

————. 1947. Adaptation-level as frame of reference for prediction of psychophysical data. *Amer. J. Psychol.*, 60, 1–29.

————. 1948. Adaptation-level as a basis for a quantitative theory of frames of reference. *Psychol. Rev.*, 55, 297–313.

————. 1959. Adaptation-level theory. In S. KOCH (ed.), *Psychology: a study of a science*. Vol. 1. *Sensory, perceptual and physiological formulations*. New York: McGraw-Hill. Pp. 565–621.

HEMPEL, C. G. 1959. The logic of functional analysis. In L. GROSS (ed.), *Symposium on Sociological Theory*. Evanston, Ill.: Row-Peterson. Pp. 271–307.

HEMPHILL, J. K. 1955. Leadership behavior associated with the administrative reputation of college departments. *J. educ. Psychol.*, 46, 385–401.

————. 1956. Why people take leadership. *Adult Leadership*, 5, 44–46.

HENDRICK, I. 1943. The discussion of the "instinct to master." *Psychoanal. Quart.*, 12, 561–65.

HENLE, MARY, and MICHAEL, MIRIAM. 1956. The influence of attitudes on syllogistic reasoning. *J. soc. Psychol.*, 44, 115–27.

HERBART, J. F. 1816. *Textbook in psychology*. Translated by MARGARET K. SMITH. New York: Appleton, 1891.

HERNANDEZ-PEON, R., SCHERRER, H., and JOUVET, M. 1956. Modification of electric activity in cochlear nucleus during "attention" in unanesthetized cats. *Science*, 123, 331–32.

HERON, W., DOANE, B. K., and SCOTT, T. H. 1956. Visual disturbance after prolonged perceptual isolation. *Canad. J. Psychol.*, 10, 13–18.

HEYTING, A. 1930. Die formalen Regeln der intuitionische Logik. *Sitzungsber. preuss. Akad. Wiss.* Berlin, 42–56.

HILGARD, E. G. 1956. *Theories of learning*. New York: Appleton-Century-Crofts.

HOBBES, T. 1651. Leviathan. Cambridge, England: Cambridge University Press, 1904.

HOBHOUSE, L. T. 1901. *Mind in evolution*. New York: Macmillan.

HOIJER, H. 1953. The relation of language to culture. In A. L. KROEHER (ed.), *Anthropology today*. Chicago: University of Chicago Press.

HOLT, E. B. 1931. *Animal drive and the learning process*. New York: Holt.

HOVLAND, C. I. 1936. "Inhibition of reinforcement" and phenomena of experimental extinction. *Proc. nat. Acad. Sci.*, 22, 430–33.

HOVLAND, C. I., HARVEY, O. J., and SHERIF, M. 1957. Assimilation and contrast effects in reactions to communication and attitude change. *J. abnorm. soc. Psychol.*, 55, 244–52.

HOVLAND, C. I., and PRITZKER, H. A. 1957. Extent of opinion change as a function of amount of change advocated. *J. abnorm. soc. Psychol.*, 47, 581–88.

HOWARD, T. W., and SOMMER, R. A critical examination of "Ideology, personality, and institutional policy in the mental hospital." Unpub. ms. (referred to by JACKSON and MESSICK, 1958).

HOYLE, E. 1748. *The Accurate Gamester's Companion.* London.

HUIZINGA, J. 1950. *Homo ludens, a study of the play element in culture.* Boston: Beacon Press.

HULL, C. L. 1943. *Principles of behavior.* New York: Appleton-Century.

————. 1952. *A behavior system.* New Haven: Yale University Press.

HUMPHREYS, L. G. 1939. The effect of random alternation of reinforcement on the acquisition and extinction of conditioned eyelid reactions. *J. exp. Psychol., 25,* 141–58.

HUNT, J. McV. 1945. Experimental psychoanalysis. In P. L. HARRIMAN (ed.), *Encyclopedia of psychology.* New York: Philosophical Library, pp. 140–56.

HUNT, J. McV. 1960. Experience and the development of motivation: some reinterpretations. *Child. Develpm., 31,* 489–504.

————. 1961. *Intelligence and experience.* New York: Ronald Press.

HUNT, J. McV., and QUAY, H. C. 1961. Early vibratory experience and the question of innate reinforcement value of vibration and other stimuli: a limitation on the discrepancy (burnt soup) principle in motivation. *Psychol. Rev., 68,* 149–56.

HURWITZ, H. M. B. 1960. The effect of illumination conditions on the effectiveness of light-onset as a reinforcer: a test of the Bevan-Adamson reinforcement theory. *Brit. J. Psychol., 51,* 341–46.

HUTCHESON, E. 1907. *Elements of piano technique.* New York: Kranz and Co.

HUTCHINSON, G. E. 1959. Homage to Santa Rosalia, or Why are there so many kinds of animals? *American Naturalist,* 145–59.

HUXLEY, T. Letter to Charles Kingsley, September 23, 1860. In M. L. SCHUSTER (ed.), *The world's great letters,* 1940. New York: Simon & Schuster.

HYDEN, H. 1958. Biochemical changes in glial cells and nerve cells at varying activity. *Proc. Int. Congr. Biochem., 4th Congr.* Vienna, 3, 64–89 (published 1959).

————. 1960. The neuron. In J. BRACHET and A. E. MIRSKY (eds.), *The cell: biochemistry, physiology, morphology.* Vol. 4. *Specialized cells: part 1.* New York: Academic Press. Chap. 5.

HYMAN, R. 1953. Stimulus information as a determinant of reaction time. *J. exp. Psychol., 45,* 188–96.

ILG, F. L., and AMES, L. B. 1955. *Child behavior.* New York: Harper.

IRWIN, F. W., and SMITH, W. A. S. 1957. Value, cost, and information as determiners of decision. *J. exp. Psychol., 54,* 229–32.

JACKSON, D. N., and MESSICK, S. J. 1958. Content and style in personality assessment. *Psychol. Bull., 55,* 243–52.

JACOBSEN, C. F., WOLFE, J. B., and JACKSON, T. A. 1935. An experimental analysis of the functions of the frontal association area in primates. *J. nerv. ment. Dis., 82,* 1–14.

JAMES, W. 1890. *Principles of Psychology.* New York: Holt (Dover Publication edition).

JANET, P. M. F. 1925. Psychological healing. Translated by EDEN and CEDAR PAUL. 2 vols. New York: Macmillan.

JASKOWSKI, S. 1934. On the rules of suppositions in formal logic. *Studia Logica,* No. L, Warsaw.

JENKINS, W. O., McFANN, H., and CLAYTON, F. L. 1950. A methodological study of extinction following aperiodic and continuous reinforcement. *J. comp. physiol. Psychol., 43,* 82–86.

JENKINS, W. O., and STANLEY, J. C., JR. 1950. Partial reinforcement: a review and critique. *Psychol. Bull., 47,* 193–234.

JERSILD, A. T., and HOLMES, FRANCES B. 1935. Children's fears. *Child Develpm. Monogr.,* No. 20.

JONES, H. E., and JONES, MARY C. 1928. Fear. *Childh. Educ., 5,* 136–43.

KAADA, B. R., PRIBRAM, K. H., and EPSTEIN, J. A. 1949. Respiratory and vascular responses to monkeys from temporal pole, insula, orbita surface, and cingulate gyrus: a preliminary report. *J. Neurophysiol.*, *12*, 347–56.

KANT, I. 1791. *Critique of pure reason*. New York: Macmillan, 1929.

KARDINER, A. 1945. *Psychological frontiers of society*. New York: Columbia University Press.

KATZ, D., MACCOBY, N., and MORSE, NANCY C. 1950. *Productivity, supervision and morale in an office situation: Part 1*. Ann Arbor, Mich.: The Survey Research Center, University of Michigan.

KATZ, R., and TYSON, R. 1950. *Gestalt psychology*. New York: Ronald Press.

KAUFMANN, F., 1944. *Methodology of the social sciences*. New York: Oxford University Press.

KAUFMANN, M. 1957. *Remember me to God*. New York: Lippincott.

KELLY, G. A. 1955. *A psychology of personal constructs*. New York: Norton.

KENNEDY, J. F. 1956. *Profiles in courage*. New York: Harper.

KESSEN, W. 1953. Response strength and conditioned stimulus intensity. *J. exp. Psychol.*, *45*, 82–86.

KIMBLE, G. A. 1956. *Principles of general psychology*. New York: Ronald Press, 205–15.

KIVY, P. N., EARL, R. W., and WALKER, E. L. 1950. Stimulus context and satiation. *J. comp. physiol. Psychol.*, *49*, 90–92.

KLING, F. R. 1958. *Chess with traitors*, unpublished mimeographed manuscript.

KLUCKHOHN, C., and MURRAY, H. A. 1948. *Personality in nature, society, and culture*. New York: Knopf.

————. 1954. A conception of personality. In C. KLUCKHOHN, H. A. MURRAY, and D. M. SCHNEIDER (eds.), *Personality in nature, society, and culture*. New York: Knopf.

KLÜVER, H. 1941. Visual functions after removal of the occipital lobes. *J. Psychol.*, *11*, 23–45.

KOCHIN, M., and GALENTER, E. H. 1958. The acquisition and utilization of information in problem solving and thinking. *Information and Control*, *1*, 267–88.

KOFFKA, K. 1922. Perception: an introduction to the Gestalt theory. *Psychol. Bull.*, *19*, 531–85.

KÖHLER, W. 1925. *The mentality of apes*. New York: Harcourt Brace.

KRAEHENBUHL, D., and COONS, E. 1959. Information as a measure of the experience of musics. *J. of Aesthetics and Art Criticism*, *17*, 510–22.

KRECH, D., and CRUTCHFIELD, R. S. 1948. *Theory and problems of social psychology*. New York: McGraw-Hill.

KUNO, Y. 1956. *Human perspiration*. Springfield, Ill.: Charles C Thomas.

LACEY, J. I. 1959. Psychophysiological approaches to the evaluation of psychotherapeutic process and outcome. In E. RUBENSTEIN and M. B. PARLOFF (eds.), *Research in psychotherapy*. Washington, D. C.: American Psychological Association. Pp. 160–208.

LANDIS, C. 1932. Electrical phenomena of the skin. *Psychol. Bull.*, *29*, 693–752.

LANIER, L. H. 1941. An experimental study of "affective conflict." *J. Psychol.*, *11*, 199–217.

LANSING, R. W., SCHWARTZ, E., and LINDSLEY, D. B. 1956. Reaction time and EEG activation. *Amer. Psychol.*, *11*, 433.

LASHLEY, K. S. 1917. The accuracy of movement in the absence of excitation from the moving organ. *Amer. J. Physiol.*, *43*, 169–94.

————. 1938. Experimental analysis of instinctive behavior. *Psychol. Rev.*, *45*, 445–71.

————. 1952. In search of the engram. *Society of experimental biology*. Symposium No. 4: *Physiological mechanisms of animal behavior*. Cambridge: Cambridge University Press. Pp. 454–82.

LAWSON, R. 1957. Brightness discrimination performance and secondary reward strength as a function of primary reward amount. *J. comp. physiol. Psychol.*, *50*, 35–39.

————. 1960. *Learning and behavior.* New York: Macmillan. P. 254.

LEEPER, R. W. 1948. A motivational theory of emotion to replace "emotion as disorganized response." *Psychol. Rev., 55,* 5–21.

LEUBA, C. 1955. Toward some integration of learning theories: the concept of optimal stimulation. *Psychol. Rep., 1,* 27–33.

LEVIN, H., and SEARS, R. R. 1956. Identification with parents as a determinant of doll play aggression. *Child Develpm., 27,* 135–53.

LEVINSON, D. J. 1957. Authoritarian personality and foreign policy. *J. Conflict Resolution, 1,* 37–47.

LEVY, D. M. 1955. Oppositional syndromes and oppositional behavior. In P. H. HOCH and J. ZURBIN (eds.), *Psychopathology of childhood.* New York: Grune.

LEWIN, K. 1935. *A dynamic theory of personality.* New York: McGraw-Hill.

————. 1936. *Principles of topological psychology.* New York: McGraw-Hill.

LEWIN, K., LIPPIT, R., and WHITE, R. 1939. Patterns of aggressive behavior in experimentally designed social climates. *J. soc. Psychol., 10,* 271–99.

LILLY, J. C. 1956. Mental effects of reduction of ordinary levels of stimuli on intact healthy persons. *Psychiat. Res. Repts., 5,* 1–9.

LINDSLEY, D. B. 1944. Electroencephalograph. In J. McV. HUNT (ed.), *Personality and the behavior disorders.* New York: Ronald Press. Chap. 33.

————. 1951. Emotion. In S. S. STEVENS (ed.), *Handbook of experimental psychology.* New York: Wiley. Chap. 14.

————. 1956. Physiological psychology. *Annu. Rev. Psychol., 7,* 323–48.

————. 1957. Psychophysiology and motivation. In M. R. JONES (ed.), *Nebraska symposium on motivation.* Lincoln, Neb.: University of Nebraska Press.

————. 1958. Psychophysiology of perception. In R. A. PATTON (ed.), *Current trends in the description and analysis of behavior.* Pittsburgh, Pa.: University of Pittsburgh Press.

LIPSET, S. M. 1960. *Political man.* Garden City, N. Y.: Doubleday.

LORENZ, K. Z. 1935. Der Kumpan in der Umwelt des Vögels. *J. Orn., 83,* 137–214, 289–413 (cited by THORPE, 1956).

————. 1950. The comparative method in studying innate behavior patterns. In *Symposia of the Society for Experimental Biology.* No. 4. *Physiological mechanisms in animal behavior.* New York: Academic Press.

LOWE, A. 1961. Individual differences in reaction to failure: Mode of coping with anxiety and interference proneness. *J. abnorm. soc. Psychol., 62,* 303–08.

MACCOBY, E. E. 1959. Role taking in childhood and its consequences for social learning. *Child Development, 30,* 239–52.

MACDONALD, ANNETTE. 1946. The effect of adaptation to the unconditioned stimulus upon the formation of conditioned avoidance response. *J. exp. Psychol., 36,* 1–12.

MACINTOSH, A. 1942. Differential effect of the status of the competing group upon the level of aspiration. *Amer. J. Psychol., 55,* 546–54.

MACMURRAY, J. 1956. *The self as agent.* London: Faber.

MAGENDIE, F. 1822. Experiences sur les fonctions des racines des nerfs rachidiens. *J. Physiol. exper. path., 2,* 276 (cited by BRAZIER, 1959).

MALMO, R. B. 1958. Measurement of drive: an unsolved problem in psychology. In M. R. JONES (ed.), *Nebraska symposium on motivation.* Lincoln, Neb.: University of Nebraska Press. Pp. 229–65.

MANN, J., and SEMERAD, E. V. 1948. The use of group therapy in psychoses. *J. Social Casework, 29,* 176.

MARCH, J. G., and SIMON, H. 1958. In collaboration with GUETZKOW. *Organizations.* New York: Wiley.

MARSCHAK, J. Towards an economic theory of organization and information. In R. M. THRALL, C. H. COOMBS, and R. L. DAVIS (eds.), 1954. *Decision processes.* New York: Wiley.

MARTIN, E., and HILL, W. F. 1957. Toward a theory of group development: Six phases of therapy group development. *Int. J. Group Psychotherapy, VII,* No. *1,* January.

MASLOW, A. H. 1943. A dynamic theory of human motivation. *Psychol. Rev., 50,* 370–96.

————. 1954. *Motivation and Personality.* New York: Harper.

McCLELLAND, D. C., ATKINSON, J. W., CLARK, R. A., and LOWELL, E. L. 1953. *The achievement motive.* New York: Appleton-Century-Crofts.

McDOUGALL, W. 1908. *Social psychology.* Boston: J. W. Luce.

————. 1923. *Outline of psychology.* New York: Scribner.

McREYNOLDS, P. 1956. A restricted conceptualization of human anxiety and motivation. *Psychol. Rep., 2,* 293–312.

McREYNOLDS, P., and BRYAN, J. 1956. Tendency to obtain new percepts as a function of the level of unassimilated percepts. *Percept. mot. Skills, 6,* 183–86.

MEAD, G. H. 1934. *Mind, self and society.* Chicago: University of Chicago Press.

MEAD, MARGARET. 1935. *Sex and temperament in three primitive societies.* New York: Morrow.

MEEHL, P. E. 1954. *Clinical vs. statistical prediction.* Minneapolis: University of Minn. Press.

MELTON, A. W. 1941. Learning. In W. S. MUNROE (ed.), *Encyclopedia of educational research.* New York: Macmillan.

MELZACK, R. The genesis of emotional behavior: an experimental study of the dog. *J. comp. physiol. Psychol., 47,* 166–68.

MEYER, D. R., and NOBLE, M. E. 1958. Summation of manifest anxiety and muscular tension. *J. exp. Psychol., 55,* 599–602.

MEYERS, A. K., and MILLER, N. E. 1954. Failure to find learned drive based on hunger: evidence for learning motivated by "exploration." *J. comp. physiol. Psychol., 47,* 428–36.

MILES, R. C. 1958. Learning in kittens with manipulatory, exploratory, and food incentives. *J. comp. physiol. Psychol., 51,* 39–42.

MILLER, G. A., GALANTER, E., and PRIBRAM, K. H. 1960. *Plans and the structure of behavior.* New York: Holt.

MILLER, J. G. 1955. Toward a general theory for the behavioral sciences. *Amer. Psychol., 10,* 513–31.

MILLER, N. E. 1944. Experimental studies of conflict. In J. McV. HUNT (ed.), *Personality and the behavior disorders.* New York: Ronald Press. Chap. 14.

————. 1948. Studies of fear as an acquirable drive: I, fear as motivation and fear-reducing as reinforcement in the learning of new responses. *J. exp. Psychol., 38,* 89–101.

————. 1951. Learnable drives and rewards. In S. S. STEVENS (ed.), *Handbook of experimental psychology.* New York: Wiley. Chap. 13.

MILLER, N. E., and DOLLARD, J. 1941. *Social learning and imitation.* New Haven, Conn.: Yale University Press.

MILNER, B. 1958. Psychological defects produced by temporal lobe excision. In *The brain and human behavior.* Baltimore: Res. Publ. Assoc. Nerv. Ment. Dis. Pp. 244–57.

MISCHEL, W., and SCHOPLER, J. 1959. Authoritarianism and reactions to "aputniks." *J. abnorm. soc. Psychol., 59,* 142–45.

MISHKIN, M. 1954. Visual discrimination performance following partial ablations of the temporal lobe: II, ventral surface vs. hippocampus. *J. comp. physiol. Psychol., 47,* 187–93.

MONTESSORI, MARIA. 1907. *The Montessori method.* Translated from the Italian by FLORENCE SIMMONDS. New York: Frederick A. Stokes, 1909.

————. 1913. *Pedagogical anthropology.* Translated from the Italian by F. T. COOPER. New York: Frederick A. Stokes.

————. 1915. *The advanced Montessori method: Spontaneous activity in education.* Translated from the Italian by FLORENCE SIMMONDS. New York: Frederick A. Stokes, 1917.

MONTGOMERY, K. C. 1952. A test of two explanations of spontaneous alteration. *J. comp. physiol. Psychol.*, 45, 287–93.

――――. 1953a. Exploratory behavior as a function of "similarity" of stimulus situations. *J. comp. physiol. Psychol.*, 46, 129–33.

――――. 1953b. The effect of hunger and thirst drives upon exploratory behavior. *J. comp. physiol. Psychol.*, 46, 315–19.

――――. 1954. The role of exploratory drive in learning. *J. comp. physiol. Psychol.*, 47, 60–64.

――――. 1955. The relation between fear induced by novel stimulation and exploratory behavior. *J. comp. physiol. Psychol.*, 48, 254–60.

MONTGOMERY, K. C., and MONKMAN, J. A. 1955. The relation between fear and exploratory behavior. *J. comp. physiol. Psychol.*, 48, 132–36.

MONTGOMERY, K. C., and SEGALL, M. 1955. Discrimination learning based upon the exploratory drive. *J. comp. physiol. Psychol.*, 48, 225–28.

MONTGOMERY, K. C., and ZIMBARDO, P. G. 1957. Effect of sensory and behavioral deprivation upon exploratory behavior in the rat. *Percept. mot. Skills*, 7, 223–29.

MOORE, O. K. 1961. Orthographic symbols and the preschool child—a new approach. In P. TORRENCE (ed.), The Proceedings of the Third Minnesota Conference on Gifted Children. Minneapolis, Minn.

――――. 1962, forthcoming. *Automated responsive environments: An application of sociology to the problem of designing optimal environments for learning complex cognitive skills.* National Educational Association monograph.

MOORE, O. K., and ANDERSON, A. R. 1960a. *Early reading and writing, Part 1: Skills* (motion picture). Basic Education, Inc., 20 Augur Street, Hamden, Conn.

――――. 1960b. *Early reading and writing, Part 2: Teaching methods* (motion picture). Basic Education, Inc., 20 Augur Street, Hamden, Conn.

――――. 1960c. *Early reading and writing, Part 3: Development* (motion picture). Basic Education, Inc., 20 Augur Street, Hamden, Conn.

――――. 1962. Some puzzling aspects of social interaction. *The Review of Metaphysics*, 15, 409–33.

MORGAN, C. L. 1894. *Introduction to comparative psychology.* London: Scott.

MORGAN, C. T. 1943. *Physiological psychology.* New York: McGraw-Hill.

――――. 1959. Physiological theory of drive. In S. KOCH (ed.), *Psychology: a study of a science.* Vol. 1. *Sensory, perceptual, and physiological formulations.* New York: McGraw-Hill. Pp. 644–71.

MORGAN, J. J. B., and NORTON, J. T. 1944. The distortion of syllogistic reasoning produced by personal convictions. *J. soc. Psychol.*, 20, 39–59.

MORUZZI, G., and MAGOUN, H. W. 1949. Brain stem reticular formation and activation of the EEG. *EEG clin. Neurophysiol.*, 1, 455–73.

MOSS, F. A. 1924. Study of animal drives. *J. exp. Psychol.*, 7, 165–85.

MOTE, F. A., and FINGER, F. W. 1942. Exploratory drive and secondary reinforcement in the acquisition and extinction of a simple running response. *J. exp. Psychol.*, 31, 57–69.

MOWRER, O. H. 1939. A stimulus-response analysis of anxiety and its role as a reinforcing agent. *Psychol. Rev.*, 46, 553–66.

――――. 1947. On the dual nature of learning: a reinterpretation of "conditioning" and "problem-solving." *Harvard Educ. Rev.*, 17, 102–48.

――――. 1952. Motivation. *Annu. Rev. Psychol.*, 3, 419–38.

――――. 1960. *Learning theory and behavior.* New York: Wiley.

MUENZINGER, K. F. 1946. Reward and punishment. *Univ. Colo. Stud., Gen. Sec.*, 27, No. 4, 1–16.

MURPHY, G. 1947. *Personality: a biosocial approach.* New York: Harper.

――――. 1953. *In the minds of men.* New York: Basic Books, Inc.

MYERS, A. K., and MILLER, N. E. 1954. Failure to find a learned drive based on hunger: evidence for learning motivated by "exploitation." *J. comp. physiol. Psychol.*, 47, 428–36.

NAGEL, E. 1957. A formalization of functionalism. *Logic Without Metaphysics,* 247–83. Glencoe, Ill.: The Free Press.

NEIMARK, E. 1959. Information gathering in diagnostic problem-solving. Unpublished manuscript, New York University.

NETTLER, G. A. 1957. A measure of alienation. *Amer. Soc. Rev.,* 22, 670–77.

NEUMANN, J. VON. 1928. Zur Theorie der Gesellschaftsspiele. *Math. Annalen, 100,* 295–320.

NEUMANN, J. VON, and MORGENSTERN, O. 1952. *Theory of games and economic behavior* (2nd ed.). Princeton: Princeton University Press.

NEUMANN, S. 1932. *Die Deutschen Parteien: Wesen und Wandel nach dem Kriege.* Berlin: Junker und Dunnhaupt Verlag.

NEWCOMB, T. M. 1950. *Social psychology.* New York: Dryden.

————. 1953. An approach to the study of communicative acts. *Psychol. Rev., 60,* 393–404.

————. 1961. *The acquaintance process.* New York: Holt, Rinehart & Winston.

NEWELL, A., SHAW, J. C., and SIMON, H. A. 1958. Elements of a theory of human problem solving. *Psychol. Rev., 65,* 151–66.

NICHOLS, I., and HUNT, J. McV. 1940. A case of partial bilateral frontal lobectomy: a psychopathological study. *Amer. J. Psychiat., 96, 1063–83.*

NISSEN, H. W. 1930. A study of exploratory behavior in the white rat by means of the obstruction method. *J. genet. Psychol., 37,* 361–76.

————. 1954. The nature of drive as innate determinant of behavioral organization. In M. R. JONES (ed.), *Nebraska symposium on motivation.* Lincoln, Neb.: University of Nebraska Press. Pp. 281–320.

OLDS, J. 1958. *The growth and structure of motives.* Glencoe, Ill.: Free Press.

ORE, O. 1953. *Cardano: the gambling scholar.* Princeton: Princeton University Press.

OSGOOD, C. E., and TANNENBAUM, P. H. 1955. The principle of congruity in prediction of attitude change. *Psychol. Rev., 62,* 42–55.

OSGOOD, C. E., SUCI, G. J., and TANNENBAUM, P. H. 1957. *The measurement of meaning.* Urbana, Ill.: University of Illinois Press.

OSSORIO, P. 1961. Meanings in ordinary language. Unpublished Ph.D. dissertation, University of California (Los Angeles).

PARSONS, T. 1953. The superego and the theory of social systems. In T. PARSONS, R. F. BALES, and E. A. SHILS (eds.), *Working papers in the theory of action.* Glencoe, Ill.: Free Press. Pp. 13–29.

————. 1955. Family structure and the socialization of the child. In T. PARSONS and R. F. BALES (eds.), *Family, socialization and interaction process.* Glencoe, Ill.: Free Press. Pp. 35–131.

————. 1959. Voting and the equilibrium of the American political system. In E. BURDICK and A. BRODBECK (eds.), *American Voting Behavior.* Glencoe: Free Press.

PARSONS, T., SHILS, E., NAEGELE, K. D., and PITTS, J. 1961. *Theories of society.* New York: Free Press.

PASCAL, B. 1819. *Oeuvres,* Vol. 4. Paris: Hachette.

PAVLOV, I. P. 1927. *Conditioned reflexes.* Translated by G. B. ANREP. London: Oxford University Press.

————. 1928. *Lectures on conditioned reflexes.* Translated by W. H. GANTT. New York: International Publishers.

PERIN, C. T. 1942. Behavior potentiality as a joint function of the amount of training and the degree of hunger at the time of extinction. *J. exp. Psychol., 32,* 95–109.

PIAGET, J. 1926. *The language and thought of the child.* New York: Harcourt Brace.

————. 1929. *The child's conception of the world.* New York: Harcourt Brace.

————. 1932. *Moral judgment of the child.* New York: Harcourt Brace.

————. 1936. *The origins of intelligence in children.* Translated by MARGARET COOK. New York: International Universities Press, 1952.

————. 1937. *The construction of reality in the child.* Translated by MARGARET COOK. New York: Basic Books, 1954.

————. 1945. *La formation du symbole chez l'enfant.* Translated as *Play, dreams, and imitation in childhood* by C. GATTEGNO and F. M. HODGSON. New York: Norton, 1951.

————. 1951. Principal factors determining intellectual evolution from childhood to adult life. In M. D. RAPAPORT (ed.), *Organization and Pathology of Thought.* New York: Columbia University Press.

PILLSBURY, W. B. 1907. The ego and empirical psychology. *Philos. Rev., 16,* 387–407.

POINCARÉ, H. The value of science. Translated by G. B. HALSTEAD. In *The foundations of science.* New York: Science Press, 1929. Pp. 201–354.

POLEZHAYEV, E. F. 1958. The role of the orientation reflex in the coordination of the cerebral cortex. In L. G. VORONIN et al. (eds.), *The orienting reflex and exploratory behavior.* Moscow: Akad. Pedag. Nauk RSFSR (cited by RAZRAN, 1961).

————. 1959. Novelty as a stimulus for special reactions. *Byull. Eksptl. Brol. i. Med., 2,* 9–14.

POPOV, N. A. 1953. Electroencephalographic observations of human cortical reaction. *Annee Psychol., 53,* 415–29.

PRESTON, M. G., and BAYTON, J. A. 1941. Differential effect of a social variable upon three levels of aspiration. *J. exp. Psychol., 29,* 351–69.

PRIBRAM, K. H. 1958. Neocortical function in behavior. In H. F. HARLOW and C. N. WOOLSEY (eds.), *Biological and biochemical bases of behavior.* Madison, Wis.: University of Wisconsin Press. Pp. 151–72.

————. 1960. A review of theory of physiological psychology. *Annu. Rev. Psychol., 11,* 1–40.

PRIBRAM, K. H., and KRUGER, L. 1954. Functions of the "olfactory brain." *Ann. N. Y. Acad. Sci., 58,* 109–38.

PRUITT, D. G. 1957. An exploratory study of individual differences in sequential decision-making. Unpublished Ph.D. dissertation, Yale University.

————. 1961. Information requirements in making decisions. *Amer. J. Psychol., 74,* 433–39.

RAZRAN, G. 1961. The observable unconscious and the inferable conscious in current Soviet psychophysiology: interoceptive conditioning, semantic conditioning, and the orienting reflex. *Psychol. Rev., 68,* 81–147.

RICHTER, C. P. 1922. A behavioristic study of the activity of the rat. *Comp. Psychol. Monogr., 1,* No. 2.

————. 1927. Animal behavior and internal drives. *Quart. Rev. Biol., 2,* 307–43.

————. 1936. Increased salt appetite in adrenalectomized rats. *Amer. J. Physiol., 115,* 155–67.

————. 1942. Total self regulatory functions in animals and human beings. *The Harvey Lecture Series, 38,* 63–103.

RICHTER, C. P., and ECKERT, J. F. 1939. Mineral appetite of parathyroid-ectomized rats. *Amer. J. med. Sci., 198,* 9–16.

RIESEN, A. H. 1947. The development of visual perception in man and chimpanzee. *Science, 106,* 107–8.

ROBERTS, J. M., ARTH, M. J., and BUSH, R. R. 1959. Games in culture. *American Anthrop., 66,* 597–605.

ROBERTS, J. M., and SUTTON-SMITH, B. 1962a. Child training and game involvement. *Ethnology, 1,* 166–85.

ROGERS, C. R. 1951. *Client-centered therapy.* Boston: Houghton Mifflin.

————. 1959. A theory of therapy, personality, and interpersonal relationships, as developed in the client-centered framework. In S. KOCH (ed.), *Psychology: A study of science.* Vol. 3. New York: McGraw-Hill.

ROKEACH, M. 1960. *The open and closed mind.* New York: Basic Books.

ROMANES, G. J. 1883. *Mental evolution in animals.* New York: Appleton, 1884.

ROSE, J. E., and WOOLSEY, C. N. 1949. The relations of thalamic connections, cellular structure and evocable electrical activity in the auditory region of the cat. *J. comp. Neurol., 91,* 441–66.

ROSENBERG, M. J. 1956. Cognitive structure and attitudinal affect. *J. abnorm. soc. Psychol., 53,* 367–72.

ROSENMAN, S. 1954. The multiplicity of the normal ego-structure. *J. Psychol., 38,* 389–419.

ROSENZWEIG, S. 1944. An outline of frustration theory. In J. McV. HUNT (ed.), *Personality and the behavior disorders.* New York: Ronald Press. Chap. 11.

SANTAYANA, G. 1962. *Reason in common sense.* New York: Collier Books.

SARBIN, T. R. 1952. A preface to a psychological analysis of the self. *Psychol. Rev., 59,* 11–22.

————. 1954. Role theory. In G. LINDZEY (ed.), *Handbook of social psychology.* Vol. 1. Cambridge, Mass.: Addison-Wesley. Pp. 253–58.

SAVAGE, L. J. 1954. *The foundations of statistics.* New York: Wiley.

SCHACHTER, S. 1951. Deviation, rejection, and communication. *J. abnorm. soc. Psychol., 46,* 190–207.

SCHACHTER, S., and SINGER, J. E. 1962. Cognitive, social, and physiological determinants of emotional state. *Psychol. Rev., 69,* 379–99.

SCHILDER, P. 1951. *Psychoanalysis, man, and society.* New York: Norton.

SCHILLINGER, J. 1948. *The mathematical basis of the arts.* New York: Philosophical Library.

SCHLOSBERG, H. 1954. Three dimensions of emotion. *Psychol. Rev., 61,* 81–88.

SCHUTZ, A. 1932. *Der sinnhafte Aufbau der sozialen Welt.* Vienna: Verlag von Julius Springer.

————. 1943. The problem of rationality in the social world, *Economica,* May 10, 130–49.

————. 1944. The stranger. *Amer. J. Sociology, 48,* 499–507.

————. 1945a. Some leading concepts in phenomenology. *Social Research, 12,* 77–79.

————. 1945b. On multiple realities. *Phil. and Phenomenological Res., 4,* 533–75.

————. 1951. Choosing among projects of action. *Phil. and Phenomenological Res., 12,* 161–84.

————. 1953. Common sense and scientific interpretation of human action. *Phil. and Phenomenological Res., 14,* 1–37.

————. 1954. Concept and theory formation in the social sciences. *Amer. J. of Philosophy, 51,* 257–74.

————. 1955. Symbol, reality, and society. In LYMAN BRYSON and OTHERS (eds.), *Symbols and Society, Fourteenth Symposium of the Conference on Science, Religion, and Philosophy.* New York: Harper. Pp. 135–202.

————. 1958. *F. I. R. O.: A three-dimensional theory of interpersonal behavior.* New York: Rinehart.

SCODEL, A., RATOOSH, J., and MINAS, J. S. 1959. Some personality correlates of decision-making under conditions of risk. *Beh. Sci., 4,* 19–28.

SCOTT, W. A. 1959. Cognitive consistency, response reinforcement, and attitude change. *Sociometry, 22,* 219–29.

————. 1960. Properties of cognitive structure. Paper read at meeting of Rocky Mountain Psychological Association.

————. 1961a. Cognitive complexity and cognitive balance. Unpublished manuscript.

————. 1961b. Cognitive complexity and cognitive flexibility. Unpublished manuscript.

————. 1962. Cognitive structure and social structure: some concepts and relationships. In N. F. WASHBURNE (ed.), *Decisions, values, and groups.* Vol. 2. New York: Pergamon.

————. 1963. Psychological structure and social correlates of international images.

In H. C. KELMAN (ed.), *International behavior.* New York: Holt, Rinehart & Winston (in preparation).

SCOTT, W. A., and WERTHEIMER, M. 1962. *Introduction to psychological research.* New York: Wiley.

SEARS, R. R., MACCOBY, ELEANOR, E., and LEVIN, H. 1957. *Patterns of child rearing.* Evanston, Ill.: Row, Peterson.

SEARS, R. R., WHITING, J. W. M., NOWLIS, V., and SEARS, P. S. 1953. Some child-rearing antecedents of aggression and dependency in young children. *Genet. Psychol. Monogr., 47,* 135–234.

SECHENOV, I. M. 1863. Reflexes of the brain. Medizinsky Vestnik. English translation in: *Sechenov's Selected Works* (p. 263). Moscow-Leningrad: State Publiacitons House, 1935 (from BRAZIER, 1959).

SHANNON, C. E., and WEAVER, W. 1949. *The mathematical theory of communication.* Urbana, Ill.: University of Illinois Press.

SHARPLESS, S., and JASPER, H. H. 1956. Habituation of the arousal reaction. *Brain, 79,* 655–80.

SHAW, M. E. 1959. Acceptance of authority, group structure, and the effectiveness of small groups. *J. Personality, 27,* 196–210.

SHERIDAN, R. B. B. 1775. *The Rivals.* London: printed for JOHN WILKIE. St. Paul's Church Yard. As it is acted at the Theatre-Royal in Covent Garden.

SHERIF, M. 1935. A study of some social factors in perception. *Arch. Psychol.,* No. 187.

————. 1936. *The psychology of social norms.* New York: Harper.

SHERIF, M., and CANTRIL, H. 1947. *The psychology of ego-involvements.* New York: Wiley.

SHERIF, M., and HARVEY, O. J. 1952. A study in ego functioning: Elimination of stable anchorages in individual and group situations. *Sociometry, 15,* 272–305.

SHERIF, M., and SHERIF, C. W. 1956. *An outline of social psychology* (rev. ed.). New York: Harper.

SHERIF, M., WHITE, B. J., and HARVEY, O. J. 1955. Status in experimentally produced groups. *Amer. J. Sociol., 60,* 370–79.

SHERRINGTON, C. S. 1906. *The integrative action of the nervous system.* New York: Scribners.

SHILS, E. 1951. The study of the primary group. In DANIEL LERNER and HAROLD LASSWELL (eds.), *The Policy Sciences.* Stanford, Calif.: Stanford University Press.

SHUFORD, E. H., and HALL, W. J. 1960. Bayes estimation of proportion: The performance criterion. Paper presented at meeting of Eastern Psychological Association.

SIMMEL, G. 1956. *Conflict and the web of group affiliations.* Glencoe, Ill.: Free Press.

SIMON, H. A. 1957. *Models of man.* New York: Wiley.

SKINNER, B. F., and FERSTER, C. B. 1957. *Schedules of reinforcement.* New York: Appleton-Century-Crofts.

SMITH, M. B., BRUNER, J. S., and WHITE, R. K. 1956. *Opinions and personality.* New York: Wiley.

SMOCK, C. D., and HOLT, BESS GENE. 1962. Children's reactions to novelty: an experimental study of "curiosity motivation." *Child Develpm., 33,* 631–42.

SPENCE, K. W. 1956. *Behavior theory and conditioning.* New Haven: Yale University Press.

SPENCER, H. 1897. *The principles of psychology.* New York: Appleton-Century (authorized edition).

SPIEGELBERG, H. 1960. *The phenomenological movement: a historical introduction.* The Hague: Nijhoff. Pp. 655–701.

SPIRO, M. E. 1961. An overview and a suggested reorientation. In F. L. K. HSU (ed.), *Psychological anthropology: Approaches to culture and personality.* Homewood, Ill.: Dorsey Press, Inc.

SPITZ, R. A. 1946a. Anaclitic depression. *Psychoanal. Stud. Child.*, 2, 313–42.

—————. 1946b. The smiling response: a contribution to the ontogenesis of social relations. *Genet. Psychol. Monogr.*, 34, 67–125.

—————. 1949. The role of ecological factors in emotional development in infancy. *Child Develpm.*, 20, 145–54.

SROLE, L. 1956. Social integration and certain corollaries: An exploratory study. *Amer. Soc. Rev.*, 21, 709–16.

STAGNER, R. 1951. Homeostasis as a unifying concept in personality theory. *Psychol. Rev.*, 58, 5–18.

STAGNER, R., and KARWOSKI, T. F. 1952. *Psychology.* New York: McGraw-Hill.

STANDING, E. M. 1957. *Maria Montessori: her life and work.* London: Hollis & Carter.

STELLAR, E. 1954. The physiology of motivation. *Psychol. Rev.*, 61, 5–22.

STRAUSS, A. 1960. *Mirrors and masks.* Glencoe, Ill.: The Free Press.

TANNER, W. P., JR., and SWETS, J. A. 1954. A decision-making theory of visual detection. *Psychol. Rev.*, 61, 401–9.

TAYLOR, D. W. 1960. Toward an information processing theory of motivation. In M. R. JONES (ed.), *Nebraska symposium on motivation.* Lincoln, Neb.: University of Nebraska Press. Pp. 51–79.

TERRELL, G. 1959. Manipulatory motivation in children. *J. comp. physiol. Psychol.*, 52, 705–9.

THACKRAY, R. I., and MICHELS, K. M. 1958. Externally-aroused drives in the raccoon. *Anim. Behav.*, 6, 160–63.

THELEN, H. A., and DICKERMAN, W. 1949. Stereotypes and the growth of groups. *Educ. Leadership*, 6, 309–16.

THIBAUT, J., and KELLEY, H. H. 1959. *The social psychology of groups.* New York: Wiley.

THORNDIKE, E. L. 1898. Animal intelligence: an experimental study of the associative processes in animals. *Psychol. Rev.*, Monogr. Suppl., No. 4.

—————. 1913. *The psychology of learning.* Vol. 2. *Educational psychology.* New York: Teachers College.

—————. 1949. *Selected writings from a connectionist's psychology.* New York: Appleton-Century-Crofts. Chap. 1.

THORPE, W. H. 1956. *Learning and instinct in animals.* London: Methuen.

THRASHER, F. M. 1927. *The gang.* Chicago: University of Chicago Press.

TITUS, H., and HOLLANDER, E. P. 1957. The California F Scale in psychological research: 1950–1955. *Psychol. Bull.*, 54, 47–64.

TOLMAN, E. C. 1925. The nature of fundamental drives. *J. abnorm. soc. Psychol.*, 20, 349–58.

TOLMAN, E. C., and HONZIG, C. H. 1930. Introduction and removal of reward, and maze performance in rats. *Univ. Calif. Publ. Psychol.*, 4, 257–75.

ULEHLA, Z. J. 1961. Individual differences in information yields of raters. Unpublished Master's thesis, University of Colorado.

VAN OSTRAND, D. 1960. Reactions to positive and negative information about the self as a function of certain personality characteristics of the recipient. Unpublished Master's thesis, University of Colorado.

VERBA, S. 1961. *Small groups and political behavior: A study of leadership.* Princeton, N. J.: Princeton University Press.

VINOGRADOVA, O. S. 1958. On the dynamics of the orienting reflex in the formation of conditioned connections. In L. G. VORONIN et al. (eds.), *The orienting reflex and orienting investigatory activity.* Moscow: Akad. Pedag. Nauk RSFSR.

VORONIN, L. G., LEONT'YEV, A. N., LURIA, A. R., SOKOLOV, E. N., and VINOGRADOVA, O. S. (eds.). 1958. *The orienting reflex and orienting investigatory activity.* Moscow: Akad. Pedag. Nauk RSFSR.

WALKER, A. E., and WEAVER, T. A., JR. 1940. Ocular movements from the occipital lobe in the monkey. *J. Neurophysiol.*, 3, 353–57 (cited by PRIBRAM, 1958).

WALKER, E. L., DEMBER, W. N., EARL, R. W., and KAROLY, A. J. 1955. Choice alternation: I, stimulus vs. place vs. response. *J. comp. physiol. Psychol.*, 48, 19–23.

WALKER, E. L., DEMBER, W. N., EARL, R. W., FLIEGE, S. E., and KAROLY, A. J. 1955. Choice alternation: II, exposure to stimulus or stimulus and place without choice. *J. comp. physiol. Psychol.*, 48, 24–28.

WARDEN, C. J. 1931. *Animal motivation: experimental studies on the albino rat.* New York: Columbia University Press.

WATSON, J. B. 1916. The place of the conditioned-reflex in psychology. *Psychol. Rev.*, 23, 89–116.

————. 1924. *Behaviorism.* New York: Norton.

WATSON, J. B., and RAYNOR, R. 1920. Conditioned emotional reactions. *J. exp. Psychol.*, 3, 1–14.

WEBER, M. 1946. The social psychology of the world religions. In H. H. GERTH and C. W. MILLS, *From Max Weber: Essays in Sociology.* New York: Oxford University Press. Pp. 267–301.

WEISS, P. 1939. *Principles of development.* New York: Holt.

WEISS, R. S. 1956. A structure-function approach to organization. *J. soc. Issues,* 12, 66.

WELKER, W. I. 1956a. Some determinants of play and exploration in chimpanzees. *J. comp. physiol. Psychol.*, 49, 84–89.

————. 1956b. Variability of play and exploratory behavior in chimpanzees. *J. comp. physiol. Psychol.*, 49, 181–85.

————. 1956c. Effects of age and experience on play and exploration of young chimpanzees. *J. comp. physiol. Psychol.*, 49, 223–26.

WENGER, M. A. 1948. Studies of autonomic balance in Army Air Force personnel. *Comp. Psychol. Monogr.*, 19, No. 4 (Serial No. 101).

WERNER, H. 1957. *Comparative psychology of mental development* (rev. ed.). New York: International Universities Press.

WHITE, R. W. 1959. Motivation reconsidered: the concept of competence. *Psychol. Rev.*, 66, 297–333.

————. 1960. Competence and the psychosexual stages of development. In Nebraska Symposium on Motivation. Lincoln, Neb.: University of Nebraska Press.

WHITING, J. W. M., and MOWRER, O. H. 1943. Habit progression and regression—a laboratory study of some factors relevant to human socialization. *J. comp. Psychol.*, 36, 229–53.

WHORF, B. 1956. *Language, thought and reality* (ed.), J. CARROL. New York: Wiley.

WHYTE, W. F. 1943. *Street corner society.* Chicago: University of Chicago Press.

WIENER, N. 1948. *Cybernetics.* New York: Wiley.

WILKINS, E. J., and DE CHARMS, R. 1961. Authoritarianism and power cues. ONR Technical Report, No. 12.

WILLIS, T. 1672. *De anima brutorum* (*de scientia seu cognitione brutorum*). London: Davis (cited by BRAZIER, 1959).

WINTERBOTTOM, MARIAN R. 1953. The relation of need for achievement to learning experiences in independence and mastery. Thesis published in J. W. ATKINSON (ed.), *Motives in fantasy, action, and society.* Princeton, N. J.: Van Nostrand, 1958. Chap. 33.

WOODWORTH, R. S. 1918. *Dynamic psychology.* New York: Columbia University Press.

————. 1928. How emotions are identified and classified. In M. L. REYMERT (ed.), *Feelings and emotions: the Wittenberg symposium.* Worcester, Mass.: Clark University Press.

————. 1947. Reinforcement of perception. *Amer. J. Psychol.*, 60, 119–24.

————. 1958. *Dynamics of behavior.* New York: Holt.

WRIGHT, J. M. 1958. Extrapunitiveness and authoritarianism: Changes in attitudinal correlates as a result of frustration. ONR Technical Report, No. 7. Vanderbilt University. Contract NONR 2149(02).

YERKES, R. M., and DODSON, J. D. 1908. The relation of strength of stimulus to rapidity of habit formation. *J. comp. Neurol. and Psychol., 18,* 459–82.

YOSHII, N. K., and TSUKIYAMA, K. 1952. EEG studies on conditioned behavior of the white rat. *Jap. J. Physiol., 2,* 186–93 (cited by BERLYNE, 1960).

YOUNG, P. T. 1936. *Motivation of behavior.* New York: Wiley.

————. 1943. *Emotion in man and animal.* New York: Wiley.

————. 1944. Studies of food preference, appetite and dietary habit: (1) running activity and dietary habit of the rat in relation to food preference. *J. comp. Psychol., 37,* 327–70.

————. 1949a. Food-seeking drive, affective process, and learning. *Psychol. Rev., 56,* 98–121.

————. 1949b. Emotion as disorganized response—a reply to Professor Leeper. *Psychol. Rev., 56,* 184–91.

————. 1959. The role of affective processes in learning and motivation. *Psychol. Rev., 66,* 104–25.

————. 1961. *Motivation and emotion: a survey of the determinants of human and animal society.* New York: Wiley.

ZAJONC, R. B. 1960. The process of cognitive tuning in communication. *J. abnorm. soc. Psychol., 61,* 159–67.

ZEIGARNIK, B. 1927. Über das Behalten von erledigten und unerledigten Handlungen. *Psychol. Forsch., 9,* 1–85.

ZIMBARDO, P. G., and MILLER, N. E. 1958. Facilitation of exploration by hunger in rats. *J. comp. physiol. Psychol., 51,* 43–46.

ZIMBARDO, P. G., and MONTGOMERY, K. C. 1957. The relative strengths of consummatory responses in hunger, thirst, and exploratory drive. *J. comp. physiol. Psychol., 50,* 504–08.

Author Index

Subject Index

Adaptation, repeated reinforcement, 28
Adaptation level
   optimal discrepancy from, 74
   principle of pooling, 20–22
   reinforcement, 25–27
Alienation, 124
Anomie, 124, 125, 220
Arousal
   collative variables, 78–79
   curiosity and exploration, 290
   emotion, 57
   expressive indicators, 57
   frustration, relation to, 56–58
   generalized drive, 57
   incongruity, 60, 61–63
   long term incongruity, 63–60
   optimum of, 76–78, 265, 290
   perception, 290
   performance, 22
   search behavior, 264
   short-term incongruity, 61–63
   uncertainty, effect of, 262
Assessment
   cognitive complexity, 278, 285
   convergent validity, 273
   discriminant validity, 274
   instrument contamination, 274
   instrument refinement vs. general applicability, 275
   integration, 282
   introspective data, 271
   isomorphism between construct and measure, 269
   judgmental vs. objective, 272
   need for, 268
   psychological variables, 268
Attitude
   conditions of confusion, 217–235
   daily life, 210–214, 217
   goal choice, 88
   modifications of, 235–238
   perception of others, 88
   response choice, 88
   salience of, 280
Autocracy, 150, 151, 153, 154, 155, 164
Autotelic, 91, 168, 184

Cognitive
   consistency, 283, 285
   differentiation-integration, 112–113, 114, 134, 277, 279, 280, 282
   hierarchic organization, 284
   relatedness, 114, 280
   structure, 266–267, 276
Collative variables, 60, 78–79
Concepts
   confirmation of, 106–110
   and conflict, 5, 58, 59
   constitutive order of, 190, 206
   construal of events, 101–102
   defined, 99
   differentiation-integration of, 112–113, 114, 134, 277, 279, 280, 282
   directionality, 106–108
   evolution of, 112–113, 138
   motivation, 12–15, 105–106
   refutation of, 106–110
   resistance to change, 103–105
   and self definition, 102–103
   structural, 266
   of trust, 190–193
Conceptual systems
   abstract functioning, 116–117, 134
   anomie, 124–126
   as cause, 162
   centrality-peripherality, 115
   clarity-ambiguity, 114
   compartmentalization, 114
   concrete functioning, 115–116, 134
   concreteness-abstractness, 113, 118–122, 123, 139, 140
   curiosity and exploration, 132–133
   functions of, 99–103
   interrelatedness, 114, 280
   openness-closedness, 115
   stages, 118–122, 135
Conflict
   expressive indexes, 59
   interference, 58
   neurosis, 58
Cortical activity
   arousal, 9–10
   stimulation, 9–10